HEINEMANN PHYSICS 12

SKILLS AND ASSESSMENT

Doug Bail

VCE Units 3 and 4

Written for the VCE Physics Study Design 2024–2027

Pearson Australia
(a division of Pearson Australia Group Pty Ltd)
459–471 Church Street
Level 1, Building B
Richmond, Victoria 3121
www.pearson.com.au

First published 2023 by Pearson Australia
2026 2025 2024 2023
10 9 8 7 6 5 4 3 2 1

VCE Heinemann Project Leads: Fiona Cooke, Bryonie Scott, Misal Belvedere, Malcolm Parsons
Content and Learning Specialists: Sam Trafford, Zoe Hamilton
Development Editor: Lucy Bates
Schools Programme Manager: Michelle Thomas
Production Editor: Chris Woods
Editor: Margaret Trudgeon
Series Designer: Anne Donald
Rights & Permissions Editor: Amirah Fatin Binte Mohamed Sapi'ee and Jes Sensberg
Production Services Desktop Operator: JitPin Chong
Illustrators: Bruce Rankin, DiacriTech, QBS Learning
Proofreader: Jane Fitzpatrick
Printed in Malaysia (CTP–PJB)

ISBN 978 0 6557 0029 6

Pearson Australia Group Pty Ltd ABN 40 004 245 943

Disclaimer
The selection of internet addresses (URLs) provided for this book was valid at the time of publication and was chosen as being appropriate for use as a secondary education research tool. However, due to the dynamic nature of the internet, some addresses may have changed, may have ceased to exist since publication, or may inadvertently link to sites with content that could be considered offensive or inappropriate. While the authors and publisher regret any inconvenience this may cause readers, no responsibility for any such changes or unforeseeable errors can be accepted by either the authors or the publisher.

Indigenous Australians
We respectfully acknowledge the traditional custodians of the lands upon which the many schools throughout Australia are located. We acknowledge traditional Indigenous Knowledge systems are founded upon a logic that developed from Indigenous experience with the natural environment over thousands of years. This is in contrast to Western science, where the production of knowledge often takes place within specific disciplines. As a result, there are many cases where such disciplinary knowledge does not reflect Indigenous worldviews, and can be considered offensive to Indigenous peoples.

Some of the images used in *Heinemann Physics 12 Skills and Assessment* might have associations with deceased Indigenous Australians. Please be aware that these images might cause sadness or distress in Aboriginal or Torres Strait Islander communities.

Practical activities
All practical activities, including the illustrations, are provided as a guide only and the accuracy of such information cannot be guaranteed. Teachers must assess the appropriateness of an activity and take into account the experience of their students and facilities available. Additionally, all practical activities should be trialled before they are attempted with students and a risk assessment must be completed. All care should be taken and appropriate personal protective clothing and equipment should be worn when carrying out any practical activity. Although all practical activities have been written with safety in mind, Pearson Australia and the authors do not accept any responsibility for the information contained in or relating to the practical activities, and are not liable for loss and/or injury arising from or sustained as a result of conducting any of the practical activities described in this book.

Attributions
We thank the following for their contributions to our skills and assessment book:

The following abbreviations are used in this list: t = top, b = bottom, l = left, r = right, c = centre.

Cover: Science Photo Library: Parker, David.

Alamy Stock Photo: Alchemy, pp. 57t, 57b; Parker, David, pp. 150–1, 208–9.

Cross, Malcolm: pp. 154tl, 154tc.

Getty Images: Rooney, Quinn, p. 3.

Science Photo Library: Andrew Lambert Photography, p. 62b; Trevor Clifford Photography, p. 58tl.

Shutterstock: Everett Collection, p. 16; HTU, pp. 1, 50–2, 108–9; noolwlee, pp. 137.

Victorian Curriculum and Assessment Authority (VCAA): Victorian Curriculum and Assessment Authority (VCAA): Selected examination questions and extracts from the VCE Physics Study Design (2023–2027) are copyright Victorian Curriculum and Assessment Authority (VCAA), reproduced by permission. VCE® is a registered trademark of the VCAA. The VCAA does not endorse this product and makes no warranties regarding the correctness or accuracy of its content. To the extent permitted by law, the VCAA excludes all liability for any loss or damage suffered or incurred as a result of accessing, using or relying on the content. Current VCE Study Designs and related content can be accessed directly at www.vcaa.vic.edu.au.

Contents

Contents

Unit 4 How have creative ideas and investigation revolutionised thinking in physics?

AREA OF STUDY 1

How has understanding about the physical world changed?

AREA OF STUDY 2

How is scientific inquiry used to investigate fields, motion or light?

ISBN 978 0 6557 0029 6

How to use this book

The *Heinemann Physics 12 Skills and Assessment* book provides the opportunity to practise, apply and extend your learning through a range of supportive and challenging activities. These activities reinforce key concepts and skills, and enable a flexible approach to learning. There are also regular opportunities for reflection and self-evaluation in the final worksheet in each area of study.

This resource has been written to the VCE Physics Study Design 2024–2027 and is divided into five areas of study—three in Unit 3 and two in Unit 4. Areas of Study 1–3 in Unit 3 and Area of Study 1 in Unit 4 consist of four main sections:

- key knowledge
- worksheets
- practical activities
- exam questions.

PHYSICS TOOLKIT

The Physics toolkit supports development of the skills and techniques needed to undertake practical and secondary-sourced investigations, and covers examination techniques and study skills. It also includes checklists, models, exemplars and scaffolded steps. The toolkit can serve as a reference tool and be consulted as needed.

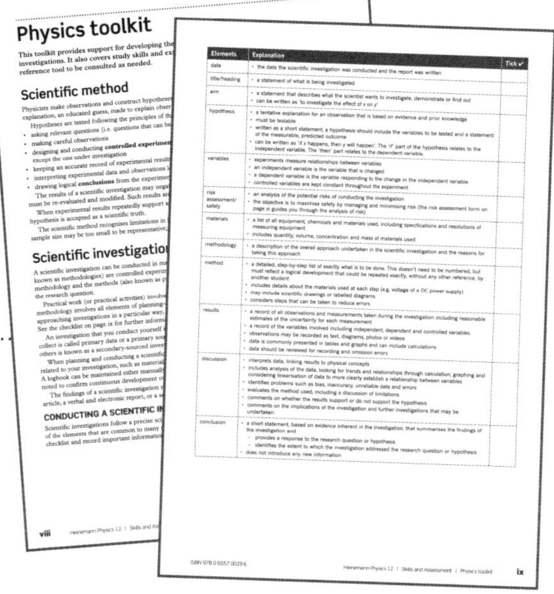

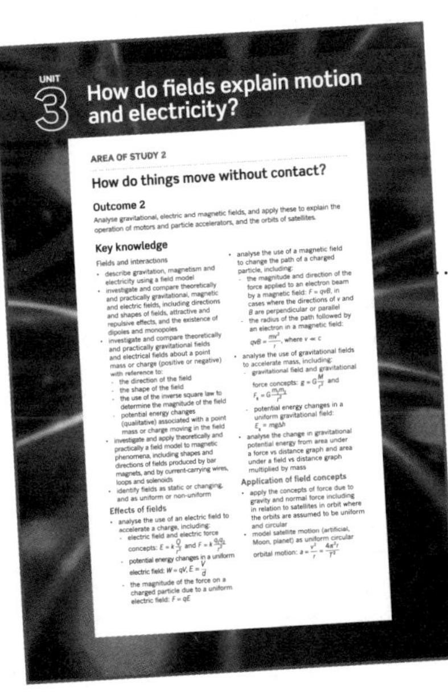

AREA OF STUDY OPENER

Heinemann Physics 12 Skills and Assessment is structured to follow the Study Design units and areas of study. The area of study opening page lists the Study Design key knowledge for easy reference to the activities that follow.

KEY KNOWLEDGE

Each area of study begins with a key knowledge section. This consists of a set of summary notes that cover the key knowledge for that area of study. Key terms are in bold and are included in the glossary of the student book. The section also serves as a ready reference for completing the worksheets and practical activities.

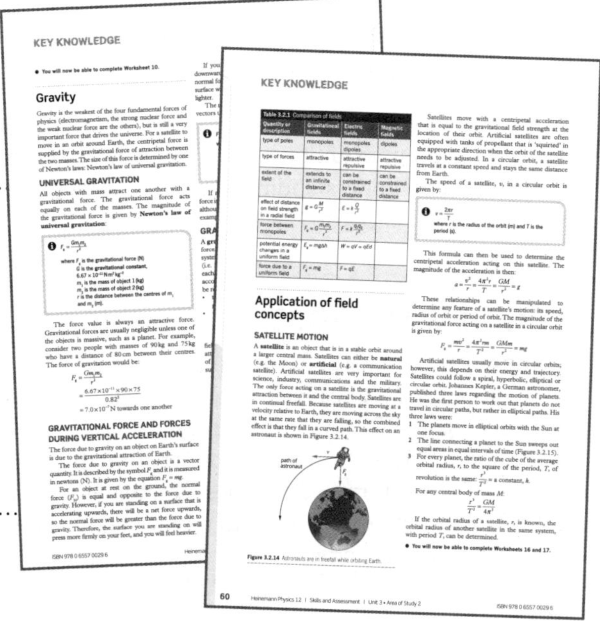

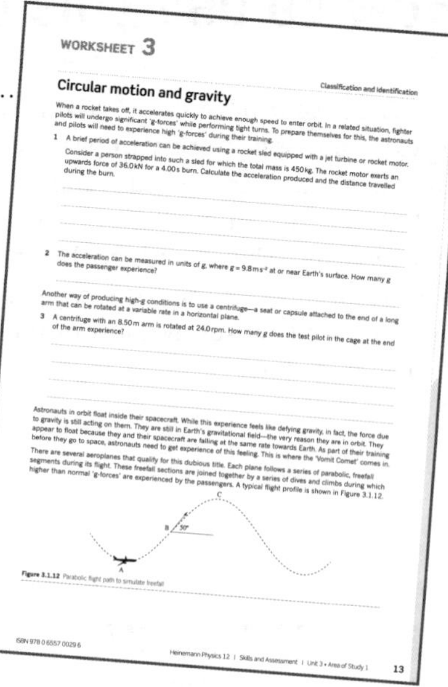
WORKSHEET 3

Circular motion and gravity

Classification and identification

Figure 3.1.12 Parabolic flight path to simulate freefall

WORKSHEETS

The worksheets feature questions that allow you to practise and apply your knowledge and skills. Each area of study includes a 'Knowledge review' worksheet to activate prior knowledge, a 'Literacy review' worksheet that provides opportunities for vocabulary and literacy support, and a 'Reflection' worksheet, which you can use for self-assessment. Other worksheets provide opportunities to revise, consolidate and further your understanding. All worksheets function as formative assessment and are clearly aligned with the Study Design. A range of questions building from foundation to challenging is included in each worksheet.

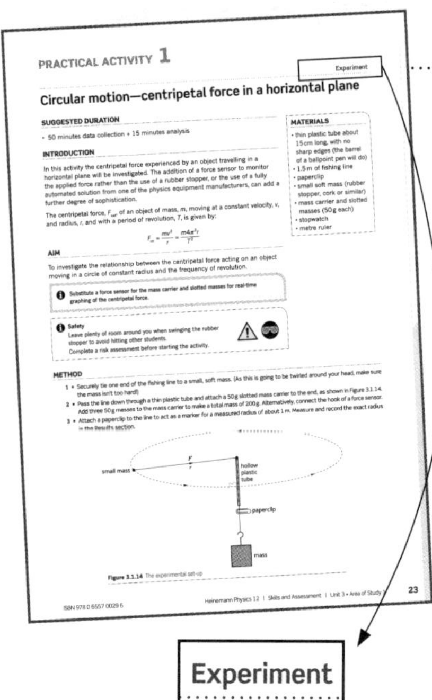
PRACTICAL ACTIVITY 1

Experiment

Circular motion—centripetal force in a horizontal plane

SUGGESTED DURATION

INTRODUCTION

MATERIALS

AIM

METHOD

Figure 3.1.14 The experimental set-up

Experiment

PRACTICAL ACTIVITIES

Practical activities offer you the chance to complete practical work related to the various themes covered in the Study Design. You have the opportunity to design and conduct scientific investigations, generate, evaluate and analyse data, appropriately record results, and prepare evidence-based conclusions. Where relevant, you will also need to conduct risk assessments to identify any potential hazards.

Each practical activity includes a suggested duration. Together with the Unit 4 Area of Study 2 scientific investigation, the practical activities meet the 30 hours of practical work mandated for Units 3 and 4 in the Study Design.

METHODOLOGIES

Each worksheet and practical activity is mapped to one or more of the scientific investigation methodologies outlined in the Study Design. Completing these activities gives you experience in applying the methodologies in a wide variety of contexts and prepares you for designing and conducting your own scientific investigation in Unit 4 Area of Study 2.

EXAM QUESTIONS

Each area of study finishes with a selection of exam questions. These give you the opportunity to gain valuable experience applying your knowledge and understanding to exam questions.

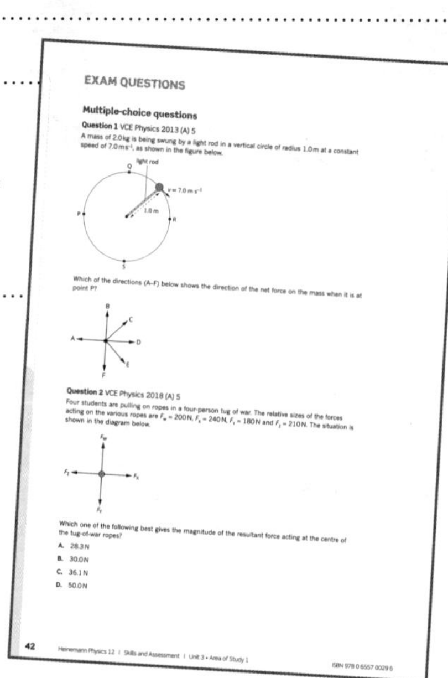
EXAM QUESTIONS

Multiple-choice questions

Question 1 VCE Physics 2013 (A) 5

Question 2 VCE Physics 2018 (A) 5

A. 28.3 N

B. 30.0 N

C. 36.1 N

D. 50.0 N

TEACHER SUPPORT

Comprehensive answers and fully worked solutions for all worksheets, practical activities and exam questions are provided via the *Heinemann Physics 12 eBook + Assessment* or Pearson Places. In-depth support for Unit 4 Area of Study 2 in the form of samples, templates and teacher notes is also included, along with an interactive SPARKlab for every practical activity.

ISBN 978 0 6557 0029 6

Physics toolkit

This toolkit provides support for developing the skills required to undertake scientific investigations. It also covers study skills and examination preparation. The toolkit can serve as a reference tool to be consulted as needed.

Scientific method

Physicists make observations and construct hypotheses to account for their observations. A **hypothesis** is a possible explanation, an educated guess, made to explain observations.

Hypotheses are tested following the principles of the **scientific method**. These include:

- asking relevant questions (i.e. questions that can be tested)
- making careful observations
- designing and conducting **controlled experiments**; in controlled experiments all **variables** are kept constant, except the one under investigation
- keeping an accurate record of experimental results
- interpreting experimental data and observations logically
- drawing logical **conclusions** from the experimental results.

The results of a scientific investigation may negate or refute the hypothesis being tested. In this case, the hypothesis must be re-evaluated and modified. Such results are useful in redirecting scientific investigation.

When experimental results repeatedly support a hypothesis, it may become a **theory** or **principle**; that is, the hypothesis is accepted as a scientific truth.

The scientific method recognises limitations in investigations. For example, some factors cannot be measured; a sample size may be too small to be representative; or unknown factors may influence investigations.

Scientific investigation

A scientific investigation can be conducted in many ways. Examples of scientific investigation approaches (also known as methodologies) are controlled experiments, literature reviews and modelling. The scientific investigation methodology and the methods (also known as procedures) selected will depend on the aim of the investigation and the research question.

Practical work (or practical activities) involves direct experiences or hands-on activities. Scientific investigation methodology involves all elements of planning—it considers the focus of the investigation and the rationale for approaching investigations in a particular way, for example, through controlled experiments, fieldwork or modelling. See the checklist on page ix for further information about methodology versus method in scientific investigations.

An investigation that you conduct yourself is known as a primary investigation, and the data and information you collect is called primary data or a primary source. An investigation that involves the analysis of data collected by others is known as a secondary-sourced investigation (see page xvii).

When planning and conducting a scientific investigation, you must maintain a logbook to record information related to your investigation, such as materials and methods, raw data, data analysis, and sources of information. A logbook can be maintained either manually or electronically. In either case, a record of dates of all work should be noted to confirm continuous development over a period of time.

The findings of a scientific investigation may be presented in a variety of formats, such as a scientific report, an article, a verbal and electronic report, or a scientific poster.

CONDUCTING A SCIENTIFIC INVESTIGATION

Scientific investigations follow a precise scientific method. The checklist on the following page provides a summary of the elements that are common to many scientific investigation methodologies and scientific reports. Refer to the checklist and record important information as you conduct your scientific investigation.

 ISBN 978 0 6557 0029 6

Elements	Explanation	Tick ✔
date	• the date the scientific investigation was conducted and the report was written	
title/heading	• a statement of what is being investigated	
aim	• a statement that describes what the scientist wants to investigate, demonstrate or find out • can be written as 'to investigate the effect of *x* on *y*'	
hypothesis	• a tentative explanation for an observation that is based on evidence and prior knowledge • must be testable • written as a short statement, a hypothesis should include the variables to be tested and a statement of the measurable, predicted outcome • can be written as 'if *x* happens, then *y* will happen'. The 'if' part of the hypothesis relates to the independent variable. The 'then' part relates to the dependent variable.	
variables	• experiments measure relationships between variables • an independent variable is the variable that is changed • a dependent variable is the variable responding to the change in the independent variable • controlled variables are kept constant throughout the experiment	
risk assessment/ safety	• an analysis of the potential risks of conducting the investigation • the objective is to maximise safety by managing and minimising risk (the risk assessment form on page xi guides you through the analysis of risk)	
materials	• a list of all equipment, chemicals and materials used, including specifications and resolutions of measuring equipment • includes quantity, volume, concentration and mass of materials used	
methodology	• a description of the overall approach undertaken in the scientific investigation and the reasons for taking this approach	
method	• a detailed, step-by-step list of exactly what is to be done. This doesn't need to be numbered, but must reflect a logical development that could be repeated exactly, without any other reference, by another student • includes details about the materials used at each step (e.g. voltage of a DC power supply) • may include scientific drawings or labelled diagrams • considers steps that can be taken to reduce errors	
results	• a record of all observations and measurements taken during the investigation including reasonable estimates of the uncertainty for each measurement • a record of the variables involved including independent, dependent and controlled variables. • observations may be recorded as text, diagrams, photos or videos • data is commonly presented in tables and graphs and can include calculations • data should be reviewed for recording and omission errors	
discussion	• interprets data, linking results to physical concepts • includes analysis of the data, looking for trends and relationships through calculation, graphing and considering linearisation of data to more clearly establish a relationship between variables • identifies problems such as bias, inaccuracy, unreliable data and errors • evaluates the method used, including a discussion of limitations • comments on whether the results support or do not support the hypothesis • comments on the implications of the investigation and further investigations that may be undertaken	
conclusion	• a short statement, based on evidence inherent in the investigation, that summarises the findings of the investigation and – provides a response to the research question or hypothesis – identifies the extent to which the investigation addressed the research question or hypothesis • does not introduce any new information	

RISK ASSESSMENT

Five levels of safety should be considered before carrying out a scientific investigation. The inverted pyramid ranks these levels in order of importance. The school and your teacher are responsible for reducing most risks. As a student scientist, you can take measures to reduce the risks shown at the bottom of the hierarchy.

A risk assessment should be completed prior to conducting an investigation to determine the risks involved. Copy the risk assessment form on page xi into your logbook and use it to identify possible risks for which you can take responsibility, and to think of ways you can reduce risks to create a safe environment.

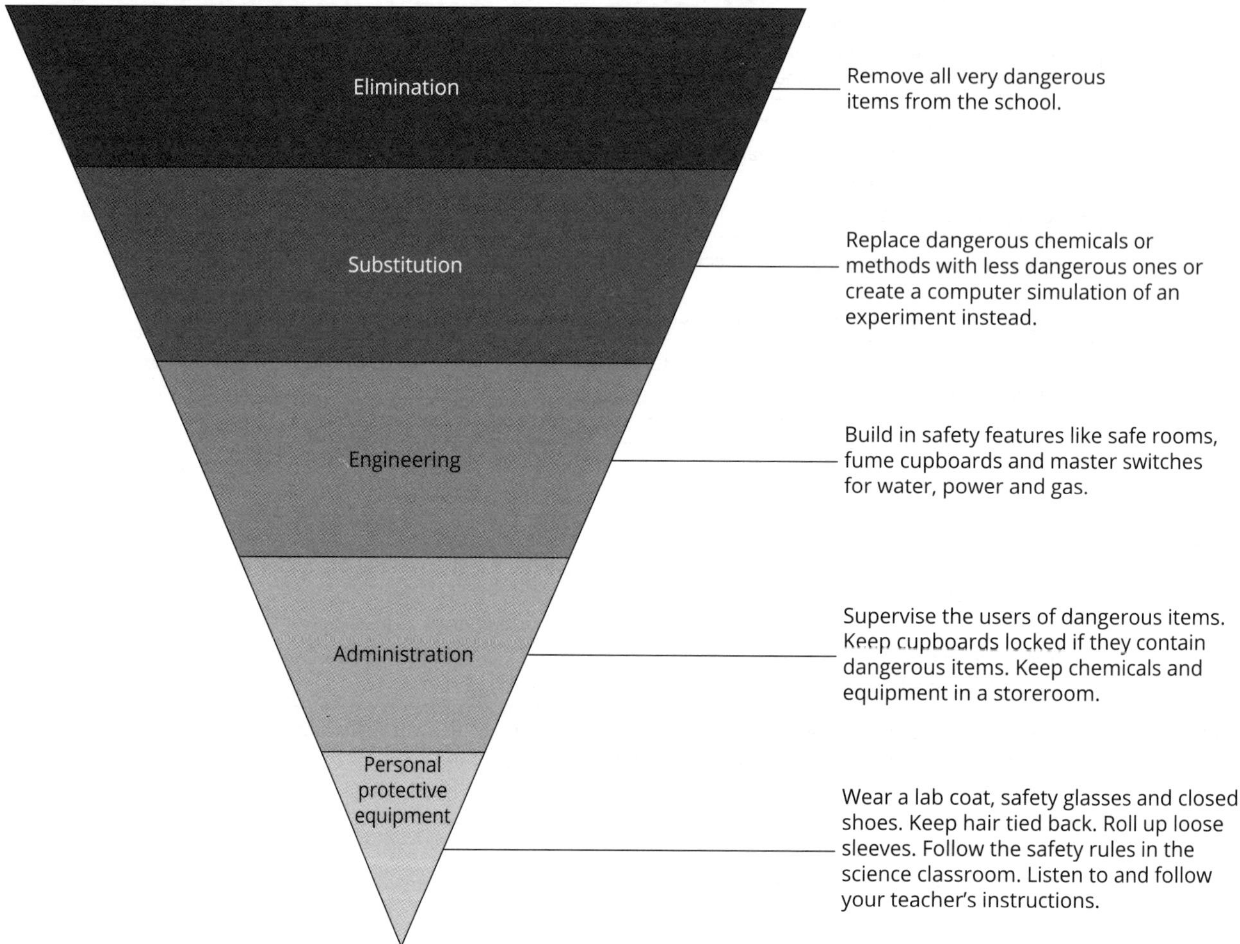

ISBN 978 0 6557 0029 6

Risk assessment form		
What activity are you doing?		
Title or description of the investigation:		
List ...	**Identify any risks**	**State how you will ...**
equipment you will be using:		use each piece:
chemicals you will be using:		carefully use each chemical: carefully dispose of the chemicals:
ethical issues you need to consider:		ethically use animals in the laboratory: ethically use human participants in the investigation:
outdoor or fieldwork activities:		reduce these risks:
any other possible risks:		reduce these risks:

EXAMPLES OF SCIENTIFIC REPORTS

It can be difficult to gauge whether you have attained a high standard in your completed scientific report. Looking at sample scientific reports can help you identify what is required. Two sample scientific reports—a high-standard and low-standard report—are provided below. They include annotations to draw your attention to key points to note on each scientific report. These points are also reflected in the checklist, so you are able to use this as a tool to evaluate whether you have completed all requirements of the scientific investigation.

High-standard practical report

Heading is clear and short.

The reason for doing the investigation is stated.

The hypothesis is based on the aim of the investigation.

The different variables are identified.

All materials are listed, including numbers of specific items.

Warnings are given of potential hazards and how these can be reduced or eliminated.

The overall approach undertaken has been described

Clear instructions are provided for each step of the experiment. These have been written in recipe style, with easy-to-follow, detailed instructions.

Results have been checked for consistency between trials. The number of significant figures shown indicates a good understanding of the limitations of the measuring technique.

If you take multiple measurements, calculating the mean (or average) gives a single representative value and can provide a clearer understanding of the data.

Investigation of motion using timed intervals

Aim

To investigate the motion of a student using timed intervals of measured distance.

Hypothesis

If the position of an object is known at regular timed intervals, the velocity can be calculated using the equations of motion.

Variables

Independent variable: Distance travelled

Dependent variable: Time

Controlled variables: Student running, the student at each distance interval

Materials

- 7 plastic cones or other position markers
- 30-metre tape measure
- stopwatches

Risk assessment

Make sure the space is clear of trip hazards before running. If a student trips, report this to the teacher immediately.

Methodology

Controlled experiment measuring distance and time.

Method

1 In a large, clear space, stretch out the tape measure on the ground in a straight line. Mark out the beginning and end of the distance, as well as every 5-metre interval.

2 Station a student with a stopwatch at each 5-metre marker. Zero each stopwatch and ensure that students are familiar with the basic operation of the stopwatch.

3 Select a student for testing and position them ready to run, walk, crawl or hop from the start of the 30 metres. On a call of 'GO', the student starts to move along the marked distance, and all student timers start their stopwatches.

4 As the moving student passes each 5-metre marker, have each student timer stop their stopwatch and note the time. Collate all times for the first trial.

5 Repeat the trial two or three times. Repeat any trials where times noted are incomplete or obviously wrong.

6 Average your results and use them to graph position versus time either manually or using a calculator or computer. Using the position–time graph, construct a graph of velocity versus time for a particular trial.

Results

Table 1 Results of trials

Distance travelled (m)	Trial 1 Time taken (s)	Trial 2 Time taken (s)	Trial 3 Time taken (s)	Trial 4 Time taken (s)	Average time taken (s)
0.0	0.0	0.0	0.0	0.0	0.0
5.0	2.3	2.2	2.3	2.4	2.3
10.0	4.2	4.1	4.2	4.3	4.2
15.0	6.5	6.6	6.4	6.5	6.5
20.0	8.4	8.4	8.3	8.4	8.4
25.0	10.3	10.2	10.4	10.3	10.3
30.0	14.2	14.1	14.3	14.2	14.2

ISBN 978 0 6557 0029 6

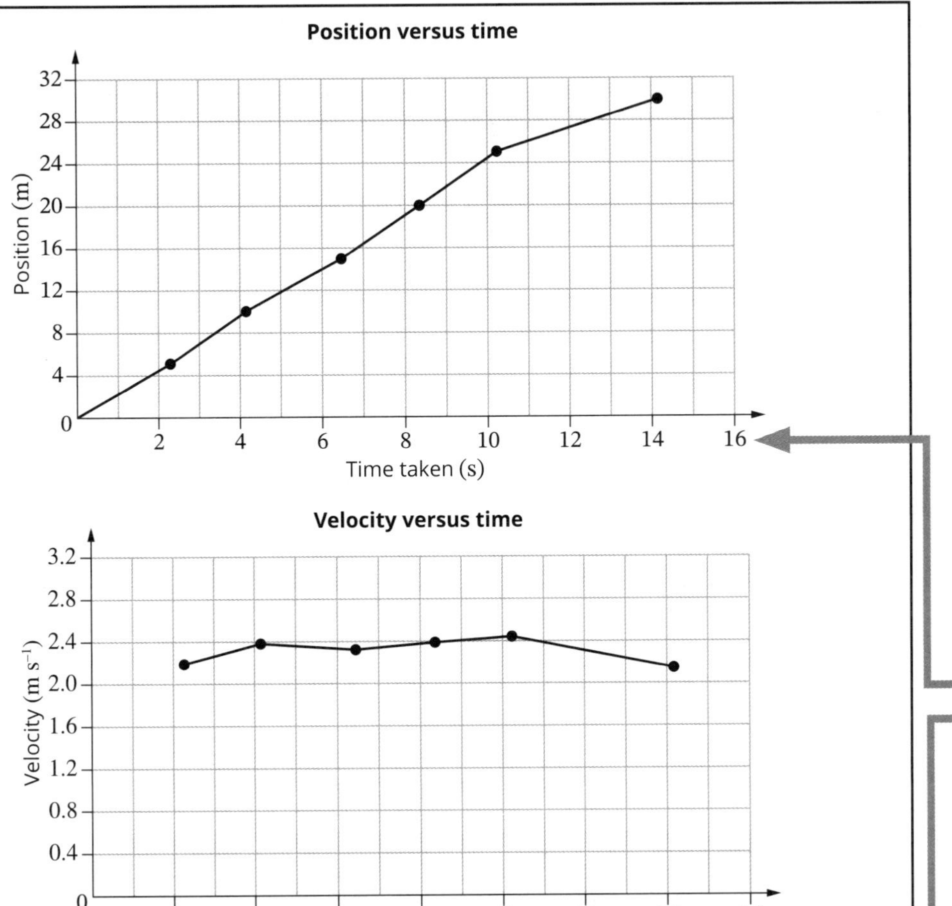

Axes have been labelled correctly and the graph includes a suitable descriptive title.

An appropriate scale has been chosen to make best use of the space available.

Discussion

Discussion shows good understanding of the method and consideration of real sources of error. Avoid general comments unrelated to the specific investigation.

1 Describe the means by which you found velocity from the position versus time graph.

The gradient of a position–time graph can be used to calculate velocity because the change in position is displacement. Alternatively, the individual 5-metre intervals can be used to calculate the velocity for each interval, i.e. $v = \frac{\Delta s}{\Delta t} = \frac{5}{t}$.

2 Comment on the reliability of this means of measuring position, time and velocity.

The error in position can be expected to be small using a 30-metre tape to mark 5-metre intervals. Hand-held timing and watching students pass each marker introduces errors that can be significant if the student's velocity is large.

3 What is the major source of error in this activity?

Timing errors are the largest. A reaction time of 0.2 s is a large part of the time per interval.

4 Suggest an alternative that would improve the reliability of results.

Electronic timing methods such as a timing gate, as used in electronics, would eliminate errors associated with hand-held timing.

Conclusion

The conclusion relates back to the purpose and states whether the hypothesis was supported or not supported. It also outlines the experimental evidence to support this.

This controlled experiment investigated the motion of a student over a 30 metre distance. The investigation demonstrated the connection between distance travelled and velocity of a moving object. The velocity was successfully calculated from the generated position data and the equation $v = \frac{\Delta s}{\Delta t}$.

The experimental evidence shows that for a linear relationship between position and time, the velocity will be constant.

Low-standard practical report

Hypothesis not stated at the beginning of the investigation.

Materials list doesn't include specific details, such as the length of the tape measure.

Risk assessment notes are absent.

The selected methodology is not outlined.

Investigation of motion using timed intervals

Aim

To investigate the motion of a student using timed intervals of measured distance.

Materials

- plastic cones or other position markers
- tape measure
- stopwatches

Method

1 In a large, clear space, stretch out the tape measure on the ground in a straight line. Mark out the beginning and end of the distance, as well as every 5-metre interval.

2 Station a student with a stopwatch at each 5-metre marker.

3 Select a student for testing and position them ready to run, walk, crawl or hop from the start. On a call of 'GO', the student starts to move along the marked distance, and all student timers start their stopwatches.

4 As the moving student passes each 5-metre marker, have each student timer stop their stopwatch and note the time.

5 Repeat the trial two or three times.

6 Construct a graph of velocity versus time for a particular trial.

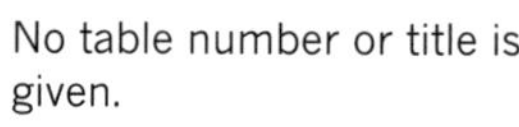

No table number or title is given.

Units are not included with data.

Check data carefully to be sure that it is entered in the appropriate row and column; data has clearly been entered incorrectly in trial 1.

No average column is included in table.

The number of significant figures shown in trial 4 is greater than the precision allowed for by the measuring technique.

Distance travelled	Trial 1 Time taken	Trial 2 Time taken	Trial 3 Time taken	Trial 4 Time taken
0	1.5	0	0	0.000
5	2.3	2.2	2.3	2.356
10	4.2	4.1	4.2	4.323
15	6.5	6.6	6.4	6.523
20	6.5	8.4	8.3	8.421

Graph should have a descriptive title and include a scale that uses the graph area available.

Labelling of axes is incomplete. Include both what is being graphed and the respective units. Scale should be clearly shown.

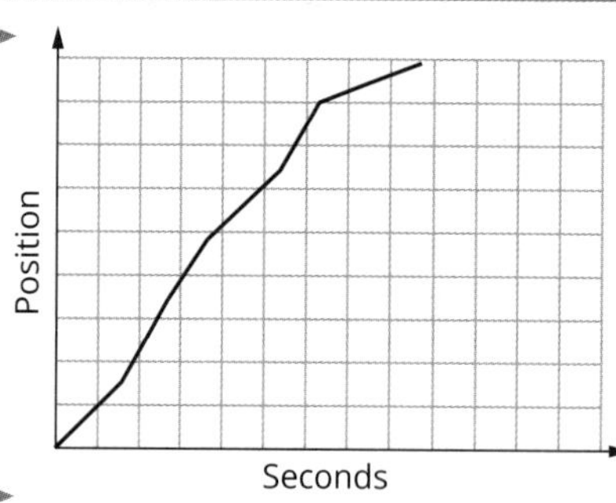

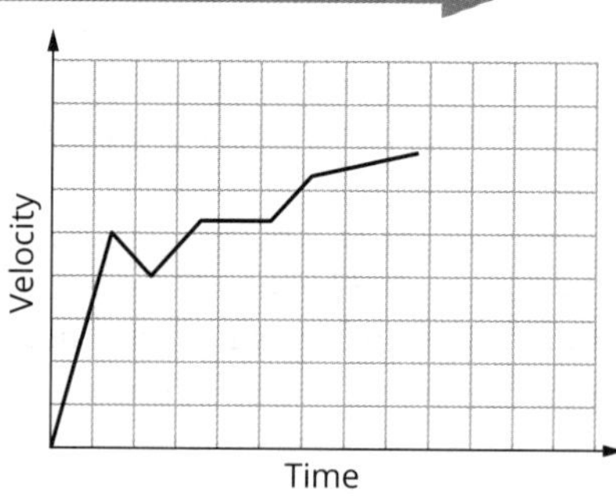

Discussion

1 Comment on the reliability of this means of measuring position, time and, hence, velocity.

There were some big errors because the answers didn't match.

2 What is the major source of error in this activity?

I think the biggest errors came from not reading the instructions. Also the timing was hard and not everybody tried.

3 Suggest alternatives that would improve the reliability of results.

You could try measuring it again or maybe try a different method.

This conclusion is vague—it doesn't respond specifically to the aim of the investigation, nor state whether the hypothesis was supported or not supported. It doesn't use the experimental results to support the conclusion.

Conclusion

We succeeded in completing this investigation.

ISBN 978 0 6557 0029 6

STUDENT-DESIGNED INVESTIGATION

You will be required to design and conduct a scientific investigation based on the concepts you have learnt in either Unit 3 or Unit 4, or across both Units 3 and 4. This assessment task gives you the opportunity to apply key science skills and to pursue an area of interest to you, based on the key knowledge addressed during the course. You will be required to develop a question that drives your investigation, state an aim and hypothesis, select appropriate methodology and methods, and generate and collect primary quantitative data, recording important information in your logbook. You will then present your investigation as a scientific poster with a maximum word count of 600 words. It will be helpful to refer to page ix to review what to include in a scientific investigation and report.

It will be important to carefully select the appropriate methodology and methods for your investigation. You will need to be clear about the difference between the two.

- **Methodology:** describes the overall approach undertaken in a scientific investigation; it considers the investigation more broadly, and includes the reasons for taking the chosen approach, for example, it will identify and describe strategies, such as the methods used to obtain data and the reasons why this is important to achieve the aim of your scientific investigation and address the question under investigation.
- **Method:** describes the specific procedure or steps taken to collect data during a scientific investigation.

DETERMINING YOUR RESEARCH QUESTION

As you develop a question for your scientific investigation, be aware of the depth of thinking it will require. The table on the following page provides support in writing questions at different levels of thinking or complexity. It also provides some key words to help target these thinking levels and gives some examples of questions.

When developing your question for investigation, be conscious of the level at which you are pitching it. Questions for scientific investigation should generally be at the analysis level.

Level of question complexity	Type of thinking	Words that might be used		Examples of questions and commands
Simple	**Retrieval:** • remembering, producing information on demand	• who • where • list • show • describe • select • complete • define	• what • when • label • demonstrate • name • state • recognise • identify	**1** Define the term 'momentum'. **2** What factors affect inertia in a collision? **3** Identify the vector quantities in a straight-line motion. **4** What variables affect the degree of diffraction when light passes through a small gap?
	Comprehension: • the ability to understand information	• who • where • explain • represent • show how	• what • when • summarise • draw • describe	**1** Explain why metals have different threshold frequencies. **2** Describe the movement of electrons in a magnetic field.
	Application: using knowledge in new situations, including: • testing a hypothesis - solving a problem - experimenting and using data	• why • investigate • find out about • test • solve • develop • decide • construct	• how • research • experiment • predict • adapt • judge	**1** Investigate the behaviour of a transformer in a DC circuit and an AC circuit. **2** Research the development of our understanding of the dual nature of light.
	Analysis: • scrutinising and breaking something into its smaller parts, including: - comparing - classifying - identifying errors - concluding - predicting	• why • categorise • contrast • sort • organise • generalise • evaluate • edit • assess • judge	• how • compare • distinguish • discriminate between • deduce • critique • identify misunderstandings	**1** Compare a solenoid with an electromagnet. **2** Compare and contrast ideas about the wave and particle behaviour of light.
Complex (requires more thinking)	**Synthesis:** • combining knowledge and proposing new solutions, including: - problem solving - decision making	• justify • evaluate • design • create • investigate	• construct • simulate • how • why • what	**1** Some scientists believe that adopting nuclear energy in Australia is necessary to limit carbon emissions. Construct an argument for or against this statement. **2** Early scientists believed that heat energy was transferred by the spilling of 'caloric'. Construct an argument for or against this statement.

SECONDARY-SOURCED INVESTIGATION

Some scientific investigations require the collation and analysis of data that others have collected. Data or information that was collected by someone else is known as secondary data, or a secondary source. An investigation that uses secondary data is known as a secondary-sourced investigation. An example of a scientific investigation methodology that involves collating and analysing secondary sources is a literature review. This section guides you in conducting a secondary-sourced investigation.

Activities such as investigating an issue are likely to rely on secondary sources of information. Such investigations require you to think carefully about the topic; find, collect and organise information; analyse and synthesise findings; and present your ideas.

The process for undertaking a secondary-sourced investigation is summarised in the following flow chart. A secondary-sourced investigation is not necessarily a straightforward linear process, as shown in the flow chart. You can move back and forth between steps as needed.

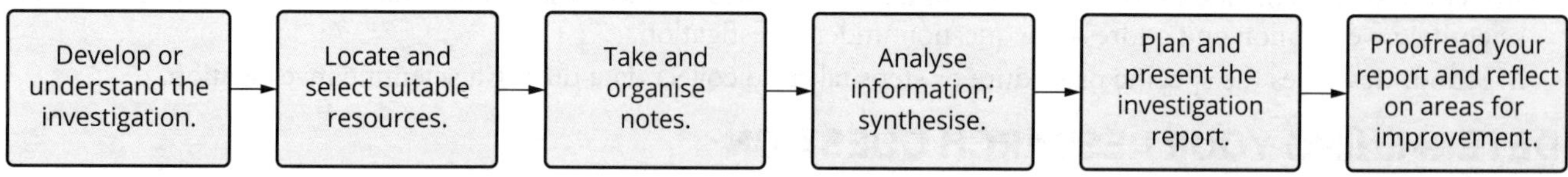

SOURCING INFORMATION

The resources you refer to in investigations may be primary and/or secondary.

Primary sources of information are created by a person directly involved in an investigation or study. Examples of primary sources are results from experiments (such as raw data or photographs), reports of scientific investigations, and peer-reviewed scientific articles reporting the results of an investigation.

Secondary sources of information are a synthesis, review or interpretation of primary sources. Secondary sources include textbooks, biographies, documentaries, newspaper articles and websites.

Refer to the following two checklists. The first shows features to look for when assessing and selecting the best sources of information. The second shows how to set out the information that is required for the references section of your report in American Psychological Association (APA) seventh edition style. This is only one of several referencing systems that you might be required to use throughout your career.

Selecting resources for the investigation	Tick ✓
The resource is:	
• **credible** and I can identify the author, author's expertise and publisher	
• **current** because the date of publication of the material is provided and is recent	
• **factual** and I know that it is objective material and not biased	
• **accurate** and all information is correct	
• **relevant** and covers the area I am investigating	
• **readable** and neither too simple nor too complex in its coverage of the material	

Examples of information required for references and bibliographies (APA style)
Article in scientific magazine Author, initials. (year). Title of article. *Journal title, volume number*(issue number), page numbers. Digital object identifier (DOI) or URL. Kensrud, J.R., Nathan A.M., & Smith L.V. (2017). Oblique collisions of baseballs and softballs with a bat. *American Journal of Physics, 85(*8). 503–509. https://doi.org/10.1119/1.4982793
Book Author, initials. (year). *Title of book* (edition, if not first). Publisher. Black, L., Dommel, A., Dommel, N., Fisher, T., Jobson, K., Lewis, G., Moran, G, Nardelli, D., & White, G. (2022). *Heinemann Physics 12* (5th ed.). Pearson Australia. Include names of all authors or editors up to 20. Special rules apply for 21 or more authors. You can find information about the rules online.
Internet Author, initials/name of organisation. (year). *Title of webpage or web document.* <URL> American Institute of Physics (2017). *Periodic table.* httwp://history.aip.org/history/exhibits/electron/

Always remember to record the above details for each resource you use. It is important to accurately cite resources in your reference section, as it can be time-consuming and difficult to find this information later.

 ISBN 978 0 6557 0029 6

NOTE-TAKING AND ORGANISING NOTES

Note-taking and organising require skill. Good note-taking helps you avoid plagiarism and provides excellent information to support your scientific report writing. Plagiarism is when you take someone else's ideas and words and present them as your own work. You plagiarise if you copy sections or sentences from sources or you cut and paste from the internet. It is acceptable to use the ideas of others, but you must state clearly where the information has come from in your reference section.

The following table provides examples of original text, plagiarised text and acceptably rephrased text.

Original text	Plagiarised text	Rephrased text
Waves on water, in a string and in air are examples of mechanical waves. Waves are classified by what they move through. Electromagnetic waves, or light waves, are able to travel without the need for a medium.	Waves are classified by what they move through. Electromagnetic waves, also known as light waves, are able to travel without the need for a medium. Waves on water or in a string and in air are mechanical waves.	Waves can be both mechanical and electromagnetic. This classification comes from the medium the waves move through. Mechanical waves need a medium such as water, a string or air. Electromagnetic waves do not require a medium.

There are various approaches to effective note-taking. Whatever technique you use, try to keep your notes brief and focus on key points. Some examples include:

- dot point summaries
- underlining or highlighting text
- labelled diagrams
- flow charts—to show sequences
- concept maps—to show connections between ideas
- Venn diagrams—to show similarities and differences
- tables—useful for summarising longer and more complex information that has subparts and can incorporate any of the other note-taking techniques. Adapt the table to suit your style and the task.

The following (partially completed) table shows how this technique can be used to take notes for a secondary-sourced investigation.

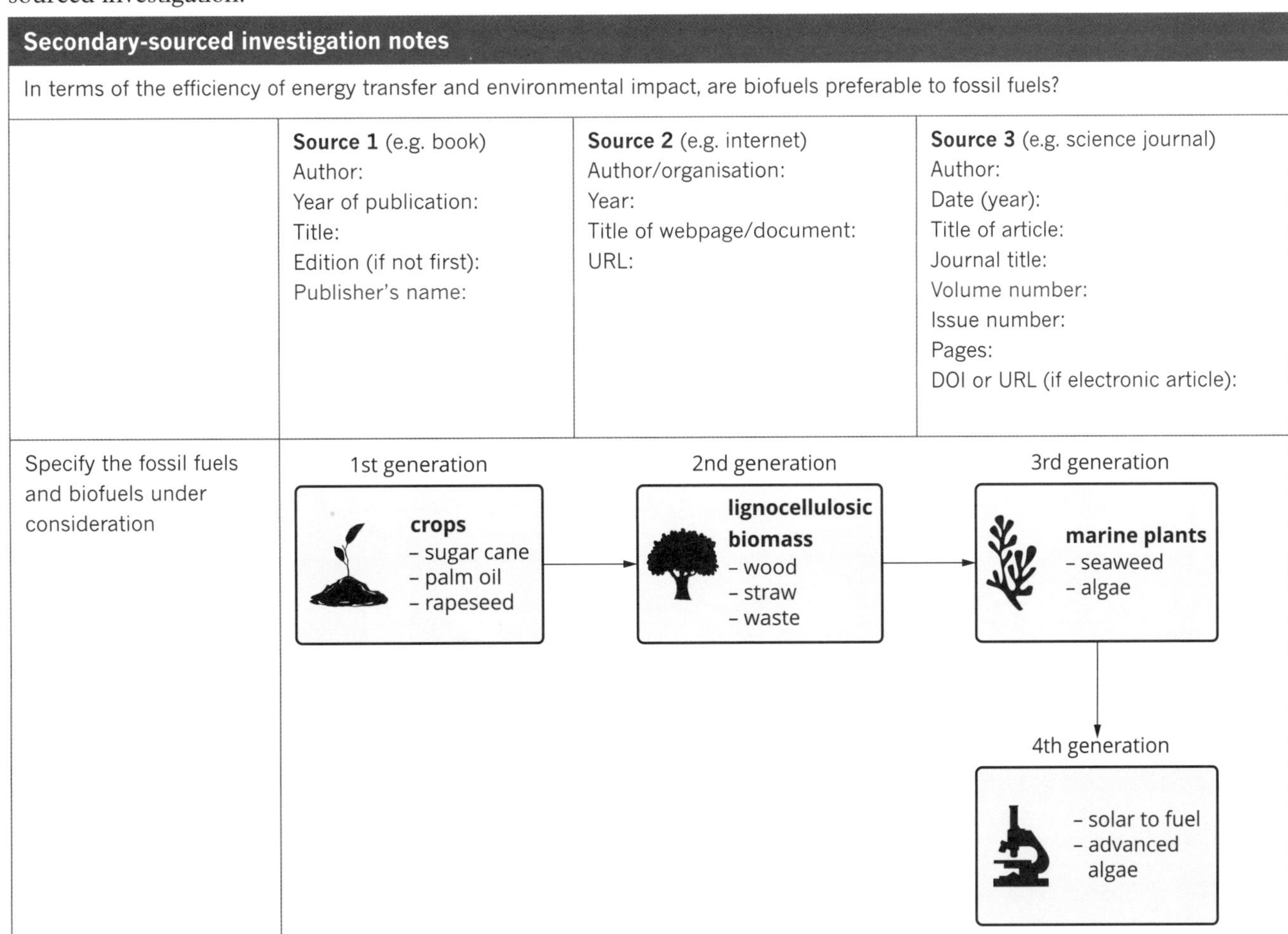

Secondary-sourced investigation notes			
In terms of the efficiency of energy transfer and environmental impact, are biofuels preferable to fossil fuels?			
	Source 1 (e.g. book) Author: Year of publication: Title: Edition (if not first): Publisher's name:	**Source 2** (e.g. internet) Author/organisation: Year: Title of webpage/document: URL:	**Source 3** (e.g. science journal) Author: Date (year): Title of article: Journal title: Volume number: Issue number: Pages: DOI or URL (if electronic article):
Specify the fossil fuels and biofuels under consideration	1st generation **crops** – sugar cane – palm oil – rapeseed	2nd generation **lignocellulosic biomass** – wood – straw – waste	3rd generation **marine plants** – seaweed – algae 4th generation – solar to fuel – advanced algae

Secondary-sourced investigation notes			
Pros and cons of fossil fuels in terms of efficiency	Biofuels can be replenished much faster than fossil fuels.	Global average efficiency is 36% for all fossil fuels.	
Pros and cons of biofuels in terms of efficiency	Biofuels can be replenished much faster than fossil fuels.		
Pros and cons of fossil fuels in terms of environmental impact			Cons • air pollution • contribute to climate change
Pros and cons of biofuels in terms of environmental impact			

SCIENTIFIC WRITING

Scientists have a particular writing style. You should use this distinctive style to communicate your ideas. Scientific writing is:

- objective—it describes events rather than what people think or feel and is as free as possible of bias or personal opinion
- precise—it avoids exaggeration and uses qualified language
- formal—it uses scholarly language rather than colloquial or everyday language
- concise—it conveys information in short, clearly understandable sentences without unnecessary information
- simple—it uses short sentences where possible
- predominantly written in passive voice, although sometimes active voice can be used to avoid confusion
- structured to include headings, tables, diagrams and mathematical calculations.

Examples of unscientific and scientific writing are demonstrated in the following table.

Unscientific writing	Scientific writing
Subjective, biased writing: • The results were fantastic. • This produced a disgusting odour.	Objective, unbiased writing: • The results showed... • This produced a pungent odour.
Exaggerated writing: • The object weighed a huge amount. • The magnesium burst into huge flames. • Safety crisis ...	Accurate, precise writing: • The mass of the object was 250 kg. • The magnesium burnt vigorously. • Safety issue...
Everyday, informal language: • The experiment didn't work and we have no idea why. • The results don't... • We guessed that... • Previous researchers were slack and missed...	Formal language: • Further research is needed to fully determine why the results of the experiment were not as expected. • The results do not... • It was hypothesised that... • Previous researchers have not found...

ISBN 978 0 6557 0029 6

PRESENTING A REPORT ON A SCIENTIFIC INVESTIGATION

Scientific findings may be presented in a variety of ways. A common presentation format at science conferences is a poster. Posters can get ideas across to a large audience in an organised, concise and creative way. Other common presentation formats are essays, reports, oral presentations and articles. Each presentation format has its own conventions. The following table summarises the characteristics of a number of presentation formats.

Presentation format	Characteristics/inclusions	
poster	• balance of text and visuals • title, subheadings • balanced layout • captions for figures and tables	• references • hierarchy of font size according to subheading level • consistent font style—no more than three fonts
report/article	• structured with an introduction, paragraphs and conclusion • includes subheadings	• mainly text • can include diagrams, graphs and tables
essay	• structured with an introduction, paragraphs and conclusion • introduction states focus of essay • each paragraph makes a new point supported by evidence	• each paragraph links back to last paragraph • a text-style presentation format—visuals at end in appendix • conclusion draws all ideas together but does not include any new information
oral presentation	• needs to be engaging • refer to cue cards but do not read from them • watch audience as you speak	• stand still and avoid fidgeting • look at audience and appear confident

PROOFREADING

After you have completed the investigation and prepared your presentation, it is important to think about and check what you have done.

Proofread your work to minimise errors and maximise effective communication of the ideas from your investigation. Use the following questions as a proofreading checklist.

Proofreading checklist	Tick ✔
Have I:	
• investigated the question fully?	
• expressed myself clearly to communicate my ideas well?	
• used the scientific writing style?	
• included data analysis?	
• checked spelling, punctuation and grammar?	
• included references?	
• met the requirements of the presentation format?	

ISBN 978 0 6557 0029 6

Study skills

There is a variety of techniques and strategies you can use to help you study. You may find that you use different strategies in different situations. For example, you may prefer to highlight key phrases in your notebook throughout the year, but make summaries of topics before an examination. The strategies you choose will depend on personal preference and may not be the same as those used by your classmates.

Effective study skills involve more than the learning strategies you use. Equally important is when you use those skills. It is more effective to apply study skills throughout the year, revising and consolidating your knowledge as you progress through the course, rather than doing a rushed cram just before the examination. Revise your work regularly. Being organised and setting up a study plan is key to reducing your stress.

GETTING ORGANISED

To get yourself organised, try the following steps.

- Use a diary to write down all homework and assessment tasks as soon as you get them. Note due dates and what is required.
- Be specific about the tasks you need to do. Rather than writing 'do biology', it is more effective to note things, such as which questions to answer and which page to look at in your student book.
- Write a list of everything you need to do each day. Tick off or cross out items as you complete them.
- Break down larger tasks into smaller separate parts that are manageable.
- Make sure your lists and planners are realistic. Do not set yourself more than you can actually do.

STUDY TECHNIQUES

Studying requires concentration. Remove any distractions and factor in some breaks. Allow a 10-minute break every hour. Vary your study technique depending on the content to be learnt and your personal preference. Although you may have already found a study technique that works for you, also consider the following options.

Study technique	Tips
Highlighting **Fields** Fields can either be monopoles (meaning one pole) or dipoles (meaning two poles). Electric fields can be either of these. For example, a point charge will be a monopole, while two charges separated a distance *r* will create a dipole. Gravitational and magnetic fields cannot be both a monopole and a dipole. Gravitational fields consist of monopoles, where the field is pointed towards a centre of mass.	Highlight or underline key points as you read your notes or text.
Summary notes *VECTOR VERSUS SCALAR QUANTITIES* • *Scalar quantities are fully defined by magnitude only* • *Vector quantities require a magnitude and direction* • *The direction can be in terms of a full circle or quadrant bearing* • *Vector quantities include displacement, velocity, force and acceleration* • *Equivalent scalar quantities are distance, speed, force and acceleration (show magnitude only)*	• Create a list of key headings and add some dot points about each heading. • Write your own summary of the key ideas in each chapter. • Use headings and subheadings. • Underline key words and key phrases. • Use simple diagrams. • Remember, the most effective chapter summaries are clear, concise and uncluttered.
Diagrams Lowest energy orbit where electron is normally found + Higher energy orbits	• Diagrams can be used as a summary of key concepts. • Diagrams are useful memory triggers. • Diagrams cover a lot of information in a visual way, with minimal text.

ISBN 978 0 6557 0029 6

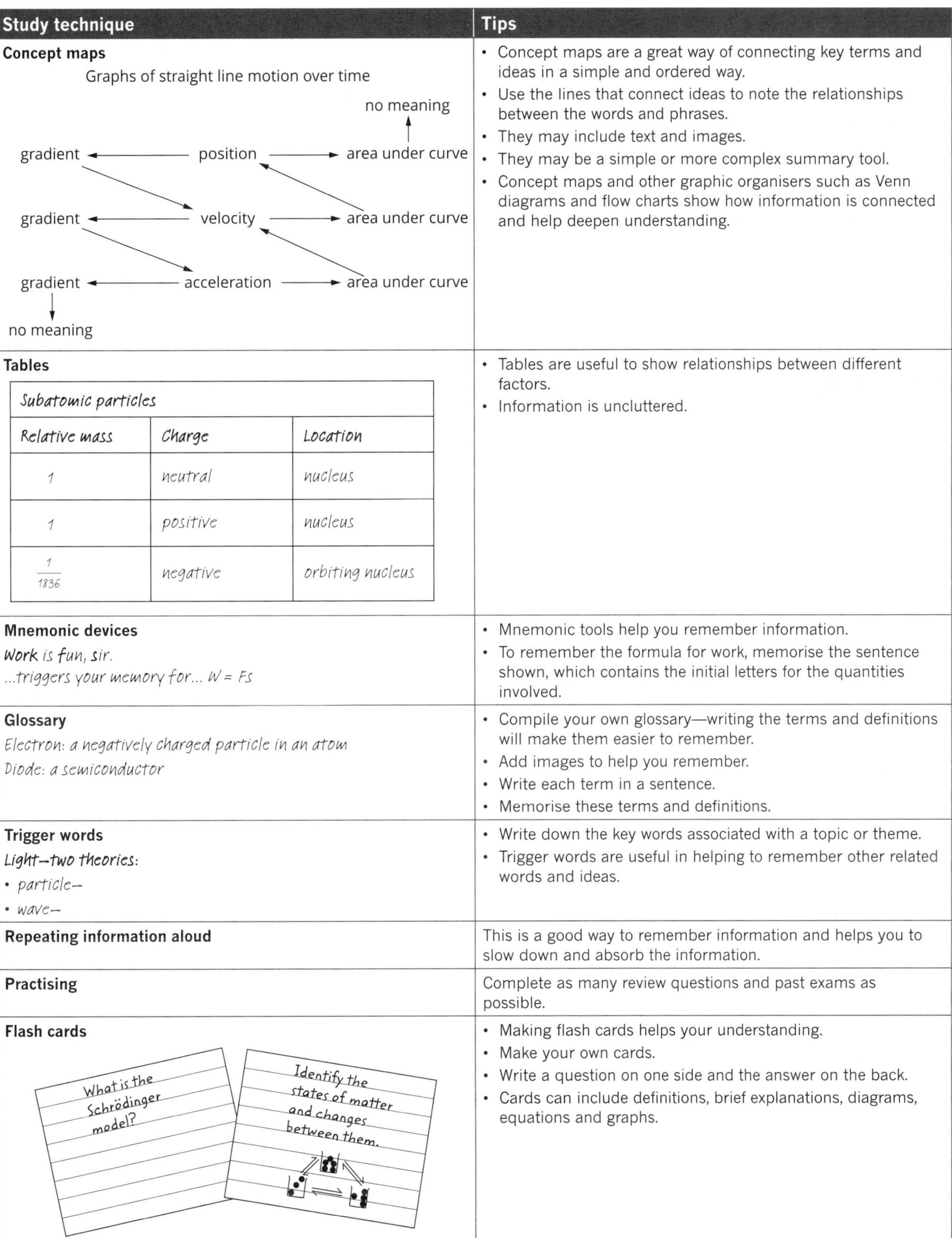

Study technique	Tips
Concept maps Graphs of straight line motion over time no meaning gradient ← position → area under curve gradient ← velocity → area under curve gradient ← acceleration → area under curve no meaning	• Concept maps are a great way of connecting key terms and ideas in a simple and ordered way. • Use the lines that connect ideas to note the relationships between the words and phrases. • They may include text and images. • They may be a simple or more complex summary tool. • Concept maps and other graphic organisers such as Venn diagrams and flow charts show how information is connected and help deepen understanding.
Tables *Subatomic particles* *Relative mass* | *Charge* | *Location* *1* | *neutral* | *nucleus* *1* | *positive* | *nucleus* $\frac{1}{1836}$ | *negative* | *orbiting nucleus*	• Tables are useful to show relationships between different factors. • Information is uncluttered.
Mnemonic devices *Work is fun, sir.* *...triggers your memory for... W = Fs*	• Mnemonic tools help you remember information. • To remember the formula for work, memorise the sentence shown, which contains the initial letters for the quantities involved.
Glossary *Electron: a negatively charged particle in an atom* *Diode: a semiconductor*	• Compile your own glossary—writing the terms and definitions will make them easier to remember. • Add images to help you remember. • Write each term in a sentence. • Memorise these terms and definitions.
Trigger words *Light—two theories:* • *particle—* • *wave—*	• Write down the key words associated with a topic or theme. • Trigger words are useful in helping to remember other related words and ideas.
Repeating information aloud	This is a good way to remember information and helps you to slow down and absorb the information.
Practising	Complete as many review questions and past exams as possible.
Flash cards *What is the Schrödinger model?* *Identify the states of matter and changes between them.*	• Making flash cards helps your understanding. • Make your own cards. • Write a question on one side and the answer on the back. • Cards can include definitions, brief explanations, diagrams, equations and graphs.

continues over

Study technique	Tips
Teaching someone	• Teach friends or family members. • Teaching a difficult concept to someone means you must first understand the concept yourself.
Handwriting notes	• Handwrite rather than type summary notes. • Remember, the examination requires you to write answers. • Practise writing for long stretches of time and make sure your writing is legible.
Responding to feedback and self-correcting	• Check through all feedback from your teacher. • Highlight what was right or wrong. • Attempt to identify where you have errors and rework the answer to get it right.

Examination preparation

In the weeks before the examination, begin your exam preparation. The earlier you begin revising, the easier it will be. It is also helpful to begin practising exam-style questions as early as possible, not just in the weeks before the exam.

Like most skills, practice will improve your ability to do exams and to handle different types of exam questions. Doing practice exams is vital because you gain experience in:

- using reading time effectively
- allocating the right amount of time to each question
- working to a time limit
- reading and interpreting questions
- understanding what is required for each question
- planning answers
- deciding on relevant information
- proofreading/checking your answers
- writing efficiently for the duration of the exam.

Use your practice exam experience not only to revise but also to analyse your strengths and weaknesses, and to assess how you managed your time.

Use the following checklist as a reminder of your study program.

Study program checklist	Tick ✔
Have I:	
• revised all areas of the course?	
• highlighted important points?	
• made a summary of the important points in each topic?	
• read over my revision notes?	
• looked at and worked through practice exam papers?	
• answered practice exam questions within the appropriate time limit?	

ISBN 978 0 6557 0029 6

EXAMINATION STRATEGIES

Familiarise yourself with the conditions of the examination well before the day you sit the exam. You should know:

- the number of exams for the subject
- the amount of reading time allowed in the exam before writing begins
- the amount of writing time allocated
- any particular equipment allowed and/or required, such as a calculator, pencils, pens and ruler
- strategies to tackle the exam.

Exam strategies are listed in the following table.

Exam strategies
Reading time • You will be given reading time at the beginning of the exam (usually 15 minutes). • Remember that no writing at all is allowed during this time—no note-taking, no highlighting or underlining. • Read the instructions. • Read through the short-answer questions first—this will give you an overall sense of the themes of questions that require written responses. • Read the multiple-choice questions next. • Decide the order in which you will answer questions. Start with what you consider to be the easiest question to build confidence.
Writing time • You will be given 2.5 hours of working time. • Begin with the multiple-choice questions. • Answer every multiple-choice question, even if you can only make an educated guess. • If you are unsure of an answer to a multiple-choice question, mark it so you can come back to it if time allows. • Attempt the short-answer questions next. • Attempt the easiest short-answer questions first and work your way to the more challenging questions.
Tips for answering questions • Carefully read each question, underlining key words. • Be aware that most questions are structured so they become more challenging towards the end. You may not be able to answer the last part of a question, but you will have earned most of the marks by answering earlier parts. • Look carefully at any diagrams, pictures, tables and graphs and make sure you understand their relevance to the questions involved. • For questions with graphs, read the graph title and the labels on the axes carefully so that you can establish the relationship the graph is showing. • For questions with tables, read the headings on the columns and rows carefully so that you can analyse the content of the table effectively. • Check for key words in a question. Highlight them, but do not colour the whole question. • Use correct spelling—it can mean the difference between scoring a point and not scoring a point, for example, 'neutrin' could be a misspelling for either 'neutron' or 'neutrino', and consequently would score zero. • Plan your answers before you write, remembering to address the exam criteria. • For questions with parts, read the whole question first. This gives you an overall picture of the question. It will also help to ensure that you do not repeat yourself in subsequent parts of the question. • Make sure you actually answer the question that is asked. • Once you have answered the question, re-read your answer and then re-read the question to ensure that you have actually answered all of the question. • When writing a definition, avoid using the word you are defining in your definition. • If giving values from a graph, use a ruler to line up points with the axes so you can be accurate, and always include units in your answer. • Be sure to attempt all questions. • Read over your answers to pick up careless errors—the mind is faster than the hand and you may not always write what you intend (especially when you have limited time). • Write legibly. Exams are scanned and marked online. If the assessor can't read your answer, they can't mark it as correct. • Keep an eye on the time. • Never leave an exam early. Use any spare time to re-read and check your answers.
Exam cues • The number of marks allocated to a question provides a clue about how much you are expected to write. Two marks usually means you need to make a minimum of two points. • The number of lines allowed for the answer indicates the length of the expected answer. If your writing is large, you may need to turn the page over and continue on the back. Make sure you indicate to the examiner that they must turn to the back of the page for the rest of the answer. Where the answer continues, clearly state that it is the continuation of the question and state the question number.

HANDLING EXAM QUESTIONS

The exam is divided into two sections. Section A consists of multiple-choice questions and Section B contains a series of short-answer questions.

Multiple-choice questions	Short-answer questions
• In many cases you can use your basic knowledge of the subject to cancel out one or two options. • Mark an answer to every question on your answer sheet as you go through them. This avoids leaving any questions unanswered if you run out of time, and avoids getting out of order by leaving blank rows. You can always go back and change the answers you were unsure about. • Circle the letter of your answer to the question on the exam paper as well, so you can easily check if you get out of sync on the answer sheet. • If you are finding a question difficult, do not spend too much time on it as it is only worth 1 mark. Make your best educated guess, if necessary, and then mark the question on your paper and come back to it later if you have time. • If you have time at the end of the exam, redo the questions with your original answer covered and compare.	• Be careful to do what the question asks. For example, do you need to identify, describe, explain or compare? Each requires a different response. • When in doubt, point it out, that is, give a thorough answer. Dot points and labelled diagrams are acceptable as long as you fully address the question. • Tailor your answer specifically to the question being asked. Do not rely on a general answer when given a specific scenario. For example, indicate the direction in which a force is acting and what provided it; do not just say a force acted. • Look at the marks allocated for an indication of the level of detail required. Generally, 1 mark = 1 key point, 2 marks = 2 key points, etc. • Give full explanations and show your working. This makes it easier for you to check your answer and you often gain part marks and consequential marks if the marker can see where you made an error.

Every year, examiners comment that many students fail to answer the question: that is, students' answers are 'not relevant' or are 'off the point'. Giving a relevant answer to a question is vital and depends on:

- choosing appropriate content
- using content purposefully to do what is asked (see the key action words list below).

Key action words	
analyse	break down into key points; show the essence of; inquire into; identify components and the relationship between them; draw out and relate implications
compare	show points of similarity
contrast	show points of difference
describe	give the features/characteristics of
design	provide steps for an experiment or procedure
evaluate	make a judgement based on criteria; determine the value of
explain	provide details to give the reader an understanding of; relate cause and effect; make the relationships between things evident; provide why and/or how
justify	demonstrate the correctness of (by giving evidence); give evidence in support of an argument or conclusion
suggest	put forward ideas, proposals or recommendations

EXAMPLES OF EXAM RESPONSES

Each year the examiners write an assessment report on the most recent exam. Reading these reports is a good way to understand what the examiners expect in the answers. The reports indicate where students showed strong responses and where answers could be improved.

Looking closely at sample responses will help you identify what is required to gain full marks. Two sample responses are provided below: one has room for improvement (low-level response) while the other is well done (high-level response). The annotations draw your attention to key points to note in each response.

Question 1 (9 marks)

In Millikan's oil-drop experiment, charged drops were suspended within an electric field, like in the diagram below.

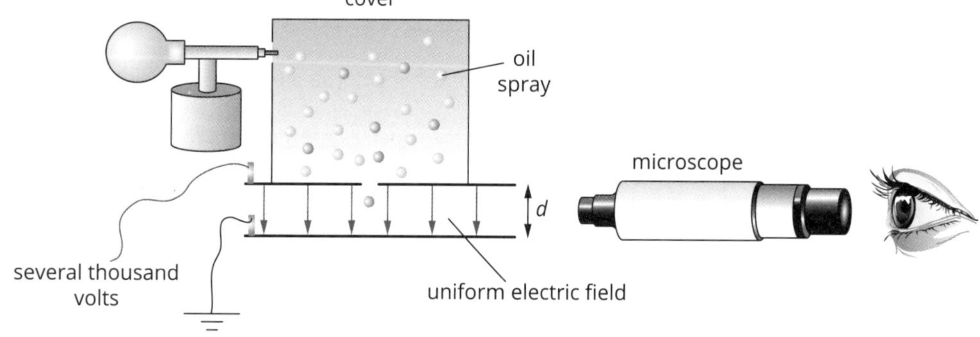

 ISBN 978 0 6557 0029 6

A group of scientists attempted to recreate Millikan's experiment by calculating the force due to gravity on different drops that become suspended between a potential difference when the electric field strength is increased. They created the following hypothesis and purpose:

If a droplet of oil spray is successfully suspended within an electric potential, then at this point the force due to gravity must be balanced by the electrostatic force felt by the particle. The electrostatic force is governed by the elementary charge q_e, which will be determined experimentally by finding the force due to gravity on suspended particles at different potential differences.

After completing their experiment, the following table was created:

Electric field strength ($\times 10^5$ V m^{-1})	Force due to gravity ($\times 10^{-14}$ N)
1.25	2.01
1.50	2.42
1.75	2.72
2.00	3.22
2.25	3.62

High-level responses

Question 1

a Plot the data and draw a line of best fit.

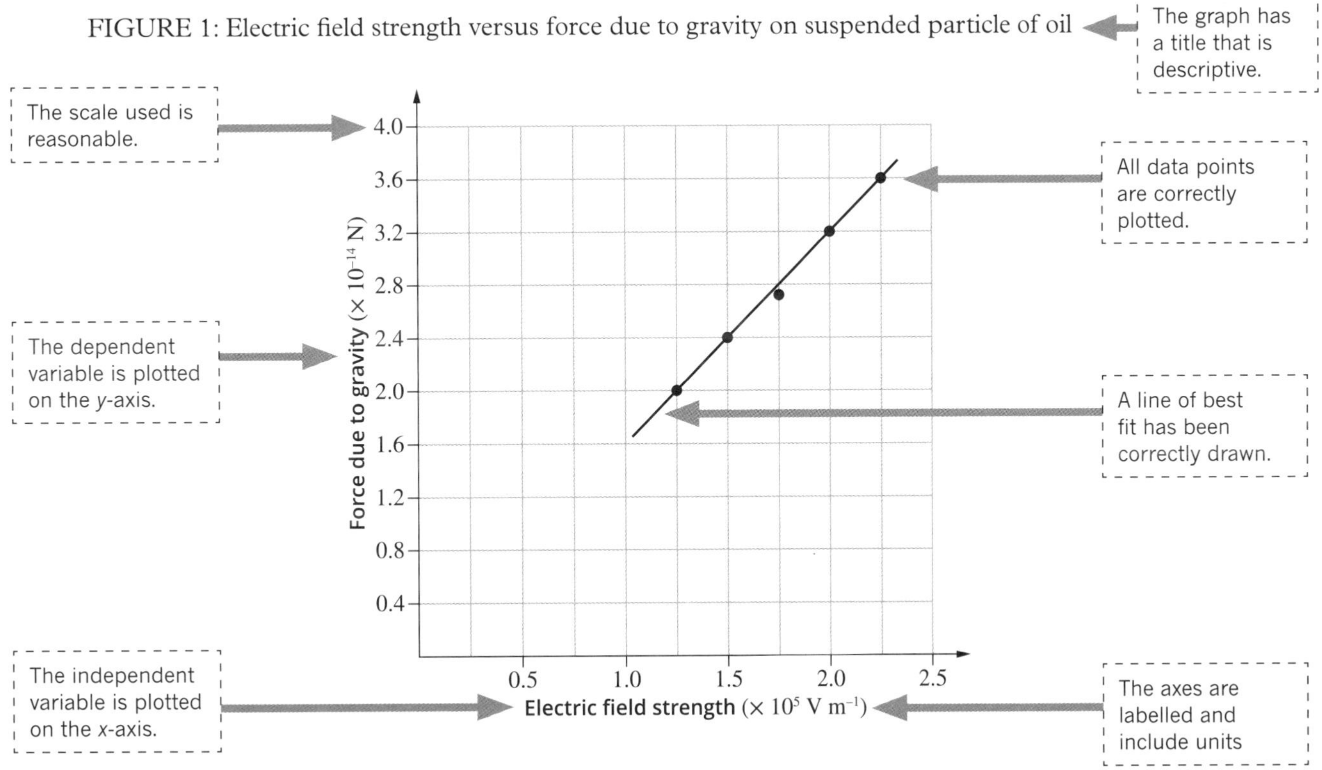

b Describe qualitatively the relationship between the electric field strength and the force due to gravity on the oil drop. In your response, explain what variable the gradient of the graph represents.

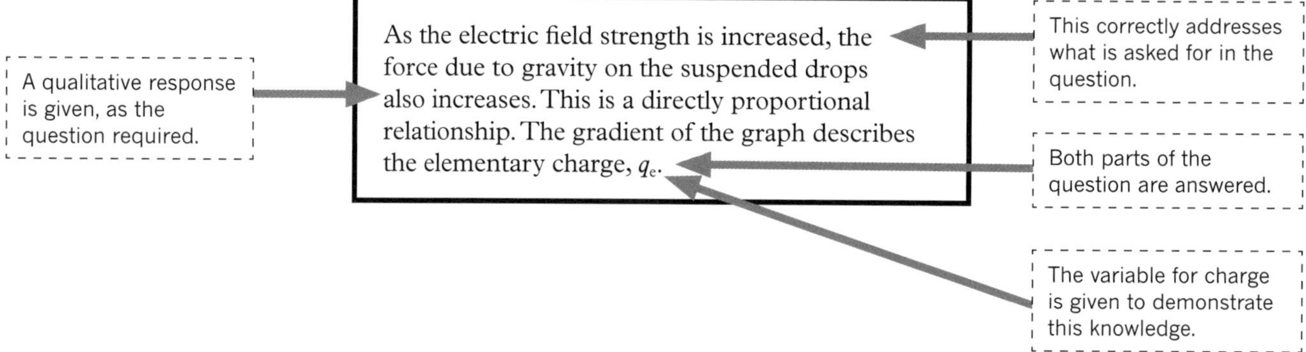

c Compare the value of the elementary charge determined by this experiment to the theoretical value of the charge of an electron.

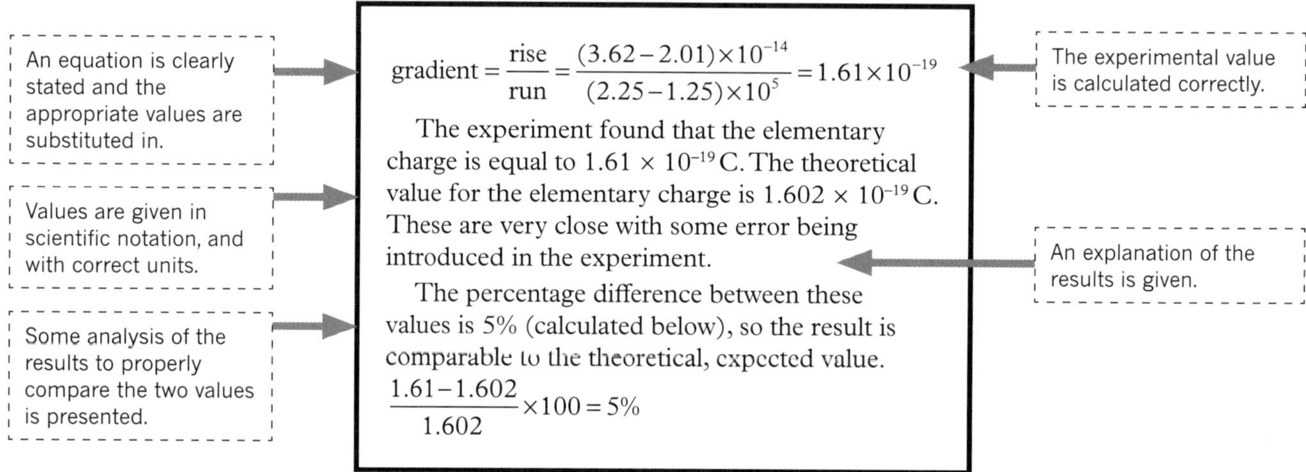

d Define the term validity and describe the validity of these results.

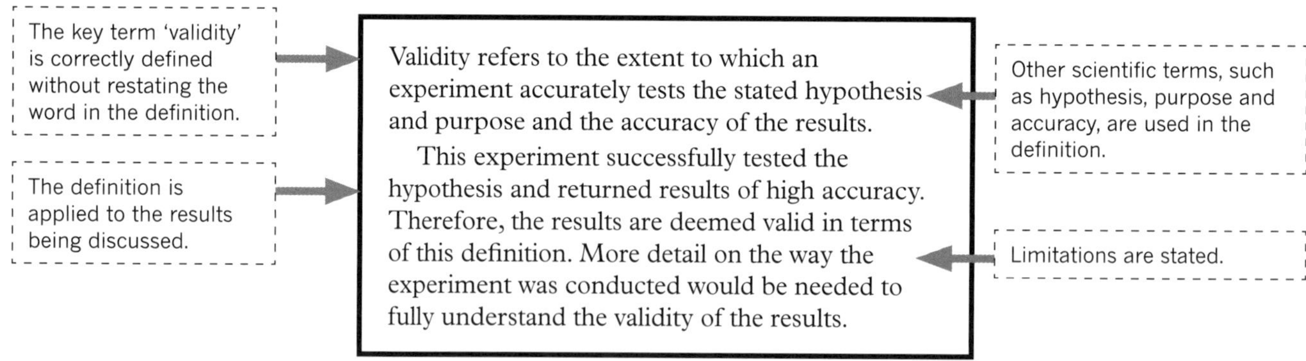

ISBN 978 0 6557 0029 6

Low-level responses

Question 1

a Plot the data and draw a line of best fit.

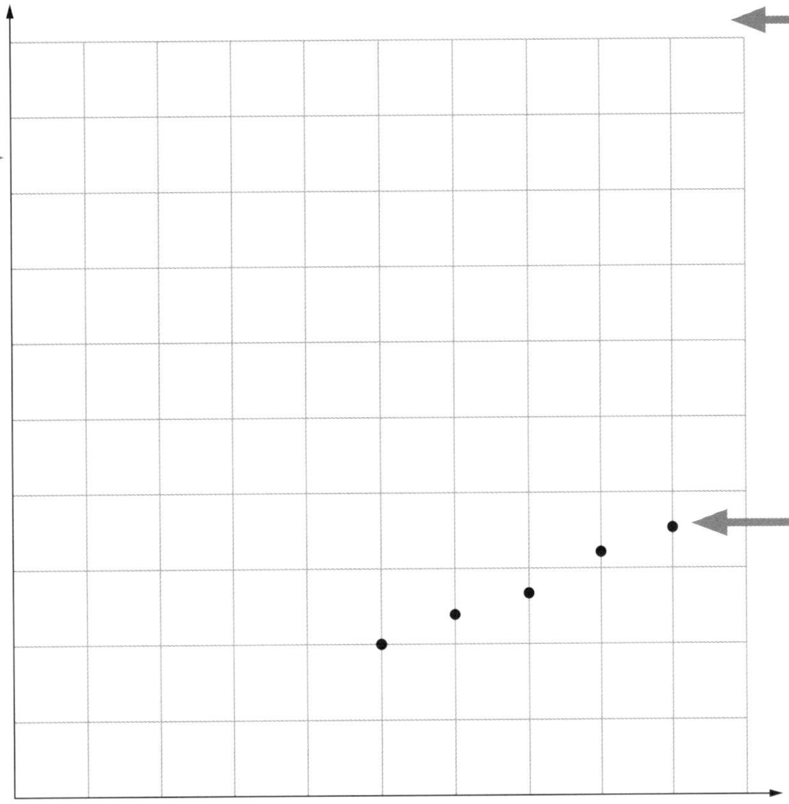

The scale of the *y*-axis is not appropriate for the data, making it hard to accurately plot the data points. It also makes interpreting the graph difficult.

The axes are not labelled, meaning the graph cannot be accurately interpreted as the reader doesn't know which axis each variable is plotted on.

No descriptive title is given.

The question has not been fully answered as no line of best fit has been drawn.

b Describe qualitatively the relationship between the electric field strength and the force due to gravity on the oil drop. In your response, explain what variable the gradient of the graph represents.

The equation given describes the quantitative relationship between the variables, but the question explicitly asked for a qualitative analysis.

> The relationship between the electric field strength and the force due to gravity can be given by the following equation: $F_g = 1.61E$.

The gradient is given in the equation, but the answer doesn't explain what it represents.

Neither part of the question is answered satisfactorily.

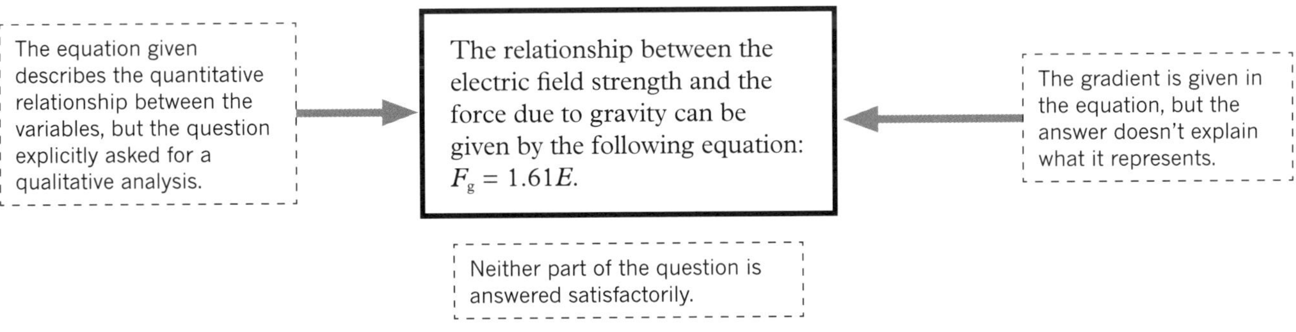

c Compare the value of the elementary charge determined by this experiment to the theoretical value of the charge of an electron.

> $$\text{gradient} = \frac{\text{rise}}{\text{run}} = \frac{3.62 - 2.01}{2.25 - 1.25} = 1.6$$
>
> The experiment found that the elementary charge is equal to 1.6×10^{-19}. The theoretical value for the elementary charge is 1.602×10^{-19}.

The question asks for a comparison, so more analysis is needed for a high-quality response. This simply states the answer

The experimental value of the charge should be given to three significant figures as the precision of the original data was to three significant figures.

Units were not given in the response.

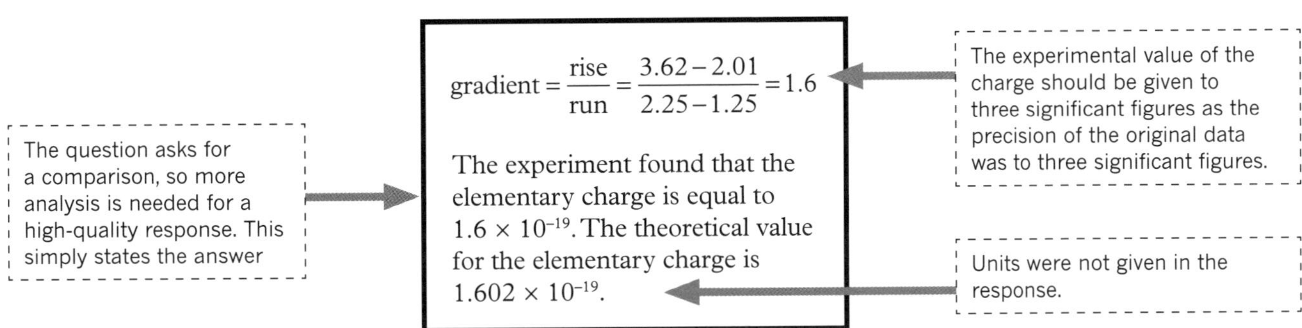

d Define the term validity and describe the validity of these results.

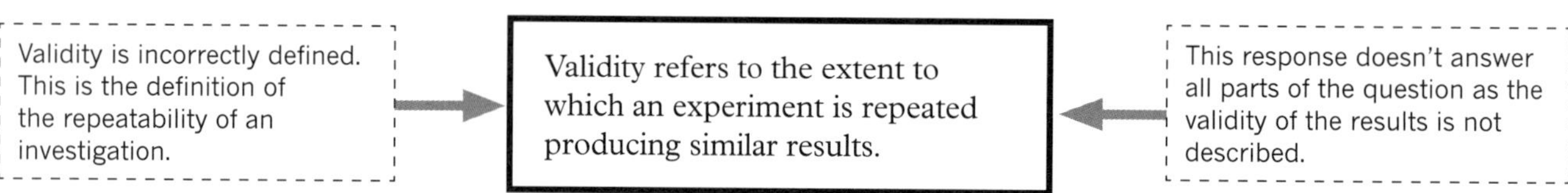

Whenever you are providing a worded response, stick to the question and answer the question only! Think carefully about what the examiner is asking and what directly answers the question. Avoid copying from your notes.

Getting ready

Once you have finished revising and feel confident with the material, use the following checklist to make sure you are prepared before exam day arrives.

The exam itself	Tick ✔
Have you:	
• checked the exact exam requirements?	
• obtained and carefully read the instruction cover sheet from previous exams? (Check that no changes are expected for your exam.)	
• planned how to best use your reading time?	
Practical steps	**Tick ✔**
Have you:	
• assembled all materials required and allowed? This includes:	
– pens to write your answers	
– pencils of the correct lead for the multiple-choice answer sheet	
– sharpeners, erasers, rulers and other permissible materials, such as calculators and spare batteries	
– a water bottle (Check that your bottle meets the requirements—it may need to be clear with no label.)	
– a watch to keep track of the time (Mobile phones are not permitted.)	
• double-checked dates, times and locations for each exam?	
• remembered your student number?	
• packed a form of photo ID (if required)?	
• arranged transport, allowing ample time to avoid rushing and to manage possible delays? (Be sure to arrive early to settle your nerves and gather your thoughts.)	
• planned for appropriate meals, snacks and drinks? (Exam times vary. Eating heavy meals before exams can make you sleepy, so avoid doing this.)	

ISBN 978 0 6557 0029 6

UNIT 3

How do fields explain motion and electricity?

AREA OF STUDY 1

How do physicists explain motion in two dimensions?

Outcome 1

Investigate motion and related energy transformations experimentally, and analyse motion using Newton's laws of motion in one and two dimensions.

Key knowledge

Newton's laws of motion

- investigate and apply theoretically and practically Newton's three laws of motion in situations where two or more coplanar forces act along a straight line and in two dimensions
- investigate and analyse theoretically and practically the uniform circular motion of an object moving in a horizontal plane: $\left(F_{net} = \frac{mv^2}{r}\right)$ including:
  - a vehicle moving around a circular road
  - a vehicle moving around a banked track
  - an object on the end of a string
- model natural and artificial satellite motion as uniform circular motion
- investigate and apply theoretically Newton's second law to circular motion in a vertical plane (forces at the highest and lowest positions only)
- investigate and analyse theoretically and practically the motion of projectiles near Earth's surface, including a qualitative description of the effects of air resistance
- investigate and apply theoretically and practically the laws of energy and momentum conservation in isolated systems in one dimension

Relationships between force, energy and mass

- investigate and analyse theoretically and practically impulse in an isolated system for collisions between objects moving in a straight line: $F\Delta t = m\Delta v$
- investigate and apply theoretically and practically the concept of work done by a force using:
  - work done = force × displacement
  - work done = area under force vs distance graph (one dimensional only)
- analyse transformations of energy between kinetic energy, elastic potential energy, gravitational potential energy and energy dissipated to the environment (considered as a combination of heat, sound and deformation of material):
  - kinetic energy at low speeds: $E_k = \frac{1}{2}mv^2$; elastic and inelastic collisions with reference to conservation of kinetic energy
  - elastic potential energy: area under force–distance graph, including ideal springs obeying Hooke's Law: $E_s = \frac{1}{2}kx^2$
  - gravitational potential energy: $E_g = mg\Delta h$ or from area under a force–distance graph and area under a field–distance graph multiplied by mass.

- **You will now be able to complete Worksheet 1.**

Newtonian theories of motion

NEWTON'S LAWS OF MOTION

Newton's laws describe how forces can be used to explain the motion of bodies. Newton's first law states that every object continues to be at rest, or continues with constant velocity, unless it experiences an unbalanced force. This is also called the law of inertia.

Newton's second law states that the acceleration of a body experiencing an unbalanced force is directly proportional to the net force acting on it and inversely proportional to the mass of the body, $F_{net} = ma$.

Newton's third law states that when one body exerts a force on another body (an action force), the second body exerts an equal force in the opposite direction on the first (the reaction force). Action–reaction pairs must act on different bodies. This can be written as $F_{\text{on A by B}} = -F_{\text{on B by A}}$.

CIRCULAR MOTION IN A HORIZONTAL PLANE

Uniform circular motion is motion along a circular path in which there is no change in speed, only a change in direction. For example, consider an athlete in a hammer throw event, swinging a steel ball in a horizontal circle with a constant speed. The velocity of the hammer at any instant is tangential (at a tangent) to its path (Figure 3.1.1). At one instant (point A), the hammer is travelling at $25\,m\,s^{-1}$ north, then an instant later (point B) at $25\,m\,s^{-1}$ west, then $25\,m\,s^{-1}$ south (point C), and so on.

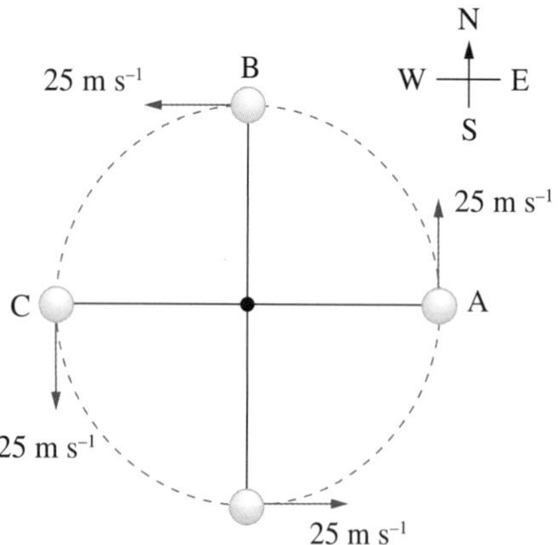

Figure 3.1.1 The velocity of the hammer (steel ball) at any instant is tangential to its path and is continually changing, even though it has constant speed. This changing velocity means that the hammer is accelerating.

Period, T, is the time for one revolution and is measured in seconds. **Frequency**, f, is the number of revolutions each second and is measured in hertz (Hz). The relationship between T and f is:

$$f = \frac{1}{T} \text{ and } T = \frac{1}{f}$$

An object moving with a uniform speed in a circular path of radius, r, and with a period, T, has an average speed that is given by:

$$v = \frac{2\pi r}{T}$$

Because an object moving in a circular path is always changing its direction of motion, even if it is travelling with a constant speed it must have a non-zero acceleration. This acceleration is directed towards the centre of the circular path and is called **centripetal acceleration**, a:

$$a = \frac{v^2}{r}$$

Centripetal acceleration is a consequence of a **centripetal force** acting to make an object move in a circular path. Centripetal forces are directed towards the centre of the circle and their magnitude can be calculated by using Newton's second law for the net force of the object:

$$F_{net} = ma = \frac{mv^2}{r}$$

By substituting the relationship between speed and period into the equations for acceleration and the net force, you can also find the following:

$$a = \frac{4\pi^2 r}{T^2} \text{ and } F = \frac{4\pi^2 rm}{T^2}$$

Centripetal force is always supplied by a real force, the nature of which depends on the situation. The real force is commonly friction, gravitation or the tension in a string or cable.

- **You will now be able to conduct Practical activity 1.**

A similar example of circular motion is the conical pendulum. A conical pendulum is a mass that travels in a horizontal circle on a string. The tension in the string supplies the force to counter the force of gravity and also supplies the centripetal force. Its construction is like an ordinary pendulum; however, instead of swinging back and forth, the mass of the conical pendulum moves at a constant speed in a circle with the string tracing out a cone. The closer the mass is to the horizontal, the more the speed increases. If the angle of the conical pendulum is known, trigonometry can be used to find the radius of the circle and the forces involved. An example of a conical pendulum is shown in Figure 3.1.2 on the opposite page.

 ISBN 978 0 6557 0029 6

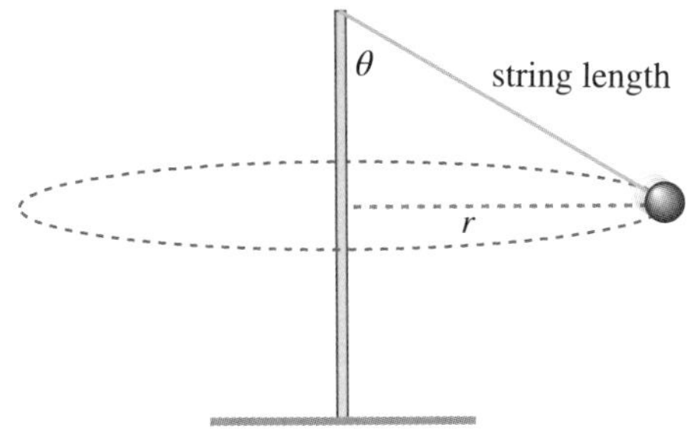

Figure 3.1.2 Conical pendulum

If both the angle and length of the string are known, the radius, r, of the circle can be found using a simple trigonometric ratio (Figure 3.1.3a). Trigonometric ratios can also be used to find the other forces involved if one of the forces is known.

For example, if the mass of the ball is 0.200 kg, the force due to gravity acting on it will be $F_g = mg = 0.200 \times 9.8 = 1.96$ N downwards. Then, as the mass of the ball (considering the string to be negligible mass) and the angle the ball is swinging at are both known, trigonometry can be used to determine the centripetal force and tension in the string (see Figure 3.1.3b).

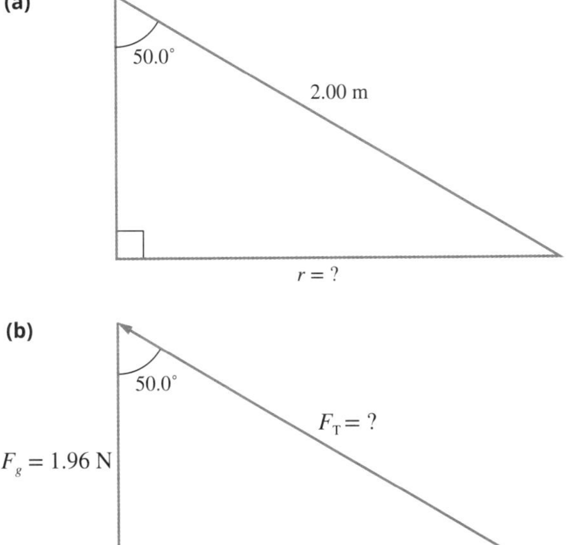

Figure 3.1.3 Trigonometry can be used to find (a) the radius of the circular motion, as well as (b) the different forces acting: the force due to gravity F_g, the tension of the string F_T and the net or centripetal force F_{net}.

CIRCULAR MOTION ON BANKED TRACKS

On many road bends, the road is not horizontal, but is at a small angle to the horizontal. This is called a banked track, and it enables vehicles to travel at higher speeds when cornering, with less chance of skidding than on a horizontal curved path. Banked tracks reduce a vehicle's dependence on friction to safely navigate a curve.

An example of this effect can be seen at a cycling velodrome like that shown in Figure 3.1.4, where the banked corners allow cyclists to travel at much higher speeds than if the track were flat.

Figure 3.1.4 The Australian women's pursuit track cycling team in action on a banked velodrome track

Banking a track eliminates the need for a sideways frictional force to turn. When cars travel in circular paths on horizontal roads, they are relying on the force of friction between the tyres and the road to provide the sideways force that keeps the car turning on a circular path. Both the normal force F_N and force due to gravity on the car F_g are balanced, so the only force allowing the car to turn is friction. A banked track means that the normal force has an inwards component, enabling the car to turn the corner (Figure 3.1.5).

When the speed and angle are such that there is no sideways frictional force, the speed is known as the design speed. The forces acting on a vehicle travelling at the design speed on a banked track are gravity and the normal force from the track. These forces are unbalanced and add to give a net force directed towards the centre of the circular motion.

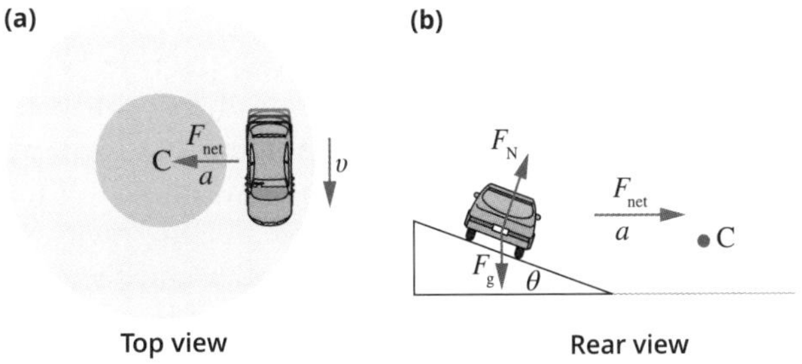

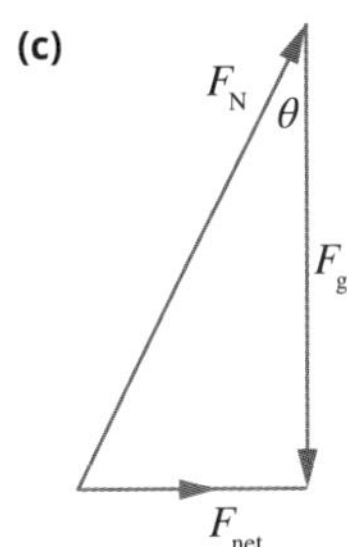

Figure 3.1.5 (a) The car is travelling in a circular path on a banked track. (b) The acceleration and net force are towards the centre of the circular motion, C. The banked track means that the normal force (F_N) has an inwards component. This is what enables the car to turn the corner. (c) Vector addition gives the net force (F_{net}) as acting horizontally towards the centre.

At the design speed, the angle of bank of the track can be determined by the following formula:

$$\theta = \tan^{-1}\frac{v^2}{rg}$$

This can therefore be rearranged to find the design speed:

$$v = \sqrt{rg\tan\theta}$$

- **You will now be able to complete Worksheet 2.**

You may come across the term 'weight' in older exams or texts to mean the force due to gravity. However, it is also commonly used in everyday speech interchangeably with mass; i.e. someone may describe their weight as 70 kg. For this reason, in VCE Physics we no longer use the term weight.

CIRCULAR MOTION IN A VERTICAL PLANE

Vertical circular paths, like horizontal circular paths, have an acceleration that is directed towards the centre of the circle. Unlike horizontal paths, however, in vertical paths the net force on the object is not constant and the speed, as well as the direction, of the object is constantly changing. Vertical circular motion is also referred to as non-uniform circular motion because of the changing relationship of the forces involved.

To understand this, consider the strong forces you would experience when travelling both through dips and over humps on a rollercoaster ride.

When you travel through dips, you feel as though you are getting pushed down into the seat, but when you travel over humps you feel like you are being lifted up. Your experience of heaviness or lightness happens when the normal force acting on you is not equal to the force due to gravity.

The normal force varies throughout the ride. When in a dip, as in Figure 3.1.6a, there must be a centripetal force (i.e. a net force) upwards for the car to move along a circular path. This means the magnitude of the normal force is greater than the force due to gravity, so the seat will push upwards into the rider and they will feel heavier than usual. When going over a hump, as in Figure 3.1.6b, the centripetal (net) force is downwards, so the magnitude of the normal force must be less than the force due to gravity, the seat pushes into the rider less and they will feel lighter than usual.

(a)

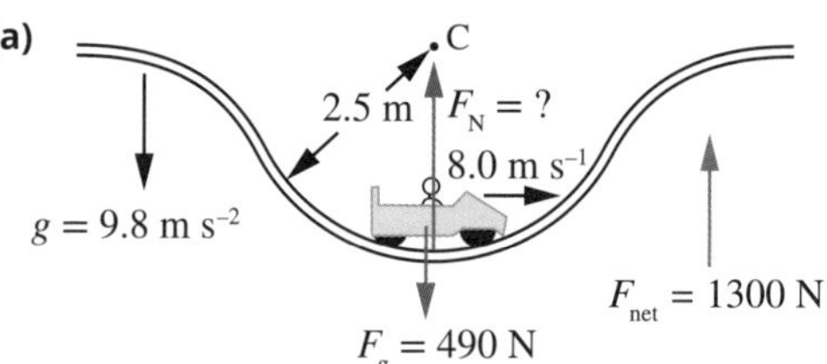

(b)

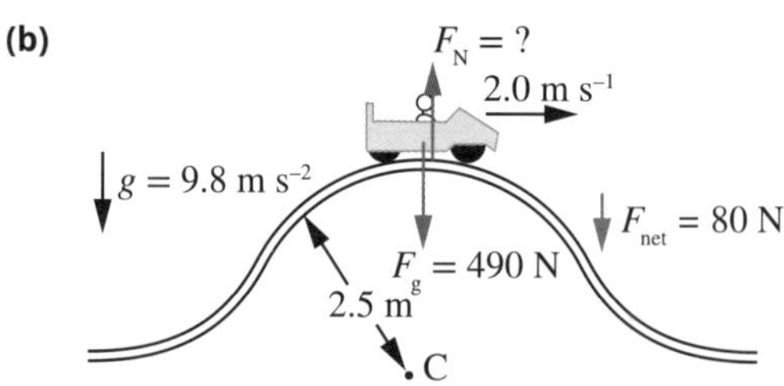

Figure 3.1.6 In (a), the centripetal acceleration is upwards towards the centre of the circle. In (b), the centripetal acceleration is downwards, so the net force is also in that direction. At this point, the magnitude of the normal force F_N is less than the force due to gravity, F_g, on the person.

As the speed is constantly changing throughout a rollercoaster ride, often it is much easier to solve these types of problems using the **law of conservation of energy**. The law of conservation of energy states that energy is transferred or transformed between objects and there is always the same amount of energy at the end as there was at the start. The sum of the kinetic and potential energy (the total **mechanical energy**, E_m) of an isolated system is always conserved. This can be represented by the following:

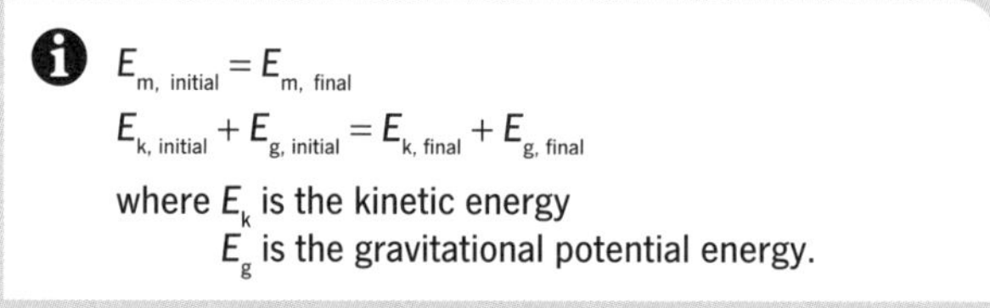

$E_{m,\ initial} = E_{m,\ final}$

$E_{k,\ initial} + E_{g,\ initial} = E_{k,\ final} + E_{g,\ final}$

where E_k is the kinetic energy
E_g is the gravitational potential energy.

Kinetic energy is the energy of motion of a body:

$$E_k = \frac{1}{2}mv^2$$

where m is the mass (kg)
v is the speed (m s^{-1}).

Close to the surface of Earth, where the force of gravity can be assumed to be constant, the change in gravitational potential energy of an object of mass m is dependent on the height from a given surface Δh and the acceleration due to gravity g:

$$E_g = mg\Delta h$$

 ISBN 978 0 6557 0029 6

KEY KNOWLEDGE

The variable Δh is always given against some reference level, so gravitational potential energy can be positive or negative. A negative potential energy just means that the object will have travelled below the reference level. Ground level is often used as the reference point.

Consider the rollercoaster ride again. There are times where the car has only potential energy (so the kinetic energy is zero) and times where the car has only kinetic energy (so the potential energy is zero). Therefore, by assuming at the start of the ride that kinetic energy is zero, only potential energy is acting, which indicates the total energy in the system. If the total energy in the system is known, this can be used to find the kinetic energy at other times during the ride, which means the speed can be found. Then the speed can be substituted into the centripetal force formula to calculate the net force.

Work is the transfer of energy from one object to another and/or the transformation of energy from one form to another. Work, W, is a scalar variable and is measured in joules (J). A force does work on an object when it acts on a body causing a displacement in the direction of the force. A centripetal force does no work on an orbiting object, as the force and displacement are perpendicular.

- **You will now be able to conduct Practical activity 2 and complete Worksheet 3.**

PROJECTILES LAUNCHED HORIZONTALLY

A **projectile** is any object that is thrown or projected into the air and has no power source driving it. If air resistance is ignored, the only force acting on a projectile is the force due to gravity, F_g. This force can be assumed to be constant and is always directed vertically downwards with the **acceleration due to gravity** being $9.8\,m\,s^{-2}$. Projectiles move in parabolic paths that can be analysed by considering the horizontal and vertical components of their motion. The two factors that affect a projectile's motion are the angle at which it is launched and its initial velocity.

Projectiles can be launched at any angle. The launch velocity needs to be resolved into vertical and horizontal components using trigonometry to complete most problems. For projectiles launched horizontally, the horizontal velocity is constant if air resistance is ignored, and is equal to the horizontal launch velocity; the initial vertical velocity is zero and will increase during the flight. A parabolic path is traced by an object accelerating only in the vertical direction while moving at constant velocity in the horizontal direction. The following equations of motion for uniform acceleration must be used for the vertical component of the motion.

$v = u + at$

$s = ut + \frac{1}{2}at^2$

$v^2 = u^2 + 2as$

where s is the displacement (m)
u is the initial velocity ($m\,s^{-1}$)
v is the final velocity ($m\,s^{-1}$)
a is the acceleration ($m\,s^{-2}$)
t is the time (s)

As the horizontal velocity of a projectile remains constant throughout its flight, the following equation for average velocity can be used for this component of the motion:

$$v_{av} = \frac{s}{t}$$

To solve a projectile motion problem, a diagram should be constructed where the direction convention is clearly specified (whether up or down is the positive or negative direction). The information supplied for the horizontal and vertical components should be drawn separately.

For example, a ball is hit horizontally from the top of a 40 m–high cliff with a speed of $25\,m\,s^{-1}$ (Figure 3.1.7). Use acceleration due to gravity of $9.8\,m\,s^{-2}$ and ignore air resistance. To calculate the time it takes the ball to land and the distance it has travelled from the base of the cliff, there are a few steps you should take.

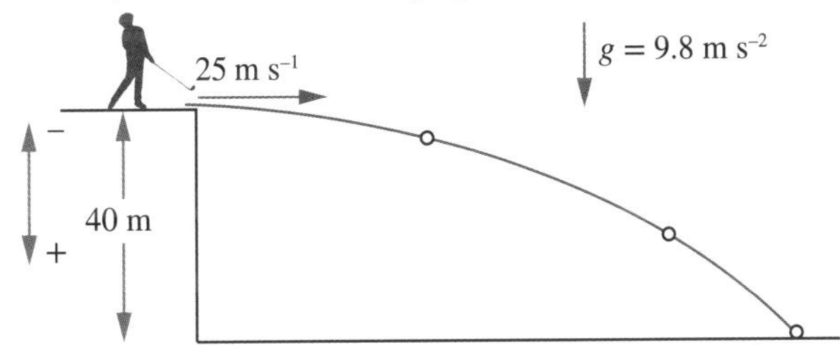

Figure 3.1.7 Parabolic motion with initial horizontal velocity only

By first writing out the variables that are known, you can then decide on the equations of motion that are best suited to finding the answers. Remember to keep the horizontal and vertical components of motion separate.

The time can then be found using the vertical components of motion and the equation: $s = ut + \frac{1}{2}at$.

$$40 = 0 + \frac{1}{2} \times 9.8 \times t^2$$

$$t = \sqrt{\frac{40}{4.9}}$$

$$= 2.9\,s$$

Similarly, to calculate the horizontal displacement (i.e. how far the ball travelled from the base of the cliff), you can use the equation: $v_{av} = \frac{s}{t}$.

$$25 = \frac{s_H}{t}$$

$$s = 25 \times 2.9$$

$$= 71\,m$$

KEY KNOWLEDGE

Generally, vector answers need both their magnitude and direction, so pay close attention to how a question is written to know what information is needed in your solution. In the example given above, you were asked for the distance travelled, not the horizontal displacement, so the answer is given as a scalar.

The effects of air resistance

Air resistance, or drag force, is a retarding force that acts in the opposite direction to the motion of an object. The interaction between a projectile and the air can have a significant effect on the motion of the projectile, particularly if the projectile has a large surface area and a relatively low mass. If you try to throw an inflated party balloon, it will not travel very far compared to throwing a marble at the same speed.

The size of the air resistance that acts on an object as it moves depends on several factors:

- The speed, v, of the object. The faster an object moves, the greater the drag force becomes.
- The cross-sectional area of the object in its direction of motion. Greater area means greater drag.
- The aerodynamic shape of the object. A more streamlined shape experiences less drag.
- The density of the air. Higher air density means greater drag.

- **You will now be able to conduct Practical activity 3 and complete Worksheet 4.**

PROJECTILES LAUNCHED OBLIQUELY

The previous section looked at projectiles launched horizontally. A more common situation is projectiles that are launched obliquely (at an angle), by being thrown forwards and upwards at the same time, as shown in Figure 3.1.8. For objects initially launched at an angle to the horizontal, it is useful to calculate the initial horizontal and vertical velocities using trigonometry. The initial velocity can be broken down into its perpendicular horizontal (u_H) and vertical (u_V) components using the trigonometric relationships below:

$$\sin\theta = \frac{\text{opposite}}{\text{hypotenuse}} = \frac{u_V}{u} \qquad u_V = u\sin\theta$$

$$\cos\theta = \frac{\text{adjacent}}{\text{hypotenuse}} = \frac{u_H}{u} \qquad u_H = u\cos\theta$$

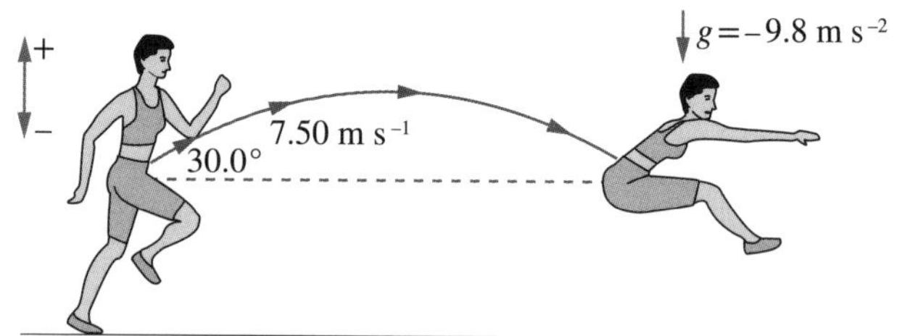

Figure 3.1.8 Projectiles can also be launched obliquely (at an angle).

As with projectiles launched horizontally, if air resistance is negligible the only force that is acting on a projectile is gravity, F_g. Therefore, the horizontal velocity of a projectile remains constant throughout its flight, i.e. $v_{av} = \frac{s}{t}$ is used. At its highest point, the projectile is only moving horizontally, so the vertical component of the velocity is zero at this point. Overall, the assumptions that must be made when analysing a projectile problem are as follows.

Air resistance is negligible.

If an object is dropped, $u = 0\,\text{m s}^{-1}$

At the highest point of a projectile's path, $v_V = 0\,\text{m s}^{-1}$

Final velocity = negative initial velocity, i.e. $u = -v$

In the example given in Figure 3.1.8, in order to find the maximum height reached, you would first need to break the initial velocity into its vertical and horizontal components.

$$u_V = u \times \sin\theta$$
$$u_V = 7.50 \times \sin 30° = 3.75\,\text{m s}^{-1}$$

The vertical displacement can then be calculated using the formula $v^2 = u^2 + 2$ as:

$$0^2 = 3.75^2 + 2 \times -9.8 \times s$$
$$s = 0.72\,\text{m upwards}$$

This means that the centre of mass of the person jumping will travel upwards to a maximum of 0.72 m above their starting height. If the centre of mass is originally 1 m off the ground, then the maximum height reached will be 1.72 m.

- **You will now be able to conduct Practical activity 4 and complete Worksheet 5.**

The relationship between force, energy and mass

CONSERVATION OF ENERGY AND MOMENTUM

Momentum is the product of an object's mass and velocity. It is a vector quantity and is calculated using the equation:

 $p = mv$

where m is the mass (in kg)
v is the velocity (in m s^{-1}).

ISBN 978 0 6557 0029 6

KEY KNOWLEDGE

An object in motion has momentum, and if this momentum changes the object must experience a force. Force is equal to the rate of change of momentum.

The momentum of a system will be **conserved** in any interaction or collision. The law of **conservation of momentum** can be represented by:

$$\Sigma p_{\text{initial}} = \Sigma p_{\text{final}}$$

where Σp is the sum of the momentum of objects in a system. Table 3.1.1 outlines the application of the conservation of momentum to a variety of different situations.

Table 3.1.1 Conservation of momentum in different collisions

Situation	Change in momentum
two objects collide and remain separate	$m_1u_1 + m_2u_2 = m_1v_1 + m_2v_2$
two objects collide and combine together	$m_1u_1 + m_2u_2 = m_3v_3$
one object breaks apart into two objects in an explosive collision	$m_1u_1 = m_2v_2 + m_3v_3$

The principle of conservation of mechanical energy states that the total mechanical energy in a system remains constant if the only forces acting are conservative forces.

In **elastic collisions**, no kinetic energy is lost, while in **inelastic collisions**, kinetic energy is lost to the environment. This means in an elastic collision, there's no permanent deformation of any of the objects. Both momentum and kinetic energy are conserved quantities in elastic collisions.

IMPULSE

Change or transfer in momentum, Δp, is also known as **impulse**. It is a vector quantity. A change or transfer in momentum occurs when an object changes its velocity.

The equation for impulse is:

$$\Delta p = mv - mu = m(v - u)$$

Change in velocity is determined by:

$$\Delta v = \text{final velocity} - \text{initial velocity}$$

Newton's second law describes the relationship between impulse, force and the period of time during which the force acts:

$$\Delta p = m(v - u) = ma\Delta t$$

$$\therefore \Delta p = F\Delta t$$

There are a few important things to note about this relationship:

- The same mass changing its velocity by the same amount will have a constant change in momentum or impulse.
- The faster a mass changes its velocity, the greater the force required to change the velocity in that period of time.
- An object colliding with a hard surface stops in a short time, but an object colliding with a soft surface takes a longer time to stop.
- The period of time taken to stop is proportional to the force involved. A shorter time means a greater force, while a longer time means a smaller force.

This concept can be used to explain the different effects of impacts. For example, it explains why an egg dropped on a hard floor breaks, but an egg dropped on a pillow does not. In both cases, m and Δv are the same. However, the pillow greatly increases the time the egg takes to stop, so the force acting on the egg is much less.

In most problems it is assumed that the force remains constant throughout the collision, but in reality this is not always the case. Forces can change during a collision. The impulse over a period of time can be found by calculating the area under the line on a force versus time graph (Figure 3.1.9).

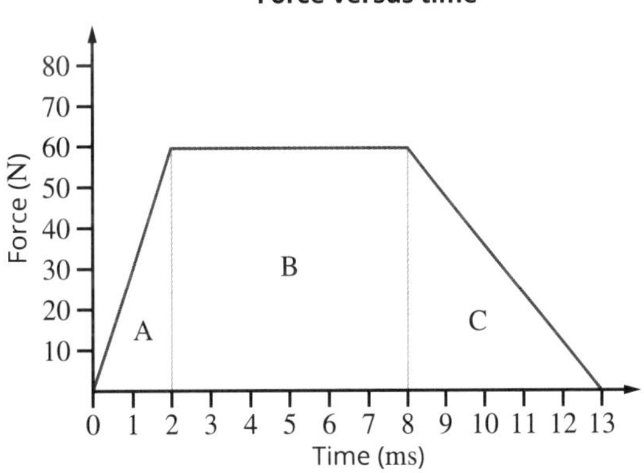

Figure 3.1.9 The area under a force–time graph gives the total impulse of the event.

WORK DONE

In physics, work cannot be done without energy, and vice versa. Work is equal to the change in energy, and therefore its unit is also the joule. Work is done when:

- energy is transferred or transformed
- a force causes an object to be displaced.

Work is the product of net force, F, and displacement, s: $W = Fs$. The unit for work is joules and the units for force and displacement are newtons and metres, so from this formula you can see that 1 J is equivalent to 1 N m.

When a force produces no displacement, no work is done. For example, if you hold a box at a constant height, no work is being done on the box even though there are energy transformations going on inside your body to hold the box in position.

If the force is applied at an angle to the displacement, only the component of the force in the direction of the displacement contributes to the work done. That is, if the force and displacement vectors are at an angle θ with respect to each other, then $F\cos\theta$ is the component of force that does work:

> $W = Fs\cos\theta$
>
> where W is the work done by the force (J)
> F is the magnitude of the constant force (N)
> s is the displacement (m)
> θ is the angle between the force vector and the displacement vector

While both force and displacement are vectors, work and energy are scalar quantities that are measured in joules (J).

Where the force–distance relationship is represented graphically, the work done is the area under the force–distance graph.

- **You will now be able to conduct Practical activity 5 and complete Worksheet 6.**

ELASTIC POTENTIAL ENERGY

Initially, it is relatively easy to start stretching a spring, but more and more force is required for each incremental amount of extension. This is expressed in Hooke's law:

> $F = -kx$
>
> where F is the force exerted by the spring (N)
> k is the spring constant ($N\,m^{-1}$)
> x is the displacement (the extension or compression) of the spring (m)

The force exerted by a spring is directly proportional to, but opposite in direction to, the spring's extension or compression. The spring constant k is a measure of the stiffness of the spring. The behaviour of a spring under force is often illustrated graphically by plotting the force applied versus the extension achieved, as shown in Figure 3.1.10. Notice that a stiffer spring has a larger spring constant, and the spring constant is represented by the gradient (slope) of the graph.

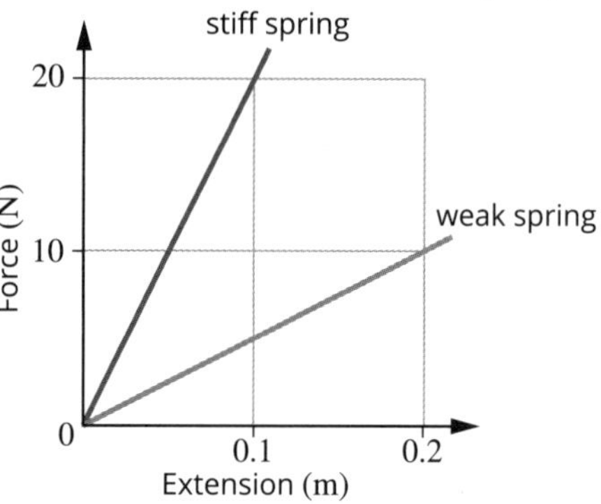

Figure 3.1.10 Both springs represented in this graph are ideal. The springs obey Hooke's law because they both have linear graphs, but they have different degrees of stiffness. The stiff spring has a spring constant of 200 $N\,m^{-1}$. The spring constant of the other spring is just 50 $N\,m^{-1}$. The stiffer spring has the higher gradient (steeper line) on the F–x graph.

When considering the work done in deforming a spring, the force applied is in the direction of the displacement and hence the negative sign in $F = -kx$ falls away. The applied force is a linear function of distance and, as discussed in the previous section, when force is not constant the work done by the force may be calculated from the area under the force–distance curve. Hence, this technique can be used to determine the work required to extend or compress a spring.

This leads us to an expression for the work done in stretching a spring, and the **elastic potential energy** which is then stored in the spring:

$$E_s = \frac{1}{2} \times \text{height} \times \text{base}$$

$$E_s = \frac{1}{2} F \times x$$

$$= \frac{1}{2} kx \times x$$

> The elastic potential energy, E_s, is calculated using:
>
> $E_s = \frac{1}{2}kx^2$
>
> where k is the spring constant ($N\,m^{-1}$)
> Δx is the spring extension (m)

- **You will now be able to complete Worksheets 7 and 8.**

 ISBN 978 0 6557 0029 6

WORKSHEET 1

Knowledge review—kinematics and dynamics

1 From a platform 24.5 m above the ground, a stone is thrown straight up at 19.6 m s^{-1}.

a How long will the stone be in the air?

b Calculate its velocity as it hits the ground.

2 A 540 kg cable car is suspended from the middle of a light cable, with each half of the cable making an angle of 12.0° to the horizontal. Draw a force diagram of the situation and calculate the size of the tension in the cable.

3 Consider a 100 g teacup sitting on a kitchen bench.

a What is its force due to gravity?

b What is the size of the force of the benchtop on the cup? In which direction does it act?

c Explain why these two forces do *not* make an action–reaction pair in the sense of Newton's third law. What are the action–reaction pairs here?

ISBN 978 0 6557 0029 6

4 The velocity–time graphs for three balls, A, B and C, dropped from the same height are shown in Figure 3.1.11.

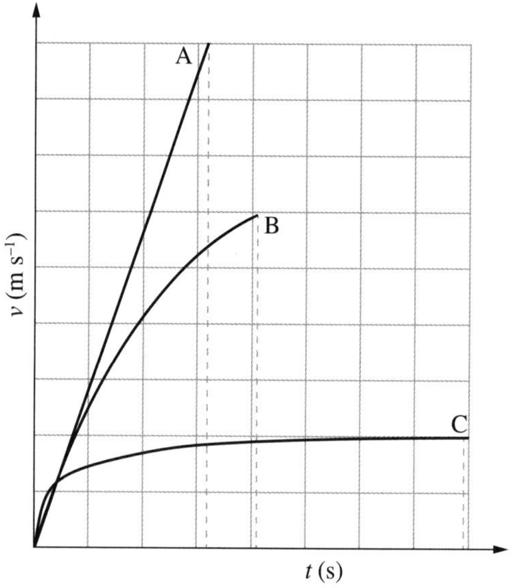

Figure 3.1.11 Velocity–time for three balls

a What physical quantity is represented by the gradient of graph A?

b What do the areas underneath the graphs represent? How do they compare with each other?

c Given that ball C is a table tennis ball, explain what is happening to it.

5 The foundations of a large building are often built on supports known as 'piles', which are driven down into the ground by a pile-driver. In one case, a pile-driver of mass 4.50×10^3 kg falls through a height of 40.0 cm before colliding with the top of a pile. The mass drives the pile 30.0 cm into the ground, then both the pile and the mass come to rest.

a Calculate the pile-driver's loss of potential energy.

b Calculate the average resistance force of the ground.

c What is the momentum of the pile-driver as it hits the ground?

 ISBN 978 0 6557 0029 6

WORKSHEET 2

Modelling

Going around corners

For a body to travel in a circle or part of a circle, a centripetal force must be exerted on the object. This can be the pull of gravity for planets, the tension in a wire for a hammer thrower, or the reaction force of a surface in contact with the object. In the case of a car going around a corner, the centripetal force must come from the sideways component of reaction from the road surface or the friction of the car tyres against the road surface.

The diagram below depicts a car travelling away from the viewer and turning to the left.

1 Draw and label the force vectors acting on the car at this instant.

2 Consider a car negotiating a suburban roundabout. The path taken has a radius of curvature of 8.0 m and the coefficient of friction, μ, between the tyre and the road is 0.72. What is the maximum speed the car can travel (in $km\,h^{-1}$) and still remain on the circular path? (Hint: The force of friction, F_f, is calculated using the equation $F_f = \mu F_N$, where F_N is the normal force.)

3 Why was the mass of the car not required in Question **2**? What does this mean for road design?

4 Consider a racing car. The coefficient of friction, μ, between a Formula One tyre and the asphalt track is typically 1.5. Calculate the minimum radius of curvature that can be taken by a Formula One car at $120\,km\,h^{-1}$.

5 Formula One cars are fitted with various aerofoils and body shaping that can generate considerable downforce. Find how much downforce (as a fraction of the force due to gravity on the car) would be needed to negotiate the same corner at a 30% greater speed.

6 When a motorcycle goes around a corner, the rider needs to lean over into the corner. On the diagram of a cornering motorcycle below, draw and label the forces acting on the motorcycle and the rider. (Point C, 0.65 m from the contact point, is the centre of mass of the bike and rider.)

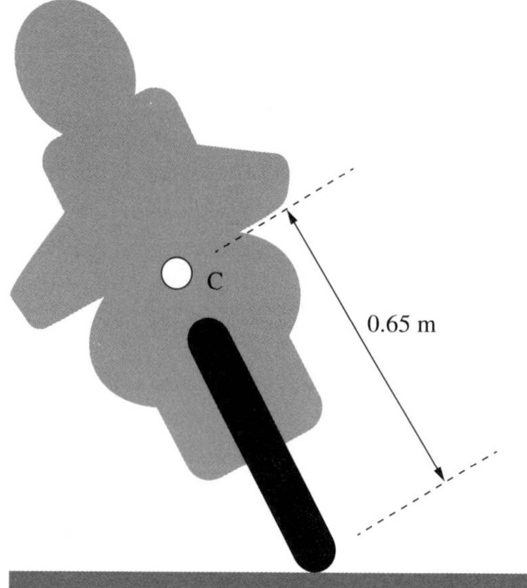

7 Assuming that the motorcycle's tyres are able to generate as much friction with the road as the tyres of the car from Question **2**, find the angle of lean of the motorcycle from the vertical as it takes the corner.

Bicycles can travel faster around a bend by 'banking' the track, as seen in a velodrome. The ideal situation on a banked curve is for the bike to be perpendicular to the track surface. The Dunc Gray Velodrome in Sydney was the venue for the track cycling in the 2000 Olympic Games. The maximum angle of bank in the end curves is 42°, while the straights are angled at 12.5°.

8 Anna Meares takes a path with a radius of curvature of 22 m, where the track is banked at 42°. Find the greatest speed at which she can travel safely.

There are many further points to consider when investigating how vehicles can be helped to negotiate corners.

- When a car first enters a bend and when it leaves the bend, it is usually travelling faster. This means the radius of curvature of the road needs to vary, and should be smallest at the apex of the corner.
- The radius of curvature of a velodrome track also changes as the banking angle varies from the straights to the ends.
- The greater the angle of bank, the harder a car is 'pushed' down onto the track. If pushed too far, the car body will touch the track and the tyres may lose adhesion.
- Car test tracks are generally constructed with variable banking on bends. The track has a curved profile that gets steeper the further it is from the centre.
- If a cyclist leans on a banked curve, they can generate more friction and take the curve even faster—provided they can pedal fast enough!

 ISBN 978 0 6557 0029 6

Circular motion and gravity

When a rocket takes off, it accelerates quickly to achieve enough speed to enter orbit. In a related situation, fighter pilots will undergo significant 'g-forces' while performing tight turns. To prepare themselves for this, the astronauts and pilots will need to experience high 'g-forces' during their training.

1 A brief period of acceleration can be achieved using a rocket sled equipped with a jet turbine or rocket motor.

Consider a person strapped into such a sled for which the total mass is 450 kg. The rocket motor exerts an upwards force of 36.0 kN for a 4.00 s burn. Calculate the acceleration produced and the distance travelled during the burn.

2 The acceleration can be measured in units of g, where $g = 9.8\,\text{m}\,\text{s}^{-2}$ at or near Earth's surface. How many g does the passenger experience?

Another way of producing high-g conditions is to use a centrifuge—a seat or capsule attached to the end of a long arm that can be rotated at a variable rate in a horizontal plane.

3 A centrifuge with an 8.50 m arm is rotated at 24.0 rpm. How many g does the test pilot in the cage at the end of the arm experience?

Astronauts in orbit float inside their spacecraft. While this experience feels like defying gravity, in fact, the force due to gravity is still acting on them. They are still in Earth's gravitational field—the very reason they are in orbit. They appear to float because they and their spacecraft are falling at the same rate towards Earth. As part of their training before they go to space, astronauts need to get experience of this feeling. This is where the 'Vomit Comet' comes in.

There are several aeroplanes that qualify for this dubious title. Each plane follows a series of parabolic, freefall segments during its flight. These freefall sections are joined together by a series of dives and climbs during which higher than normal 'g-forces' are experienced by the passengers. A typical flight profile is shown in Figure 3.1.12.

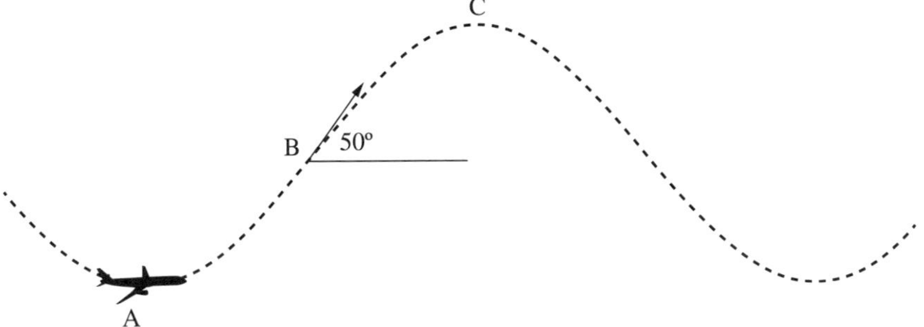

Figure 3.1.12 Parabolic flight path to simulate freefall

ISBN 978 0 6557 0029 6

4 Consider point A at the bottom of the dive phase where the aeroplane is travelling at 720 km h^{-1}. A 65.0 kg person lying on the floor of the cabin experiences 1.80g. Draw a diagram showing the forces acting on them.

5 Calculate the radius of curvature of the flight path at that point.

6 From that point the aeroplane begins to climb at an increasing angle until it reaches an elevation of 50° at point B. At this point it begins the parabolic trajectory phase by reducing engine power. Assuming the passenger still experiences 1.80g just before the engines are throttled back, draw a new diagram showing the forces acting on them then.

7 During this part of the flight, the engine power is reduced—but not to zero. If the aeroplane is entering freefall, explain why the plane still needs the thrust of the engines.

8 Typically, the parabolic trajectory phase lasts 20 s: 10 s up and 10 s down. Calculate the velocity the plane will need at point B to allow the passengers to 'float' for this duration.

9 Explain what would happen if the aeroplane was to fly a bit too fast at the top of the parabolic section of the flight at point C.

 ISBN 978 0 6557 0029 6

WORKSHEET 4

Case study

Projectile motion—is it safe?

A group of students intends to fire a small missile with a velocity of $40.0\,m\,s^{-1}$ at an angle of 60.0° from the horizontal from a point on the oval. They intend to aim at the windowless wall of a building 45.0 m away from the launch site, so that there is no danger of the missile hitting anyone. The building is 36.0 m high.

1 Construct a diagram of the situation, showing all known variables.

2 Prove that the projectile will travel over the height of the building and hence that this situation is unsafe.

3 As this situation is unsafe, make two possible recommendations in order to make it safe. Show calculations to prove that your proposal is safe, and note any assumptions.

WORKSHEET 5

Modelling

Projectile motion—human cannonball data analysis

Human 'cannonballs' used to be a common feature of circuses and fairs (Figure 3.1.13)—risk assessments and ever-increasing insurance premiums mostly brought an end to them. More than 30 people have died performing this stunt over the years since the first human cannonball, a 14-year-old girl, was launched at the Royal London Aquarium in 1877.

Figure 3.1.13 A human cannonball

These days, however, some stunt performers still maintain the tradition, as shown in Figure 3.1.13. The human cannonball is fired from a specially designed cannon, and lands on a horizontal net or inflated bag. Amazingly, the official world record stands at 59.05 m.

The data below was collected from the launch of a human cannonball of mass 80 kg blasted towards the east from a cannon and landing in a safety net. The height of the net was equal to the launch height. The angle of launch was 45° and the initial speed was 28 m s^{-1}. In your calculations, ignore air resistance unless otherwise instructed and use $g = 9.8$ m s^{-2}.

Time after launch (s)	Speed (m s^{-1})
0	28.0
1.0	22.4
2.0	20.0
3.0	22.4
4.0	28.0

 ISBN 978 0 6557 0029 6

WORKSHEET 5

1 On the graph below, draw a graph of vertical acceleration versus time for the human cannonball for the 4.0 s of motion. Use up as positive and ensure that your graph is appropriately labelled.

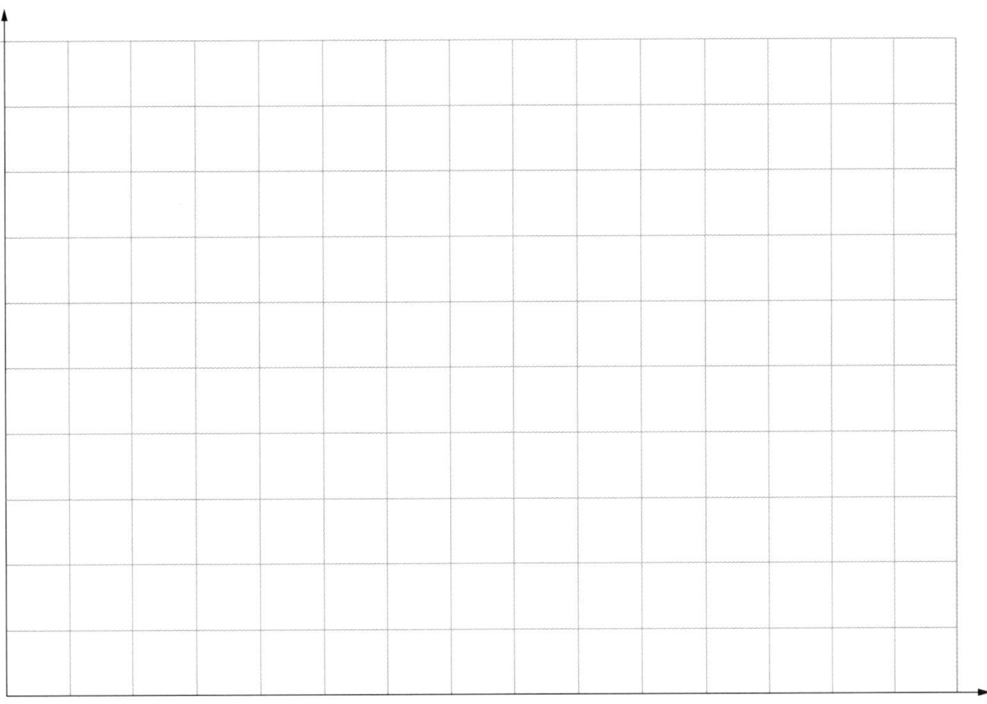

2 Using an energy approach, determine the:

a total mechanical energy of the human cannonball

b gain in gravitational potential energy of the human cannonball as they reach the maximum height

c change in height the human cannonball achieved from launch.

3 Determine the height above the initial launch height after:

a 2.0 s

b 3.5 s

4 Calculate the speed of the human cannonball after:

a 2.0 s

b 3.5 s

5 What is the velocity and acceleration of the human cannonball at the maximum height?

6 Discuss the forces that are acting on the human cannonball when passing through the highest point in the trajectory if air resistance is ignored. State the magnitude and direction of the net force acting at this point.

7 Discuss the forces that are acting on the human cannonball when passing through the highest point in the trajectory if air resistance is taken into account.

ISBN 978 0 6557 0029 6

Impulse and momentum—a modelling exercise

This worksheet requires you to use *reasonable estimates* to determine the magnitude of the force to the nearest power of 10 in an *inelastic* collision using an understanding of the relationship between impulse and momentum.

1 Describe a realistic *inelastic* collision between two objects. Include reasonable estimates of the mass of the objects and the initial velocity of each object respectively. Use a diagram to assist your description.

Object 1 mass: ________________ kg   Initial velocity: ______________ $m\,s^{-1}$

Object 2 mass: ________________ kg   Initial velocity______________ $m\,s^{-1}$

2 Determine the initial momentum of each object and the total momentum of the system.

3 Based on your description of the collision, make a reasonable estimate of the final velocities of each object and, hence, determine the final momentum of the system.

Object 1 final velocity: ______________ $m\,s^{-1}$

Object 2 final velocity: ______________ $m\,s^{-1}$

4 State the relationship between the change in momentum and the impulse during a collision.

5 Define the difference between an elastic and an inelastic collision in terms of conservation of momentum and conservation of energy.

6 State the additional quantity that you will need to estimate in order to determine the size of the force experienced during the collision.

7 State a reasonable estimate of the additional quantity, including units. Using this estimate, calculate the force experienced between the objects to the nearest magnitude of 10 (e.g. 10^1, 10^2, 10^3, ...)

Estimate: ________________

ISBN 978 0 6557 0029 6

Modelling

Hooke's law—data analysis

A student is conducting an experiment to test Hooke's law for two different springs. The student adds 50 g masses to the end of each spring, and measures the extension of the springs (i.e. Δx_1 and Δx_2).

1 Complete the table.

Mass (g)	Force due to gravity (N)	Δx_1 (cm)	Δx_2 (cm)
50		0.8	0.5
100		1.7	1.0
150		2.5	1.5
200		3.5	2.1
250		4.7	2.7
300		5.6	3.2

2 Graph the data for the two springs on the same set of axes below.

3 Calculate the spring constant of each spring.

4 Qualitatively describe the energy transformations that occur in a spring if it bounces as a mass is added to it.

 ISBN 978 0 6557 0029 6

Literacy review—talking motion

Complete the statements below using the list of words provided. Some words may not be used and others may be used more than once.

gravity	freefall	speed	range	velocity	mass
horizontal	radius	angle	acceleration	circular	constant
diameter	parabolic	tension	vertical	linear	elliptical
centripetal force	centrifugal force				

1 When a ball falls vertically to the floor, we say it is in a ________________ state of motion. When we launch a projectile horizontally, its ________________ velocity is ________________. The shape of the ball's flight is referred to as its trajectory and is ________________ in shape. The maximum ________________ of flight depends on the launch ________________ and the launch ________________. The force due to ________________ directly relates to the freefall acceleration of the ball.

2 The force that acts through a string is referred to as ________________. If an object is tied to a string such that its speed remains constant as it travels around a central point, it undergoes uniform ________________ motion. Even though the object's ________________ is constant, its ________________ is constantly changing. The tension in the string supplies the ________________________________.

3 An inward, or centre-seeking, force is called ________________. A constant force means a constant ________________, which makes sense if the object undergoing circular motion has a constantly changing ________________. If the centripetal force is kept constant then variables such as ________________ and ________________ are proportional to the time it takes to complete a revolution.

4 Centripetal and centrifugal forces are real and imaginary forces respectively that are used in discussions of circular motion. Find the derivation of each word and from this, its definition.

WORKSHEET 9

Reflection—How do physicists explain motion in two dimensions?

The following table lists the key knowledge covered in this area of study.

1 Reflect on how well you understand the concepts listed. Rate your learning by shading the circle that corresponds to your current level of understanding for each one.

Key knowledge	Not confident ◄				► Very confident
Applying Newton's three laws of motion	○	○	○	○	○
Uniform circular motion in a horizontal plane	○	○	○	○	○
Modelling satellite motion as uniform circular motion	○	○	○	○	○
Circular motion in a vertical plane	○	○	○	○	○
Projectile motion near Earth's surface	○	○	○	○	○
Laws of conservation of energy and conservation of momentum	○	○	○	○	○
Impulse in collisions in a straight line	○	○	○	○	○
The work done by a force	○	○	○	○	○
Energy transformations in elastic and inelastic collisions	○	○	○	○	○
Hooke's law, including elastic potential energy $E_s = \frac{1}{2}kx^2$	○	○	○	○	○
Energy transformations due a change in vertical position above Earth's surface	○	○	○	○	○

2 Consider the points you have shaded from Not confident to Very confident. List specific ideas you can identify that were challenging.

____

____

3 Write down two different strategies that you will apply to help further your understanding of these ideas.

____

____

ISBN 978 0 6557 0029 6

PRACTICAL ACTIVITY 1

Experiment

Circular motion—centripetal force in a horizontal plane

SUGGESTED DURATION

- 50 minutes data collection + 15 minutes analysis

MATERIALS

- thin plastic tube about 15 cm long, with no sharp edges (the barrel of a ballpoint pen will do)
- 1.5 m of fishing line
- paperclip
- small soft mass (rubber stopper, cork or similar)
- mass carrier and slotted masses (50 g each)
- stopwatch
- metre ruler

INTRODUCTION

In this activity the centripetal force experienced by an object travelling in a horizontal plane will be investigated. The addition of a force sensor to monitor the applied force rather than the use of a rubber stopper, or the use of a fully automated solution from one of the physics equipment manufacturers, can add a further degree of sophistication.

The centripetal force, F_{net}, of an object of mass, m, moving at a constant velocity, v, and radius, r, and with a period of revolution, T, is given by:

$$F_{net} = \frac{mv^2}{r} = \frac{m4\pi^2 r}{T^2}$$

AIM

To investigate the relationship between the centripetal force acting on an object moving in a circle of constant radius and the frequency of revolution.

Substitute a force sensor for the mass carrier and slotted masses for real-time graphing of the centripetal force.

Safety

Leave plenty of room around you when swinging the rubber stopper to avoid hitting other students.

Complete a risk assessment before starting the activity.

METHOD

1. Securely tie one end of the fishing line to a small, soft mass. (As this is going to be twirled around your head, make sure the mass isn't too hard!)
2. Pass the line down through a thin plastic tube and attach a 50 g slotted mass carrier to the end, as shown in Figure 3.1.14. Add three 50 g masses to the mass carrier to make a total mass of 200 g. Alternatively, connect the hook of a force sensor.
3. Attach a paperclip to the line to act as a marker for a measured radius of about 1 m. Measure and record the exact radius in the Results section.

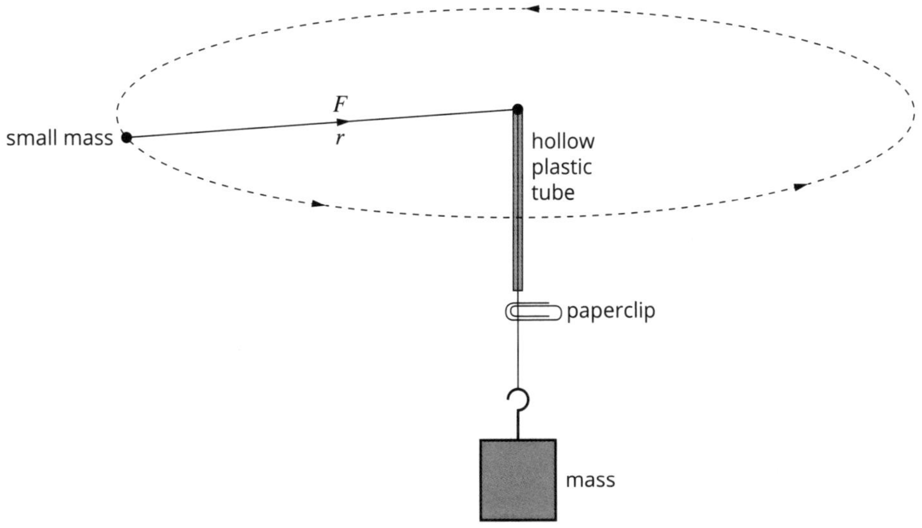

Figure 3.1.14 The experimental set-up

4 ▪ Twirl the stopper in a horizontal circular path at a speed that pulls the paperclip up to, but not touching, the bottom of the tube. Get a partner to keep an eye on the position of the clip to ensure that the speed of rotation stays quite constant. Practise doing this for a while before trying any measurements.

5 ▪ Maintain the speed of revolution and measure the time taken for 20 revolutions of the small mass. Record this time in the table below, along with an estimate of the uncertainty in the mass, diameter and time.

6 ▪ Add an extra 50 g to the mass carrier and repeat steps 4 and 5.

7 ▪ Keep adding an extra 50 g mass to the mass carrier, until the mass carrier is full.

RESULTS

Measured radius of revolution: ________ m

List the variables associated with this experimental method.

Independent: ____________________

Dependent: ____________________

Controlled: ____________________

1 Define the force that the mass carrier provides in this experiment.

____

____

2 If using a force sensor, additional masses won't be added. Describe the changes you would make instead to increase the applied force.

____

3 The force of gravity on the suspended mass is providing the centripetal force. Calculate the force due to gravity acting on each mass using $g = 9.8\,m\,s^{-2}$. Alternatively, if using a force sensor, record the average recorded force for each test as the centripetal force. Complete the table below with the calculated results.

Results of F_{net} versus period					
Mass (kg) ±	F_{net} (N) ±	Time for 20 revolutions (s) ±	Period, T, for one revolution (s) ±	$f = \frac{1}{T}$ (Hz)	f^2 (Hz)^2

 ISBN 978 0 6557 0029 6

4 Plot a graph of frequency, f, versus centripetal force, F_{net}, on the grid provided. Draw appropriate error bars for each point. Comment on the relationship the shape of the graph suggests.

Frequency versus centripetal force

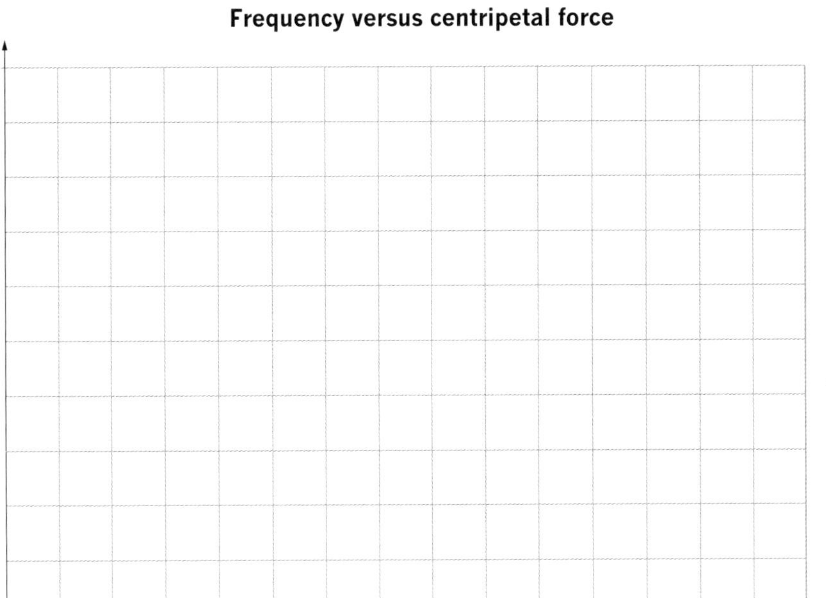

5 Plot a graph of frequency squared, f^2, versus centripetal force, F_{net}, on the grid provided. Draw a line of best fit.

Frequency squared versus centripetal force

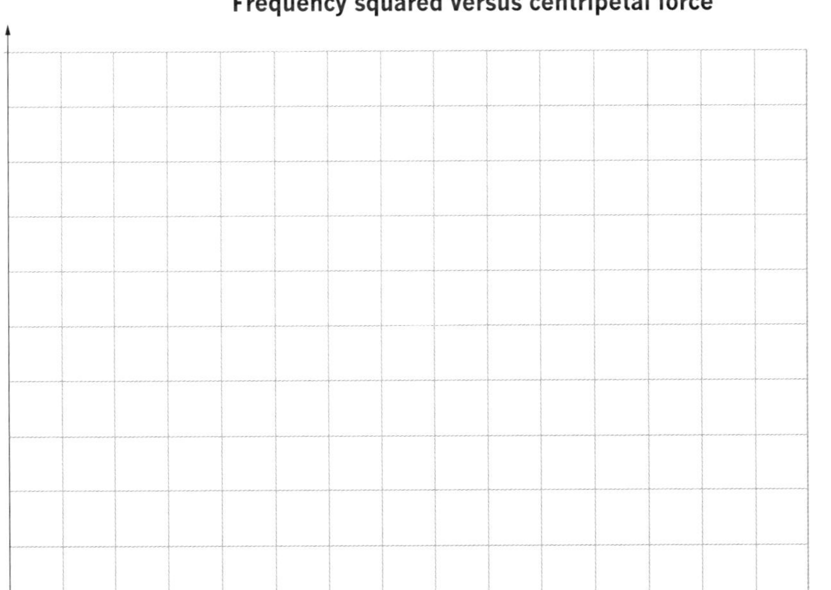

a State whether the shape of the graph confirms the relationship $F_{net} \propto f^2$.

b Define the value that the gradient of this graph should approximate.

ISBN 978 0 6557 0029 6

DISCUSSION

1 Based on your results, state the relationship between centripetal force and the frequency of rotation, including the constant of proportionality. Discuss whether your results confirm what was expected from theory. Comment on any discrepancies.

2 The radius of revolution will not actually be quite what was measured, nor will the tension in the string be exactly F_{net}. Explain why this is so.

3 Discuss the likely effect this will have on your results.

CONCLUSION

 ISBN 978 0 6557 0029 6

PRACTICAL ACTIVITY 2

Experiment

Circular motion—centripetal force in a vertical plane

SUGGESTED DURATION

- 50 minutes data collection + 15 minutes analysis

MATERIALS

- string
- small mass
- alligator clip
- stopwatch
- metre ruler

INTRODUCTION

In this activity, the centripetal force experienced by an object travelling in a vertical plane will be investigated.

AIM

To investigate the non-uniform nature of the forces acting in vertical circular motion.

As an option for more accurate timing, phones and tablets can be used to video the motion for video analysis. Use a bright coloured mass against a plain background to allow for auto tracking by video analysis tools.

Safety

Leave plenty of room around you when swinging the mass to avoid hitting other students.

Complete a risk assessment before starting the activity.

METHOD

1. Tie the string to the mass and measure the length of the string to the centre of the mass. Mark the string in 20 cm segments.
2. To reduce the friction between the string and your fingers, fasten the alligator clip at one of the 20 cm marks. This will give a better defined radius of the mass and reduces friction, allowing a more constant speed of rotation and greatly improving accuracy.
3. Rotate the mass in a vertical circle. With practice, you can feel the change in tension in the string at the top of the circle compared with that at the bottom. Keep the rotation as even as possible.
4. Time the period of rotation for 20 revolutions and then find the average period. Repeat five times for each particular radius. You may need to add rows to the table if results are recorded for more than four radii.
5. Record your results in the table in the Results section.

RESULTS

Radius and period

Radius r (m) ±	Time for 20 revolutions (s) ±			Average time for 20 revolutions (s)	Period, T, for one revolution (s)
	Trial 1	Trial 2	Trial 3		

ISBN 978 0 6557 0029 6

PRACTICAL ACTIVITY 2

Plot a graph of period versus radius on the grid provided. Draw appropriate uncertainty bars for each point and, hence, draw a line of best fit. Determine the gradient of the line of best fit.

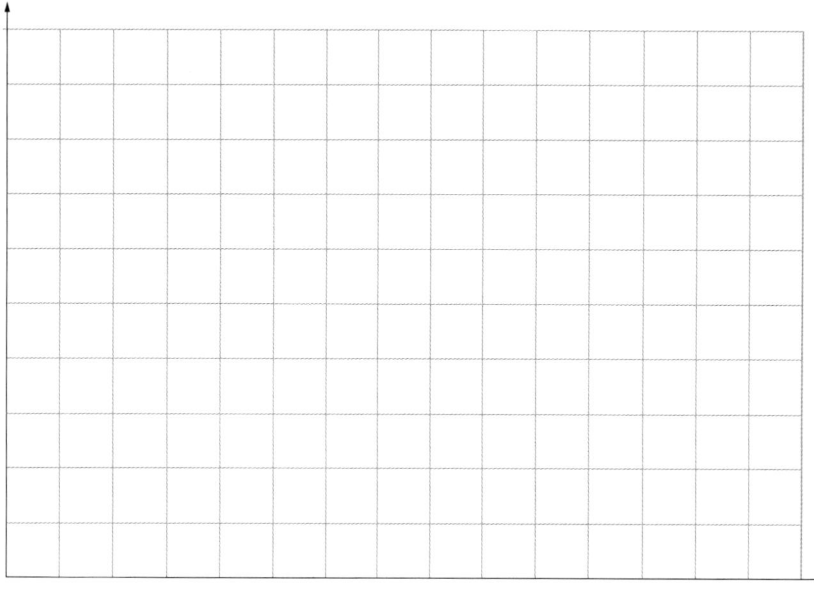

DISCUSSION

1 Why is a graph of period versus radius being plotted?

2 Based on your graph, comment on the relationship between period and radius. Do your results confirm what was expected from theory? Comment on any discrepancies.

CONCLUSION

ISBN 978 0 6557 0029 6

PRACTICAL ACTIVITY 3

Experiment

Projectile motion—an introduction

SUGGESTED DURATION

- 45 minutes data collection + 15 minutes analysis

MATERIALS

- ramp or board
- small ball (each group may use one or more of different size and mass)
- stopwatch
- horizontal bench or table
- polystyrene cup and Blu Tack®

INTRODUCTION

In this activity you will conduct a practical investigation to collect primary data to validate the relationship between time of flight, height and range.

AIM

To confirm the dependence of the range of a projectile (the horizontal distance it travels) on its time of flight and launch velocity by predicting the landing point of a projectile and then testing the prediction.

Safety
Ensure that the path of the projectile is clear.
Complete a risk assessment before starting the activity.

METHOD

Consider the situation in Figure 3.1.15. A small ball rolls down a ramp, then across a flat surface at a known speed, and then moves off the end of the table and falls to the floor. While it is in flight, the only external forces acting on the ball are gravity and air resistance. Air resistance should be ignored in this investigation.

Figure 3.1.15 The experimental set-up

Part A • Determining the launch velocity

1. Mark a point on the ramp from which the ball can be consistently released at the same position. Measure the horizontal distance from the end of the ramp to the edge of the table. Record this in the Results section.
2. Release the ball and time how long it takes to travel the horizontal distance from the base of the ramp to the edge of the table. Do not let the ball fall to the floor while recording this time.
3. Repeat the test a number of times, recording each trial in the table in the Results section.
4. Complete the table by calculating the velocity across the tabletop for each trial and then finding the average velocity.

Part B • Predicting and testing the range

1. Record the height the ball will fall from the table to the floor.
2. Calculate the time of flight and hence the distance the ball will travel in the horizontal direction (the range) while it is in the air. Show your working in the Results section.
3. Measure out the calculated landing distance on the floor and place a polystyrene cup at the predicted point. Attach the cup to the floor with some Blu Tack® so it won't move when the ball hits it or lands in it.
4. Test your prediction by releasing the ball from the same spot on the ramp as used in Part **A**.

RESULTS

Part A • Determining the launch velocity

List the variables associated with this experimental method.

Independent: ________________

Dependent: ________________

Controlled: ________________

1 Complete the table by calculating the velocity across the tabletop for each trial and, hence, find the average velocity

Distance across the tabletop: $s =$ __________ m

Data collected for Part A		
Trial number	**Time, *t*, taken to travel across tabletop (s)**	**Velocity across tabletop ($m\,s^{-1}$)** $v = \frac{s}{t}$
1		
2		
3		
4		
5		
Average		

2 Is the velocity being calculated the velocity of the ball at the edge of the table? If not, is it a reasonable approximation? Explain your answer.

3 What effect would increasing the horizontal distance have on the reliability of your measurements?

Part B • Predicting and testing the range

1 Record the height the ball will fall from the table to the floor, including an estimate of the uncertainty.

Height above the ground = __________ ± ______ m

2 Describe how you measured the height to ensure that it is as accurate as possible.

 ISBN 978 0 6557 0029 6

3 Calculate the time it takes for the ball to fall from the table to the floor.

4 Calculate the distance the ball will travel in the horizontal direction, i.e. the range.

DISCUSSION

1 State whether your prediction was successful and describe any difficulties encountered in testing the prediction.

2 In this experiment, the assumption was made that there is negligible effect from air resistance. Would the effect of air resistance be more significant if the ball was released from a height of 30 cm up the ramp or 15 cm? Explain.

3 Discuss the major potential source of uncertainties in this experiment and the steps that were taken to minimise them.

CONCLUSION

PRACTICAL ACTIVITY 4

Experiment

Projectile motion—the effect of launch angle on range

SUGGESTED DURATION

- 50 minutes data collection + 15 minutes analysis

INTRODUCTION

In this activity students will use electronic means to:

- measure the initial velocity of a projectile
- measure the time of flight of a projectile
- interpret data to predict the angle that will give the longest range
- calculate the appropriate angle in order to hit a target at a given range.

AIM

To investigate the relationship between the launch angle of a projectile, its motion and the range of the projectile.

Safety

Always wear safety glasses when using any kind of projectile launcher. Never look down the barrel of a mechanical projectile launcher.

Complete a risk assessment before starting the activity.

MATERIALS

- data-collection system
- projectile launcher (commercial or improvised, e.g. poly tube)
- projectile
- photogate/s and (optional) time-of-flight pad or stopwatch
- angle indicator
- tabletop or bench
- table clamp or burette stand and clamps
- A4 paper
- tape measure
- sticky tape
- carbon paper (optional)

METHOD

1. Start a new experiment on your data-collection system. Connect the photogates to your system following the manufacturer's instructions.
2. Select 'velocity between gates' if prompted by your data-collection system. Ensure the 'space between gates' parameter on your data-collection system is set to the measured space between your photogates.
3. Put your data-collection system into manual sampling mode with manually entered data. Name the manually entered numerical data 'Angle' measured in degrees. Construct a table to record angle, velocity, distance and time of flight or use Table 1 in the Results section to write down your results. Record an estimate of the uncertainty in each measurement.
4. Attach the projectile launcher to a table so that the projectiles travel across the longest part of the table. One suitable arrangement of the launcher is shown in Figure 3.1.16. Use the equipment available to you to arrange the launcher to 'fire' down the length of the table and through the photogates. Be careful to avoid firing the projectile at classmates!

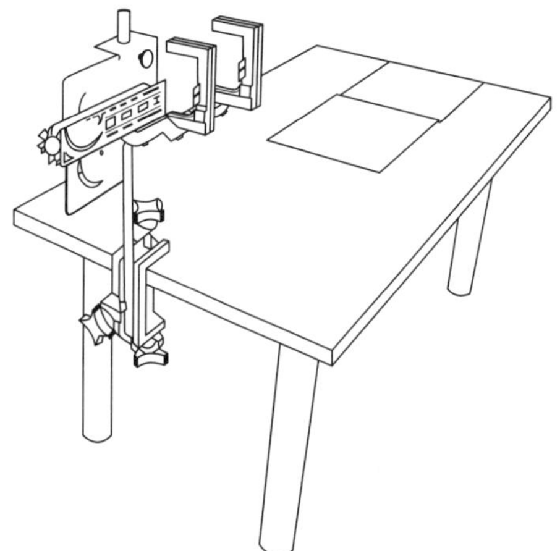

Figure 3.1.16 The projectile launcher set-up

 ISBN 978 0 6557 0029 6

5 ▪ Place sheets of paper end-to-end in a line across the length of the table in front of the projectile launcher, and secure them in place with tape.

6 ▪ Measure the height from the point where the ball is released to the tabletop, and record this value in the Results section.

7 ▪ Mount the photogates to the launcher. Be sure to mount the first named photogate in your data analysis software closest to the launcher.

Part A • Distance versus angle

1 ▪ Set the launcher in the horizontal position with a launch angle of 0°.

2 ▪ Load a projectile into the launcher, and ensure that the launcher is set to its maximum compression or distance setting.

3 ▪ Launch the projectile, and note the point of impact on the paper.

4 ▪ Lay a sheet of carbon paper on top of the white paper over the point of impact, carbon-side down, so that when a ball lands on it there will be a mark on the paper. Place a sheet of paper over the carbon paper to prevent damage to the carbon paper by the projectile.

If carbon paper is not available, look for a small indentation on the paper where the ball hits. Highlight the point with a pencil or marker when the projectile lands. Before continuing, answer Question **1** in the Results section.

5 ▪ Start recording with the data-collection system and launch the projectile.

Record the sampled 'velocity between gates' data point, and enter the corresponding angle value in Table 1 in the Results section.

6 ▪ Move the carbon paper, and measure the distance to the mark. Write the angle next to the mark on the paper.

7 ▪ Use the angle indicator on the launcher to position the launcher at the next angle, 10°.

8 ▪ Repeat the data-collection steps, increasing the angle of inclination by 10° each time until you have recorded a data point every 10° from 0° to 80°.

9 ▪ Measure and enter the horizontal distance for each angle value into Table 1. Draw a graph of distance versus angle and a graph of velocity versus angle in the grids provided.

Part B • Time of flight

1 ▪ If a time-of-flight pad is available, remove one photogate and attach the time-of-flight pad. Alternatively, a hand-held stopwatch or other timing mechanism can be used. Position the time-of-flight pad over the landing point recorded for an angle of 0° and reset the launcher to an angle of 0°. Before continuing, answer Question **2** in the Discussion section.

2 ▪ Start a new data-collection session. Launch the ball from the launcher and using the time-of-flight pad, or a stopwatch, record the time the ball is in flight in Table 1.

3 ▪ Use the angle indicator on the launcher to position the launcher at the next angle, and repeat the data-collection steps until you have recorded a data point every 10° from 0° to 80°. Record the time of flight for each angle in Table 1 of the Results section. Draw a graph of time of flight versus angle in the grid provided.

RESULTS

List the variables associated with this experimental method.

Independent: ______

Dependent: ______

Controlled: ______

Ball release height: ______(m)

1 What launch angle do you predict will yield the greatest range (horizontal distance)?

______

2 Complete Table 1, below, including an estimate of the uncertainty in each measurement.

Table 1 Collected data for your projectile

Angle (°) ±	v (m s^{-1})				s (m)				Time of flight, t (s)			
	Trial 1	Trial 2	Trial 3	Average	Trial 1	Trial 2	Trial 3	Average	Trial 1	Trial 2	Trial 3	Average
0°												
10°												
20°												
30°												
40°												
50°												
60°												
70°												
80°												

Plot the relevant data points on a graph of distance versus angle, initial velocity versus angle and time of flight versus angle in the spaces provided. (You may also be able to print these graphs from your data-collection system and paste them over the grids.)

Draw the corresponding uncertainty bars for each data set and, hence, find a line of best fit for each graph.

Distance versus angle

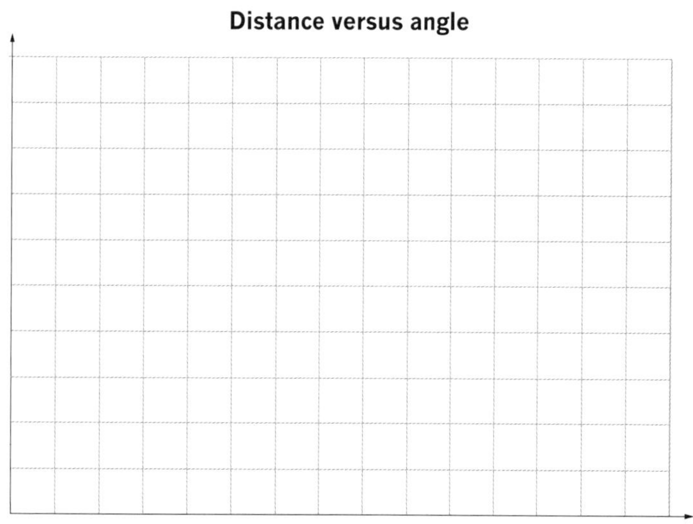

Initial velocity versus angle

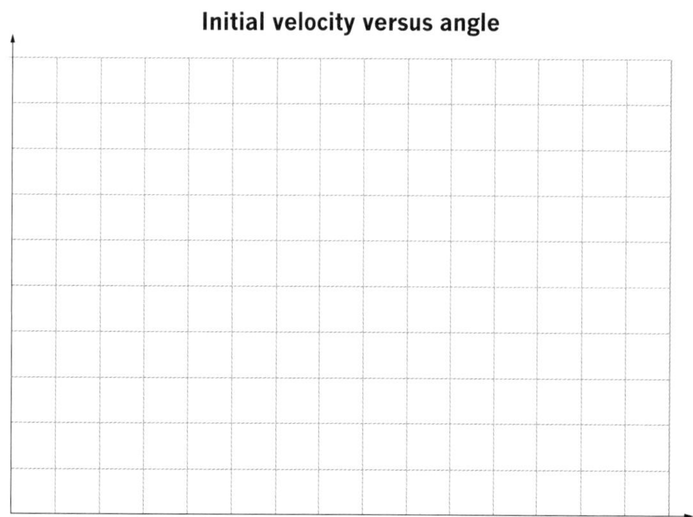

 ISBN 978 0 6557 0029 6

3 Choose one of the angles other than 0° and draw to scale a vector diagram for your projectile at the launch position showing both the horizontal and vertical component velocities. Show how you would determine the average initial velocity, and draw the resultant velocity on the diagram.

4 Use the horizontal distance and time of flight to calculate the average horizontal velocity for each angle, and fill in the corresponding column in Table 2, on the following page. Explain why this is referred to as the average horizontal velocity over the flight of the projectile.

5 Using the initial vertical velocity and the height of the launcher for each launch angle, calculate the theoretical time of flight of an object shot straight up. Record the results in Table 2.

PRACTICAL ACTIVITY 4

Table 2 Projectile data calculations

Angle (°) ±	Horizontal velocity ($m\,s^{-1}$)	Vertical velocity ($m\,s^{-1}$)	Average horizontal velocity ($m\,s^{-1}$)	Theoretical time of flight (s)
0°				
10°				
20°				
30°				
40°				
50°				
60°				
70°				
80°				

DISCUSSION

1 Compare the measured horizontal velocities to the average horizontal velocities.

2 Based on your data, state the launch angle that will yield the maximum horizontal range

3 Based on your results, determine whether there are launch angles that yield the same horizontal range. Explain the relationship between these angles.

CONCLUSION

ISBN 978 0 6557 0029 6

PRACTICAL ACTIVITY 5

Experiment

Elastic and inelastic collisions

SUGGESTED DURATION

50 minutes data collection + 20 minutes analysis

INTRODUCTION

Elastic and inelastic collisions are performed with two dynamics carts of different masses. Magnetic bumpers are used in the elastic collision and Velcro® bumpers are used in the completely inelastic collision. In both cases, momentum is conserved.

Cart velocities can be measured using a motion sensor or a built-in position sensor. These add no additional frictional losses and, since the velocities are continuously monitored, any deceleration due to friction can be measured. The total kinetic energy before and after the collision is also studied.

The momentum, *p*, of a cart depends on its mass and velocity.

$$p = mv \qquad (1)$$

The direction of the momentum is the same as the direction of the velocity. During a collision, the total momentum of the system of both carts is conserved because the net force on the two-cart system is zero. This means that the total momentum just before the collision is equal to the total momentum just after the collision. If the momentum of one cart decreases, the momentum of the other cart increases by the same amount. This is true regardless of the type of collision, and even in cases where kinetic energy is not conserved. The law of conservation of momentum is stated as

$$\Sigma p_{\text{initial}} = \Sigma p_{\text{final}} \qquad (2)$$

where $\Sigma p_{\text{initial}}$ is the total momentum before the collision and Σp_{final} is the total momentum after the collision.

The kinetic energy of a cart also depends on its mass and speed but kinetic energy is a scalar.

$$E_k = \frac{1}{2}mv^2 \qquad (3)$$

The total kinetic energy of the system of two carts is found by adding the kinetic energies of the individual carts.

MATERIALS

- 2 × dynamics carts and track. At least one of the carts should have a spring-loaded plunger. Both should have Velcro® and magnetic bumpers available.
- 2 × cart masses to suit the carts
- end stops for the track (if using smart dynamic carts)
- electronic balance
- electronic measurement system including either motion sensors or sensors in the carts to allow continuous monitoring of the velocity of both carts.

AIM

To investigate the energy changes in elastic and inelastic collisions between two dynamics carts.

Safety

Avoid dropping masses and carts or letting carts roll off benches. The equipment may be damaged and may injure students.

Complete a risk assessment before starting the activity.

METHOD

1 ▪ Start a new experiment on your data collection system. Connect the motion sensors or 'smart' carts to your system following the manufacturer's instructions. If using motion sensors, place one at each end of the track. Angle each motion sensor slightly downwards to be sure it's focused on the cart at the same end. The motion sensors can also act as end stops.

2 ▪ Use the balance to measure the mass of each cart and record them in the Results section.

3 ▪ Using your manufacturer's software, create a graph of velocity versus time, putting the velocity of both carts on the same vertical axes.

4 ▪ Check the signs of the velocities. The goal is to have the velocities of both carts be positive to the right.

Start recording and push both carts to the right. Check that both velocities are positive and adjust in your software as needed. This establishes the coordinate system to have positive *x* to the right for both carts.

PRACTICAL ACTIVITY 5

Part A • 'Explosive' force

I Equal mass carts

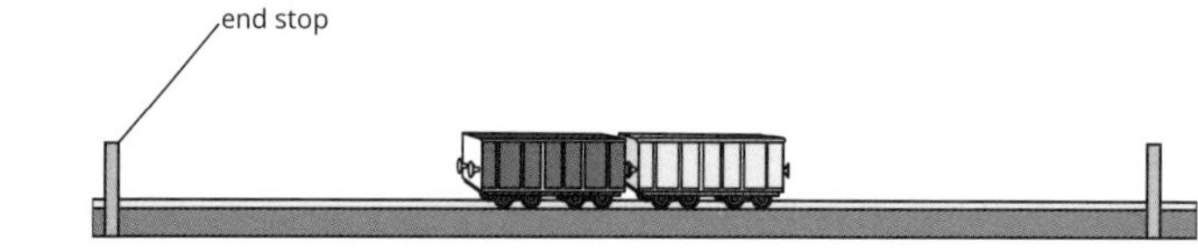

Figure 3.1.17 Equal mass carts—elastic collision

1 ▪ Depress the plunger on one cart about half-way—don't use the maximum amount as the force may be too large, depending on the carts available. Place the two carts in contact with each other in the centre of the track, as shown in Figure 3.1.17.

2 ▪ Start recording with your data collection system and tap the trigger release to launch the carts. Hitting the trigger with a mass bar works well.

3 ▪ Stop recording before either cart reaches the end of the track.

4 ▪ On the velocity vs time graph, use the graph tools available to find the velocity of both carts just after the initial impulse from the plunger. Record these in Table 1 in the Results section.

II Unequal mass carts

Figure 3.1.18 Unequal mass carts—elastic collision

5 ▪ Use the balance to find the mass of two mass bars, and then place them both on one of the carts, as shown in Figure 3.1.18.

6 ▪ Repeat steps 1 to 4 from Part **I**. Record these in Table 1.

Part B • Inelastic collisions

This part uses the Velcro® bumpers so the carts 'stick' together on impact.

I Equal mass carts

Figure 3.1.19 Equal mass carts—inelastic collision

1 ▪ Place the two carts at rest on the track as shown in Figure 3.1.19, with the Velcro® bumpers facing each other.
Check the properties in your data collection system so that the positive direction is the same for each cart. This will mean reversing that for the right-hand cart from the settings in Part **A**.

2 ▪ Start recording and give the left-hand cart a push towards the other cart. Stop recording after the carts collide and before either cart reaches the end of the track.

3 ▪ On the velocity vs time graph, find the velocity of the left-hand cart just before and just after the collision. It may be helpful to expand the graph, to see just that area you are interested in.
Record the velocities of each cart in Table 1.

II Unequal mass carts

Figure 3.1.20 Unequal mass carts—inelastic collision

4 ▪ Place the two mass bars in the right-hand cart, as shown in Figure 3.1.20, and repeat the method from Part **I**. Record the velocities in Table 1.

 ISBN 978 0 6557 0029 6

Part C • Elastic collisions

This section requires magnetic, or similar, bumpers on the carts.

I Equal mass carts

1 ▪ Place the carts at rest on the track, as shown above, with the magnetic bumpers facing each other. Check the properties in your data collection system so that the positive direction is the same for each cart. This may mean reversing that for the left-hand cart from the earlier settings.

2 ▪ Start recording and give the left-hand cart a push towards the other cart.

3 ▪ Record while the carts collide and stop recording before either cart reaches the end of the track.

4 ▪ On the velocity vs time graph, find the velocity of each cart just before and just after the collision. It may be helpful to expand the graph, to see just that area you are interested in.

II Unequal mass carts

5 ▪ Place the two mass bars in the right-hand cart and repeat the method from Part **I**. Record the velocities in Table 1.

RESULTS

Mass of cart 1: ______________ kg

Mass of cart 2: ______________ kg

Mass of additional mass bars: ______________ kg

Table 1 Cart momentum

Cart	Initial velocity ($m\,s^{-1}$)	Final velocity ($m\,s^{-1}$)	Initial *p* ($kg\,m\,s^{-1}$)	Final *p* ($kg\,m\,s^{-1}$)	% difference
Part A I, left-hand cart					
Part A I, right-hand cart					
Part A II, left-hand cart					
Part A II, right-hand cart					
Part B I, left-hand cart					
Part B I, right-hand cart					
Part B II, left-hand cart					
Part B II, right-hand cart					
Part C I, left-hand cart					
Part C I, right-hand cart					
Part C II, left-hand cart					
Part C II, right-hand cart					

PRACTICAL ACTIVITY 5

1 Calculate the initial and final momentum for each cart for each of the collisions and add the results to Table 1.

2 Calculate the percentage difference between the total initial momentum and the total final momentum for each collision and add your results to Table 1:

$$\text{percentage difference} = \frac{(p_{\text{initial}} - p_{\text{final}})}{p_{\text{initial}}} \times 100\%.$$

Table 2 Cart kinetic energy

Cart	Initial velocity ($m\,s^{-1}$)	Final velocity ($m\,s^{-1}$)	Initial E_k (J)	Final E_k (J)	% difference
Part A I, left-hand cart					
Part A I, right-hand cart					
Part A II, left-hand cart					
Part A II, right-hand cart					
Part B I, left-hand cart					
Part B I, right-hand cart					
Part B II, left-hand cart					
Part B II, right-hand cart					
Part C I, left-hand cart					
Part C I, right-hand cart					
Part C II, left-hand cart					
Part C II, right-hand cart					

3 Calculate the initial and the final kinetic energy for each cart for each of the collisions and add the results to Table 2, above.

4 Calculate the percentage of the total kinetic energy lost for each collision and add the results to Table 2.

DISCUSSION

Summarise your findings on conservation of momentum and kinetic energy in different types of collisions:

1 State whether momentum was conserved for all types of calculations. Justify your statement with reference to your results.

ISBN 978 0 6557 0029 6

PRACTICAL ACTIVITY 5

2 State whether kinetic energy was conserved for all types of calculations. Justify your statement with reference to your results.

3 Explain what happens to the initial kinetic energy that is lost in a collision.

CONCLUSION

EXAM QUESTIONS

Multiple-choice questions

Question 1 VCE Physics 2013 (A) 5

A mass of 2.0 kg is being swung by a light rod in a vertical circle of radius 1.0 m at a constant speed of 7.0 m s^{-1}, as shown in the figure below.

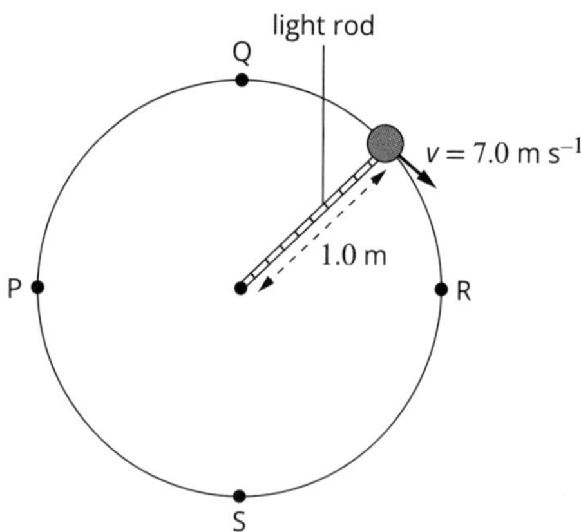

Which of the directions (A–F) below shows the direction of the net force on the mass when it is at point P?

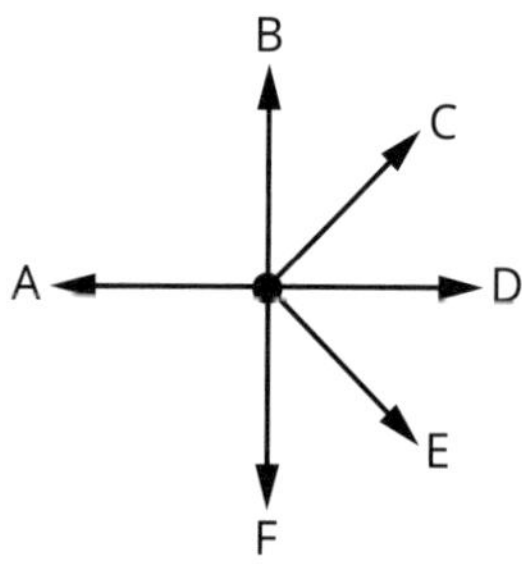

Question 2 VCE Physics 2018 (A) 5

Four students are pulling on ropes in a four-person tug of war. The relative sizes of the forces acting on the various ropes are $F_W = 200$ N, $F_X = 240$ N, $F_Y = 180$ N and $F_Z = 210$ N. The situation is shown in the diagram below.

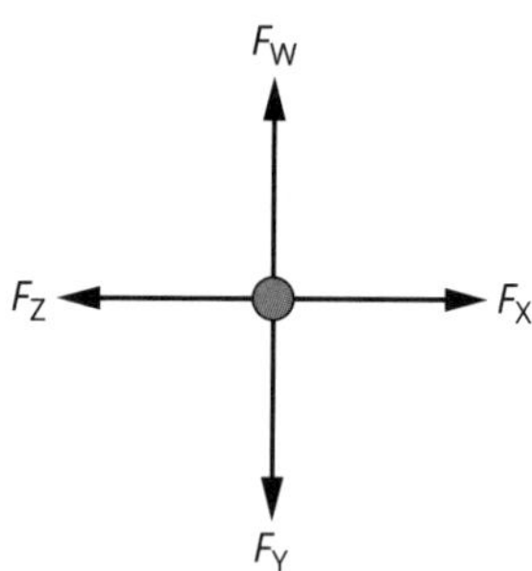

Which one of the following best gives the magnitude of the resultant force acting at the centre of the tug-of-war ropes?

A. 28.3 N

B. 30.0 N

C. 36.1 N

D. 50.0 N

 ISBN 978 0 6557 0029 6

EXAM QUESTIONS

Use the following information to answer Questions 3 and 4.

A railway truck X of mass 10 tonnes, moving at 6.0 m s^{-1}, collides with a stationary railway truck Y of mass 5 tonnes. After the collision, the trucks are joined together and move off as one. The situation is shown below.

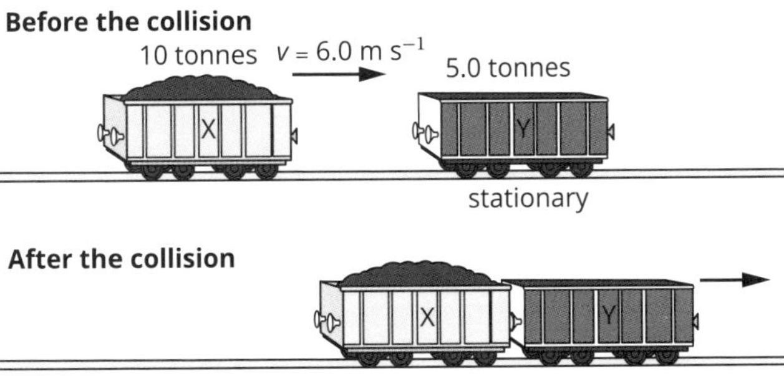

Question 3 VCE Physics 2018 (A) 8

The final speed of the joined railway trucks after the collision is closest to:

A. 2.0 m s^{-1}

B. 3.0 m s^{-1}

C. 4.0 m s^{-1}

D. 6.0 m s^{-1}

Question 4 VCE Physics 2018 (A) 9

The collision of the railway trucks is best described as one where:

A. kinetic energy is conserved but momentum is not conserved.

B. kinetic energy is not conserved but momentum is conserved.

C. neither kinetic energy nor momentum is conserved.

D. both kinetic energy and momentum are conserved.

Question 5 VCE Physics 2020 (A) 8

A ball is attached to the end of a string and rotated in a circle at a constant speed in a vertical plane, as shown in the diagram below.

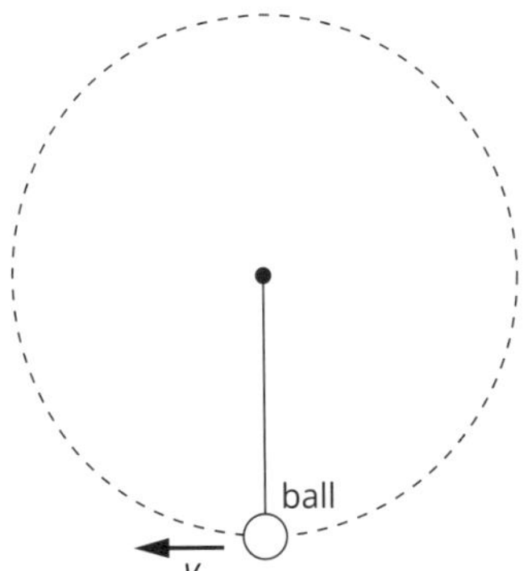

EXAM QUESTIONS

The arrows in options A to D below indicate the direction and the size of the forces acting on the ball.

Ignoring air resistance, which one of the following best represents the forces acting on the ball when it is at the bottom of the circular path and moving to the left?

A.

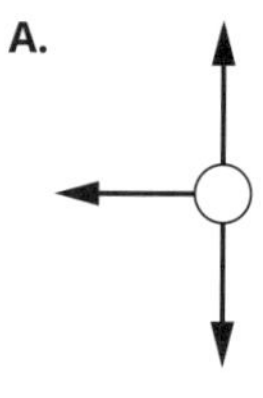

B.

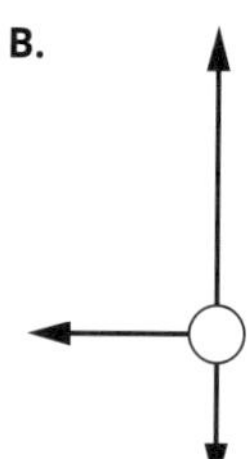

C.

D.

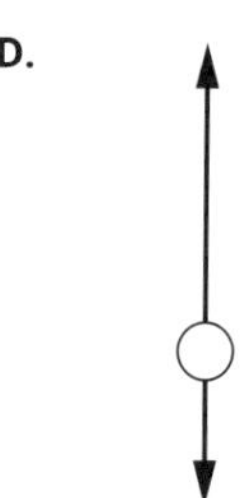

Use the following information to answer Questions 6 and 7.

Two blocks of mass 5 kg and 10 kg are placed in contact on a frictionless horizontal surface, as shown in the diagram below. A constant horizontal force, *F*, is applied to the 5 kg block.

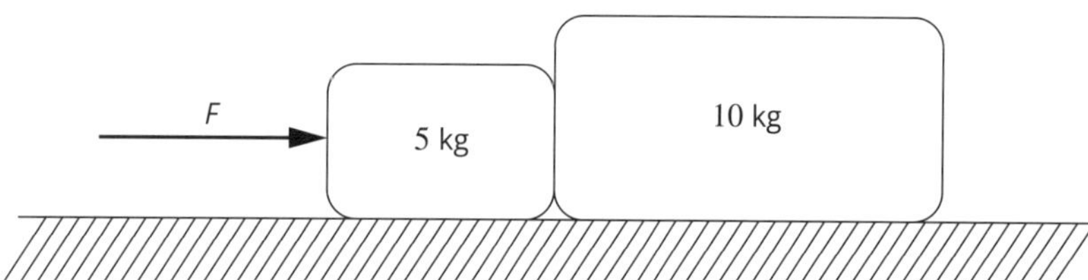

Question 6 VCE Physics 2020 (A) 9

Which one of the following statements is correct?

A. The net force on each block is the same.

B. The acceleration experienced by the 5 kg block is twice the acceleration experienced by the 10 kg block.

C. The magnitude of the net force on the 5 kg block is half the magnitude of the net force on the 10 kg block.

D. The magnitude of the net force on the 5 kg block is twice the magnitude of the net force on the 10 kg block.

Question 7 VCE Physics 2020 (A) 10

If the force *F* has a magnitude of 250 N, what is the work done by the force in moving the blocks in a straight line for a distance of 20 m?

A. 5 kJ

B. 25 kJ

C. 50 kJ

D. 500 kJ

ISBN 978 0 6557 0029 6

EXAM QUESTIONS

Question 8 VCE Physics 2019 (A) 11

An ultralight aeroplane of mass 500 kg flies in a horizontal straight line at a constant speed of 100 m s^{-1}. The horizontal resistance force acting on the aeroplane is 1500 N.
Which one of the following best describes the magnitude of the forward horizontal thrust on the aeroplane?

A. 1500 N

B. slightly less than 1500 N

C. slightly more than 1500 N

D. 5000 N

Question 9 VCE Physics 2019 (A) 12

A small ball is rolling at constant speed along a horizontal table. It rolls off the edge of the table and follows the parabolic path shown in the diagram below. Ignore air resistance.

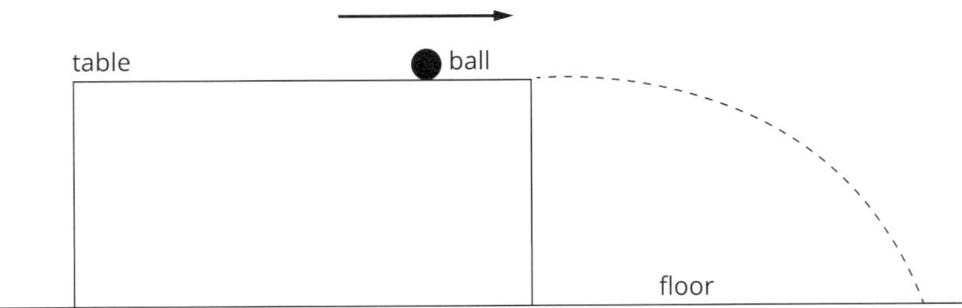

Which one of the following statements about the motion of the ball as it falls is correct?

A. The ball's speed increases at a constant rate.

B. The momentum of the ball is conserved.

C. The acceleration of the ball is constant.

D. The ball travels at constant speed.

Question 10 VCE Physics 2017 (A) 12

A model car is on a track and moving to the right. It collides with and compresses a spring that is considered ideal, as shown in the diagram below.

The car compresses the spring to 0.50 m when the car comes to rest. The force–distance graph for the spring is also shown below.

Assume that friction is negligible.

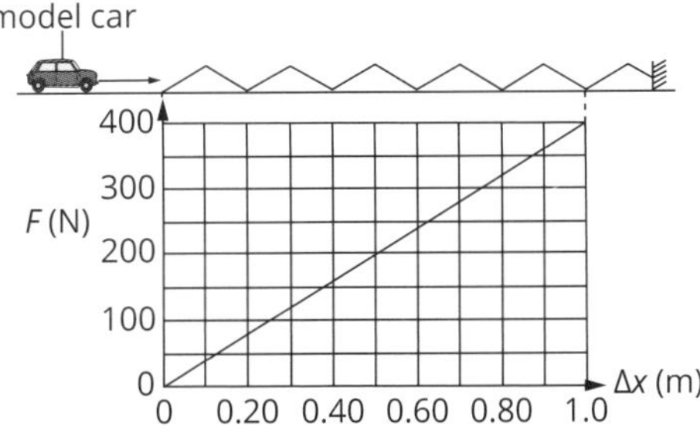

Based on the graph above, what is the best estimate of the spring constant, *k*?

A. 100 N m^{-1}

B. 200 N m^{-1}

C. 400 N m^{-1}

D. 800 N m^{-1}

EXAM QUESTIONS

Short-answer questions

Question 1 (5 marks) VCE Physics 2013 (A) 1

Students set up an inclined plane surface, as shown in the figure below. It is angled at 10° to the horizontal. They place a frictionless trolley of mass 0.50 kg at the top of the incline, so that the distance from the front of the trolley to the stopper at the bottom is 3.5 m.

They release the trolley from rest and find that it takes 2.0 s to reach the stopper at the bottom.

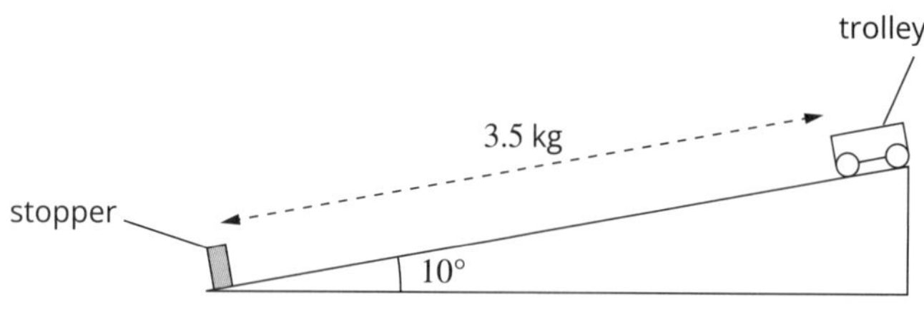

a. Calculate the acceleration of the trolley. 2 marks

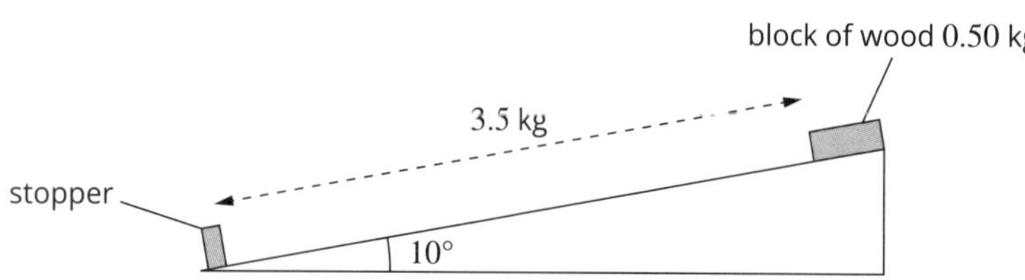

b. The students replace the frictionless trolley with a block of wood of the same mass. They release the block of wood at a distance of 3.5 m from the stopper, the same as they did with the trolley. When the block is sliding down the incline, there is a constant frictional force between it and the surface. They find that it takes 6.0 s to reach the stopper at the bottom.

Calculate the magnitude of the frictional force of the plane surface acting on the block. 3 marks

ISBN 978 0 6557 0029 6

EXAM QUESTIONS

Question 2 (5 marks) VCE Physics 2013 (A) 3

The figure below shows an experiment in which a frictionless trolley, m_1, of mass 2.0 kg, moving to the right at 6.0 m s^{-1}, collides with and sticks to an initially stationary trolley, m_2, of mass 4.0 kg and also frictionless.

$u_1 = 6.0$ m s^{-1} $u_2 = 0$

2.0 kg 4.0 kg

m_1 m_2

v_{after}

$(m_1 + m_2)$

m_1 m_2

a. Calculate the magnitude of the total momentum of the two trolleys when they stick together after the collision. 1 mark

b. Determine, by using calculations, whether this collision is elastic or inelastic. 2 marks

c. Calculate the magnitude and direction of the impulse exerted on m_1 by m_2 during the collision. 2 marks

Question 3 (6 marks) VCE Physics 2018 (B) 7

A small ball of mass 0.20 kg rolls on a horizontal table at 3.0 m s^{-1}, as shown in the figure below.

The ball hits the floor 0.40 s after rolling off the edge of the table. The radius of the ball may be ignored. In this question, take the value of g to be 10 m s^{-2}.

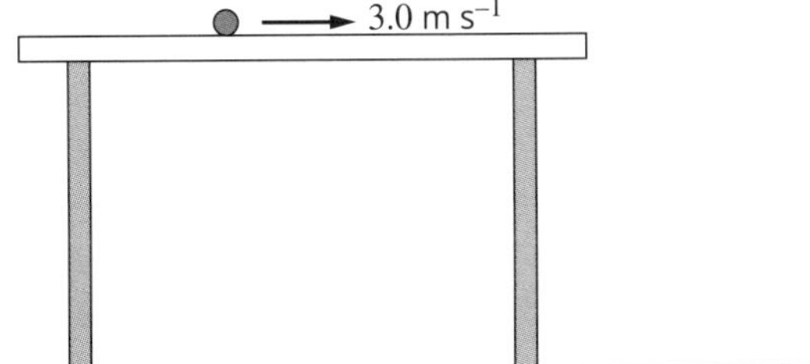

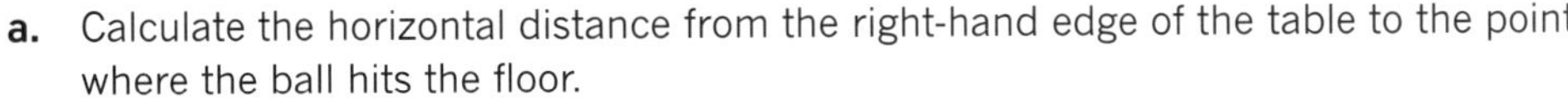

a. Calculate the horizontal distance from the right-hand edge of the table to the point where the ball hits the floor. 1 mark

b. Calculate the height of the table. Show your working. 2 marks

c. Calculate the speed at which the ball hits the floor. Show your working. 3 marks

Question 4 (10 marks) VCE Physics 2021 (B) 9

Abbie and Brian are about to go on their first loop-the-loop rollercoaster ride. As competent Physics students, they are working out if they will have enough speed at the top of the loop to remain in contact with the track while they are upside down at point C, shown in the figure below. The radius of the loop CB is *r*.

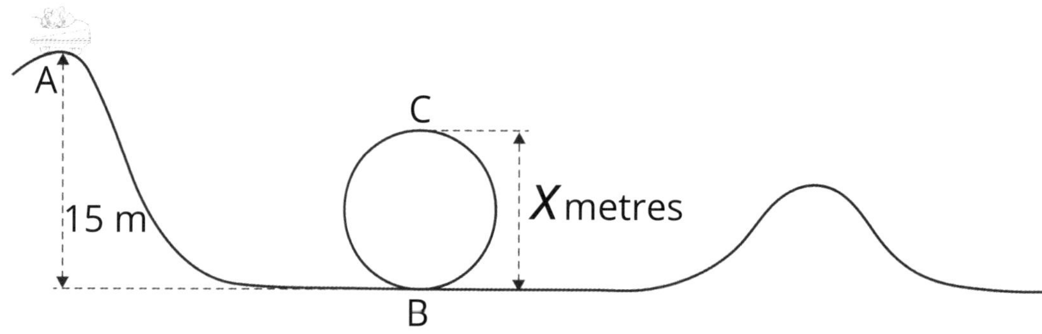

The highest point of the rollercoaster (point A) is 15 m above point B and the car starts at rest from point A. Assume that there is negligible friction between the car and the track.

a. What is the speed of the car at point B at the bottom of the loop? Show your working. 2 marks

b. By considering the forces acting on the car, show that the condition for the car to just remain in contact with the track at point C is given by $\frac{v^2}{r} = g$. Show your working. 2 marks

c. What is the maximum height of the loop (*X* metres) that will ensure that the car stays in contact with the track at point C? Show your working. 3 marks

 ISBN 978 0 6557 0029 6

d. If friction is taken into account, will Abbie and Brian need to increase or decrease their predicted value for the radius of the loop? Explain your answer. 3 marks

Question 5 (7 marks) VCE Physics 2018 (B) 6

A ball of mass 2.0 kg is dropped from a height of 2.0 m above a spring, as shown in the figure below. The spring has an uncompressed length of 2.0 m. The ball and the spring come to rest when they are at a distance of 0.50 m below the uncompressed position of the spring.

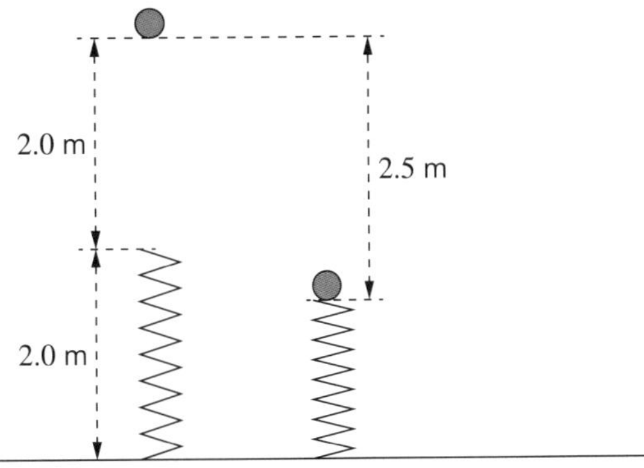

a. Using $g = 9.8\,N\,kg^{-1}$, show that the spring constant, k, is equal to $392\,N\,m^{-1}$. Show your working. 3 marks

b. Determine the acceleration of the ball when it reaches its maximum speed. Explain your answer. 2 marks

c. Calculate the compression of the spring when the ball reaches its maximum speed. Show your working. 2 marks

UNIT

3 How do fields explain motion and electricity?

AREA OF STUDY 2

How do things move without contact?

Outcome 2

Analyse gravitational, electric and magnetic fields, and apply these to explain the operation of motors and particle accelerators, and the orbits of satellites.

Key knowledge

Fields and interactions

- describe gravitation, magnetism and electricity using a field model
- investigate and compare theoretically and practically gravitational, magnetic and electric fields, including directions and shapes of fields, attractive and repulsive effects, and the existence of dipoles and monopoles
- investigate and compare theoretically and practically gravitational fields and electrical fields about a point mass or charge (positive or negative) with reference to:
  - the direction of the field
  - the shape of the field
  - the use of the inverse square law to determine the magnitude of the field
  - potential energy changes (qualitative) associated with a point mass or charge moving in the field
- investigate and apply theoretically and practically a field model to magnetic phenomena, including shapes and directions of fields produced by bar magnets, and by current-carrying wires, loops and solenoids
- identify fields as static or changing, and as uniform or non-uniform

Effects of fields

- analyse the use of an electric field to accelerate a charge, including:
  - electric field and electric force concepts: $E = k\frac{Q}{r^2}$ and $F = k\frac{q_1q_2}{r^2}$
  - potential energy changes in a uniform electric field: $W = qV$, $E = \frac{V}{d}$
  - the magnitude of the force on a charged particle due to a uniform electric field: $F = qE$
- analyse the use of a magnetic field to change the path of a charged particle, including:
  - the magnitude and direction of the force applied to an electron beam by a magnetic field: $F = qvB$, in cases where the directions of v and B are perpendicular or parallel
  - the radius of the path followed by an electron in a magnetic field: $qvB = \frac{mv^2}{r}$, where $v \ll c$
- analyse the use of gravitational fields to accelerate mass, including:
  - gravitational field and gravitational force concepts: $g = G\frac{M}{r^2}$ and $F_g = G\frac{m_1m_2}{r^2}$
  - potential energy changes in a uniform gravitational field: $E_g = mg\Delta h$
- analyse the change in gravitational potential energy from area under a force vs distance graph and area under a field vs distance graph multiplied by mass

Application of field concepts

- apply the concepts of force due to gravity and normal force including in relation to satellites in orbit where the orbits are assumed to be uniform and circular
- model satellite motion (artificial, Moon, planet) as uniform circular orbital motion: $a = \frac{v^2}{r} = \frac{4\pi^2 r}{T^2}$

- describe the interaction of two fields, allowing that electric charges, magnetic poles and current carrying conductors can either attract or repel, whereas masses only attract each other
- investigate and analyse theoretically and practically the force on a current carrying conductor due to an external magnetic field, $F = nIlB$, where the directions of I and B are either perpendicular or parallel to each other
- investigate and analyse theoretically and practically the operation of simple DC motors consisting of one coil, containing a number of loops of wire, which is free to rotate about an axis in a uniform magnetic field and including the use of a split ring commutator
- investigate, qualitatively, the effect of current, external magnetic field and the number of loops of wire on the torque of a simple motor
- model the acceleration of particles in a particle accelerator (including synchrotrons) as uniform circular motion (limited to linear acceleration by a uniform electric field and direction change by a uniform magnetic field).

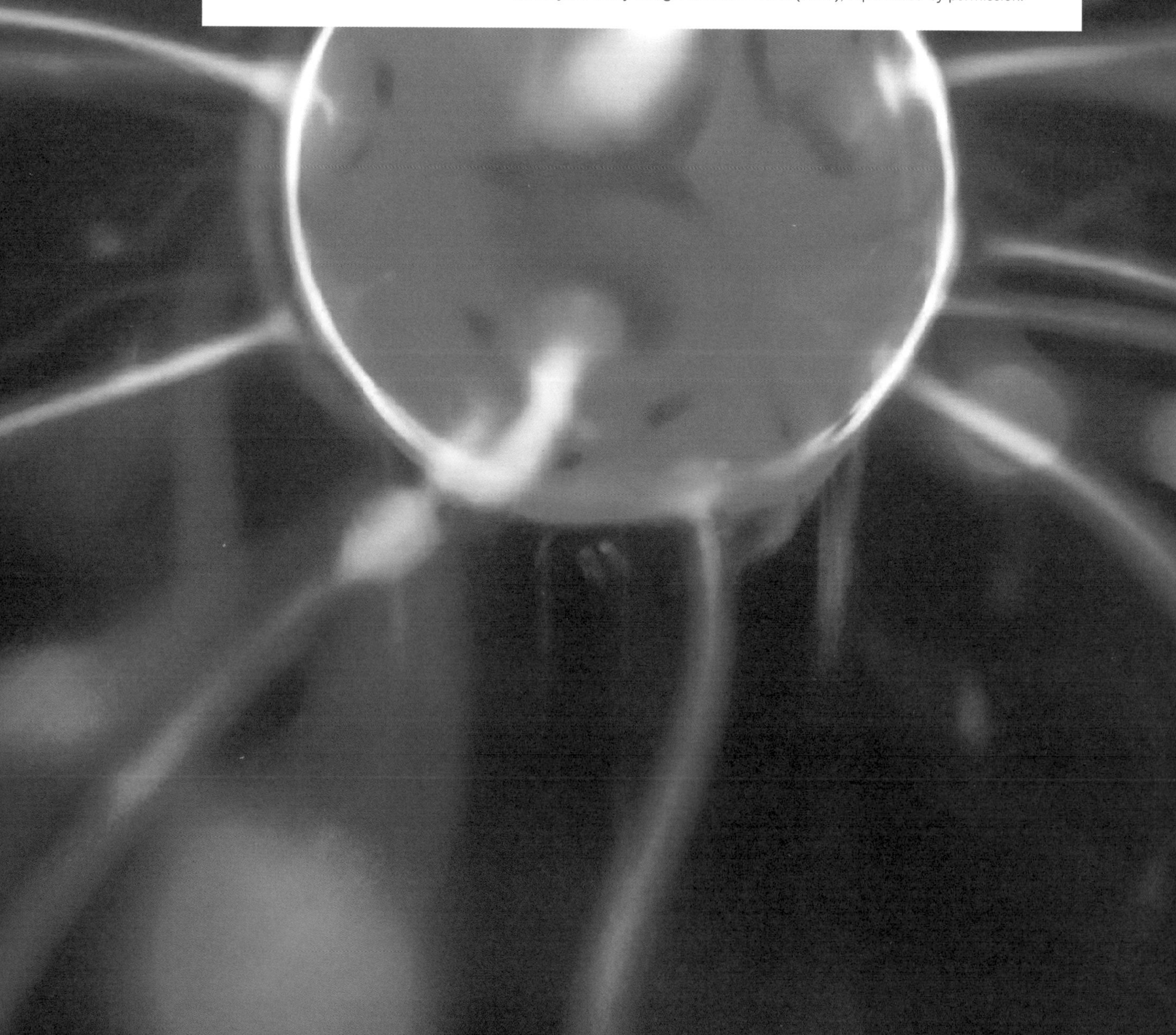

- **You will now be able to complete Worksheet 10.**

Gravity

Gravity is the weakest of the four fundamental forces of physics (electromagnetism, the strong nuclear force and the weak nuclear force are the others), but is still a very important force that drives the universe. For a satellite to move in an orbit around Earth, the centripetal force is supplied by the gravitational force of attraction between the two masses. The size of this force is determined by one of Newton's laws: Newton's law of universal gravitation.

UNIVERSAL GRAVITATION

All objects with mass attract one another with a gravitational force. The gravitational force acts equally on each of the masses. The magnitude of the gravitational force is given by **Newton's law of universal gravitation**:

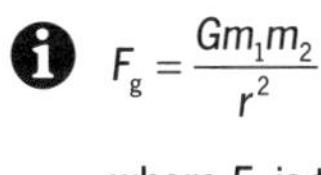

$F_g = \frac{Gm_1m_2}{r^2}$

where F_g is the gravitational force (N)
G is the **gravitational constant**, 6.67×10^{-11} N m^2 kg^{-2}
m_1 is the mass of object 1 (kg)
m_2 is the mass of object 2 (kg)
r is the distance between the centres of m_1 and m_2 (m).

The force value is always an attractive force. Gravitational forces are usually negligible unless one of the objects is massive, such as a planet. For example, consider two people with masses of 90 kg and 75 kg who have a distance of 80 cm between their centres. The force of gravitation would be:

$$F_g = \frac{Gm_1m_2}{r^2}$$

$$= \frac{6.67 \times 10^{-11} \times 90 \times 75}{0.82^2}$$

$$= 7.0 \times 10^{-7} \text{ N towards one another}$$

GRAVITATIONAL FORCE AND FORCES DURING VERTICAL ACCELERATION

The force due to gravity on an object on Earth's surface is due to the gravitational attraction of Earth.

The force due to gravity on an object is a vector quantity. It is described by the symbol F_g and it is measured in newtons (N). It is given by the equation $F_g = mg$.

For an object at rest on the ground, the normal force (F_N) is equal and opposite to the force due to gravity. However, if you are standing on a surface that is accelerating upwards, there will be a net force upwards, so the normal force will be greater than the force due to gravity. Therefore, the surface you are standing on will press more firmly on your feet, and you will feel heavier.

If you are standing on a surface that is accelerating downwards, there will be a net force downwards, so the normal force will be less than the force due to gravity. The surface will press less firmly on your feet, and you will feel lighter.

The normal force and the force due to gravity add as vectors to give the net force that causes the acceleration:

$F_{net} = F_N + F_g$

where F_N is the normal force that acts upwards on your body
F_g is the force due to gravity (which is constant in this context)
F_{net} is the net force causing the acceleration.

If a person is not touching any surface, the normal force is zero and the person may feel as if they are floating, although the force due to gravity still acts on them. An example of this is an astronaut in a space station in orbit.

GRAVITATIONAL FIELDS

A **gravitational field** is a region in which a gravitational force is exerted on all matter within that region. Some systems, such as the solar system, involve several objects (i.e. the Sun and planets) exerting attractive forces on each other at the same time. Every physical object has an accompanying gravitational field. A gravitational field can be represented by a gravitational field diagram, in which:

- the arrowheads indicate the direction of the gravitational force
- the spacing of the lines indicates the relative strength of the field. The closer the line spacing, the stronger the field.

For example, Figure 3.2.1 shows a gravitational field diagram. The arrows indicate that objects will be attracted towards the mass in the centre and the spacing of the lines shows that the force will be strongest at the surface of the central mass and weaker further away.

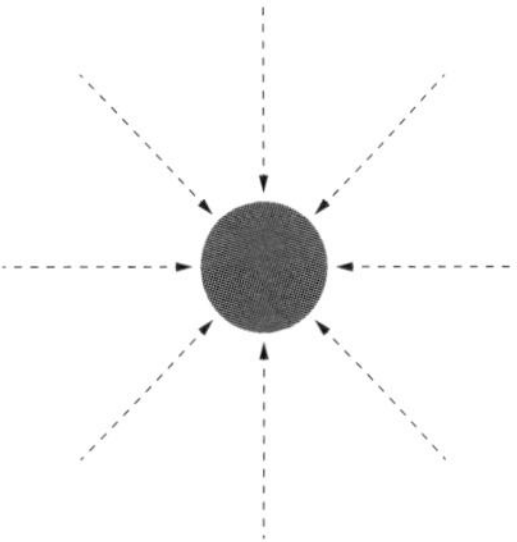

Figure 3.2.1 Gravitational field lines

The strength of a gravitational field can be calculated using the following formulas:

$g = \frac{F_g}{m}$ or $g = G\frac{M}{r^2}$

You might notice that the first part of this formula, $g = \frac{F_g}{m}$, is the equation for gravitational acceleration. In fact, the units for gravitational acceleration (m s^{-2}) and gravitational field strength (N kg^{-1}) are equivalent.

The gravitational field strength (or acceleration due to gravity of an object) near Earth's surface can be calculated using the dimensions of Earth:

$$g = \frac{Gm_{\text{Earth}}}{(r_{\text{Earth}})^2} = 9.8\ \text{N kg}^{-1} = 9.8\ \text{m s}^{-2}$$ towards the centre of Earth.

- **You will now be able to conduct Practical activity 6.**

This value for g varies from location to location and with altitude (but is consistent enough to be considered a constant for most calculations in Units 3 and 4). The gravitational field strength on the surface of any other planet depends on the mass and radius of the planet.

To find the field strength at a given altitude, the following formula can be used:

$$g = \frac{Gm_{\text{Earth}}}{(r_{\text{Earth}} + \text{altitude})^2}$$

INVERSE SQUARE LAW

In Figure 3.2.2, going from r to $2r$ to $3r$, the area shown increases from one square to four squares (2^2) to nine squares (3^2). This shows that gravitational fields follow an inverse square law. For example, at a distance $2r$ the strength of the field will be reduced to a quarter of that at r, as is the force that the field would exert. At $3r$ from the source, the field will be reduced to one-ninth of that at the source, and so on.

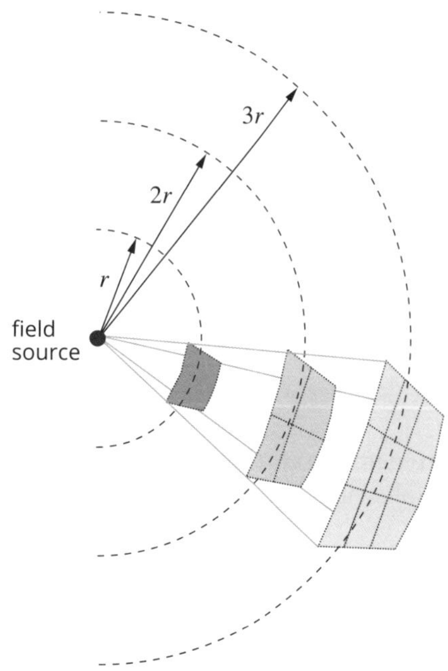

Figure 3.2.2 Gravitational fields follow an inverse square law.

WORK IN A GRAVITATIONAL FIELD

When considering **gravitational potential energy** for the motion of objects such as rockets or satellites, a larger understanding is necessary. The gravitational potential energy formula $E_g = mg\Delta h$ assumes that Earth's gravitational field is constant. This is approximately true for objects that are within a few kilometres of Earth's surface. Gravitational potential energy is important when combined with **kinetic energy**, $E_k = \frac{1}{2}mv^2$, and the conservation of mechanical energy to calculate the speed of a falling object.

Work is the transfer of energy from one object to another and/or the transformation of energy from one form to another. Work, W, is a scalar variable and is measured in joules (J). A force does work on an object when it acts on a body causing a displacement in the direction of the force.

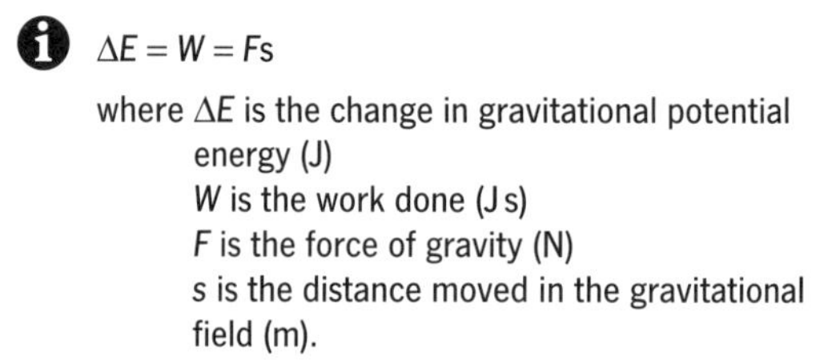

$\Delta E = W = Fs$

where ΔE is the change in gravitational potential energy (J)
W is the work done (J s)
F is the force of gravity (N)
s is the distance moved in the gravitational field (m).

Using the gravitational force vs distance graph

The area under a gravitational force–distance graph gives the change in gravitational potential energy that an object will experience as it moves through the gravitational field.

The shaded area in Figure 3.2.3 represents the decrease in gravitational potential energy of a 10 kg meteor as it falls from a distance of 2.0×10^7 m to 1.0×10^7 m from the centre of Earth. This area also represents the amount of kinetic energy that the meteor gains as it approaches Earth.

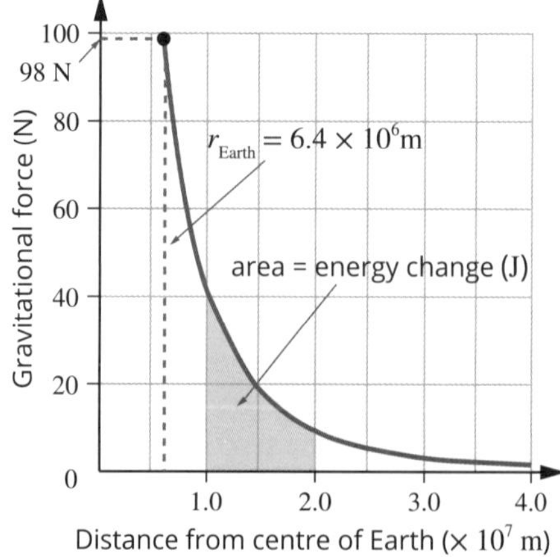

Figure 3.2.3 The gravitational force acting on a 10 kg meteor at different distances from Earth. The shaded region represents the work done by the gravitational field as the body moves between 2.0×10^7 m and 1.0×10^7 m from the centre of Earth.

 ISBN 978 0 6557 0029 6

Note that the energy change of the meteor will be the same regardless of whether the meteor falls directly towards the planet (Figure 3.2.4a) or follows a more indirect path (Figure 3.2.4b).

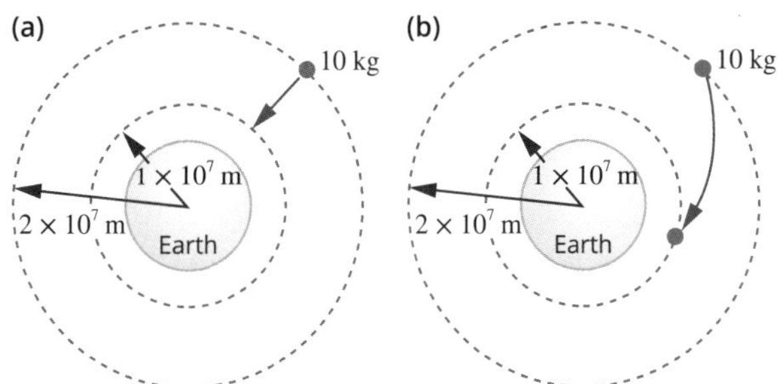

Figure 3.2.4 The shaded region on the gravitational force–distance graph in Figure 3.2.3 could represent the change in energy in the freefall situations in either (a) or (b).

Using the gravitational field strength vs distance graph

The change in gravitational potential energy of an object can also be calculated using a graph of the gravitational field strength of an object (Figure 3.2.5).

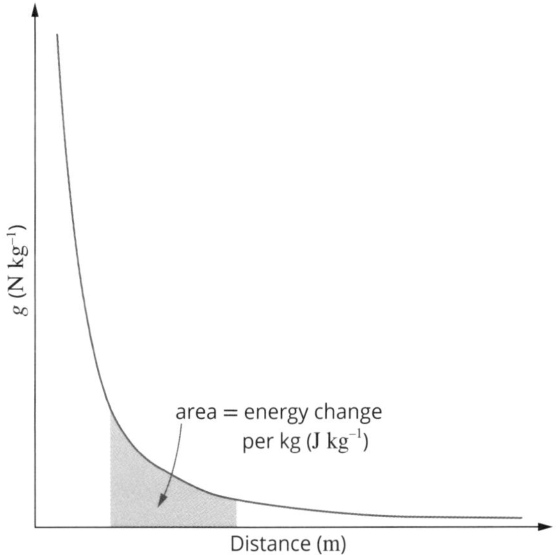

Figure 3.2.5 A graph of gravitational field strength against distance

The area under a gravitational field strength–distance graph gives a quantity that has units of $\text{N kg}^{-1}\text{m}$, equivalent to J kg^{-1}, so the area indicates the change in energy for each kilogram of the object's mass. To find the work done or energy change (J), the area (J kg^{-1}) is multiplied by the mass (kg) of the object.

Electric and magnetic fields

ELECTRIC FIELDS

An **electric field** is a region of space around a charged object in which another charged object will experience a force. An electric field has both strength and direction, which makes it a vector quantity. Electric fields are represented using field lines. Electric field lines point in the direction of the force that a positive charge within the field would experience. A positive charge experiences a force in the direction of the electric field and a negative charge experiences a force in the opposite direction to the field. The spacing between the field lines indicates the strength of the field. The closer together the lines are, the stronger the field. Figure 3.2.6 on page 56 shows an electric field between a positive plate and a negative plate, while also indicating the strength of the field.

Recall: Like charges repel and unlike (opposite) charges attract.

FORCES ON FREE CHARGES IN ELECTRIC FIELDS

If a charged particle, such as an electron, is placed within an electric field, it experiences a force. The direction of the field and the sign of the charge allow you to determine the direction of the force. The direction of the electric field, E, indicates the direction in which a force would act on a positive charge.

The magnitude of the force experienced by a charged particle due to an electric field can be determined using the equation:

$F = qE$

where F is the force on the charged particle (N)
q is the charge of the object experiencing the force (C)
E is the strength of the electric field (N C^{-1}).

This equation illustrates that the force experienced by a charge is proportional to the strength of the electric field, E, and the size of the charge, q. The force on the charged particle will cause the charged particle to accelerate in the field. This means that the particle could increase its velocity, decrease its velocity, or change its direction while in the field.

To calculate the acceleration due to the force experienced, you can use the equation from Newton's second law:

$F = ma$

where m is the mass of the accelerating particle (kg)
a is the acceleration (m s^{-2}).

WORK DONE IN UNIFORM ELECTRIC FIELDS

Electrical potential (V) is defined as the work required per unit charge to move a positive point charge from infinity to a point within the electric field. The electrical potential at infinity is defined as zero.

The potential across a distance, d, and the **electric field strength**, E, are related by the following equation:

$$E = \frac{V}{d}$$

$$V = Ed$$

where V is the difference in electrical potential (V)
E is the electric field strength (V m^{-1})
d is the distance between points, parallel to the field (m).

The electric field, E, always points in the direction from the higher potential towards the lower potential.

Between two oppositely charged parallel plates (two points), the field lines are parallel, and therefore the field has a uniform strength. Figure 3.2.6 represents a uniform electric field between two parallel plates. The potential difference is the change between these two points. The electrical potential, however, is the actual work required per charge to move a positive point charge from zero to the positively charged plate.

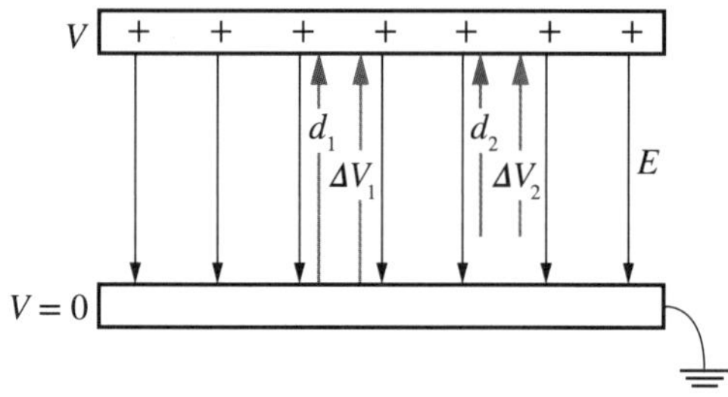

Figure 3.2.6 The potential difference between two points in a uniform electric field

Electrical potential energy is the energy a charge has due to its position relative to other charges. It is a form of energy that is stored in an electric field. Work is done on the field when a charged particle is forced to move in the electric field. Conversely, when energy is stored in the electric field, work can be done by the field on the charged particle.

$$V = \frac{W}{q}$$

$$W = qV$$

where W is the work done on a positive point charge or on the field (J)
q is the charge of the point charge (C)
V is the electrical potential (J C^{-1}) or volts (V).

Work is done whenever a force moves something over a distance. Work is a measure of the amount of energy used in moving the object.

When a charged object is moved against the direction it would naturally move in an electric field, work is done on the field. When a charged object moves in the direction it would naturally tend to move in an electric field, the field does work on the particle. For example, Figure 3.2.7 shows the motion of three protons in an electric field. A proton will naturally move towards the negative plate, so for the motion of q_1 work is done on the field, while for q_2 work is done by the field. If the charge doesn't move any distance parallel to the field, then no work is done. Charge q_3 moves perpendicular to the field, so no work is done.

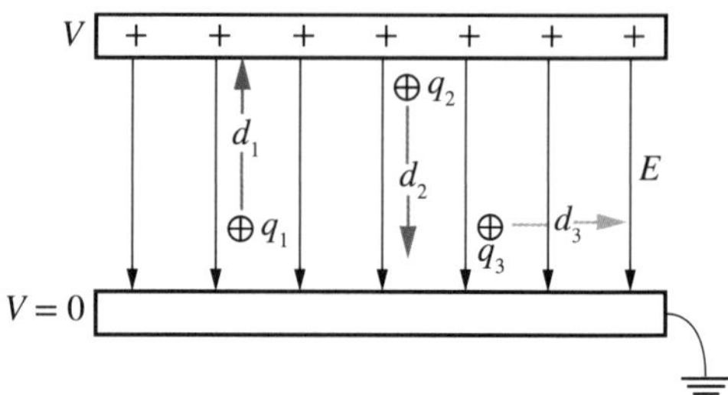

Figure 3.2.7 Work is being done on the field by moving q_1 and work is being done by the field on q_2. No work is done on q_3 because it is moving perpendicular to the field.

- **You will now be able to conduct Practical activities 7 and 8, and complete Worksheet 11.**

COULOMB'S LAW

Coulomb's law gives the force between two point charges. The force is along the line connecting the charges, and is attractive if the charges are opposite, and repulsive if the charges are like.

Coulomb's law for the force between two charges q_1 and q_2 (in C) separated by a distance of r (in m) is given by the following equation:

$$F = \frac{1}{4\pi\varepsilon_0}\frac{q_1 q_2}{r^2}$$

where ε_0 is a constant (the permittivity of free space) that is equal to 8.8542×10^{-12} C^2 N^{-1} m^{-2}.

The expression $\frac{1}{4\pi\varepsilon_0}$ at the front of Coulomb's law can be simplified to the value of k, called Coulomb's constant, which has a value of approximately 8.99×10^9 N m^2 C^{-2}. So:

$$F = k\frac{q_1 q_2}{r^2}$$

If there are multiple point charges, the forces add by superposition (the head-to-tail vector method).

The direction of the force will either describe repulsion (two like charges) or attraction (two opposite charges).

 ISBN 978 0 6557 0029 6

Coulomb's law can be combined with the definition of electric field strength, $E = \frac{F}{q}$ to find the magnitude of the electric field at a distance r from a single point charge:

$$E = k\frac{Q}{r^2}$$

where $k = 8.99 \times 10^9\,\text{N m}^2\,\text{C}^{-2}$
Q is the charge on the point creating the field.

- **You will now be able to complete Worksheet 12.**

THE MAGNETIC FIELD

Since ancient times, certain materials, called magnets, have been known to have the property of attracting iron and some other metals. This attractive property is called magnetism. Magnetism, like electrostatic force, results in a field that attracts or repels other magnetic materials. Again, similar to electrostatic forces, like magnetic poles repel and unlike magnetic poles attract. **Magnetic poles** exist only as dipoles, having both north and south poles. A single magnetic pole (monopole) is not known to exist.

In Figure 3.2.8, Earth itself can be shown to have a giant magnetic field around it.

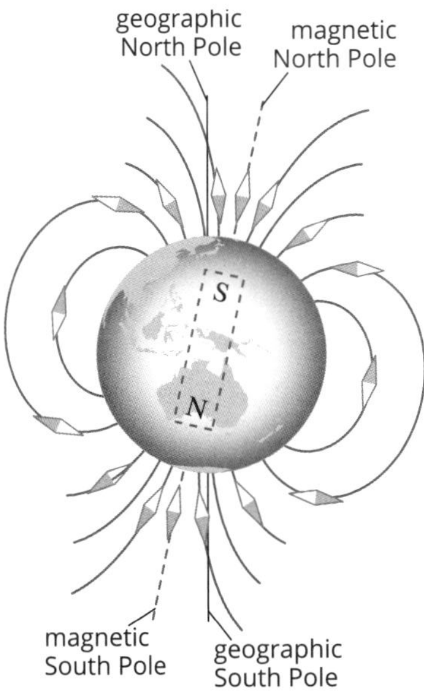

Figure 3.2.8 Earth acts somewhat like a huge bar magnet.

Magnetic field lines can be described by imagining a tiny compass placed at nearby points. The direction of a magnetic field is from the magnetic north pole to the magnetic south pole, which is the direction a compass would point. The denser (closer) lines indicate a relatively stronger magnetic field. In Figure 3.2.9, iron filings are used to highlight the magnetic field lines from the magnetic north pole to the magnetic south pole of two magnets, and the denser regions at the two pole ends. The magnetic field is a vector quantity and so has both a magnitude and a direction. The strength, or vector magnitude, of a magnetic field is denoted by the variable B and the unit is the tesla (T).

The resultant direction of the magnetic field at a particular point will be the vector addition of the individual magnetic fields acting at that point.

Figure 3.2.9 The patterns in the fields show (a) attraction and (b) repulsion between poles.

- **You will now be able to complete Worksheet 13.**

Magnetic fields and current-carrying wires

Charged particles that are moving, such as the electrons in a conductive material, create a magnetic field. This field is circular around the current-carrying conductor. An example of this is shown in Figure 3.2.10a on page 58, in which the magnetic field lines are shown by iron filings around a current-carrying wire. Figure 3.2.10b indicates the **right-hand grip rule**. If the thumb points in the direction of the conventional current (i.e. from positive to negative), the fingers curl around the conductor in the direction of the magnetic field.

This rule can also be used to find the direction of conventional current if the direction of the magnetic field is known.

Conventional current is from positive to negative, as it was originally thought that this is how current flows. It is now known that the current actually flows in the opposite direction. This actual current is called electron flow.

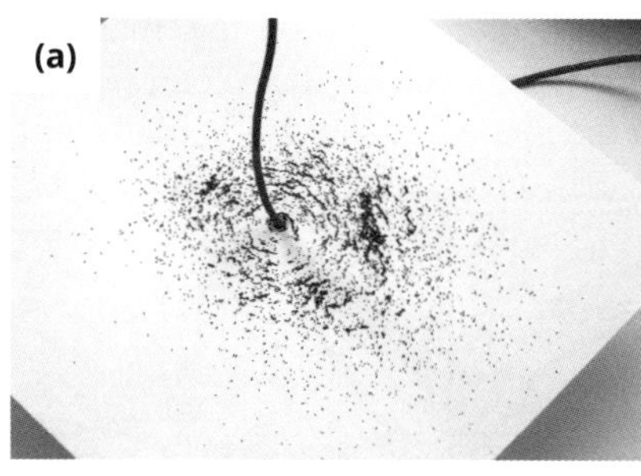

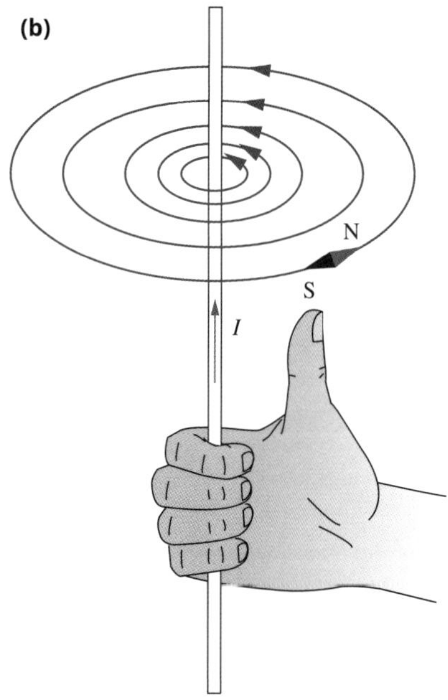

Figure 3.2.10 (a) The magnetic field lines are shown by iron filings around a current-carrying conductor. (b) The right-hand grip rule can be used to find the direction of the magnetic field.

Magnetic fields between parallel wires

When two conductors are placed parallel to each other, an interesting effect occurs. As discussed previously, if there is a current, it will have an associated magnetic field. The direction of the field can be determined using the right-hand grip rule, if the direction of the current is known. Depending on the direction of the current in the conductors (in the same direction or in opposite directions), the resulting magnetic forces will either attract or repel.

If the two parallel conductors carry current in the same direction, the forces will attract. If the two parallel conductors carry current in opposite directions, the forces will repel. This is illustrated in Figure 3.2.11. The force experienced between the two parallel conductors is equal and opposite—an example of Newton's third law; the force wire 1 exerts on wire 2 is equal and opposite to the force wire 2 exerts on wire 1.

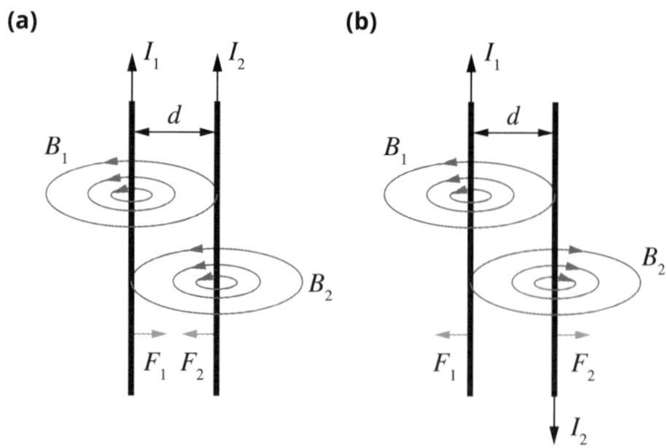

Figure 3.2.11 Two parallel conductors, with (a) current going in the same direction and (b) current going in opposite directions

The magnetic field around a solenoid

A wire bent into a single circular loop can be thought of as a series of small straight segments that create a magnetic field. A device commonly known as a **solenoid** consists of many such loops of current-carrying conductor wound into a coil (Figure 3.2.12). The direction of the field can be determined by applying the right-hand grip rule to the loops or coils. The resulting field around the solenoid is like the field around a normal bar magnet; in this case, it contains an effective north end on the left and a south end on the right. The compass points in the direction of the field lines.

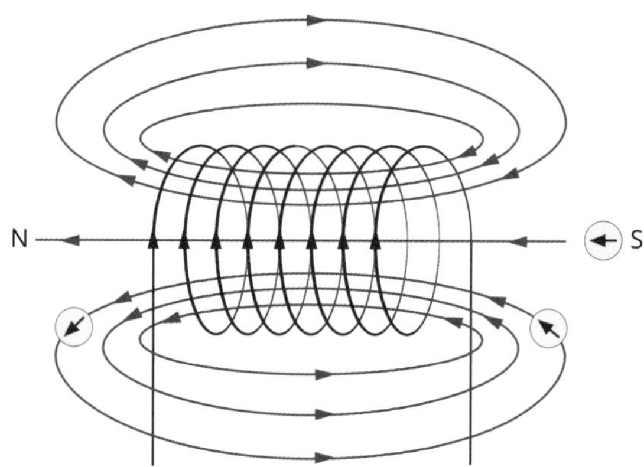

Figure 3.2.12 This solenoid has an effective 'north' end at the left and a 'south' end at the right. The compasses point in the direction of the field lines.

The strength of a magnet can be increased by wrapping a current-carrying wire around the magnet to create an **electromagnet**. The atoms in an unmagnetised magnetic material such as iron point in random directions, so that the individual magnetic fields tend to cancel each other out. However, the magnetic field produced by wires wrapped around an iron core can force the atoms within the core to point in one direction. Their individual magnetic fields add together, creating a stronger magnetic field.

- **You will now be able to conduct Practical activity 9.**

 ISBN 978 0 6557 0029 6

KEY KNOWLEDGE

FORCES ON CHARGED OBJECTS DUE TO MAGNETIC FIELDS

When a charged particle travels into a magnetic field, the force on it is perpendicular to both its direction of motion and the magnetic field lines. In comparison, a charged particle in an electric field will travel in the direction of the electric field lines.

The magnitude of the force on a charged object within a magnetic field depends on the strength of the magnetic field, B, the velocity of the charge, the angle of motion of the object with respect to the magnetic field, and the charge on the particle.

When v and B are perpendicular:

 $F = qvB$

where F is the force (N)
q is the electric charge on the particle (C)
v is the component of the instantaneous velocity of the particle that is perpendicular to the magnetic field ($m\,s^{-1}$)
B is the strength of the magnetic field (T).

This force is referred to as the Lorentz force. The force is at a maximum when the charged particle is moving at right angles to the magnetic field. The force is zero when the charged particle is travelling parallel to the magnetic field.

The **right-hand force rule** (Figure 3.2.13; sometimes called the right-hand slap rule) is used to determine the direction of the force on a positive charge moving in a magnetic field, B. Point the thumb of the right hand in the direction of the movement of a *positive charge* (conventional current direction) and the fingers in the direction of the magnetic field. The force on the charge will point out from the palm. The direction of the force on a negatively charged particle is in the opposite direction.

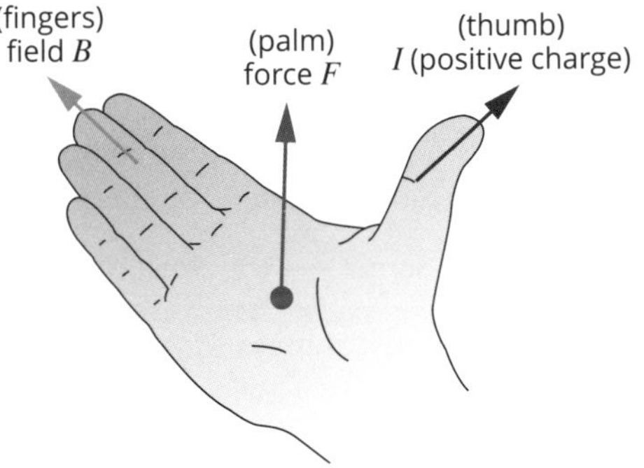

Figure 3.2.13 The right-hand force rule

THE FORCE ON A CURRENT-CARRYING CONDUCTOR

A conducting wire allows a stream of charged particles to flow in one direction. If a conductor carrying many charged particles is placed within a magnetic field, it will experience a force. This is the theory behind the operation of electric motors. The force acting on any conductor, or part of a conductor, within a magnetic field, is given by the equation:

 $F = nIlB$

where F is the force on the conductor perpendicular to the magnetic field (N)
n is the number of loops or conductors
I is the current in the conductor (A)
l is the length of the conductor (m)
B is the strength of the magnetic field (T).

The force is at a maximum when the charged particle is moving at right angles to the magnetic field. The force is zero when the charged particle is travelling parallel to the magnetic field. The right-hand rule can be used to determine the direction of the force on the charge.

- **You will now be able to conduct Practical activity 10 and complete Worksheets 14 and 15.**

COMPARING FIELDS—A SUMMARY

Fields can either be **monopoles** (meaning one pole) or **dipoles** (meaning two poles).

- Electric fields can be either of these. For example, a point charge will be a monopole, while two charges separated a distance r will create a dipole.
- Gravitational fields consist of monopoles, where the field is pointed toward a centre of mass.
- Magnetic fields always exist as dipoles, with both a north and south pole.

Another key difference between these fields is that, theoretically, a gravitational field around any mass extends an infinite distance from it. Although the shape of the field will be influenced by the field of other masses, there is no way of stopping the field. The extent of both electric and magnetic fields, while theoretically extending to infinity, can be constrained by external electric and magnetic influences.

Table 3.2.1, on the following page, outlines some of the key differences and similarities between the three different types of fields.

KEY KNOWLEDGE

Table 3.2.1 Comparison of fields

Quantity or description	Gravitational fields	Electric fields	Magnetic fields
type of poles	monopoles	monopoles dipoles	dipoles
type of forces	attractive	attractive repulsive	attractive repulsive
extent of the field	extends to an infinite distance	can be constrained to a fixed distance	can be constrained to a fixed distance
effect of distance on field strength in a radial field	$g = G\frac{M}{r^2}$	$E = k\frac{Q}{r^2}$	
force between monopoles	$F_g = G\frac{m_1m_2}{r^2}$	$F = k\frac{q_1q_2}{r^2}$	
potential energy changes in a uniform field	$E_g = mg\Delta h$	$W = qV = qEd$	
force due to a uniform field	$F_g = mg$	$F = qE$	

Application of field concepts

SATELLITE MOTION

A **satellite** is an object that is in a stable orbit around a larger central mass. Satellites can either be **natural** (e.g. the Moon) or **artificial** (e.g. a communication satellite). Artificial satellites are very important for science, industry, communications and the military. The only force acting on a satellite is the gravitational attraction between it and the central body. Satellites are in continual freefall. Because satellites are moving at a velocity relative to Earth, they are moving across the sky at the same rate that they are falling, so the combined effect is that they fall in a curved path. This effect on an astronaut is shown in Figure 3.2.14.

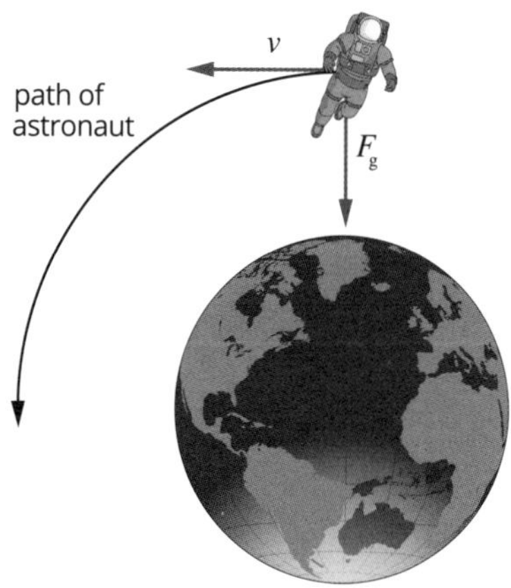

Figure 3.2.14 Astronauts are in freefall while orbiting Earth.

Satellites move with a centripetal acceleration that is equal to the gravitational field strength at the location of their orbit. Artificial satellites are often equipped with tanks of propellant that is 'squirted' in the appropriate direction when the orbit of the satellite needs to be adjusted. In a circular orbit, a satellite travels at a constant speed and stays the same distance from Earth.

The speed of a satellite, v, in a circular orbit is given by:

$$v = \frac{2\pi r}{T}$$

where r is the radius of the orbit (m) and T is the period (s).

This formula can then be used to determine the centripetal acceleration acting on this satellite. The magnitude of the acceleration is then:

$$a = \frac{v^2}{r} = \frac{4\pi^2 r}{T} = \frac{GM}{r^2} = g$$

These relationships can be manipulated to determine any feature of a satellite's motion: its speed, radius of orbit or period of orbit. The magnitude of the gravitational force acting on a satellite in a circular orbit is given by:

$$F_g = \frac{mv^2}{r} = \frac{4\pi^2 rm}{T^2} = \frac{GMm}{r^2} = mg$$

Artificial satellites usually move in circular orbits; however, this depends on their energy and trajectory. Satellites could follow a spiral, hyperbolic, elliptical or circular orbit. Johannes Kepler, a German astronomer, published three laws regarding the motion of planets. He was the first person to work out that planets do not travel in circular paths, but rather in elliptical paths. His three laws were:

1. The planets move in elliptical orbits with the Sun at one focus.
2. The line connecting a planet to the Sun sweeps out equal areas in equal intervals of time (Figure 3.2.15).
3. For every planet, the ratio of the cube of the average orbital radius, r, to the square of the period, T, of revolution is the same: $\frac{r^3}{T^2}$ = a constant, k.

   For any central body of mass M:

$$\frac{r^3}{T^2} = \frac{GM}{4\pi^2}$$

If the orbital radius of a satellite, r, is known, the orbital radius of another satellite in the same system, with period T, can be determined.

- **You will now be able to complete Worksheets 16 and 17.**

ISBN 978 0 6557 0029 6

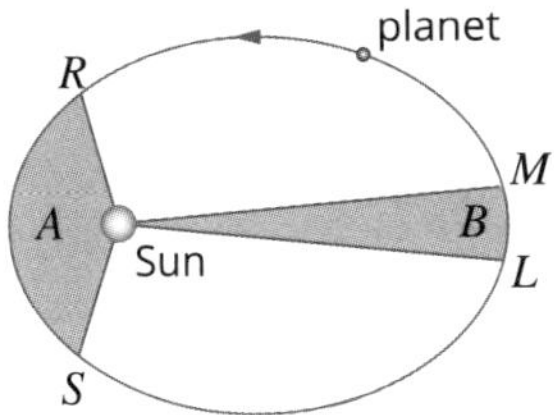

Figure 3.2.15 A line joining a planet to the Sun will sweep out equal areas in equal times. If the time taken for the planet to travel from *R* to *S* is the same as it takes to travel from *L* to *M*, then area *A* will equal area *B*.

DC MOTORS

The force produced on a current-carrying conductor leads to very important practical applications, such as the electric meter or the basic principle of operation of electric motors. Recall that the magnetic force experienced by a current-carrying conductor is given by $F = nIlB$. If a current and a magnetic field are present, the magnetic force acting on each side of a current-carrying square wire coil in a magnetic field will cause it to turn. The turning effect of a magnetic field on a coil of conducting wire is called electromagnetic **torque**. Torque is the turning effect of any force; for example, pushing on a swinging door.

Torque is defined as:

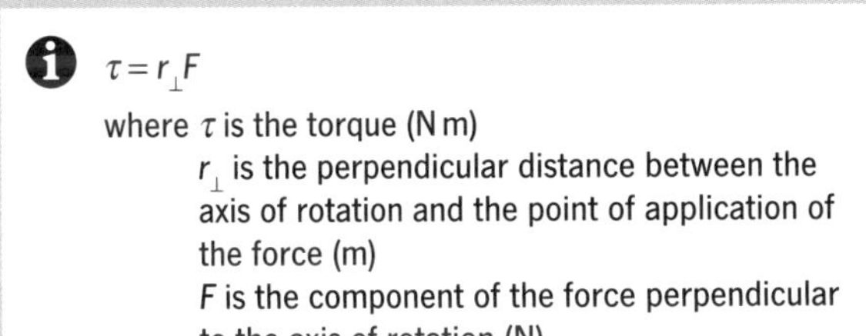

$\tau = r_{\perp}F$

where τ is the torque (N m)

$r_{\perp}$ is the perpendicular distance between the axis of rotation and the point of application of the force (m)

F is the component of the force perpendicular to the axis of rotation (N).

When the current-carrying coil is perpendicular to the magnetic field, the full magnitude of the magnetic force is experienced. When the current-carrying coil is parallel to the magnetic field, the current-carrying coil experiences no force. In the case of a single square or rectangular coil, the total torque applied to the coil will be twice that acting on one side (Figure 3.2.16).

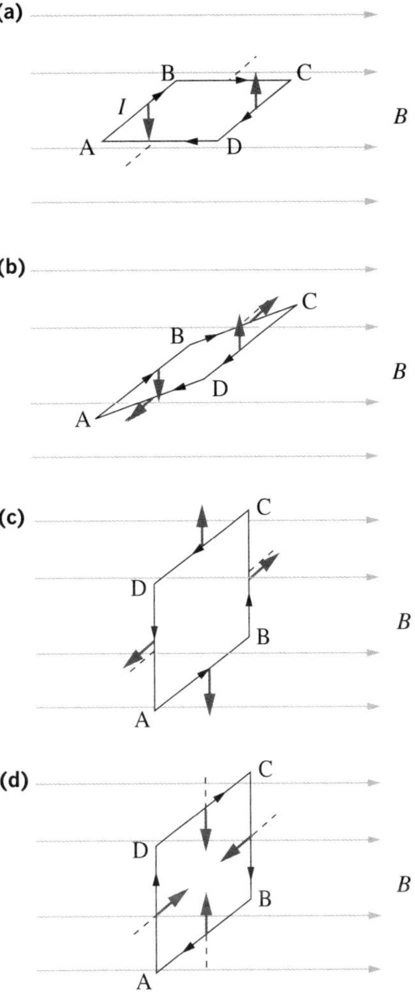

Figure 3.2.16 The magnetic force acting on each side of a current-carrying square wire coil in a magnetic field, *B*

A DC motor is a device that makes use of the motor principle but contains a switch assembly on the rotating coil shaft that allows the direction of the current through the coil to be reversed every 180°. This switch is called a **commutator**. It allows the DC motor to keep rotating because the direction of current, and hence torque, is reversed each half turn by the commutator. This is shown in Figure 3.2.17.

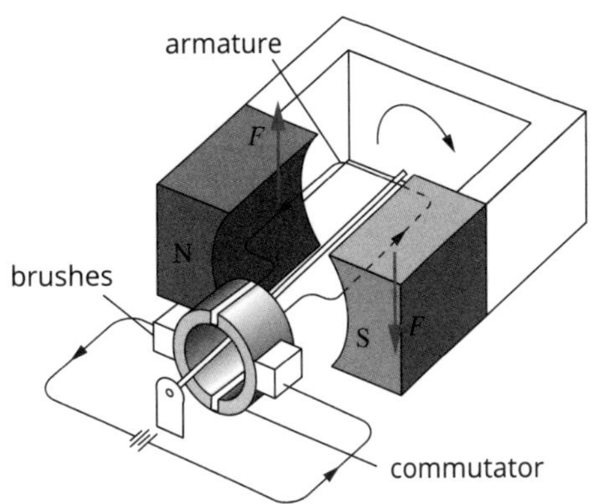

Figure 3.2.17 The main parts of a simple but practical single-coil DC electric motor

The coils are wound around a soft iron core to increase the magnetic field that passes through them. The whole arrangement of core and coils is called an **armature**. The armature of a practical motor consists of many coils that are fed current by the commutator when they are in the position of maximum torque. The total torque will be the sum of the torques on all the individual coils.

Permanent magnets are generally used to provide the magnetic field in small motors, but in larger motors electromagnets are used as they can produce larger and stronger fields. These magnets are usually stationary, as distinct from the rotating rotor or armature, and are often referred to as the **stator**.

A magnetic field is static if it has a fixed strength and position. Where the magnetic field is changing, such as that associated with an alternating current direction, the magnetic field strength will also be changing.

PARTICLE ACCELERATORS

A synchrotron is a doughnut-shaped particle accelerator designed to circulate electrons around a closed path at speeds very close to that of light. All particle accelerators require a source of charged particles. In a cathode ray tube (Figure 3.2.18), the charged particles are provided by a device called an **electron gun**. Electrons are 'boiled' off a heated wire element and then accelerated from rest across a chamber emptied of air by an electric field created between the charged plates. The force acting on the charged particles due to electric and magnetic fields will change the direction of the beam. As the charged particles are accelerated by these forces, work is done and the charges gain kinetic energy.

Figure 3.2.18 Cathode ray tube

As the work done, W, is defined as the change in energy, it is possible to find the speed of the charged particles as they are accelerated through an electrical potential, V, using the electron-gun equation:

$$\frac{1}{2}mv^2 = qV$$

Recall that because an electric current is itself a stream of moving charges, the magnitude of the force, F, on a charge, q, moving with velocity, v, perpendicular to a magnetic field of strength, B, is given by:

$$F = qvB$$

If a moving charge experiences a force of constant magnitude that remains at right angles to its motion, its direction will be changed but not its speed. In this way, bending magnets within a particle accelerator act to alter the path of the electron beam, rather than speed up the electrons. As a result, the electrons will follow a curved path of radius, r, as shown in Figure 3.2.19.

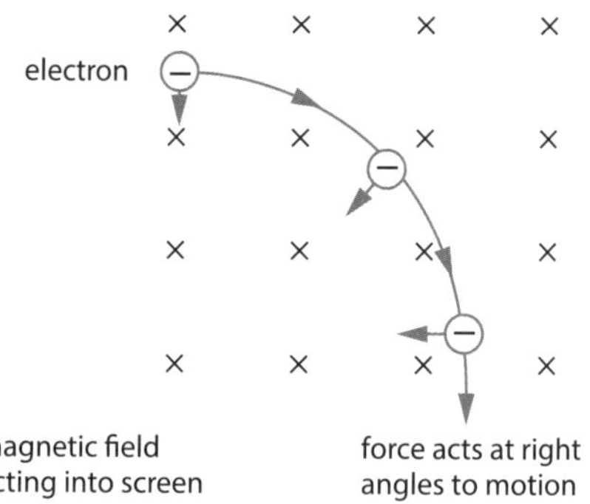

Figure 3.2.19 An electron moving in a magnetic field

When a field is running directly into or out of the plane of the page, dots are used to show a field coming out of the page and crosses are used to depict a field running directly into the page. This convention was adopted from the idea of viewing an arrow. The dot is the point of the arrow coming towards you, and the cross represents the tail feathers of the arrow as it travels away.

Combining the force on the charged particle with Newton's second law ($F = ma$) and substituting the equation for centripetal acceleration gives:

$$qvB = \frac{mv^2}{r}$$

Rearranging this equation gives an expression that predicts the radius of the path of an electron travelling at right angles to a constant magnetic field:

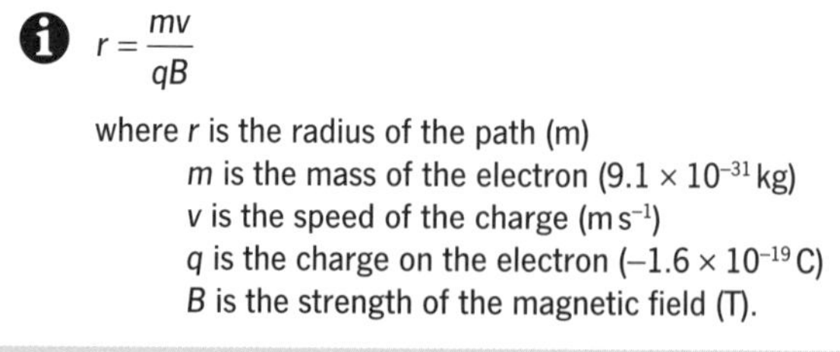

$$r = \frac{mv}{qB}$$

where r is the radius of the path (m)
m is the mass of the electron (9.1×10^{-31} kg)
v is the speed of the charge (m s^{-1})
q is the charge on the electron (-1.6×10^{-19} C)
B is the strength of the magnetic field (T).

- **You will now be able to complete Worksheets 18, 19 and 20.**

ISBN 978 0 6557 0029 6

WORKSHEET 10

Classification and identification

Knowledge review—checking up on electricity

A 24 V truck battery is connected to two resistors in series as shown in Figure 3.2.20.

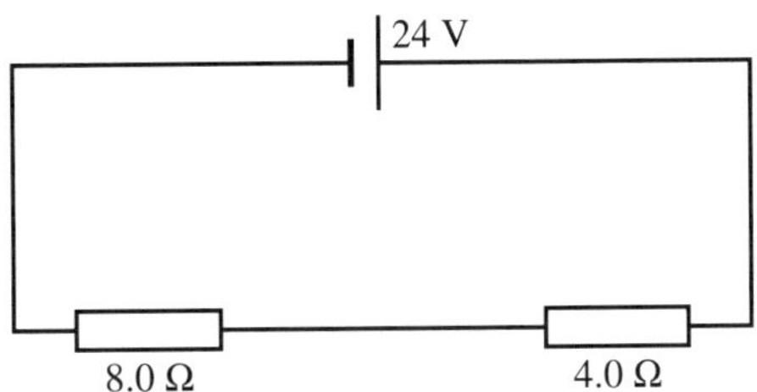

Figure 3.2.20 The circuit set-up

1 Calculate the total resistance in the circuit.

2 Determine the current flowing through the 8.0 Ω resistor.

3 Calculate the potential difference across the 4.0 Ω resistor.

4 Another 8.0 Ω resistor is placed in parallel with the 4.0 Ω resistor. Determine the new current in the circuit.

A 12.0 V DC power supply is attached to a 56.0 Ω resistor in a simple circuit.

5 Calculate the current that the power source will supply to the circuit.

6 Determine the power that is being expended in the circuit.

ISBN 978 0 6557 0029 6

7 A 33.0Ω resistor is now connected in series with the first resistor. Calculate the values for Questions **5** and **6** for this new circuit.

At a certain point in the circuit, 4.5×10^{17} electrons per second are recorded moving from left to right through a 25 cm length of wire.

8 State the direction of the conventional current in the circuit.

9 Calculate the magnitude of the current.

10 If every electron has 8.0×10^{-18} J of work done on it, find the potential difference across the length of wire.

ISBN 978 0 6557 0029 6

WORKSHEET 11

Modelling

Electric field lines

By drawing field lines, qualitatively model the direction and strength of electric fields produced by:

a single positive point charge

(+)

b single negative point charge

(−)

c two positive point charges

(+) (+)

d two negative point charges

(−) (−)

e a positive and a negative point charge (dipole)

(+) (−)

f parallel charged plates.

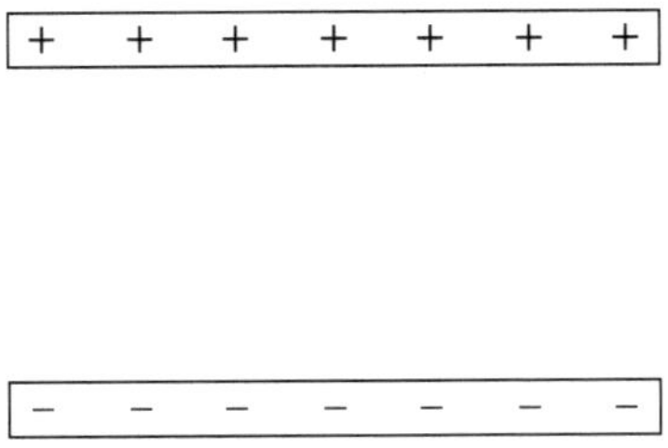

\+ + + + + + +

− − − − − − −

ISBN 978 0 6557 0029 6

WORKSHEET 12

Modelling

Forces in electric fields

Coulomb's law is used to calculate the size of the electrostatic force acting between charges. When it is applied to two charges, the direction of the force vector is along a line joining the two charges, and it is either a mutual repulsion or a mutual attraction.

When three or more charges interact, the net force on any one of them is the vector sum of the forces applied by the other charges.

The electric field is defined as the region in space in which an electric force would be experienced by a charge, and is given by the equation $E = \frac{F}{q}$.

Electric fields can be represented qualitatively by means of field lines, where the direction of the field is a tangent to the field line itself and the field strength can be judged by the density of the field lines.

A more precise representation of the field at a point is obtained by the application of the equation above. If the charge is 1.0 C, then the field can be thought of as the force on a unit charge.

1 In the diagram below there is a charge $Q = +5.0$ C at (0, 0) and a test charge $q_1 = +1.0$ C placed 3.0 m away at (0, 3).

The force on the test charge is represented by the vector F.

In the diagram, take the positive y-direction as north and the positive x-direction as east.

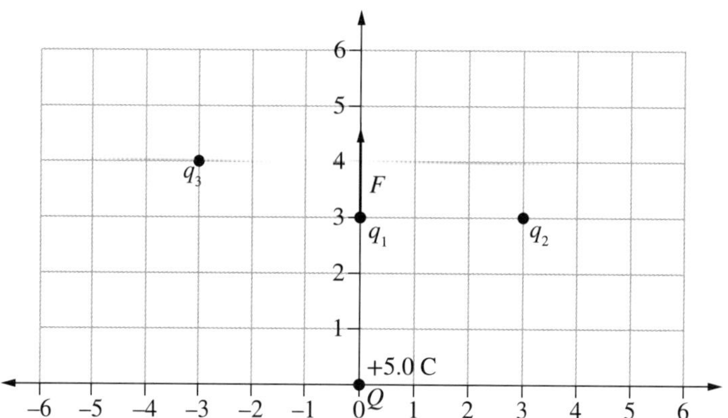

a Calculate the magnitude of F.

b What is the magnitude of the electric field E at q_1? Include the correct units.

c q_2 is also a +1.0 C test charge. It has been placed at (3, 3). Calculate the size of the electric field at that point due to its interaction with charge Q, and fully express the electric field vector.

Draw the corresponding electric field vector on the diagram above. The size of the vector you draw is not important, but the direction is very important.

ISBN 978 0 6557 0029 6

d Repeat part **c** for q_3, another test charge of +1.0 C at (–3, 4).

2 Consider the situation when two charges are creating the field being tested. In the diagram below two charges, Q_1 and Q_2, each of +5.0 C, are placed at coordinates (–3, 0) and (3, 0) respectively.

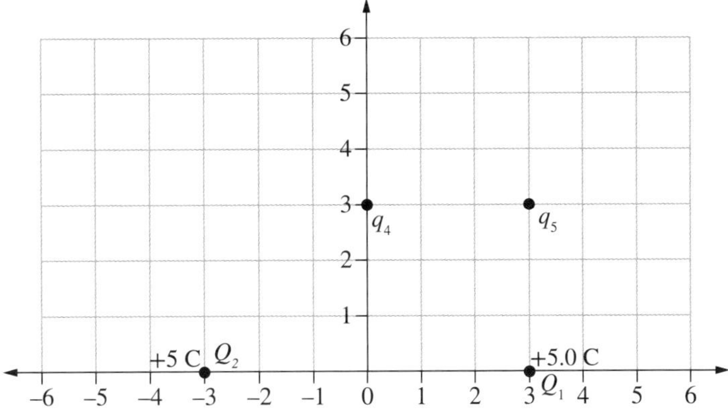

The electric field acting on charge q_4 = + 1.0 C at (0, 3) is the vector sum of the fields produced by Q_1 and Q_2. Call these fields E_{Q1} and E_{Q2}.

Find the size and direction of E_{Q1} and E_{Q2}, and draw them on the diagram. Then find the net electric field, E_4.

EXTENSION

3 **a** Repeat Question **2** for the charge q_5 = +1.0 C at (3, 3).

b The charge at (3, 0) is now replaced by a charge of –5.0 C. Describe what happens to the field at (3, 3).

WORKSHEET 13

Modelling

Magnetic fields

1 Three bar magnets are arranged end to end, as shown in the diagram below. Indicate, using an arrow pointing inwards or outwards, where the magnets will be repelling and where they will be attracting.

2 Draw the magnetic field for each of the following arrangements of bar magnets.

3

4

The circles in the following diagrams represent compasses. For each arrangement, draw in the needle of the compass, indicating the direction in which it would be pointing.

5

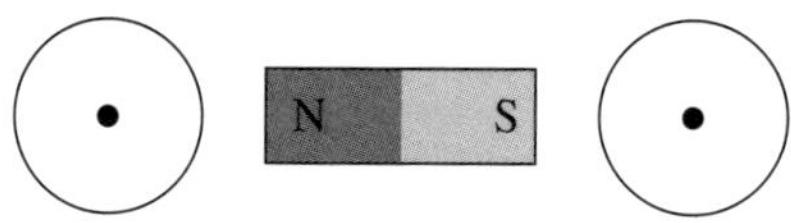

ISBN 978 0 6557 0029 6

6

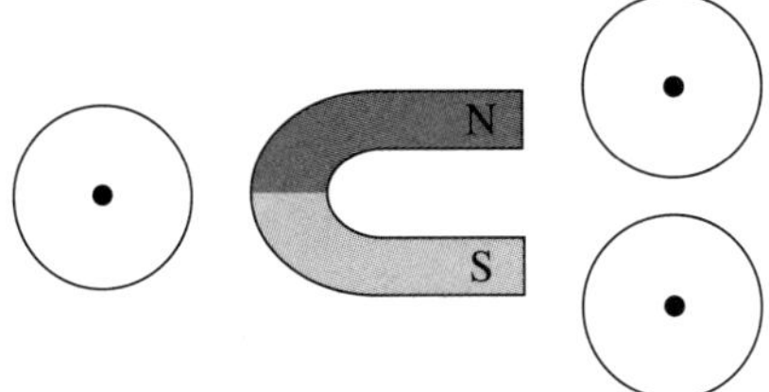

7

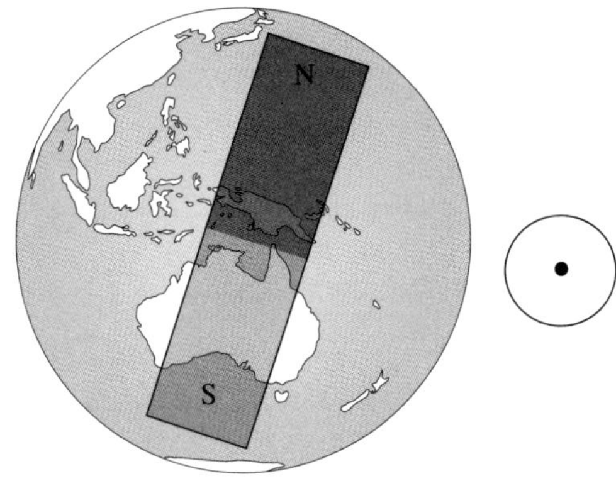

8 What rare event must have happened to make the figure in Question **7** correct?

ISBN 978 0 6557 0029 6

WORKSHEET 14

Modelling

Making it magnetic—fields and coils

1 The needle in a compass acts like a tiny bar magnet. When the needle is in a strong magnetic field, it will align itself with that field. If the black end of the needle represents the north pole of a magnet, in which direction would the black end point if the compass was placed between the poles of a horseshoe magnet, as shown in Figure 3.2.21?

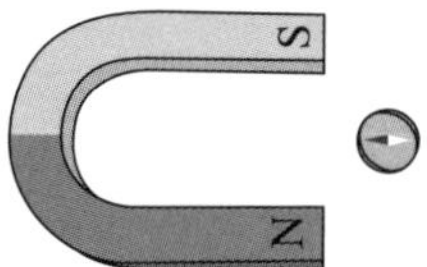

Figure 3.2.21 Horseshoe magnet and compass

2 If you had two identical bar magnets separated by distance d with the north pole of each magnet facing the other, as shown in Figure 3.2.22, in which direction would a compass point at a distance of 0.5d (i.e. exactly halfway between the magnets)? Explain your answer.

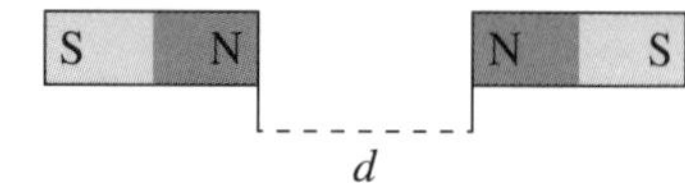

Figure 3.2.22 Two bar magnets with the same poles facing

3 Two magnets each produce a magnetic field strength of 0.25 T at a distance 0.5d. If the north and south poles of the magnets are facing each other a distance d apart, as shown in Figure 3.2.23, what is the magnetic field strength halfway between these two poles?

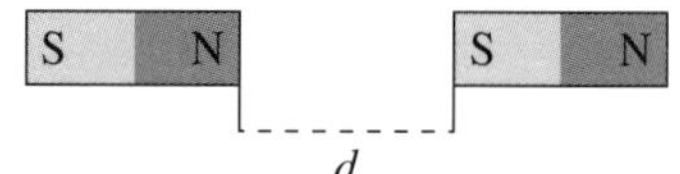

Figure 3.2.23 Two bar magnets with opposite poles facing

4 In the coil of wire shown in Figure 3.2.24, the current flows anticlockwise. In what direction is the magnetic field inside the coil?

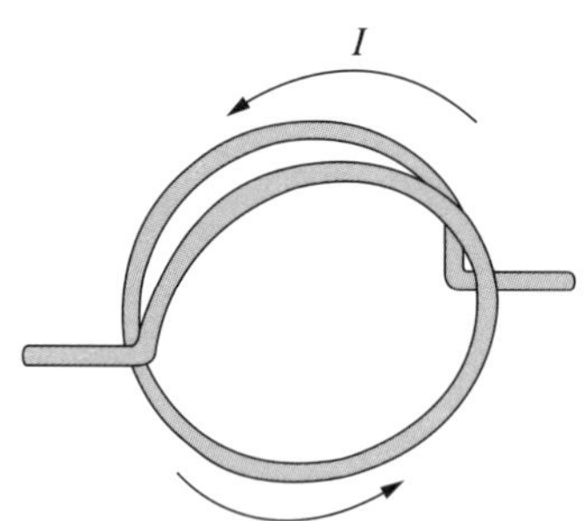

Figure 3.2.24 Loop of wire carrying a current

5 In Figure 3.2.25, the coil on the right has a radius half that of the coil on the left. What must happen to the current in the coil on the right in order to induce the same magnetic field strength in the centre of the coil as that in the centre of the coil on the left? Hint: $B \propto \frac{1}{r}$

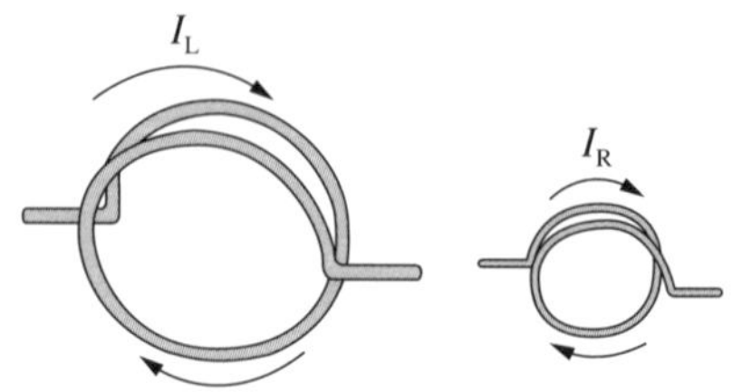

Figure 3.2.25 Two coils of wire carrying a current

ISBN 978 0 6557 0029 6

WORKSHEET 15

Modelling

Force and current

A student conducted an experiment to evaluate the magnetic field strength of a coil. This coil was 40 cm high and 5 cm wide, and had 200 turns of wire. The experiment involved connecting the coil of wire to a battery and an ammeter. The coil is suspended from a spring balance between the poles of two magnets. The spring balance readings were recorded for different currents. The apparatus and results are shown in Figure 3.2.26.

Force (N)	Current (A)
2.9	0.5
3.3	1.0
3.7	1.5
4.1	2.0
4.5	2.5
4.9	3.0
5.3	3.5
5.7	4.0
6.1	4.5
6.5	5.0

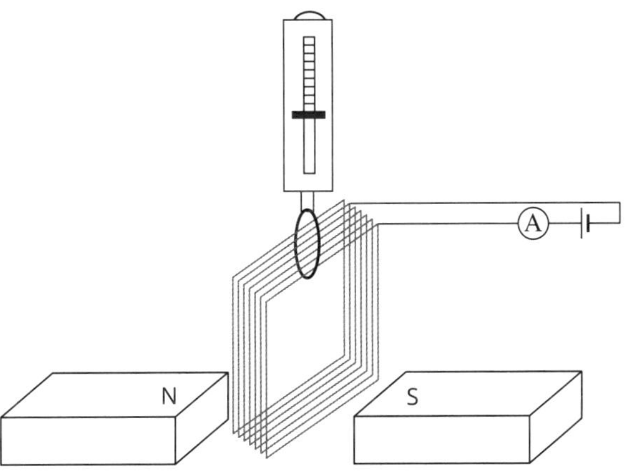

Figure 3.2.26 The experimental set-up

1 State the mathematical relationship for a force acting on any conductor placed in a magnetic field. Identify the known variables from the description above.

ISBN 978 0 6557 0029 6

2 a Graph the data given in the table above in the space provided. According to these results, what will the force be when the current is zero?

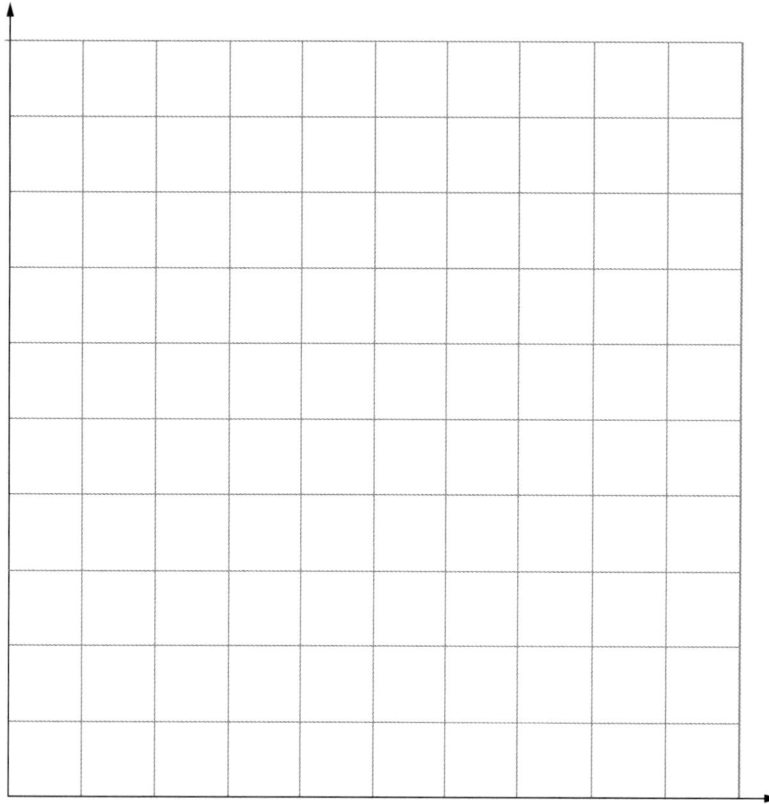

b Identify what this additional force is.

c Determine the mass of the coil. Give your answer to two significant figures.

d Evaluate the magnitude of the magnetic field strength.

 ISBN 978 0 6557 0029 6

WORKSHEET 16

Simulation

Gravitational fields

1 The planet Mercury has a mass about one-twentieth of Earth's mass and a radius of about two-fifths that of Earth. What is the approximate gravitational field on Mercury's surface?

A 0.40g

B 0.05g

C 0.13g

D 0.31g

2 A rocket-powered spacecraft of mass 125 kg (including fuel) is in Earth's orbit at an altitude of 630 km, as shown in Figure 3.2.27.
Use $r_E = 6.37 \times 10^6$ m and $M_E = 5.98 \times 10^{24}$ kg. Give your answers to three significant figures.

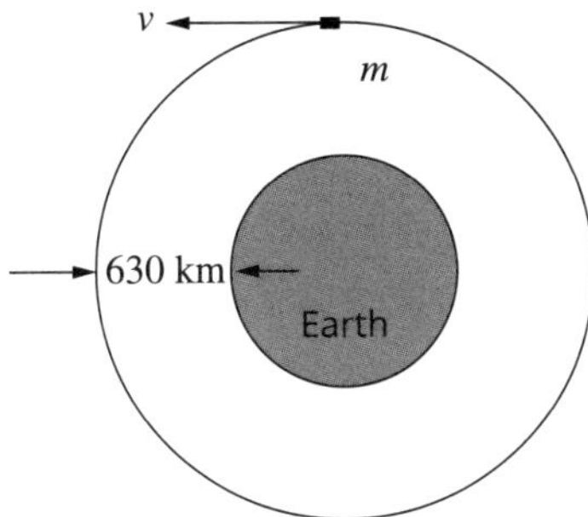

Figure 3.2.27 The orbit of the spacecraft around Earth (not to scale)

a Show that the speed v of the satellite is given by $v^2 = \frac{GM_E}{r}$.

b Calculate the speed and kinetic energy of the satellite.

The controllers at NASA want to alter the orbit to a higher path at 730 km above Earth's surface. They do this by firing the satellite's thruster engine for a short time in the direction of the satellite's velocity.

c What will be the satellite's kinetic energy in the new orbit?

d Explain how an initial increase in the satellite's speed ends in reducing its kinetic energy.

WORKSHEET 17

Modelling

Working with orbits

Getting a satellite into space is not an easy task. The objective is to achieve enough speed and height to maintain orbit. Consider the task of putting a 100 kg satellite into a circular orbit.

1 Given the radius ($r_E = 6.37 \times 10^6$ m) and mass ($M_E = 5.98 \times 10^{24}$ kg) of Earth, calculate the gravitational potential energy of the satellite before it is launched.

2 Find the total energy of the satellite once it has been placed in an orbit of altitude 100 km above Earth's surface. Use $E_g = -\frac{GMm}{2r}$.

3 Explain why these quantities are negative.

4 The difference between the two quantities found in Questions **1** and **2** is the amount of energy that needs to be imparted to the satellite by the launch vehicle. How much energy is this?

5 The satellite before launch is not really stationary—it is moving along with Earth as it rotates. Assuming that the launch pad is on the equator, find the initial kinetic energy of the satellite.

6 This initial kinetic energy can be utilised by launching the satellite in the appropriate direction. What is that direction and why is the equator the best latitude for the launch?

ISBN 978 0 6557 0029 6

7 Describe this initial kinetic energy as a percentage of the amount of energy found in Question **4**.

Now consider what is required to get such a satellite to Mars. To simplify things, first consider what energy is required to move the 100 kg satellite from Earth's orbit to the orbit of Mars.

8 Find the difference between the total energy of the satellite when it is in orbit at a distance of Earth's orbit compared to the distance when it is in Mars' orbit. (Use this data: mass of the Sun $M_S = 1.99 \times 10^{30}$ kg, radius of Earth's orbit $r_E = 1.50 \times 10^{11}$ m, radius of Mars' orbit = 2.28×10^{11} m.)

This energy difference is only a part of the story. In addition, the satellite will need to be given enough energy to escape entirely from Earth's gravity. (This is also known as escaping Earth's gravity well.) When the satellite is in Mars' orbit, its gravitational potential energy in Earth's field can be taken to be zero, as it is so far away.

9 What is the value of this escape energy? What percentage of the energy calculated in Question **8** does this represent?

EXTENSION

Consider the trajectory required for this orbital transfer. Rather than trying to travel to Mars in a straight line, the path will be determined by the relative positions of Earth and Mars, both at the time of launch and at the planned rendezvous with Mars.

The orbit required for greatest efficiency is called the Hohmann transfer orbit, shown in Figure 3.2.28. The orbits of Earth and Mars are approximately circular, but the transfer orbit is elliptical, with the perihelion (the closest point to the Sun) equal to Earth's orbital radius and the aphelion (the furthest point from the Sun) at the orbit of Mars.

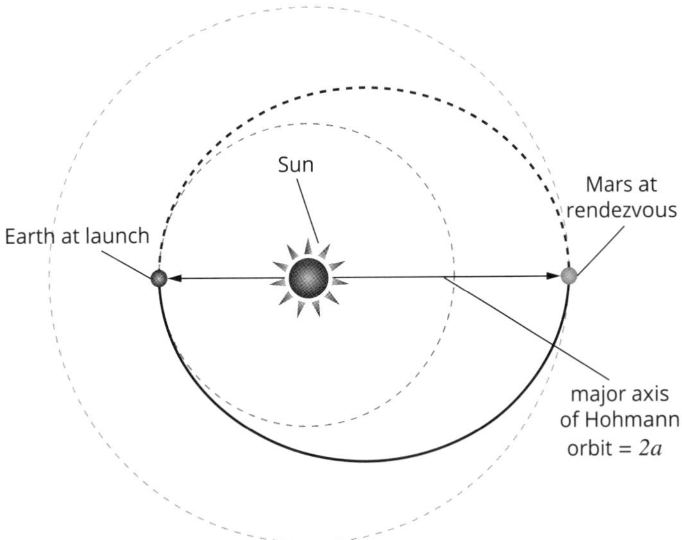

Figure 3.2.28 Hohmann transfer orbit for Earth and Mars

Kepler's third law can be used to find out roughly how long the trip to Mars would take. The third law states that for all orbits around the Sun the quantity $\frac{r^3}{T^2}$ is a constant, where r is the radius of the orbit and T is the period. Most planets have an approximately circular orbit and the application of the third law involves the orbital radius. But when the orbit is highly elliptical, the value of r needs to be replaced with the length of the semi-major axis, a. The third law then becomes $\frac{a^3}{T^2}$.

10 Find the value of the semi-major axis of the Hohmann transfer orbit. Give your answer to three significant figures.

11 Compare the value of $\frac{a^3}{T^2}$ for the satellite in the Hohmann transfer orbit with the value of $\frac{a^3}{T^2}$ for Earth, and find the duration of the Hohmann trip to Mars in units of days.

This exercise has presented some of the preliminary analyses required to plan a trip to Mars. There are many further questions that can be considered, including:

- Exactly when are both Earth and Mars in the correct positions for a launch? (This is known as the launch window.)
- You have found the energy for the transfer orbit, but at what points does this energy need to be applied?
- How much does the orbital energy of the satellite in its 100 km orbit help?
- How will the gravity well of Mars affect calculations?
- Will a trip back to Earth be needed at some stage? (This has not yet been achieved.)

 ISBN 978 0 6557 0029 6

WORKSHEET 18

Simulation

Looking for particles

One of the earliest indications that atoms were not simply tiny hard spheres came when a high voltage was applied to a glass tube containing a very low-pressure gas. The gas started to emit light consisting of several discrete colours.

Each gas emitted a different mix of wavelengths, indicating that there was a possible inner structure in the gas atoms.

Further experiments were carried out using glass tubes containing almost no gas at all. In these circumstances a green glow was observed in the tube wall near the positive electrode. It seemed as if there might be some type of emanation or radiation coming from the negative electrode—and thus cathode rays were discovered. We now know that the cathode rays are actually particles (electrons) being emitted from the negative electrode and accelerated towards the positive electrode.

1 If a potential difference of 6.0 kV is applied across an evacuated glass tube, how much energy is transferred to each electron travelling from one electrode to the other?

2 How fast would the electron be travelling when it reaches the positive electrode? (Use $m_e = 9.1 \times 10^{-31}$ kg.)

It was soon determined that the 'rays' were deflected by an external electric field in the opposite direction to the field, indicating that the rays were negatively charged. The rays were also deflected by a magnetic field. In 1897, J. J. Thomson was able to apply electric and magnetic fields to the rays and thereby find the charge-to-mass ratio $\frac{e}{m}$ for the electron.

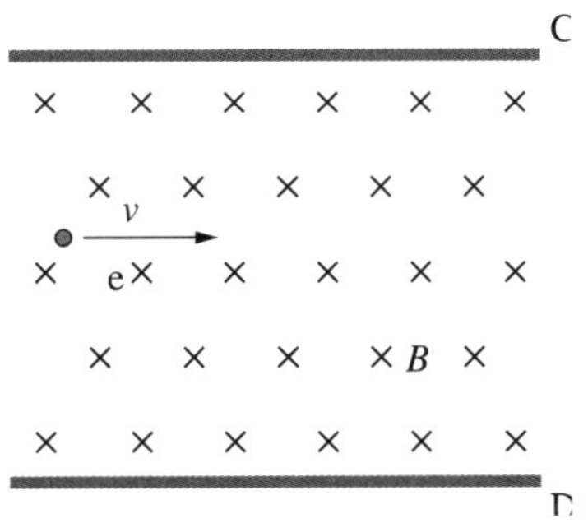

Figure 3.2.29 An electron travelling through a magnetic field

3 In Figure 3.2.29, an electron enters a region where there is a magnetic field, B. In which direction will the magnetic force act on the electron?

4 If the electric field created by the parallel plates acts in the opposite direction, which plate is positive?

5 When the fields are adjusted, the electrons can be made to travel straight through, undeflected. Show how the velocity of the undeflected electrons can be found.

6 This arrangement of fields is known as a velocity filter. Research the definition for a velocity filter and describe how it applies to this application.

The next challenge was to find the charge of the electron, as this would lead to finding its mass. In 1909, Robert Millikan's landmark experiment did just that. Millikan was able to observe microscopic oil droplets between a pair of charged plates. Many of the oil droplets were charged and were seen to move up or down at different speeds. They were so small that they reached a terminal velocity very quickly when acted upon by the forces of gravity, electrostatic attraction and air resistance.

When terminal velocity is reached, the net force is zero. The driving force, the sum of the oil droplet's force due to gravity and any electric force, is balanced by air resistance, and the size of the terminal velocity itself is proportional to the driving force.

7 Millikan found that the terminal velocities were clustered together at values that were multiples of each other. What did this clustering imply about the charge on the oil droplets?

8 Millikan then concentrated on the droplets that were moving very slowly. He adjusted the electric field between the plates until the droplets were stationary. From the size of the droplet, he could calculate its mass. Consider an oil droplet of mass 1.77×10^{-15} kg held motionless between a pair of plates 2.50 mm apart at a potential difference of 90.0 V. How many elementary charges does the droplet carry?

From 1908 to 1913, at about the same time that Millikan was performing his experiments, a pair of Ernest Rutherford's associates at the Cavendish Laboratory in England were using alpha particles to probe the atoms in a gold foil. Hans Geiger and Ernest Marsden encased an alpha particle source in a lead shield with a small hole in it. The emerging narrow beam of positively charged alpha particles was directed at very thin gold foil just hundreds of atoms thick. Most of the alpha particles passed straight through the gold foil as if it wasn't there. However, some underwent huge deflections, even emerging from the foil in the opposite direction.

9 Explain how this observation implied the existence of a very dense mass at the centre of the gold atom.

 ISBN 978 0 6557 0029 6

WORKSHEET 19

Modelling

Deflecting electrons—particle accelerators

A group of students set up an old cathode ray oscilloscope tube to study the behaviour of electrons in a magnetic field. They placed a 'horseshoe' electromagnet around the straight part of the tube, as shown in Figure 3.2.30. A DC power supply produces a current *I* in the electromagnet.

Electrons are produced in the electron gun by means of thermionic emission. The electron gun itself can be considered to be a form of particle accelerator. The electrons are accelerated by means of a high DC voltage applied across a pair of plates just outside the gun. Then the focusing electrodes within the cathode ray tube produce a beam that is focused at one point on the screen, creating a bright spot. In the absence of any external magnetic field, the spot is in the centre of the screen. When a field acts on the electron beam, the spot is deviated by a distance *d* from the centre.

1 Research and briefly explain how thermionic emission works.

____

____

____

2 Does X represent the north or south pole of the electromagnet? Explain your answer.

____

____

____

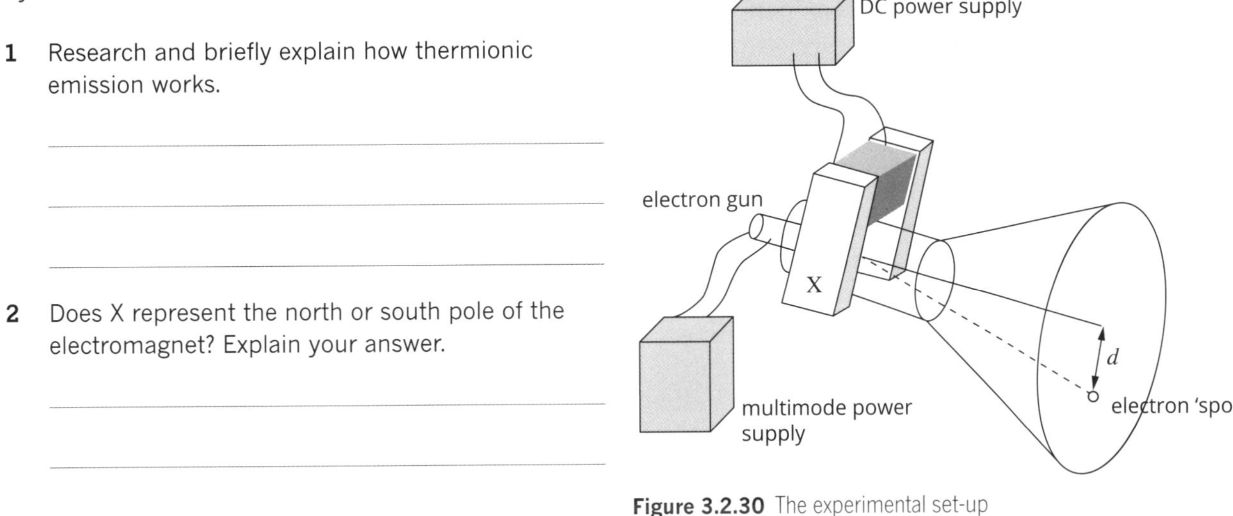

Figure 3.2.30 The experimental set-up

During the investigation, the current, *I*, in the electromagnet and the accelerating potential, *V*, were both varied systematically. At each stage, the deflection distance, *d*, was recorded. The students realised that the electrons followed a circular arc for the time they were between the poles of the magnet. By careful scale drawing and use of geometry they were able to show that the radius of curvature was given by the relationship $r = \frac{85}{d}$.

Table 1 and Table 2 display their results.

Table 1 Variation of current with a constant accelerating potential *V* of 4.0 kV

I (A)	*d* (cm)
0.21	0.9
0.34	1.7
0.43	2.1
0.57	2.8
0.70	3.1
0.84	4.1

Table 2 Variation of voltage with a constant electromagnet current *I* of 0.50 A

V (kV)	*d* (cm)
1.8	2.5
2.1	2.3
2.9	2.0
3.7	1.8
4.0	1.7
5.5	1.5

The students were keen to test whether these results were consistent with the equations they had studied for charged particles travelling in magnetic fields. First, they had to rearrange the equations.

3 Identify the independent and dependent variables in this investigation.

The following relationships relate to the movement of electrons in a cathode ray tube:

- The kinetic energy gained by each electron in the gun is given by the equation $E_k = qV = \frac{1}{2}mv^2$.
- The radius of curvature is given by the relationship $F = \frac{mv^2}{r}$.
- The magnetic force acting on each charged particle is given by $F = qvB$.
- The radius of curvature is given by $r = \frac{85}{d}$.
- The strength of the magnetic field is proportional to the current: $B \propto I$.

4 By manipulating these equations, show that $d \propto I$. (Hint: Find the relationship between B and r by equating the magnetic force on a charge to the centripetal force required. Then replace B with constant × I and r with $\frac{85}{d}$.)

5 Plot a graph of d versus I. Sketch or paste your graph in the space provided. Does it support the relationship $d \propto I$?

6 Demonstrate that $r \propto \sqrt{V}$. (Hint: First find a relationship between r and v by equating the magnetic force on a charge to the centripetal force required. Then find a relationship between v and V. Use these two relationships to find the one between r and $\sqrt{V}$.)

 ISBN 978 0 6557 0029 6

WORKSHEET 20

Literacy review—fields

1 The statement below defines some key ideas about magnetic fields. Complete the statement using some of the following key words (not all words in the list are needed).

north	strong	dipolar	monopolar	Tesla	Ampère	south	weak

Magnets come in many shapes and sizes, but all magnets are ________. A magnetic field is defined as running from ________ to ________. An example of a ________ permanent magnet is a neodymium magnet. A compass is an example of a ___________ permanent magnet. The units for magnetic field strength are named after two of the scientists who described key ideas about magnetic fields— ________ and Gauss.

2 The statement below defines some key ideas about electric fields. Complete the statement using some of the following key words (not all words in the list are needed).

scalar	vector	positive	negative	directly	inversely

The magnitude of an electric field in the space surrounding a charge is related ____________ to the magnitude of the charge and ____________ to the distance from the charge. The direction of the electric field is always in the direction that a ______________ test charge would be pushed or pulled if placed in the space surrounding the source charge. An electric field is a ____________ quantity.

3 Complete the following table with the similarities and differences between gravitational, magnetic and electric fields by indicating the form or equation each field takes.

Property	Gravitational	Magnetic	Electric
single point source			
field intensity proportional to			
range (long/short)			
strength			
direction			
attractive or repulsive forces			

WORKSHEET 21

Reflection—How do things move without contact?

On completion of Area of Study 2: How do things move without contact?, you should be able to describe, explain and apply the relevant scientific ideas. You should be able to work with data; to interpret, analyse and evaluate it.

1 The following table lists the key knowledge covered in this area of study. Reflect on how well you understand the concepts listed. Rate your learning by shading the circle that corresponds to your current level of understanding for each one.

Key knowledge	Not confident ◄				► Very confident
The similarities and differences between gravitational, electric and magnetic fields	○	○	○	○	○
The direction, shape and magnitude of gravitational and electric fields about a point mass or charge	○	○	○	○	○
The direction and shape of magnetic fields produced by bar magnets, current-carrying wires and solenoids	○	○	○	○	○
Work done in gravitational and electric fields	○	○	○	○	○
The motion of charged particles in an electric field	○	○	○	○	○
The motion of objects with mass in a gravitational field; orbits and satellite motion	○	○	○	○	○
The motion of charged particles in a magnetic field	○	○	○	○	○
The force on a current-carrying conductor in a magnetic field	○	○	○	○	○
Simple DC motors	○	○	○	○	○
Particle accelerators and uniform circular motion	○	○	○	○	○

2 Consider the points you have shaded from Not confident to Very confident. List specific ideas you can identify that were challenging.

3 Write down two different strategies that you will apply to help further your understanding of these ideas.

 ISBN 978 0 6557 0029 6

PRACTICAL ACTIVITY 6

Experiment

Gravitational acceleration

SUGGESTED DURATION

- 50 minutes data collection + 15 minutes analysis

MATERIALS

- 5 large metal nuts
- 5 m length of string
- metal baking tray
- ruler or measuring tape

INTRODUCTION

Earth's gravity exerts a force on all objects within its field. This force causes the objects to accelerate towards the ground at a constant rate of $g = 9.8\,\text{m}\,\text{s}^{-2}$, irrespective of the mass of the object.

AIM

Using the equations of motion, model the relationship between the distance an object falls and time.

Safety

Wear safety glasses to avoid potential injury to eyes.

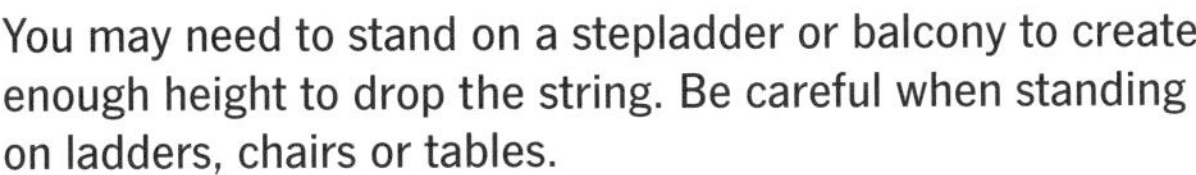

You may need to stand on a stepladder or balcony to create enough height to drop the string. Be careful when standing on ladders, chairs or tables.

Complete a risk assessment before starting the activity.

METHOD

1. Tie one nut onto the end of the string.
2. Thread the other nuts onto the string one at a time, fixing them at 50 cm intervals.
3. Place the metal baking tray on the ground upside down.
4. Standing above the tray, hold the string so that the first nut is just resting on the tray.
5. Drop the string and listen to the beats the nuts make as they hit the tray.

The sound of the nuts on the tray may be hard to hear. Discuss as a class how to produce reliable results.

6. Adjust the position of the nuts on the string so they create equally spaced beats when they hit the baking tray. You can use the equation for uniform acceleration, $s = ut + \frac{1}{2}at^2$, to make predictions about where the nuts should be tied to the string.

RESULTS

Nut number	Total string length to nut, s (m)	Time, t (s)	t^2 (s^2)
1			
2			
3			
4			
5			

PRACTICAL ACTIVITY 6

Plot a graph of the string length against time squared and draw a line of best fit.

DISCUSSION

1 Describe the relationship between distance and time when equally spaced beats are created.

2 Calculate the gradient of your graph. What does this value represent?

CONCLUSION

FURTHER INVESTIGATION

Investigate and develop a method, or methods, by which the accuracy of this experiment could be improved using electronic data collection, including such equipment as photogates and motion sensors.

Carry out your investigation and record both your method and results. Compare the potential reliability and eventual accuracy with that based on the method above.

Explain why the accelerometers in phones and other purpose-built sensors cannot be used to determine the acceleration due to gravity here on Earth.

ISBN 978 0 6557 0029 6

PRACTICAL ACTIVITY 7

Experiment

Charge and electric field

SUGGESTED DURATION

- 55 minutes data collection + 20 minutes analysis

MATERIALS

- charge sensor and data-collection system, electrometer or quantifiable electroscope
- Faraday ice pail
- charge producers, pair
- proof planes (2)
- plastic rod
- glass rod
- aluminium rod
- silk cloth
- fur cloth

INTRODUCTION

Normally, all atoms have a neutral charge, which means that the number of electrons equals the number of protons. Atoms that lose or gain electrons are electrically charged. The magnitude of the charge is proportional to the number of electrons gained or lost. If the number of protons exceeds the number electrons, or the number of electrons exceeds the number of protons, then the atom is said to have a positive charge or negative charge, respectively. Objects with like charge will repel one another, and objects with unlike charge will attract one another.

In the right conditions, an object can acquire an electric charge by rubbing it with another object, such as rubbing your shoes on carpet, sliding across a car seat, or rubbing a balloon against your hair. The charged balloon and hair will have the same amount of charge, but opposite polarities. Therefore, they will attract one another. Rubber and plastic are insulators (materials that do not transfer a charge easily), which prevents charge from easily moving through the material. In this experiment, a charge sensor, electrometer or other quantifiable electroscope and a Faraday ice pail are used to examine the transfer of electric charges from one material to another.

AIM

To quantify the charge transferred from one material to another from rubbing of one material against another.

Safety
Keep charged items away from sensitive electronics.
Complete a risk assessment before starting the activity.

METHOD

1 ▪ If using a charge sensor, start a new experiment on the data collection system and connect the charge sensor. Display the charge in a digital display. Otherwise, connect power to the electrometer as required and set it up ready for connection.

2 ▪ Connect the alligator clips from the charge sensor to the Faraday ice pail with the red lead connected to the inner screen and the black lead to the outer screen, as shown in Figure 3.2.31. For best results, the charge sensor and the Faraday ice pail should be kept as far away from each other as possible.

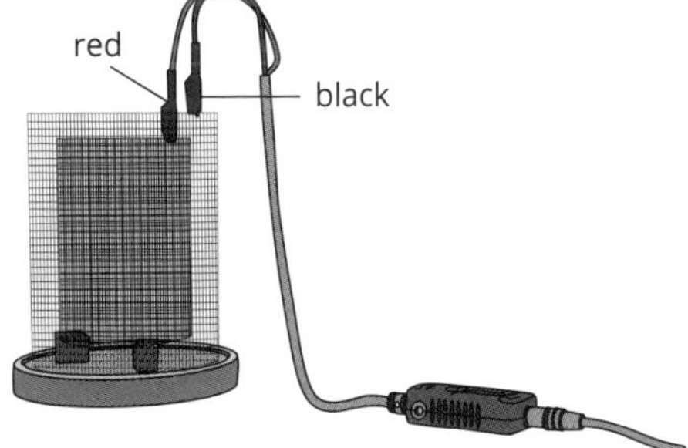

Figure 3.2.31 Leads connected to the Faraday ice pail

3 ▪ Ground the Faraday ice pail by touching the inner and outer screens of the pail with one finger at the same time. This operation technically neutralises the ice pail. To actually ground the device, the outer screen can be connected to a grounded earth.

4 ▪ Zero the charge sensor or electrometer, following the manufacturer's instructions.

5 ▪ Initially, monitor live data without recording. Verify that the charge reading on the screen is approximately zero. If not, re-ground the Faraday ice pail.

6 ▪ Rub the surfaces of the two charge producers together several times, avoiding the insulating material.

Do not touch the white insulating material on the charge producers or proof planes. Any contact with the circular end of a charge producer or proof plane can affect the charge.

7 ▪ Lower the first charge producer into the inner pail without touching the sides or bottom of the screen. Record the measured charge value in Table 1. Remove the charge producer.

8 ▪ Lower the second charge producer into the inner pail without touching the sides or bottom of the screen. Record the charge value in Table 1. Remove the charge producer.

9 ▪ Ground the round end of one of the proof planes.

10 ▪ Place the flat round surface of the second charge producer against the flat round surface of the proof plane.

11 ▪ Lower the proof plane into the inner pail without touching the sides or bottom of the screen. Record the charge value in Table 1. Remove the proof plane.

12 ▪ Ground the round end of a second proof plane.

13 ▪ Place the flat round surface of the first proof plane against the flat round surface of the second proof plane. Lower the first proof plane into the inner pail without touching the sides or bottom of the screen. Record the charge value in Table 1. Remove the proof plane.

14 ▪ Lower the second proof plane into the inner pail without touching the sides or bottom of the screen. Record the charge value in Table 1. Remove the proof plane.

15 ▪ Vigorously rub one end of the plastic rod (about ¼ of its length) with the silk cloth. Lower the rod into the inner pail without touching the sides or bottom of the screen. Record the materials used and the charge value in Table 2. Remove the rod.

16 ▪ Without rubbing the rod again, lower the unrubbed end of the plastic rod into the inner pail without touching the sides or bottom of the screen. Record the materials and charge value in Table 2. Remove the rod.

17 ▪ Repeat steps 15 and 16 for the glass rod using the silk cloth.

18 ▪ Repeat steps 15 and 16 again for the aluminium rod using the fur cloth.

19 ▪ Repeat steps 15 and 16 for the plastic rod using the silk cloth, but this time rub about $\frac{3}{4}$ of its length.

RESULTS

Table 1 Charge data for proof planes and charge producers

Parameters	Charge (nC)
charge on the first charge producer	
charge on the second charge producer	
charge on the proof plane	
charge on the first proof plane, after contact	
charge on the second proof plane, after contact	

Table 2 Charge data for rods

Parameters	Charge (nC)	Classification
plastic rod, end rubbed with silk		
plastic rod, unrubbed end		
glass rod, end rubbed with silk		
glass rod, unrubbed end		
aluminium rod, end rubbed with fur		
aluminium rod, unrubbed end		
plastic rod, end rubbed with silk (greater surface area)		

 ISBN 978 0 6557 0029 6

PRACTICAL ACTIVITY 7

DISCUSSION

1 A material that transfers charge easily is called a conductor. A material that prevents the movement of charge is an insulator. Classify each of the rod materials, and enter the classification in Table 2.

2 According to the data, identify the rod and cloth combination that obtained the greatest charge.

3 List the objects that gained electrons.

4 Identify the charge the silk gained when rubbed with a) the plastic rod, and b) the glass rod.

a

b

5 Identify the end of the plastic rod (the rubbed or unrubbed end) that indicated a larger charge.

6 Identify the material that transferred its charge more easily from one end to the other. What material did not?

7 Based on your results, discuss whether rubbing the objects longer would increase or decrease the electric charge.

8 Describe a method that would increase the amount of charge transferred between two objects.

CONCLUSION

PRACTICAL ACTIVITY 8

Experiment

Mapping electric fields

SUGGESTED DURATION

- 55 minutes data collection + 10 minutes analysis

MATERIALS

- semi-conductive paper with grid
- conductive ink pen
- metal drawing pens
- metal T-pin
- corkboard
- multimeter or voltage sensor
- banana-plug patch cords with alligator clips
- pencil
- white or light-coloured felt-tip marker
- power supply, 18 V, 3 A

INTRODUCTION

All charged objects produce electric fields in the space surrounding them. If you know the shape, direction and magnitude of an electric field, you can determine how a charged particle will interact with the field.

Electric field lines are a convenient visual way of representing an electric field. They are lines drawn to follow the path of the electric field, originating from a positive charge (or charged object) and ending at a negative charge (or charged object). The lines never cross, and the density of lines (the closeness of the lines) represents the magnitude of the field strength. Lines of equal electrical potential are known as isolines.

In this activity you will identify different isolines of electrical potential surrounding a pair of charged electrodes, then use those isolines as guides to draw electric field lines and identify the magnitude and direction of the electric field.

AIM

Using the principles of electric fields and electrical potential energy, investigate the lines of equal electrical potential surrounding oppositely charged electrodes and the shape and direction of the corresponding electric field lines.

Allow plenty of time for the conductive ink to dry completely. This may take overnight.

Safety

Wear safety glasses to avoid potential injury to eyes.

Do not connect the terminals of a power supply without a load or resistance. This will cause a short circuit, which may damage the power supply.

Complete a risk assessment before starting the activity.

METHOD

Drawing dipole electrodes with conductive ink

1. Place a sheet of semi-conductive paper flat, printed side up, on the lab bench.
2. Use the pencil to draw two small circles 10 cm apart along the horizontal centre line of the paper, as shown in Figure 3.2.32. Make each circle about 1 cm in diameter.
3. Shake the conductive ink pen (with the cap on) for 10–20 seconds, then remove the cap and press the spring-loaded tip down on the semi-conductive paper, in the centre of either circle.
4. Lightly squeeze the barrel on the pen until ink starts to slowly flow onto the paper, then move the tip of the pen around inside the circle until the circle is completely filled with the ink.
5. If the circle is not completely filled in, draw over it again with the pen. A solid, uniform circle is essential for good measurements.
6. Repeat the process for the second circle.
7. Allow the conductive ink to dry completely. During this time, you can draw parallel-plate electrodes following the steps below.

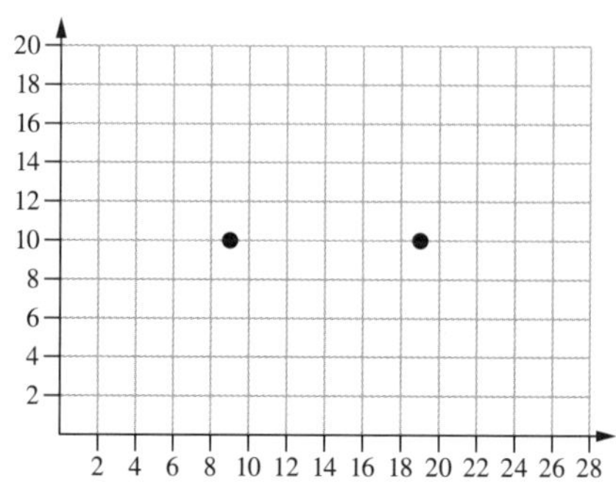

Figure 3.2.32 The dipole electrodes drawn on semi-conductive paper

ISBN 978 0 6557 0029 6

Drawing parallel-plate electrodes with conductive ink

1 ▪ Place a sheet of semi-conductive paper flat, printed side up, on the lab bench.

2 ▪ Use the ruler and pencil to draw two straight lines 10 cm long and 8 cm apart, and perpendicular to the horizontal centre line of the paper, as shown in Figure 3.2 33. Make each line about 5 mm wide.

3 ▪ Shake the conductive ink pen (with the cap on) for 10–20 seconds. Then remove the cap and press the spring-loaded tip down on the semi-conductive paper, in the centre of either line.

4 ▪ Lightly squeeze the barrel on the pen until ink starts to slowly flow onto the paper, and then move the tip of the pen back and forth inside the sketched line until it is completely filled with the ink.

5 ▪ Use care when drawing the electrodes. If the line is not uniformly thick, it may not conduct. Go back and deposit more conductive material if necessary. If the line is not completely filled in, draw over it again. A solid uniform line is essential for good measurements.

6 ▪ Repeat the process for the second line.

7 ▪ Allow the conductive ink to dry completely.

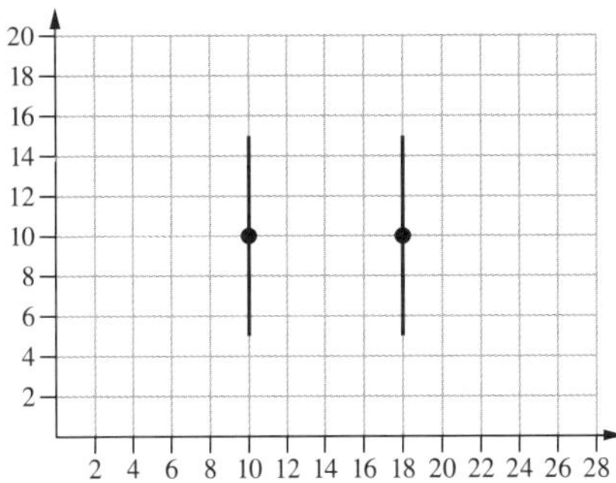

Figure 3.2.33 The parallel-plate electrodes drawn on semi-conductive paper

Part 1 • Dipole electric fields

1 ▪ Place the first sheet of semi-conductive paper with the dipole electrodes drawn on it onto the corkboard. Pin each corner of the paper to the corkboard using metal drawing pins.

2 ▪ Press a drawing pin into the centre of each electrode, making sure that the pins are pressed firmly through the paper and into the corkboard.

3 ▪ With the power supply off, connect the electrode pins to the terminals on the power supply using two patch cords and alligator clips, as shown in Figure 3.2.34. The positive terminal is connected to one electrode (which will be the positive electrode), and the negative terminal is connected to the other electrode (which will be the negative electrode).

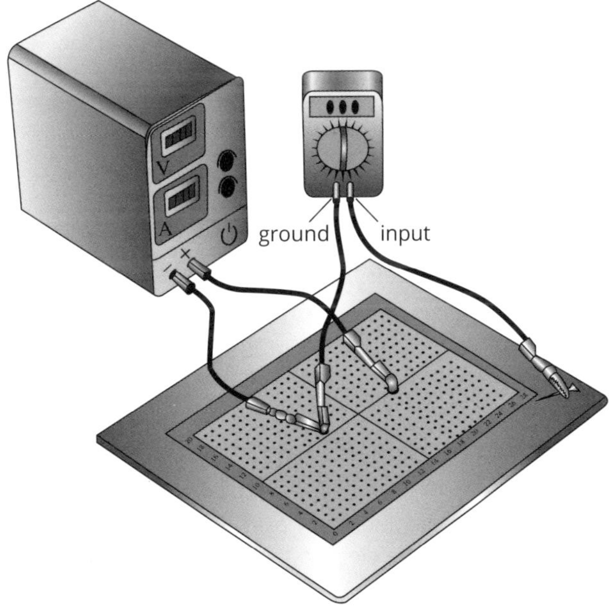

Figure 3.2.34 The electrode pins connected to the power supply and multimeter

4 ▪ Connect the two remaining patch cords to the DC voltage ports on the digital multimeter or voltage sensor, and then adjust the meter to measure DC voltage up to 10 V DC.

5 ▪ Attach alligator clips to the ends of the meter patch cords. Clip the meter 'ground' or 'COM' patch cord to the pin in the negative electrode; this is now the reference electrode. Connect the alligator clip on the other patch cord to the metal T-pin.

6 ▪ Turn on the power supply and adjust the voltage to 10 V DC.

7 ▪ Touch the tip of the T-pin to several solid black areas on the paper, and observe the voltage measurement on the meter. Repeat for a few other solid black areas. The meter should show different voltages at different points on the paper. If not, make sure all of the alligator clips and drawing pins are making good connections, then retest.

Touch the tip of the T-pin only to the solid black areas of the semi-conductive paper. Do not touch it to the paper's grid marks.

8 ▪ Use the tip of the T-pin to test different positions surrounding the electrodes until you find a location on the paper where the meter reads 1.0 V. Use the felt-tip marker to make a small mark at this position.

9 ▪ Continue moving the T-pin to different points on the paper, identifying several positions surrounding the electrodes where the voltage is at 1.0 V. Mark each new point with the felt-tip marker until there are enough marks to accurately draw a smooth line that connects them. Label the line '1.0 V'.

Be sure to probe all areas surrounding the electrodes. Isolines of electrical potential may connect in a closed path on the paper or extend off the edge of the paper and then re-enter the paper in an unexpected location.

10 ▪ Repeat the previous data-collection steps, identifying and drawing the isolines of electrical potential of 3.0 V, 5.0 V, 7.0 V and 9.0 V. Label each line with its corresponding voltage.

11 ▪ Turn the power supply off when you are finished.

Part 2 • Parallel plates

Using the second sheet of semi-conductive paper with the two parallel-plate electrodes drawn on it, repeat the set-up method outlined in Part **1**. For each line (plate), push the drawing pin into the plate about 10 mm from one end.

1 ▪ Clip the DMM ground patch cord to the drawing pin in the negative plate electrode; this is now the reference electrode.

2 ▪ Turn on the power supply and adjust the voltage to 10 V DC.

3 ▪ Using the data-collection steps in Part **1**, identify and draw the isolines of electrical potential surrounding the parallel-plate electrodes for 1.0 V, 3.0 V, 5.0 V, 7.0 V and 9.0 V.

4 ▪ Turn the power supply off when you are finished.

RESULTS

Dipoles

1 Using the pencil, draw a line starting from any point on the surface of the positive electrode and extending to the nearest isoline. Draw the line so it leaves the surface of the electrode at a right angle and intersects the first isoline at a right angle. The field line must curve smoothly, as shown in Figure 3.2.35.

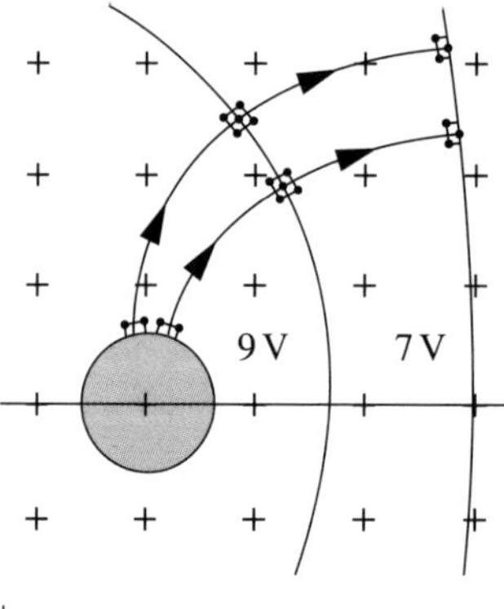

Figure 3.2.35 Field lines connecting the positive electrode and isolines

2 When you are satisfied with the shape of the line, draw over it using the felt-tip pen, and then draw an arrow head on the line indicating the direction of the electric field.

3 From the tip of the arrow you have just drawn, draw another field line like the previous one, extending from that isoline to the next, and then another field line to the next isoline, and so on until you reach the other electrode or the edge of the paper. Combine the connecting lines to form one electric field line.

4 Repeat these steps to draw a total of 10 electric field lines originating from the positive electrode, spacing the start of each line evenly along its surface.

Parallel plates

Repeat the method from the dipoles to draw 10 electric field lines from the positive parallel-plate electrode to the negative parallel-plate electrode, as follows:

1 Draw seven of the 10 field lines leaving the inner surface of the positive electrode, and the remaining three field lines leaving the outer surface of the electrode.

 ISBN 978 0 6557 0029 6

2 Space the seven lines evenly along the inner surface, and the three lines evenly along the outer surface of the positive electrode. Draw each line with a smooth curve when necessary, and include arrow heads indicating the direction of the electric field.

DISCUSSION

1 What is the convention for showing the direction of electric fields?

2 Based on your final electric field plots, what are the primary similarities and differences between the electric fields surrounding each electrode configuration?

3 Identify where the electric field was strongest in each electrode configuration. Justify your answer based on your results.

4 What can be said about the voltage at each point of an isoline of electrical potential?

5 What do the electric field lines represent?

6 How would the shape of the electric field lines in each configuration change if you increased the voltage across the electrodes? Justify your answer.

CONCLUSION

PRACTICAL ACTIVITY 9

Experiment

Magnetic field of a coil

SUGGESTED DURATION

- 45 minutes data collection + 15 minutes analysis

MATERIALS

- data-collection system
- current sensor
- magnetic field sensor
- 3 coils of varying turns but the same radius
- DC power supply (10 V 1 A minimum)
- 3 patch cords with banana plugs

INTRODUCTION

The use of coils in electromagnetic devices varies from transformers allowing electrical supply over long distances to pick-up coils in electric guitars, voice coils in loudspeakers and coils in electric motors. Coils, or solenoids as they are also known, are a key enabling technology of modern society.

The strength of the magnetic field inside a coil depends upon the number of turns of the wire, the magnitude of the current in the wire, and the radius of the coil:

$$B = N\frac{\mu_0 I}{2\pi r}$$

where B is magnitude of the magnetic field strength in Teslas (T)
N is the number of turns
μ_0 is a constant referred to as the permeability of free space ($\mu_0 = 1.257 \times 10^{-6}\,\text{N A}^{-2}$)
I is the current in amperes (A)
r is the radius of the coil in metres (m).

The magnetic field at a point well inside a solenoid is uniform and independent of the length or diameter of the solenoid. Instead, it is dependent upon the number of turns of the coil per unit length. For a solenoid of N turns and length l, the equation becomes:

$$B = \frac{\mu_0 N I}{l}$$

The more tightly wound the wire is around a solenoid, the greater the magnetic field. Solenoids can be used to generate nearly uniform magnetic fields, similar to those of bar magnets.

AIM

To experimentally investigate (a) the relationship between the magnetic field strength inside a coil and the magnitude of the current carried through the coil wire, and (b) the relationship between the number of turns of wire in a coil and the magnetic field strength within the coil.

This investigation is best performed with a data-collection system. However, if this is unavailable, reasonable comparative results can be obtained using an ammeter and a magnet suspended on a string. Record the deflection of the magnet as an alternative to magnetic field strength.

Safety

Wear safety glasses to avoid potential injury to eyes.

Strong magnetic fields will be developed within and around the coil. Keep the coil away from any sensitive electronic equipment such as phones, tablets and computers.

Keep liquids away from the power supply.

Complete a risk assessment before starting the activity.

METHOD

1 ▪ Start a new experiment in the data-collection system and connect both the magnetic field sensor and the current sensor. (Refer to the note above if these are not available to you.)

2 ▪ Set up displays in the data-collection software to show digital readings to monitor current and magnetic fields.

ISBN 978 0 6557 0029 6

Part 1 • Varying the number of turns in the coil

1 ▪ Measure the radius of the coils and record this value in the Results section.

2 ▪ Using the patch cords, connect the negative terminal from the power supply directly to one of the terminals on the first coil. Connect the positive terminal from the power supply to the positive terminal on the current sensor, and then connect the negative terminal on the current sensor to the second terminal on the coil to complete the circuit, as shown in Figure 3.2.36.

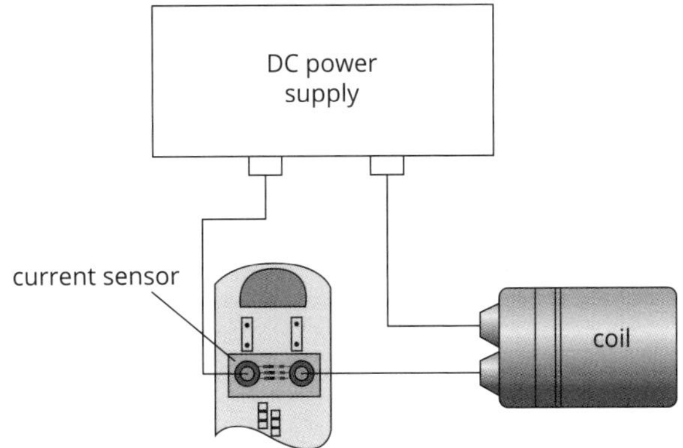

Figure 3.2.36 The circuit set-up

3 ▪ Position the tip of the magnetic field sensor inside the coil at the centre, so that the probe of the sensor is perpendicular to the plane of the coil, as shown in Figure 3.2.37.

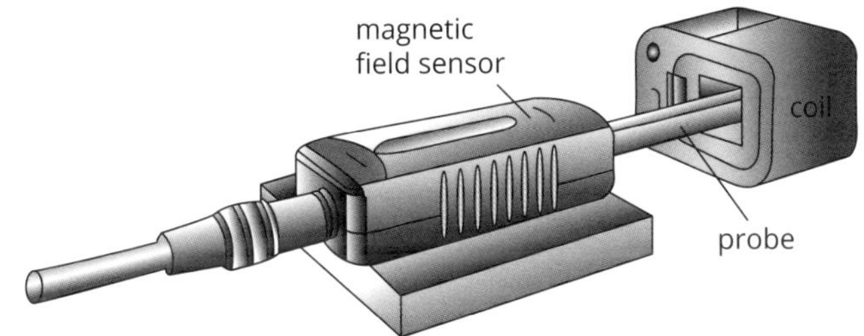

Figure 3.2.37 The probe of the magnetic field sensor positioned inside the coil

4 ▪ Turn on the power supply, and adjust the voltage until the current measured by the current sensor is approximately 0.5 A.

5 ▪ Record the current value in the Results section.

6 ▪ Record the number of turns in the coil and magnetic field strength in Table 1 in the Results section.

7 ▪ Turn off the power supply, disconnect the coil, and replace it with the next coil.

8 ▪ Reposition the coil and magnetic field sensor, and then turn the power supply back on. Adjust the voltage until the current is the same magnitude as was used with the previous coil.

9 ▪ Record the number of turns in the coil and the magnetic field strength in Table 1.

10 ▪ Turn off the power, disconnect the coil, and replace it with the last coil.

11 ▪ Reposition the coil and magnetic field sensor, and then turn the power supply back on. Adjust the voltage until the current is the same magnitude as was used with the previous coils.

12 ▪ Record the number of turns in the coil and the magnetic field strength in Table 1.

Part 2 • Varying the current through the coil

1 ▪ Using the same set-up as in Part **1** and the first coil, turn the voltage down to zero on the power supply and turn it on. Record the magnetic field strength in Table 2 in the Results section.

2 ▪ Increase the voltage slightly until the current increases to about 0.1 A. Record the magnetic field strength and current values in Table 2.

3 ▪ Adjust the voltage until the current increases approximately another 0.1 A (i.e. approximately 0.2 A in total). Once again, record the magnetic field strength and current values in Table 2.

4 ▪ Continue collecting data points every 0.1 A through to approximately 1.0 A, and then stop data collection and turn the power supply off.

Note the limit of the current sensor or ammeter carefully. Do not exceed this rating with the investigation of current range.

RESULTS

Part 1 • Varying the number of turns in the coil

1 Calculate the expected magnetic field for each coil using the theoretical formula and complete Table 1, below.

2 Compare the measured values to the calculated values for magnetic field strength within each coil. Calculate the percentage difference and add it to Table 1.

3 Sketch a graph of magnetic field strength versus number of turns on the grid below.

- Current in the coils: __________ A
- Radius of the coils: __________ m

Table 1 Number of turns and the strength of the magnetic field

Number of turns (N)	Measured magnetic field B (T)	Calculated magnetic field B (T)	% difference

Part 2 • Varying the current in the coil

1 Calculate the expected magnetic field for each coil using the theoretical formula and complete Table 2.

2 Compare the measured values to the calculated values for magnetic field strength within each coil. Calculate the percentage difference and add it to Table 2.

3 Sketch a graph of magnetic field strength versus current on the grid provided.

Radius of the coils: __________ m

Number of turns: __________

 ISBN 978 0 6557 0029 6

Table 2 Current and the strength of the magnetic field

Current (A)	Measured magnetic field B (T)	Calculated magnetic field B (T)	% difference

DISCUSSION

1 What variables can be changed in order to investigate their effect on magnetic field strength in a coil?

2 Describe the relationship between magnetic field strength and the number of turns and current in the coil, with reference to your graphs.

ISBN 978 0 6557 0029 6

3 How can any differences between measured and calculated values for the magnetic field strength be accounted for? Explain and include suggestions for improving the measured results.

CONCLUSION

 ISBN 978 0 6557 0029 6

PRACTICAL ACTIVITY 10

Experiment

A current-carrying conductor in a uniform magnetic field

SUGGESTED DURATION

- 55 minutes data collection + 20 minutes analysis

INTRODUCTION

A current-carrying wire in a magnetic field experiences a force that is usually referred to as a magnetic force. The magnitude and direction of this force depends on four variables:

- the magnitude of the current (I)
- the length of the wire (l)
- the strength of the magnetic field (B), and
- the angle between the field and the wire (θ).

This magnetic force can be described mathematically by the equation $F = IlB\sin\theta$.

AIM

To investigate the relationship between force and current for a current-carrying conductor in a magnetic field.

MATERIALS

- current balance*
- DC power supply supplying up to 5 A
- DC ammeter, current sensor or current probe measuring up to 5 A
- 0.01 g resolution beam, electronic balance or small milligram masses
- magnets or air-cored solenoid and 0–20 V power supply
- retort stand or lab stand
- connecting wires with banana plug connections

*Current balances of different design are available from various suppliers.

Effective balances can also be student-made using copper wire and stiff card or plastic sheets (non-conductive).

As the coil and beam conductors carry current, they will become warmer and their resistance will rise and the current will fall over time. If available, use 'constant current' power sources.

Safety

Follow the manufacturer's specific set-up and safety instructions when conducting this activity.

To prevent burning of the balance contact points and possible damage to the circuit board, do not pass currents in excess of the manufacturer's recommendation through the current balance.

To avoid permanent damage to the current-measuring device, be careful to keep the supplied current below the maximum limit of the measuring device.

Wear safety glasses to avoid potential injury to eyes.

Complete a risk assessment before starting the activity.

METHOD

1. Set up the current balance following the manufacturer's instructions.
2. With no current flowing, either use small masses to balance the beam or record the mass using a beam or electronic balance. Record the mass in the table in the Results section. If you are using an electronic balance, tare the balance to read zero with no current flowing. Record the uncertainty in the reading from the balance.

PRACTICAL ACTIVITY 10

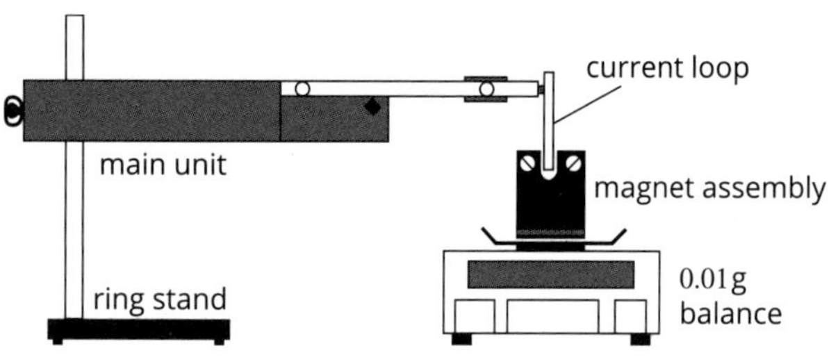

Figure 3.2.38 The experimental set-up

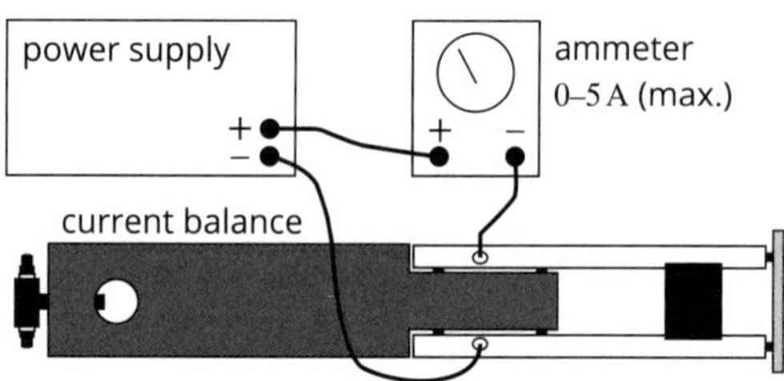

Figure 3.2.39 The current balance connected to a power supply and ammeter

3 ▪ Position the magnet assembly around the end of the straight wire at the end of the current balance, as shown in Figure 3.2.38. This may be a magnet or an air-core solenoid. If using a solenoid, connect the second power supply to the solenoid and set it at approximately 5 V.

4 ▪ Rebalance the current balance by adding or removing small masses from the opposite end of the current balance or record the new mass if using a beam balance. If using an electronic balance, tare the balance back to zero.

5 ▪ Connect the power supply and ammeter to the current balance, as shown in Figure 3.2.39.
If using a solenoid to provide the magnetic field, a second power supply should be connected to the solenoid to allow separate control.

6 ▪ Check the maximum current that your current sensor or ammeter and current balance can safely use. Set the current from the power supply to give a reading of one-tenth of the maximum range. For example, if the maximum range is 1 A, adjust the current from the power supply to read 0.1 A on the current sensor or ammeter. For a maximum range of 5 A, adjust the current to show a reading of 0.5 A on the current sensor or ammeter. Record the uncertainty in the current reading.

7 ▪ Rebalance the current balance or read the new mass on the balance. Record this value in the table in the Results section.

8 ▪ Increase the current in one-tenth increments (i.e. 0.1 A for a 1 A range). Balance the current balance with small weights or record the mass on the balance for each current setting. Do not exceed the maximum range of the ammeter or current sensor, or the safe working range of the current balance.

RESULTS

List the variables associated with this experimental method.

Independent: ______

Dependent: ______

Controlled: ______

1 When investigating the relationship between force and current, what angle should the wire along the end of the current balance make with the magnetic field? Why?

______

2 Why can the effect of the connecting wires along the length of the current balance be ignored?

______

3 Calculate the force corresponding to each measurement of mass and record it in the corresponding column of the table below. How is the force calculated?

______

 ISBN 978 0 6557 0029 6

Current (A) ±	Mass (g) ±	Force (N) ±
0		

4 Plot a graph of force versus current in the space provided, using a suitable scale.

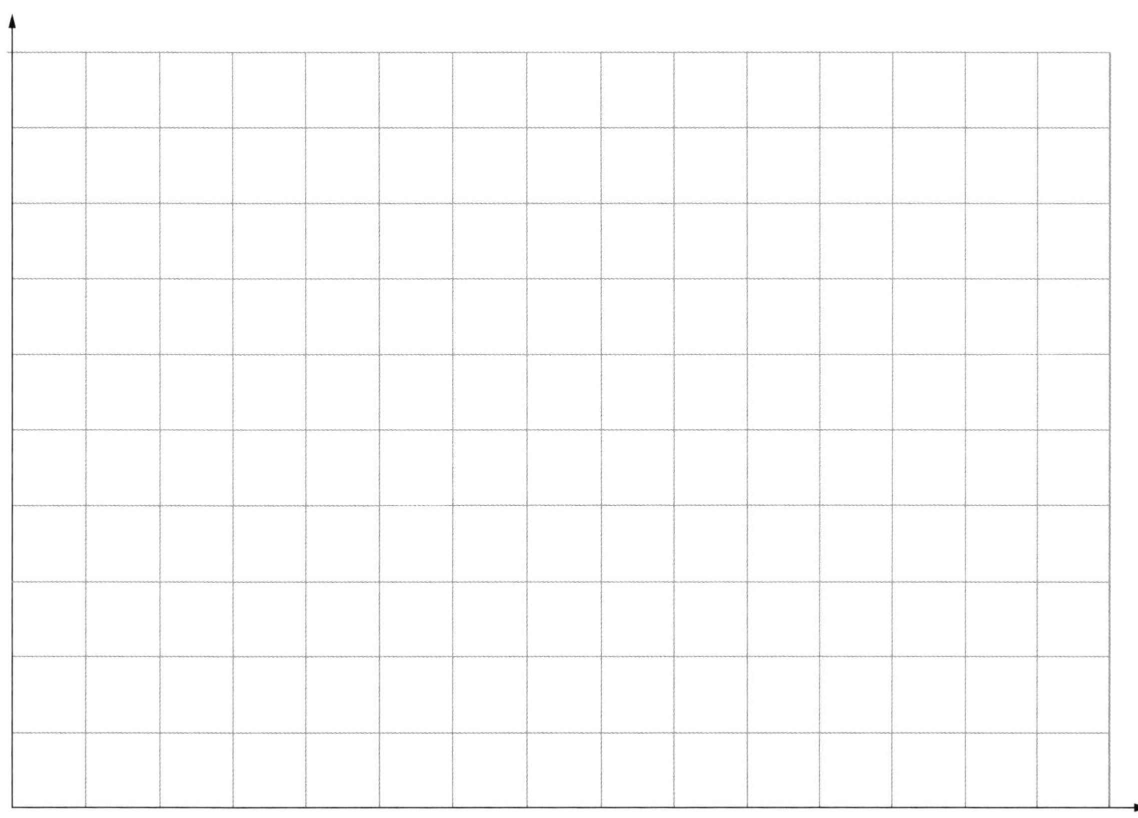

5 Draw a line of best fit and determine the equation of the relationship between the force and current for your data.

DISCUSSION

1 State the relationship between these two variables based on your experimental results.

2 Discuss the implications this relationship has in predicting how the current will affect the force acting on a wire that is inside a magnetic field.

3 Explain the significance of the gradient of the graph.

4 Discuss the reliability of the method you used.

CONCLUSION

FURTHER INVESTIGATION

In the introduction to this activity, it was discussed that the magnitude and direction of the force on a current-carrying wire in a magnetic field depends on four variables:

- the magnitude of the current (I)
- the length of the wire (l)
- the strength of the magnetic field (B), and
- the angle between the field and the wire (θ).

Investigate the relationship between the force and the strength of the magnetic field by repeating this activity, but instead of varying the current, keep the current constant and vary the strength of the magnetic field. Do this by either adding more magnets or, if using an air-cored solenoid, by varying the voltage to the solenoid. Variations in the voltage to the solenoid should be made in 1 V increments.

Investigate the relationship between the force and the length of wire in the magnetic field by again repeating this activity, but instead of varying the current, keep the current constant and vary the length of the conductor in the magnetic field.

 ISBN 978 0 6557 0029 6

EXAM QUESTIONS

Multiple-choice questions

Question 1 VCE Physics 2020 (A) 1

The diagram below shows the electric field lines between two charges of equal magnitude.

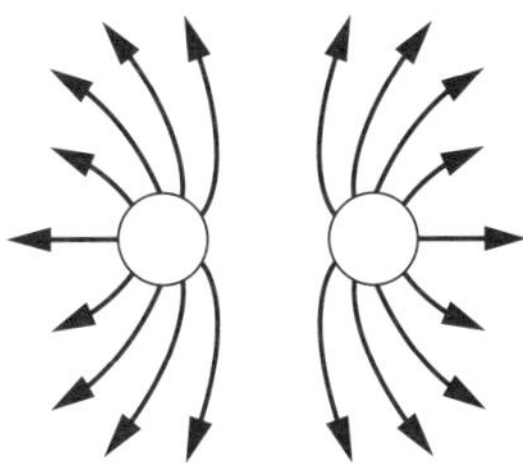

The best description of the two charges is that the:

A. charges are both positive

B. charges are both negative

C. charges can be either both positive or both negative

D. left-hand charge is positive and the right-hand charge is negative.

Question 2 VCE Physics 2017 (A) 1

A group of students is considering how to create a magnetic monopole. Which one of the following is correct?

A. Break a bar magnet in half.

B. Pass a current through a long solenoid.

C. Pass a current through a circular loop of wire.

D. It is not known how to create a magnetic monopole.

Use the following information to answer Questions 3 and 4.

A wire carrying a current of 10 A is placed in a uniform magnetic field of $B = 4.0 \times 10^{-4}$ T, as shown below. 10 cm of the wire is in the field.

Question 3 VCE Physics 2018 (A) 1

Which one of the following best gives the magnitude of the force acting on the wire?

A. 4.0×10^{-2} N

B. 4.0×10^{-4} N

C. 1.6×10^{-8} N

D. 4.0×10^{-12} N

Question 4 VCE Physics 2018 (A) 2

Which one of the following best gives the direction of the force acting on the wire?

A. out of page

B. into page

C. right

D. left

EXAM QUESTIONS

Question 5 VCE Physics 2018 (A) 3

A straight wire carries a current of 10 A.
Which one of the following diagrams best illustrates the magnetic field associated with this current?

A.

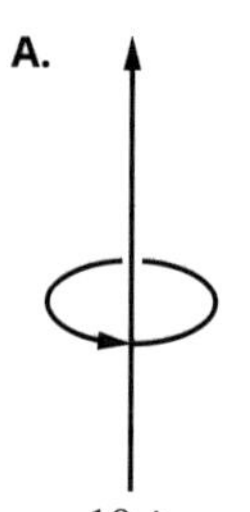

B.

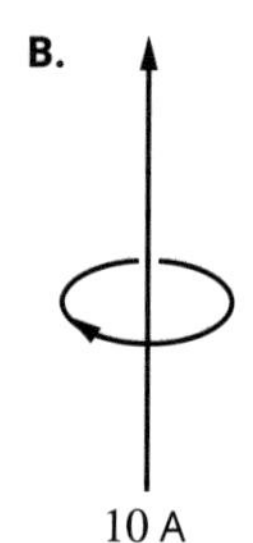

C.

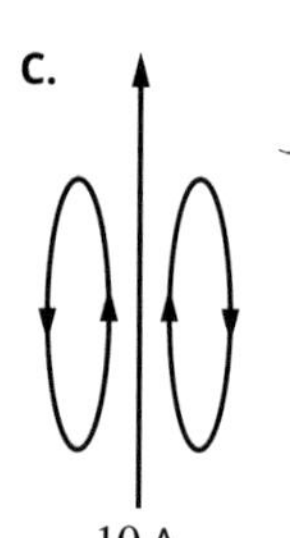

D.

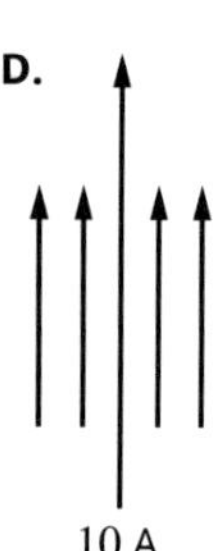

Question 6 VCE Physics 2018 (A) 4

A small sphere has a charge of 2.0×10^{-6} C on it. Take $k = 8.99 \times 10^{9}$ N m^{2} C^{-2}.
The strength of the electric field due to this charge at a point 3.0 m from the sphere is best given by:

A. 2.0×10^{-3} V m^{-1}

B. 6.0×10^{-3} V m^{-1}

C. 9.0×10^{-3} V m^{-1}

D. 2.0×10^{3} V m^{-1}

Question 7 VCE Physics 2017 (A) 2

Millikan, a famous scientist, measured the size of the electron charge by balancing an upwards electric force with a gravitational force on a small oil drop. In a repeat of this experiment, an oil drop with a charge of 9.6×10^{-19} C was placed in an electric field of 10^{4} V m^{-1}.

Which one of the following is closest to the electrical force on the oil drop?

A. 9.6×10^{-14} N

B. 9.6×10^{-15} N

C. 9.6×10^{-22} N

D. 9.6×10^{-23} N

Question 8 VCE Physics 2017 (A) 3

Two large charged plates with equal and opposite charges are placed close together, as shown in the diagram below. A distance of 5.0 mm separates the plates. The electric field between the plates is equal to 1000 N C^{-1}.

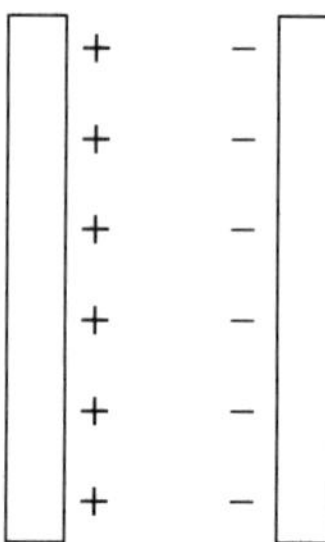

Which one of the following is closest to the voltage difference between the plates?

A. 5.0 V

B. 200 V

C. 5000 V

D. 5 000 000 V

ISBN 978 0 6557 0029 6

EXAM QUESTIONS

Question 9 VCE Physics 2020 (A) 2

Jupiter's moon Ganymede is its largest satellite.
Ganymede has a mass of 1.5×10^{23} kg and a radius of 2.6×10^{6} m.
Which one of the following is closest to the magnitude of Ganymede's surface gravity?

A. $0.8\,m\,s^{-2}$

B. $1.5\,m\,s^{-2}$

C. $3.8\,m\,s^{-2}$

D. $9.8\,m\,s^{-2}$

Question 10 VCE Physics 2018 (A) 7

At one point on Earth's surface at a distance *R* from the centre of Earth, the gravitational field strength is measured as $9.76\,N\,kg^{-1}$.

Which one of the following is closest to Earth's gravitational field strength at a distance 2*R* **above** the surface of Earth at that point?

A. $1.08\,N\,kg^{-1}$

B. $2.44\,N\,kg^{-1}$

C. $3.25\,N\,kg^{-1}$

D. $4.88\,N\,kg^{-1}$

Question 11 VCE Physics 2021 (A) 2

The diagram below shows the electric field lines between four charged spheres: P, Q, R and S. The magnitude of the charge on each sphere is the same.

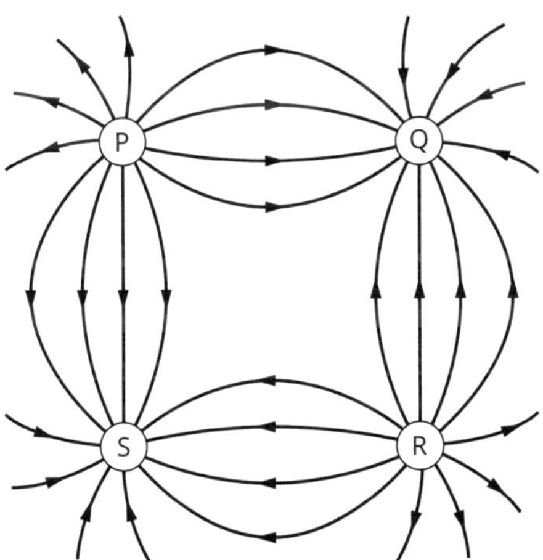

Which of the following correctly identifies the type of charge (+ positive or – negative) that resides on each of the spheres P, Q, R and S?

	P	Q	R	S
A.	–	+	–	+
B.	+	–	+	–
C.	–	–	+	+
D.	+	+	–	–

EXAM QUESTIONS

Short-answer questions

Question 1 (3 marks) VCE Physics 2021 (B) 1

Two identical bar magnets of the same magnetic field strength are arranged at right angles to each other and at the same distance from point P, as shown in the figure below.

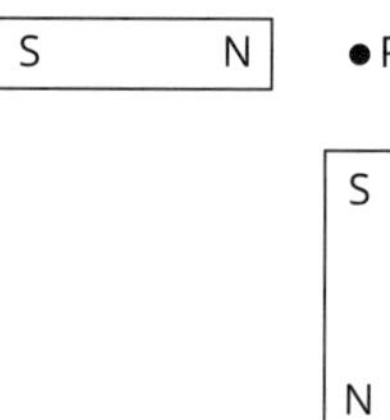

a. At point P on the figure, draw an arrow indicating the direction of the combined magnetic field of the two bar magnets. 1 mark

b. Calculate the magnitude of the combined magnetic field strength of the two bar magnets if each bar magnet has a magnetic field strength of 10.0 mT at point P. 2 marks

Question 2 (9 marks) VCE Physics 2021 (B) 5

The figure below shows a stationary electron (e^-) in a uniform magnetic field between two parallel plates. The plates are separated by a distance of 6.0×10^{-3} m, and they are connected to a 200 V power supply and a switch. Initially, the plates are uncharged. Assume that gravitational effects on the electron are negligible.

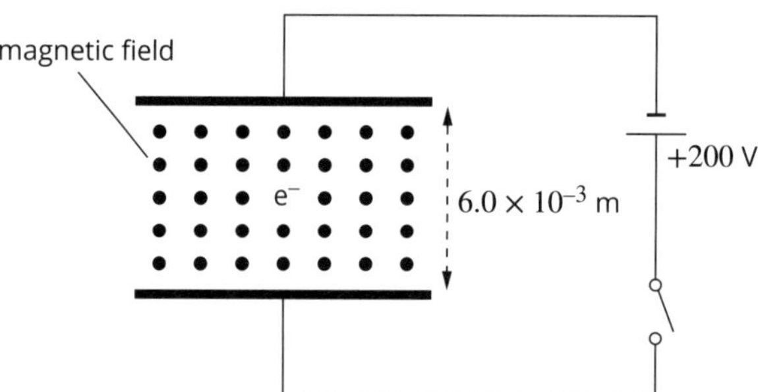

a. Explain why the magnetic field does not exert a force on the electron. Justify your answer with an appropriate formula. 2 marks

The switch is now closed.

b. Determine the magnitude and the direction of any electric force now acting on the electron. Show your working. 3 marks

 ISBN 978 0 6557 0029 6

c. Ravi and Mia discuss what they think will happen regarding the size and the direction of the magnetic force on the electron after the switch is closed.

Ravi says that there will be a magnetic force of constant magnitude, but it will be continually changing direction.

Mia says that there will be a constantly increasing magnetic force, but it will always be acting in the same direction.

Evaluate these two statements, giving clear reasons for your answer. 4 marks

Question 3 (3 marks) VCE Physics 2013 (A) 7

A satellite is in a geostationary circular orbit over Earth's equator. It remains vertically above the same point X on the equator, as shown in the figure below.

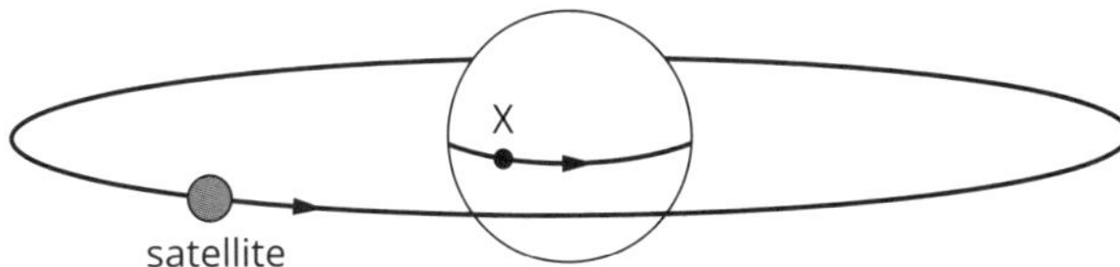

Data

mass of Earth	$M_E = 6.0 \times 10^{24}$ kg
radius of Earth	$R_E = 6.4 \times 10^{6}$ m
mass of satellite	1000 kg
universal gravitational constant	$G = 6.7 \times 10^{-11}$ N m^2 kg^{-2}

a. Calculate the period of the orbit of the satellite. 1 mark

b. Calculate the radius of the orbit of the satellite from the centre of Earth. 2 marks

Question 4 (2 marks) VCE Physics 2013 (A) 14

Two solenoids are shown in the figure below. Current is flowing through their coils and both of them are generating magnetic fields. Their combined field is much greater than Earth's field.

Sketch at least **four** field lines in the space enclosed by the dashed rectangle. Mark the direction of each field line that you draw.

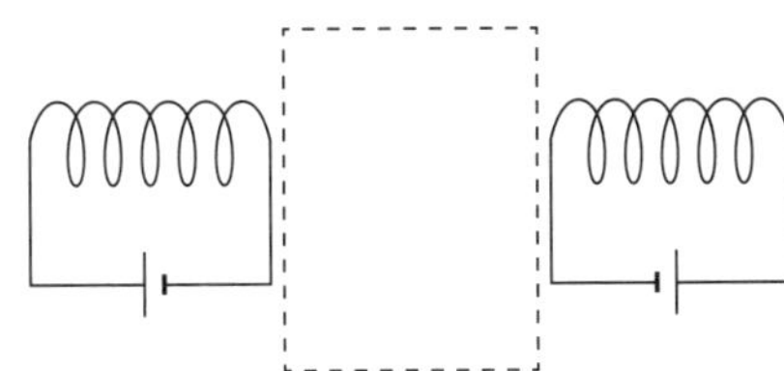

ISBN 978 0 6557 0029 6

EXAM QUESTIONS

Question 5 (5 marks) VCE Physics 2018 (B) 1

An electric field accelerates a proton between two plates. The proton exits into a region of uniform magnetic field at right angles to its path, directed out of the page, as shown in the figure below.

Data

mass of proton	1.7×10^{-27} kg
charge on proton	$+1.6 \times 10^{-19}$ C
accelerating voltage	10 kV
distance between plates	20 cm
strength of magnetic field	2.0×10^{-2} T

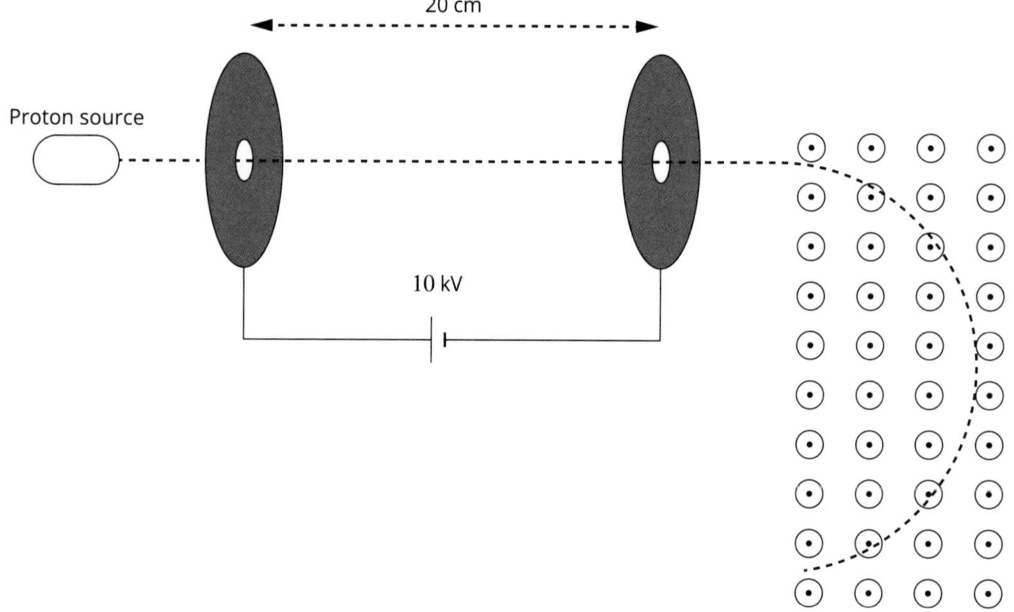

a. Calculate the strength of the electric field between the plates. 1 mark

b. Calculate the speed of the proton as it exits the electric field. Show your working. 2 marks

c. With a different accelerating voltage, the proton exits the electric field at a speed of 1.0×10^{6} m s^{-1}. Calculate the radius of the path of this proton in the magnetic field. Show your working. 2 marks

 ISBN 978 0 6557 0029 6

EXAM QUESTIONS

Question 6 (8 marks) VCE Physics 2018 (B)

The spacecraft *Juno* has been put into orbit around Jupiter. The table below contains information about the planet Jupiter and the spacecraft *Juno*. The figure below shows gravitational field strength ($N\,kg^{-1}$) as a function of distance from the centre of Jupiter.

Data

mass of Jupiter	1.90×10^{27} kg
radius of Jupiter	7.00×10^{7} m
mass of spacecraft *Juno*	1500 kg

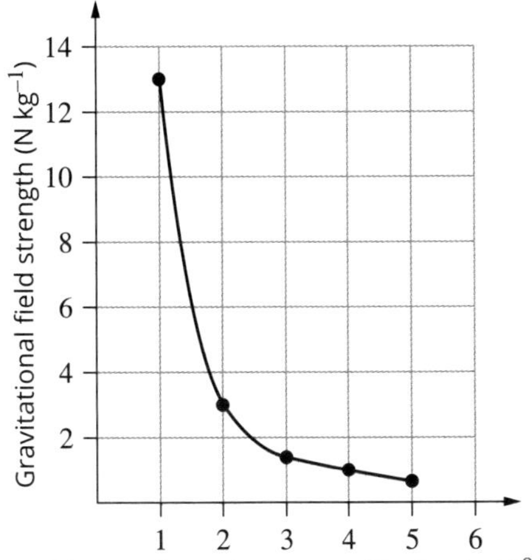

a. Calculate the gravitational force acting on *Juno* by Jupiter when *Juno* is at a distance of 2.0×10^{8} m from the centre of Jupiter. Show your working. 2 marks

b. Use the graph above to estimate the magnitude of the change in gravitational potential energy of the spacecraft *Juno* as it moves from a distance of 2.0×10^{8} m to a distance of 1.0×10^{8} m from the centre of Jupiter. Show your working. 3 marks

c. Europa is a moon of Jupiter. It has a circular orbit of radius 6.70×10^{8} m around Jupiter. Calculate the period of Europa's orbit. Show your working. 3 marks

UNIT 3

How do fields explain motion and electricity?

AREA OF STUDY 3

How are fields used in electricity generation?

Outcome 3

Analyse and evaluate an electricity generation and distribution system.

Key knowledge

Generation of electricity

- calculate magnetic flux when the magnetic field is perpendicular to the area, and describe the qualitative effect of differing angles between the area and the field: $\Phi_B = B_{\perp}A$
- investigate and analyse theoretically and practically the generation of electromotive force (EMF), including AC voltage and calculations using induced EMF: $\varepsilon = -N\frac{\Delta\Phi_B}{\Delta t}$, with reference to:
  - rate of change of magnetic flux
  - number of loops through which the flux passes
  - direction of induced EMF in a coil
- explain the production of DC voltage in DC generators and AC voltage in alternators, including the use of split ring commutators and slip rings respectively
- describe the production of electricity using photovoltaic cells and the need for an inverter to convert power from DC to AC for use in the home (not including details of semiconductors action or inverter circuitry)

Transmission of electricity

- compare sinusoidal AC voltages produced as a result of the uniform rotation of a loop in a constant magnetic field with reference to frequency, period, amplitude, peak-to-peak voltage (V_{p-p}) and peak-to-peak current (I_{p-p})
- compare alternating voltage expressed as the root-mean-square (rms) to a constant DC voltage developing the same power in a resistive component
- analyse transformer action with reference to electromagnetic induction for an ideal transformer: $\frac{N_1}{N_2} = \frac{V_1}{V_2} = \frac{I_2}{I_1}$
- analyse the supply of power by considering transmission losses across transmission lines.

- You will now be able to complete Worksheet 22.

Electromagnetic induction and transmission of electricity

In the nineteenth century, scientists studying the relatively new field of electrical currents discovered that moving charges produce magnetic effects. After this, Michael Faraday, an English scientist, was convinced that the reverse should also be true—a magnetic field should be able to produce an electric current. It was discovered that a *change* in a magnetic field, when a magnet is moved closer to a conductor, leads to an induced EMF (electromotive force), which in turn produces a current. An EMF can be induced by moving a magnet in and out of a coil or moving a straight conductor in a magnetic field.

INDUCING AN EMF IN A MAGNETIC FIELD

The production of an induced EMF, ε, by a changing magnetic flux, is called **electromagnetic induction**. **Magnetic flux** is essentially the total number of magnetic field lines passing through any given area. Figure 3.3.1a represents a strong magnetic field acting over a small area, and this has the same magnetic flux as a weaker magnetic field acting over a larger area (Figure 3.3.1b).

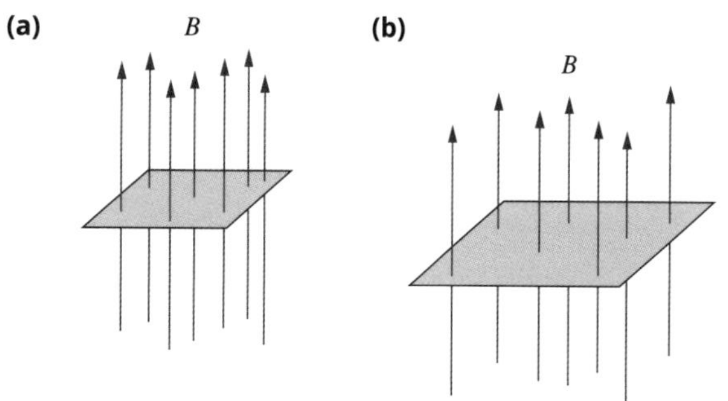

Figure 3.3.1 The magnetic flux is the same in (a) and (b).

Magnetic flux is defined as the product of the strength of the magnetic field, B, and the area of the field perpendicular to the field lines, A. It is given by the formula:

> $\Phi_B = BA$
>
> where Φ_B is the magnetic flux in weber (Wb, where 1 Wb = 1 T m^2)
> B is the magnetic field (T)
> A is the area perpendicular to the magnetic field (m^2).

A subscript $\perp$ can be included in the formula to indicate that the area referred to is perpendicular to the magnetic field ($\Phi_B = BA_\perp$), or the component of the magnetic field is perpendicular to the area ($\Phi_B = B_\perp A$).

The amount of magnetic flux varies with the angle of the field to the area under investigation. It is a maximum when the area is perpendicular (at 90°) to the field, and zero when the area is parallel to the field. This can be represented by the following formula:

$$\Phi_B = BA\cos\theta$$

In Figure 3.3.2, the charges in the wire are moving due to the force they are experiencing from the magnetic field. One end of the conductor will become more positively charged, the other more negatively charged and a potential difference, ΔV, or EMF, ε, will be induced between the ends of the conductor. This can be represented by the formula:

> $\varepsilon = lvB$
>
> where ε is the induced EMF (V)
> l is the length of the conductor (m)
> v is the speed of the conductor perpendicular to the magnetic field (m s^{-1})
> B is the strength of the magnetic field (T).

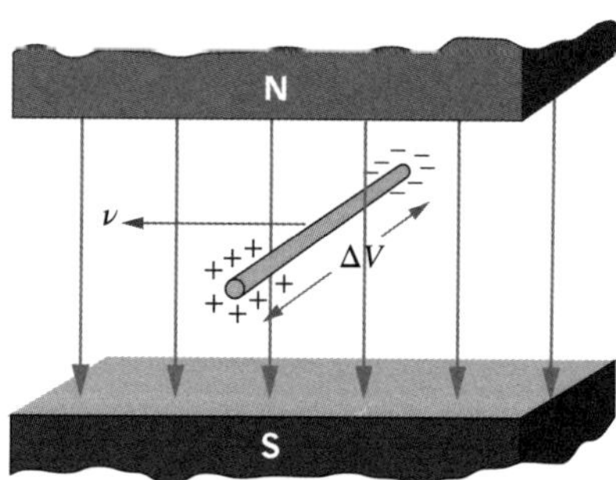

Figure 3.3.2 A potential difference, ΔV, will be produced across a straight wire moving to the left in a downwards-pointing magnetic field.

INDUCED EMF FROM A CHANGING MAGNETIC FLUX

Faraday's investigations led him to conclude that the average EMF induced in a conducting loop in which there is a changing magnetic flux is proportional to the negative rate of change of flux. This is now known as **Faraday's law** of induction and is one of the basic laws of electromagnetism. If the flux through N turns (or loops) of a coil changes from Φ_1 to Φ_2 ($\Delta\Phi_B$) during a time Δt, then the average induced EMF during this time will be:

> $\varepsilon = -N\dfrac{\Delta\Phi_B}{\Delta t}$

The negative sign in Faraday's law indicates direction. For questions involving only magnitudes, you should not use the negative sign or any negative quantities.

 ISBN 978 0 6557 0029 6

KEY KNOWLEDGE

LENZ'S LAW AND ITS APPLICATIONS

The Russian physicist Heinrich Lenz developed a law to explain how electromagnetic induction obeys the principles of conservation of energy, and which explains the direction of the induced EMF. This is known as **Lenz's law**. Lenz used the idea of nature trying to oppose any applied force. Lenz's law states that when an EMF is generated by a change in magnetic flux (Faraday's law), the induced EMF produces a current, which, in turn, produces a magnetic field that opposes the original change in flux. For example, when an induced current flows through a coil and a galvanometer, the magnetic field produced by the coil has a direction that repels the incoming pole of a permanent magnet. The same happens if the permanent magnet is pulled out of the coil; however, the magnetic field produced tries to attract the withdrawing permanent magnet back inside the coil again.

A galvanometer is a type of sensitive ammeter; it is an instrument for detecting small electric currents.

In Figure 3.3.3a, the north end of a magnet is brought towards a coil from right to left, inducing a magnetic field in which the current flows anticlockwise.

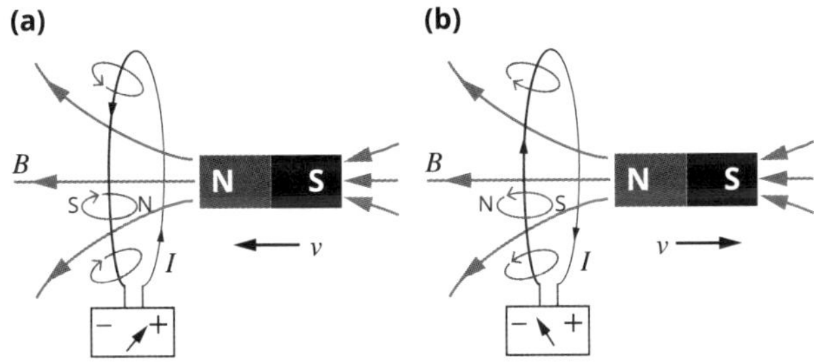

Figure 3.3.3 (a) The north end of a magnet is brought towards a coil from right to left, inducing a current that flows anticlockwise. (b) Pulling the north end of the magnet away from the coil from left to right induces a current in a clockwise direction.

There are three distinct steps to determine the induced current direction according to Lenz's law:

1 What is the change that is happening?
2 What will oppose the change and/or restore the original conditions?
3 What must be the current direction to match this opposition?

For example, consider Figure 3.3.4, in which the arrow indicates the direction the magnet is moving. In this figure, the south pole of a magnet is moved towards the horizontal coil held above it.

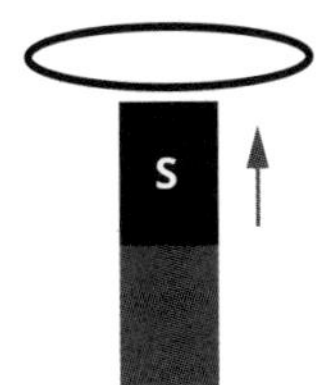

Figure 3.3.4 The south end of a magnet is brought towards a coil.

To find the direction of the induced current, the three distinct steps will be followed.

1 What is the change that is happening?

The magnetic field direction in the coil will be downwards towards the south pole of the magnet. As the magnet is brought closer to the coil, the downwards flux in the coil from the magnet will increase (the coil initially had zero magnetic field, hence zero magnetic flux). So the change in flux is increasing downwards.

2 What will oppose this change?

The magnetic flux is increasing downwards as the magnet moves towards the coil, so this means the induced magnetic field that opposes the change would act upwards.

3 What is the current direction?

In order to oppose the change, the current direction would be anticlockwise when viewed from above (using the right-hand grip rule).

It is important to note it is the flux, not the field, and the rate of change of flux, not the absolute size of the flux, that matters.

Induced current direction by changing area

As magnetic flux $\Phi_B = B_{\perp}A$, a change can be created by any method that causes a change to either of the variables B or A. So an induced EMF can be created in three ways:

1 by changing the strength of the magnetic field
2 by changing the area of the coil within the magnetic field
3 by changing the orientation of the coil with respect to the direction of the magnetic field.

Figure 3.3.5 illustrates an example of the direction of an induced current that results during a decrease in the area of a coil.

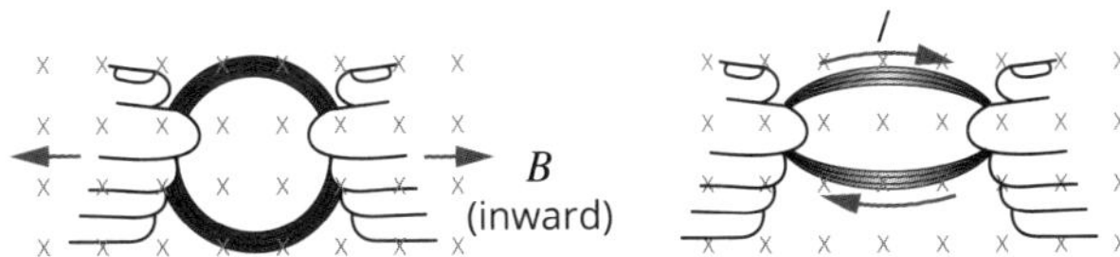

Figure 3.3.5 Inducing a current by changing the area of a coil

As the area of the coil decreases due to its changing shape, the flux through the coil (which is directed into the page) also decreases. Applying Lenz's law, the direction of the induced current would oppose this change and will be such that it acts to increase the magnetic flux through the coil inward. Using the right-hand grip rule, a current would therefore flow in a clockwise direction while the area is changing.

In Figure 3.3.6 on the following page, the coil is being rotated within the magnetic field. The effect is the same as reducing the area. The amount of flux flowing through the coil is reduced as the coil changes from being perpendicular to the field to being parallel to the field. An induced EMF would be created while the coil is being rotated. This becomes particularly important in determining the direction of the currrent in a generator.

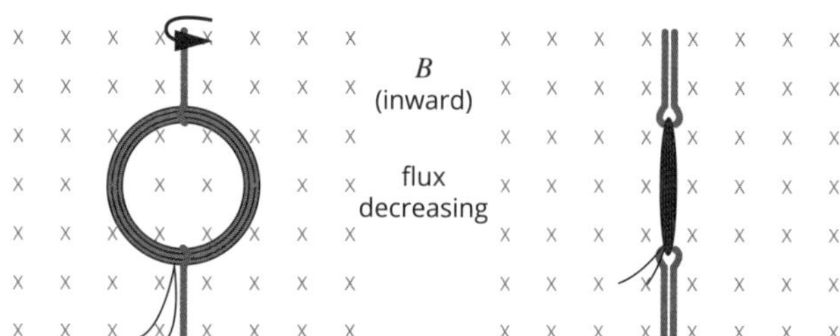

Figure 3.3.6 An EMF is induced when the orientation of a coil within a magnetic field is changed by rotating the coil, reducing the amount of flux through the coil.

- **You will now be able to conduct Practical activities 11 and 12, and complete Worksheet 23.**

Generators

A machine that converts mechanical energy into electrical energy is called a **generator** or **alternator**. The electric generator is probably the most important practical application of Faraday's discovery of electromagnetic induction. This machine relies on the induction principle between a coil and a magnetic field. The principle of electric power generators is the same whether the result is alternating current or direct current. Relative motion between a coil and a magnetic field induces an EMF in the coil.

The construction of a generator or alternator is very similar to that of an electric motor. A coil is rotated in a magnetic field, which will induce an alternating current in the coil. How that current is harnessed will determine whether the device is an AC alternator or a DC generator.

An AC alternator has slip rings that transfer the alternating nature of the current in the coil to the output (Figure 3.3.7a). A DC generator has a split ring commutator to reverse the current direction every half-turn, so that the output current is always in the same direction (Figure 3.3.7b).

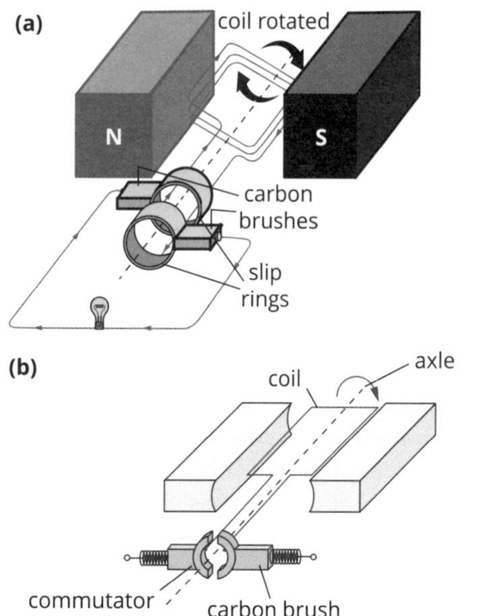

Figure 3.3.7 The main features of (a) an AC alternator and (b) a DC generator

An AC generator produces an alternating current that varies sinusoidally over time with the change in magnetic flux. The alternating current produced by power stations and supplied to cities varies sinusoidally at a frequency of 50 Hz. The peak value of the voltage of domestic power (V_p) is ±340 V, and the peak-to-peak voltage (V_{p-p}) is 680 V. This is shown in Figure 3.3.8.

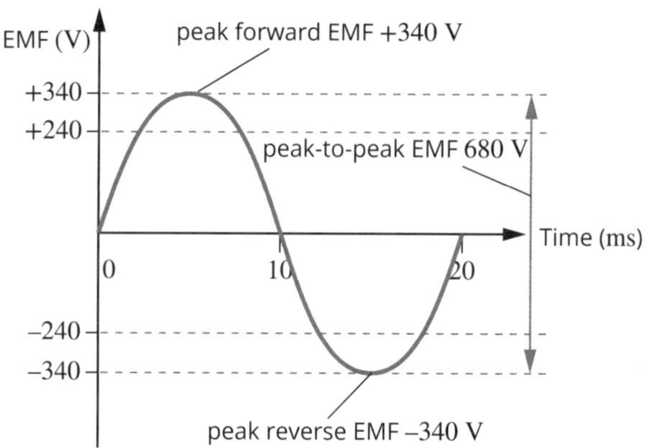

Figure 3.3.8 The voltage from Australian power points oscillates between +340 V and −340 V, 50 times each second. The value of a DC supply that would supply the same average power is 240 V.

- **You will now be able to conduct Practical activity 13 and complete Worksheets 24 and 25.**

Sometimes it is more useful to know the average power produced in a circuit. The average power can be obtained by using the **root mean square**, or rms value. The rms value of domestic mains voltage in Australia is 240 V. The root mean square voltage, V_{rms}, is the value of an equivalent steady voltage (DC) supply that would provide the same average power as the AC supply.

$$V_{rms} = \frac{V_p}{\sqrt{2}} \text{ and } I_{rms} = \frac{I_p}{\sqrt{2}}$$

where V_p is the peak voltage (V)
I_p is the peak current (A).

Electric power is the rate, per unit time, at which electrical energy is transferred by an electric current. The power supplied in an electrical circuit is given by $P = VI$.

Once the V_{rms} is known, it can be used to find the average power in a resistive AC circuit. The formula is:

$$P = V_{rms}I_{rms}$$
$$= \frac{1}{2} \times V_p \times I_p$$

 ISBN 978 0 6557 0029 6

KEY KNOWLEDGE

PHOTOVOLTAIC CELLS

Photovoltaic cells, or solar cells, generate electricity when they are exposed to light. They are made of a semiconductor material. When light hits this material, electrons are ejected from the atoms in the semiconductor. This is due to the photoelectric effect (see Unit 4 Area of Study 1). The free electrons are then able to flow through connecting wires, generating a current.

The cells produce a DC current. To convert DC to AC so that the electricity can be used in households, an inverter is used.

TRANSFORMERS AND LARGE-SCALE POWER DISTRIBUTION

A **transformer** is a device for increasing and decreasing an alternating current (AC) voltage, which is an essential part of any electrical distribution system. A transformer works on the principle of a changing magnetic flux inducing an EMF. No matter what the size or application, it will consist of two coils, known as the primary and secondary coils. These two coils are wound onto a common soft iron core (Figure 3.3.9a). If the primary coil is fed with an AC voltage, the iron core ensures that all the flux generated in the primary coil also passes through the secondary coil. Figure 3.3.9b illustrates the symbol used in circuit diagrams for an iron-core transformer.

(a)

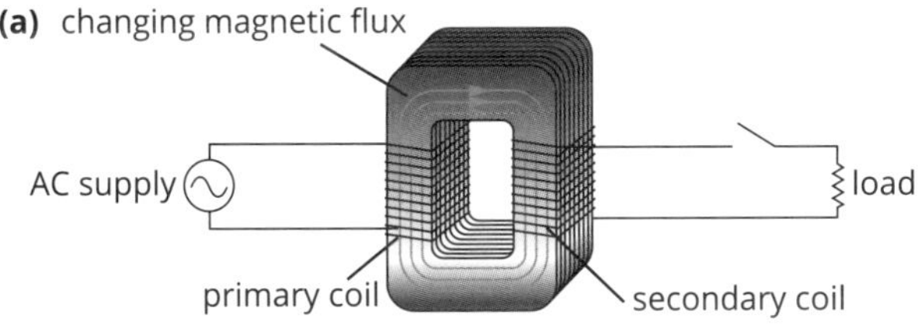

(b)

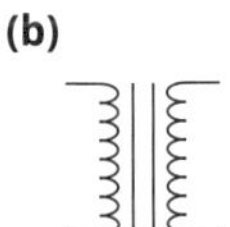

Figure 3.3.9 (a) A transformer; (b) the symbol used in circuit diagrams for a transformer

Ideal transformers are 100% efficient; real transformers are often over 99% efficient, and for this reason power losses within the transformer can be ignored in calculations.

The transformer equation can be written in different ways, but is based on:

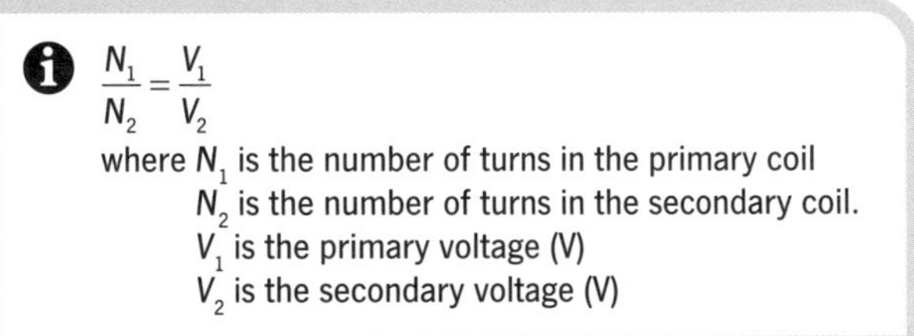

$$\frac{N_1}{N_2} = \frac{V_1}{V_2}$$

where N_1 is the number of turns in the primary coil
N_2 is the number of turns in the secondary coil.
V_1 is the primary voltage (V)
V_2 is the secondary voltage (V)

A **step-up transformer** increases the secondary voltage compared with the primary voltage. A **step-down transformer** decreases the secondary voltage compared with the primary voltage.

The transformer equation can also be written in terms of current:

$$\frac{N_1}{N_2} = \frac{I_2}{I_1}$$

POWER OUTPUT

Transformers will not work with DC voltage since it has a constant, unchanging current that creates no change in magnetic flux. A transformer works on the basis of a changing current (AC voltage) in the primary coil inducing a changing magnetic flux, which therefore induces a current in the secondary coil. The AC electrical supply from a generator is easily stepped up or down by transformers, so AC is the preferred form of electrical energy in large-scale transmission systems.

Large-scale transmission systems involve current travelling large distances and so even relatively good electrical conductors such as copper have a significant resistance. The efficient transmission of the electrical energy with the least amount of power loss over that distance is therefore important to consider.

Electrical power loss is proportional to the square of the current:

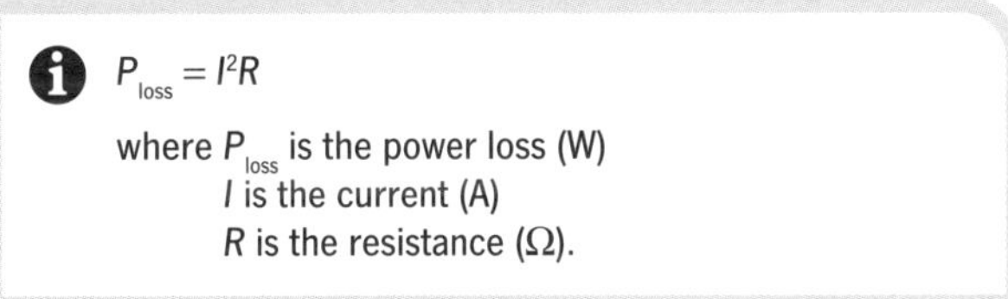

$$P_{loss} = I^2R$$

where P_{loss} is the power loss (W)
I is the current (A)
R is the resistance (Ω).

Using this equation, it can be recognised that electrical engineers use very high voltages ($P = VI$) to keep the currents small and the loss of power as heat to a minimum.

- **You will now be able to conduct Practical activities 14 and 15 and complete Worksheets 26 and 27.**

WORKSHEET 22

Knowledge review—magnets and magnetism

1 Tesla is a unit of:

A magnetic flux

B magnetic inductance

C electric vehicle performance

D magnetic flux density

2 Identify which of the following statements is correct.

A The conductivity of iron and iron compounds is better than ferromagnetic materials in general.

B The conductivity of ferromagnetic materials is better than iron and iron compounds.

C The conductivity of iron and iron compounds is very high.

D The conductivity of iron and iron compounds is the same as that of ferromagnetic materials.

3 Two south magnetic poles brought near each other will:

A attract each other

B repel each other

C form one stronger south pole

D form one stronger north pole

4 All electric currents produce a magnetic field.

true

false

5 The relationship between electricity and magnetism is termed:

A magnetic role reversal

B the electromagnetic spectrum

C electromagnetism

D scary

6 Identify which of the following is not a good conductor.

A copper

B silver

C aluminium

D plastic

7 An electromagnet is:

A a temporary magnet created when electric current flows around a ferromagnetic material

B a permanent magnet causing an electric current to flow around a ferromagnetic material

C a temporary magnet created when a ferromagnetic material is electrified

D a permanent magnet created when a ferromagnetic material is electrified

8 A simple electromagnet made from a coil of current-carrying wire around an iron nail can be made stronger by:

A adding more coils of wire to the nail

B using a battery with a smaller potential difference

C reversing the direction of the current in the wire around the nail

D removing the nail and retaining just the current-carrying wire

 ISBN 978 0 6557 0029 6

WORKSHEET 23

Inducing an EMF

1 A magnet is dropped, with the north end facing down, through a conducting coil, inducing a current. Which of the options in the table below describes the direction of the current when viewed from above the coil?

	Magnet entering the coil	Magnet exiting the coil
A	clockwise	anticlockwise
B	anticlockwise	clockwise
C	clockwise	clockwise
D	anticlockwise	anticlockwise

2 On the diagrams below, draw the direction of the induced current in a coil as it enters or exits a magnetic field.

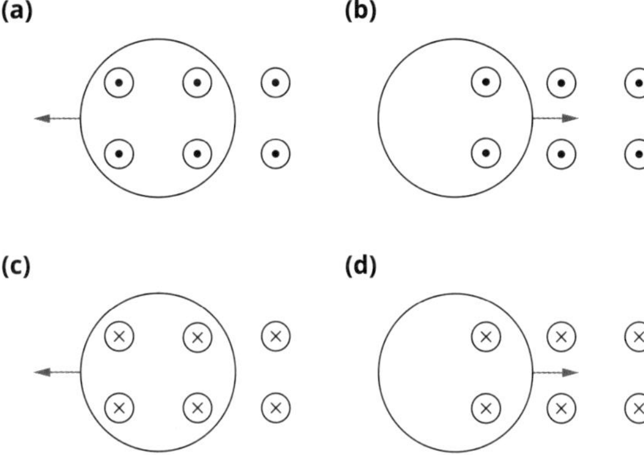

3 A square coil of 50 turns and with a side length of 3.0 cm long is moving at 12 cm s^{-1} into a uniform magnetic field of 4.0×10^{-4} T, as shown in Figure 3.3.10. The coil has a resistance of 6.0 Ω (represented by a single resistor symbol). At the instant shown, it is halfway into the field.

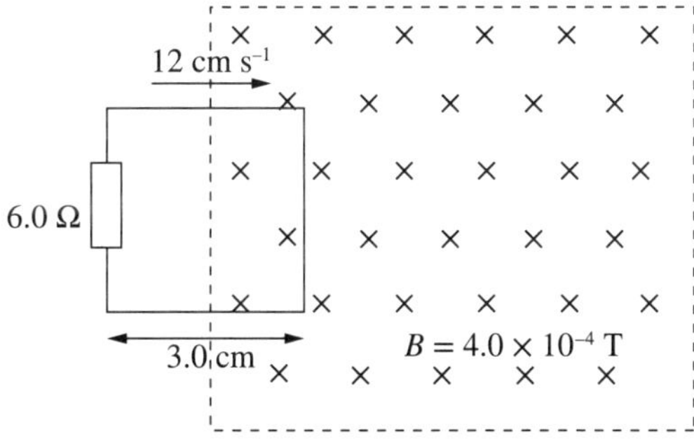

Figure 3.3.10 A coil moving into a magnetic field

a How much flux is threading the coil at the instant shown?

b What is size of the EMF generated in the coil?

c Describe and calculate the forces, if any, acting on the coil.

WORKSHEET 24

Modelling

The motor effect

Figure 3.3.11 shows a simplified view of a single square loop, SPQR, in a vertical, uniform magnetic field. The loop is free to rotate about an axis inside the field. The diagram on the right is a side-on view along the axis. Each side of the loop is 4.0 cm in length and the strength of the magnetic field is 8.0 T. The loop carries a current of 200 mA and is shown at an angle of 35° to the horizontal.

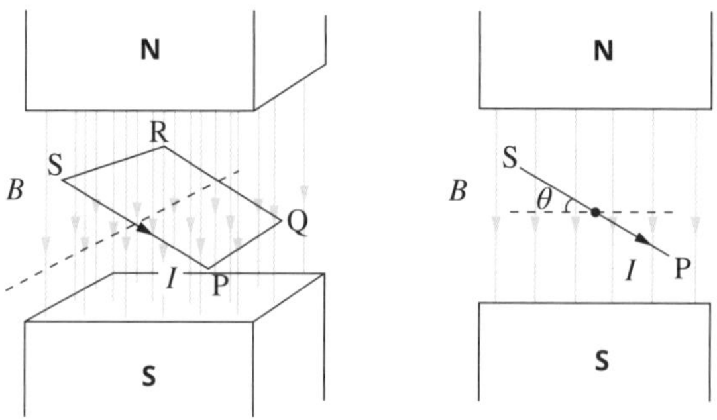

Figure 3.3.11 A simple loop of wire in a magnetic field

1 What is the magnetic force acting on side PQ? (Include a direction in your answer.)

2 What is the magnetic force acting on side RS? (Include a direction in your answer.)

3 What is the magnitude of the torque on the coil?

4 What effect will this torque have on the loop?

5 Calculate the magnetic forces acting on sides SP and QR. (Include a direction in your answer.)

6 What effect will these forces have on the loop?

7 At what angle will the torque acting on the loop be a maximum?

 ISBN 978 0 6557 0029 6

8 What happens to the forces on sides PQ and RS (and to the torque) when the angle θ is 180°?

9 Describe what happens to the forces on PQ and RS (and to the torque) when the angle θ exceeds 180°.

10 If this loop is to continue to be rotated by the magnetic forces, what needs to happen to the current? Describe how this action can be applied to the loop. What mechanism can you use to achieve this?

11 Explain three further modifications or additions that could be made to this arrangement to turn it into a practical electric motor.

WORKSHEET 25

Modelling

Back to motors and generators

1 Figure 3.3.12 shows the main features of a DC motor. Add the missing labels and describe the purpose of each feature.

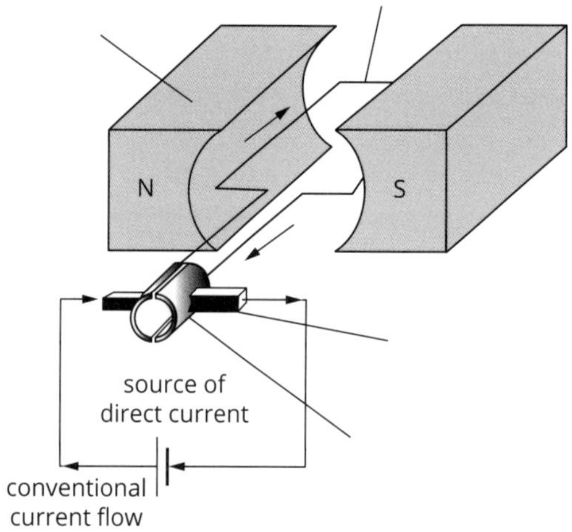

Figure 3.3.12 A simple DC motor

2 The DC motor shown has the magnetic poles shaped to create a radial field. What advantage does this have over flat magnetic poles?

3 A simple motor can be a generator and a simple generator can be a motor. Describe, in simple point form, the similarities and differences between simple motors and generators.

Similarities	Differences

4 An electric motor rotates due to the torque applied on the coil by the field as a result of the interaction of the current through the coil with the magnetic field of the motor. However, the action of the coil moving through the motor's magnetic field also causes a voltage to be induced. Name this induced voltage and state the direction in which it will act.

5 About 95% of the world's electric motors run on AC rather than DC current. In a DC motor, the magnetic field is stationary (the stator), and the coil that carries the electric current rotates (the rotor). An AC induction motor works by producing a rotating magnetic field. Describe the structure and function of the rotor and stator in an AC induction motor.

6 Describe one advantage and one disadvantage of an AC induction motor.

 ISBN 978 0 6557 0029 6

7 Figure 3.3.13 shows a simple DC generator and an AC generator.

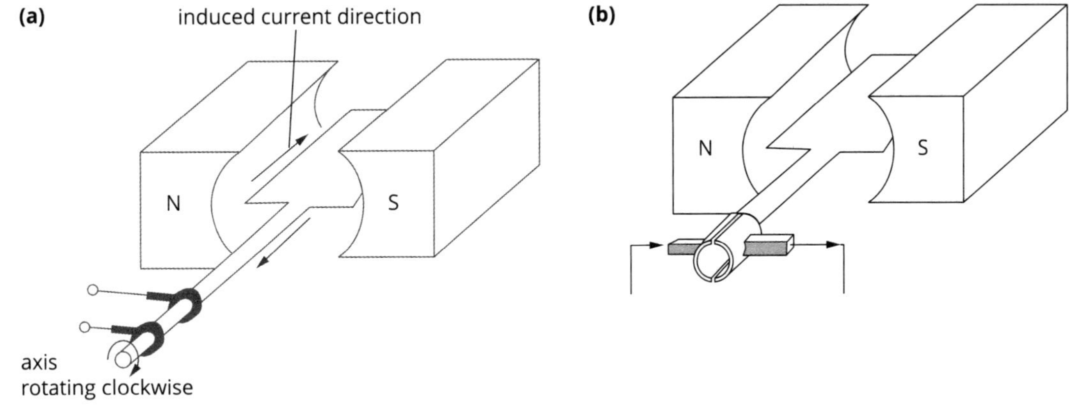

Figure 3.3.13 Simple DC and AC generators

Which of these generators is the AC generator and which is the DC generator? Explain your reasoning.

8 Sketch the output of the induced voltage from each of the generators in the space provided.

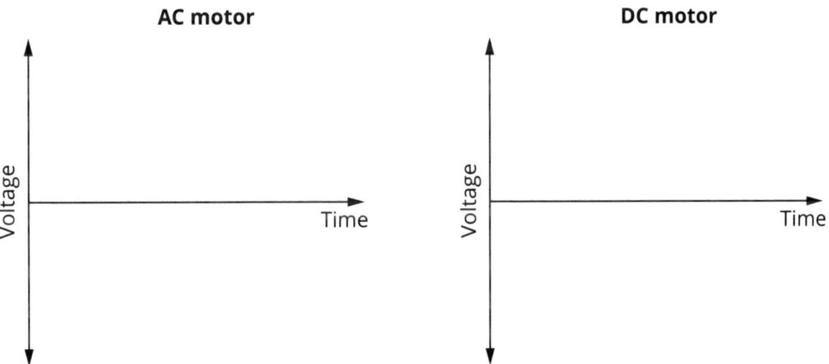

EXTENSION

9 Magnetic brakes can produce a strong braking force without the physical contact needed in standard drum or disc brakes. In the space provided, describe with the use of diagrams the operation of a magnetic brake.

WORKSHEET 26

Case study

Small-scale power transmission

A farmer has just bought a wind turbine that produces a maximum power of 12 kW at 250 V_{rms}. When the wind is not blowing well enough for this output, he plans to buy power from the grid. He also plans to sell power to the grid when he can't use all that is generated.

He places the turbine on the top of a hill behind his farmhouse, at a distance of 326 m. He buys some twin-core power cable from the local hardware store and strings it up on poles, as shown in Figure 3.3.14.

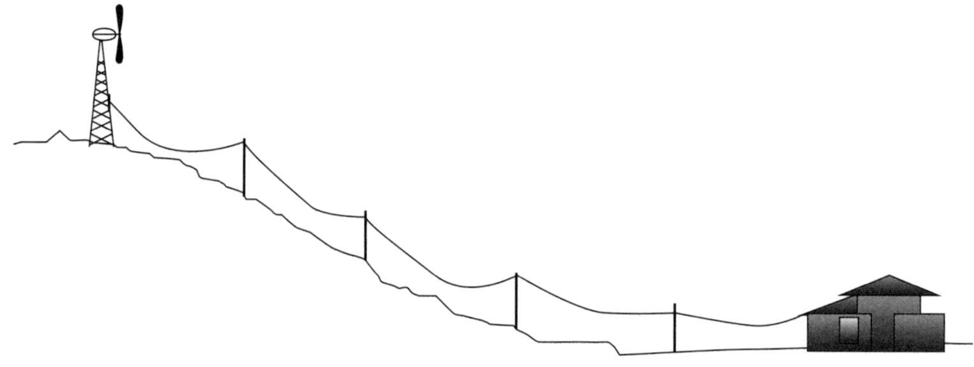

Figure 3.3.14 The wind turbine connected to the farmhouse

1 Each of the two cores within the cable has a resistance of $0.004\,\Omega\,m^{-1}$. What is the total resistance of the transmission circuit between the turbine and the house?

2 How much current does the turbine produce under optimum conditions (i.e. when operating at maximum power)?

3 Calculate the power loss in the cables.

4 What is the voltage drop across the transmission cables?

5 What voltage is available at the house?

 ISBN 978 0 6557 0029 6

After he discovers these issues, the farmer rings up his old physics teacher and asks her for help. She advises that step-up and step-down transformers with turn ratios of 25 : 1 will need to be installed so that the power can be transmitted at a higher voltage with less loss.

6 Where should these be installed and why?

A further suggestion was that another 326 m of the same twin-core cable can be strung up alongside the original cable. In this way, the two cores in each cable can be used in parallel, so that one twin cable provides the outwards path for the current and the other provides the return path.

For the remaining questions, assume that the turbine is operating at maximum power.

7 What will be the new resistance of the transmission line?

8 What will the voltages be at the input and output of the first transformer?

9 How much current will the line be carrying?

10 How much power will now be lost in transmission?

11 What will be the voltage drop across the transmission lines now?

12 What voltage will be available at the input of the second transformer?

13 What voltage will now be available at the house?

14 The farmer decides to invest in solar panels in his setup. Describe how the panels generate electricity, how they will be installed and the purpose of an inverter.

WORKSHEET 27

Literacy review—understanding electromagnetism

1 Define each of the following terms.

Term	Definition
commutator	
magnetic flux	
electromagnetic induction	
electromotive force (EMF)	
solenoid	
transformer	
peak-to-peak voltage	
root-mean-square voltage	
inverter	

2 Fill in the blanks from the following list of terms. Some terms may be used more than once.

coil	displacement	conductors	magnetic flux
attract	Faraday's	field	repel
motor	magnetic	right-hand	flux

a ____________ law defines the relationship between the number of turns in a coil, N, and the rate of change in ____________, Φ_B. ____________ is related to the strength of the ____________ field, the area enclosed by the wire loop, and the angle between them. We can say that the ____________ is proportional to the strength of the magnetic field.

b If two parallel ____________ carry current in the same direction, the forces ____________. If two parallel ____________ carry current in the opposite direction, the forces ____________. This can be proven using the ____________ rule.

ISBN 978 0 6557 0029 6

WORKSHEET 28

Reflection—How are fields used in electricity generation?

The following table lists the key knowledge covered in this area of study.

1 Reflect on how well you understand the concepts listed. Rate your learning by shading the circle that corresponds to your current level of understanding for each one.

Key knowledge	Not confident ◄				► Very confident
Calculations of magnetic flux $\Phi_B = BA$	○	○	○	○	○
Generation of an induced voltage from $\varepsilon = -N\frac{\Delta\Phi_B}{\Delta t}$	○	○	○	○	○
Operation of AC and DC generators and role of split ring commutators and slip rings $\frac{N_1}{N_2} = \frac{V_1}{V_2}$	○	○	○	○	○
Production of electricity from photovoltaic cells, including the role of the inverter	○	○	○	○	○
AC voltages, including peak and rms values	○	○	○	○	○
Transformer operation, including the transformer equation for an ideal transformer	○	○	○	○	○
Analysis and calculation of power and power losses through transmission lines	○	○	○	○	○

2 Consider the points you have shaded from Not confident to Very confident. List specific ideas you can identify that were challenging.

____

____

3 Write down two different strategies that you will apply to help further your understanding of these ideas.

____

____

PRACTICAL ACTIVITY 11

Experiment

Electromagnetic induction—the direction of the induced current in a wire

SUGGESTED DURATION

- 45 minutes data collection + 10 minutes analysis

MATERIALS

- galvanometer or current sensor
- horseshoe magnet
- electrical leads with alligator clips

INTRODUCTION

Just three years after Faraday's discovery of electromagnetic induction, Russian physicist Heinrich Lenz discovered a simple principle by which the direction of the induced EMF could be found. Lenz's law states that a current that is induced in a loop will create a flux that will oppose the change in flux that created the current.

The right-hand rule can be used to visualise the direction of the induced current. In this activity the direction of the current induced in a wire by a magnetic field is investigated.

AIM

To investigate the direction of the current induced in a wire by a magnetic field.

Safety

Complete a risk assessment before starting the activity.

METHOD

1 ▪ Connect a long copper wire to a galvanometer or current sensor using two leads with alligator clips. If using a current sensor, follow the directions of the manufacturer to set up an analogue display of current. Set a sample rate of 20–50 Hz.

2 ▪ Hold a part of the wire horizontally between the two poles of a horseshoe magnet, as shown in Figure 3.3.15.

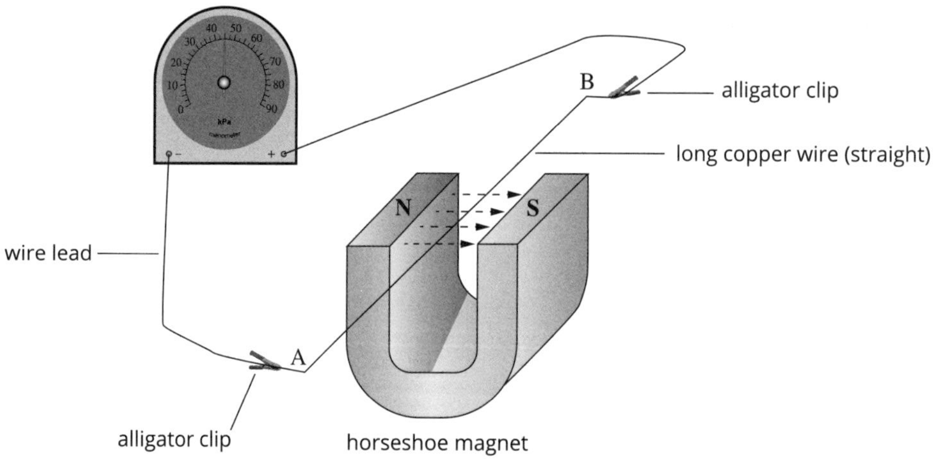

Figure 3.3.15 The experimental set-up

3 ▪ Keeping the wire horizontal and parallel to the line AB, move it vertically up and down within the magnetic field of the magnet. Observe and record the direction of the current induced in the wire as it is moved in each direction. Note the direction in the table in the Results section.

4 ▪ Keeping the wire horizontal and parallel to the line AB, move it horizontally from one pole of the magnet to the other. Observe and record the direction of the current induced in the wire as it is moved in each direction.

5 ▪ Finally, move the wire backwards and forwards along the line A–B, keeping it horizontal. Once again, observe and record the direction of the current induced in the wire as it is moved in each direction.

ISBN 978 0 6557 0029 6

PRACTICAL ACTIVITY 11

RESULTS

Movement of wire and current direction	
Direction of movement of wire	**Current direction or no current detected**
moving upwards within a magnetic field	
moving downwards within the magnetic field	
moving horizontally to the right	
moving horizontally to the left	
moving away parallel to the direction of the wire	
moving forward parallel to the direction of the wire	

DISCUSSION

Comment on the following with reference to the figure and your observations.

1 In which direction does the current flow when the wire is moved vertically upwards?

2 In which direction does current flow when the wire is moved vertically downwards?

3 What current is observed when the wire is moved horizontally within the magnetic field?

4 What current is observed when the wire is moved backwards and forwards along the line A–B within the magnetic field?

5 The relationship between the direction of the magnetic field, the direction of motion of the wire and the direction of the induced current can be shown by three mutually perpendicular arrows.

Write down what each of the arrows in the figure represents.

X ____________________

Y ____________________

Z ____________________

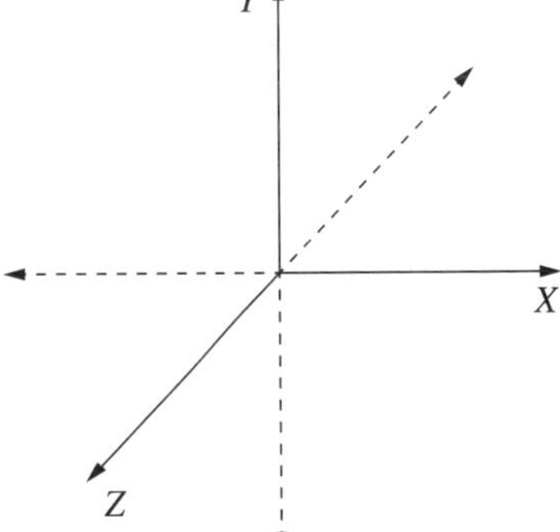

CONCLUSION

PRACTICAL ACTIVITY 12

Experiment

Faraday's law of electromagnetic induction

SUGGESTED DURATION

- 50 minutes data collection + 20 minutes analysis

INTRODUCTION

Michael Faraday (1791–1867) discovered a relationship between a changing magnetic flux, Φ_B, and the induced EMF within a conductor, ε. Known as Faraday's law, this relationship is defined by two key elements: the number of turns in a coil, N, and the change in magnetic flux, $\Delta\Phi_B$. In this activity, Faraday's law will be investigated by using magnets of different strength and increasing the rate at which the magnet passes through the coil.

AIM

To investigate quantitatively the relationship between induced voltage and magnetic flux, time and the number of turns in a coil of wire.

Safety

Be careful with magnets.

Strong magnets can disrupt electronic devices. Keep magnets away from computer hard drives, USB drives and phones.

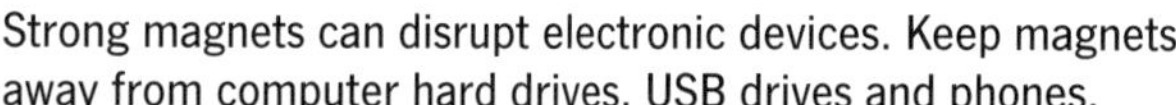

Neodymium magnets can severely pinch skin and are very fragile. Prior to starting the experiment, place the magnets in the plastic tubes—one magnet in one tube, two in the next, and so on. Seal the tubes to prevent the magnets from falling out.

Complete a risk assessment before starting the activity.

MATERIALS

- data-collection system
- voltage sensor (if not available, a CRO (cathode ray oscilloscope) or galvanometer can be used for a qualitative investigation)
- 200-, 400- and 800-turn coils (or other coils of known number of turns as available)
- neodymium magnets
- plastic tubes with lids (empty blood-test tubes from a pathology lab are ideal)
- retort stand and clamp
- paper and tape
- no-bounce or foam pad (optional)

METHOD

Part A • Varying the number of turns

1. Connect the voltage sensor to the data-analysis system following the manufacturer's guidelines and start a new experiment in the relevant software. Set the sample rate to at least 200 Hz and display a graph of voltage versus time.
2. Mount the 200-turn coil to the retort stand using the clamp, so that it is approximately 40 cm above the benchtop. If a no-bounce pad is available, place it under the coil to soften the fall of the magnet/s.
3. Connect the voltage sensor to the coil.
4. What do you expect the voltage–time graph to look like when the magnet is dropped through the coil? Before continuing, sketch your prediction in the grid supplied in the Results section.
5. Hold the magnet just above the opening of the coil, start the data-collection system and then drop the magnet through the coil. Stop collecting immediately after.
6. Replace the coil with the 400-turn coil (or the coil with the next most turns) and then repeat the data collection. Do the same for each coil.
7. Display the data on one graph, annotating each curve to identify the number of turns. Print out and paste the graph in the Results section or sketch the graphs in the space provided.

Part B • Varying the number of magnets

Use the same set-up for this part as in Part **A**, but use only the 200-turn coil (or the smallest number of turns available).

1. Hold the tube containing one magnet just above the coil opening. Start the data-collection system and then drop the magnet through the coil. Stop collecting immediately after.
2. Repeat with tubes containing two, three, four and five magnets, as available.
3. Display the data runs on the one graph, annotating each to identify the number of magnets. Print out and paste the graph in the Results section or sketch the graphs in the space provided.

 ISBN 978 0 6557 0029 6

PRACTICAL ACTIVITY 12

Part C • Varying the rate of change of flux

Use the same set-up for this part as in Part **A**, but using only the 200-turn coil (or the smallest number of turns available) and a tube with a single magnet.

1 ▪ Roll up a piece of paper into a tube, and tape it securely. The tube should be wide enough to allow your magnet to pass through freely, but narrow enough to guide the magnet through the coil, as shown in Figure 3.3.16.

2 ▪ Mark four equally spaced positions on the tube and slide the tube into the coil so that the first mark is showing just above the coil opening.

3 ▪ Hold the magnet just above the tube opening. Start the data-collection system and then drop the magnet through the coil. Stop collecting immediately after.

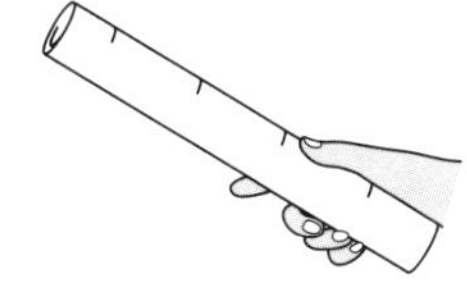

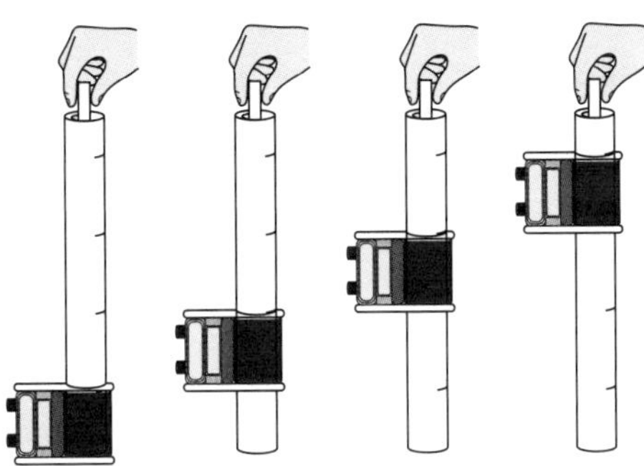

Figure 3.3.16 The magnet, paper tube and coil set-up

4 ▪ Slide the paper tube down into the coil until the next mark on the tube is just above the opening of the coil and repeat the data collection. Repeat the process for the remaining positions marked on the paper tube.

5 ▪ Display the data on one graph, annotating each to identify the height from which the magnets were dropped. Print out and paste the graph in the Results section or sketch the graphs in the space provided.

RESULTS

Part A • Varying the number of turns

1 Sketch your prediction of the voltage versus time graph.

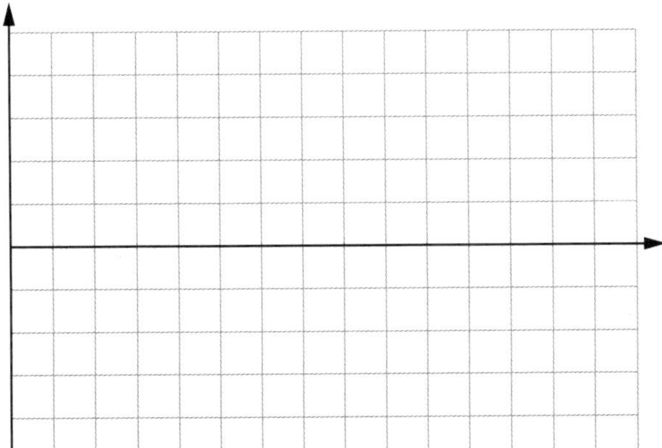

2 If a changing magnetic field causes charges to move in a conductor, and charges moving in a conductor give rise to a magnetic field, what will be the orientation of the induced magnetic field relative to the original changing magnetic field?

3 Sketch or paste your graph of the induced voltage versus time for the different number of turns in the coils.

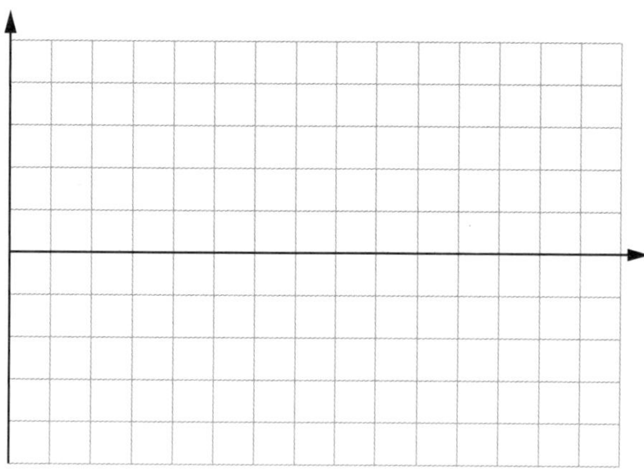

Part B • Varying the number of magnets

Sketch or paste your graph of the induced voltage versus time for a different number of magnets.

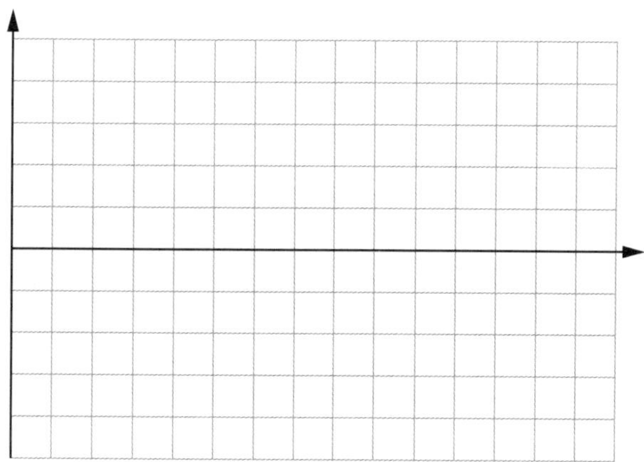

Part C • Varying the rate of change of flux

Sketch or paste your graph of the induced voltage versus time for each of the different drop heights.

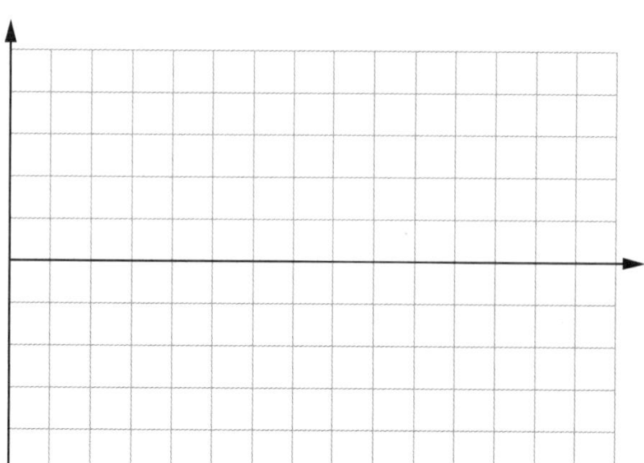

 ISBN 978 0 6557 0029 6

PRACTICAL ACTIVITY 12

DISCUSSION

1 How did your prediction compare to the actual voltage versus time graphs?

2 Describe the relationship between the number of turns in the coils and the peak voltages observed.

3 Describe the relationship between the strength of the magnets used and the peak voltages observed. What could be measured to give a more precise relationship?

4 Describe the relationship between the height above the coil from which the magnet fell and the peak voltages observed. What could be measured to give a more precise relationship?

5 The second peak of the voltage curve is always in the opposite direction to the first peak and is also a slightly larger peak. Describe why this is the case.

CONCLUSION

PRACTICAL ACTIVITY 13

Experiment

Electricity from a DC motor

SUGGESTED DURATION

- 45 minutes data collection + 20 minutes analysis

INTRODUCTION

In this activity, the basic principle of electric power generation will be investigated. A rotating-coil generator is fundamentally just an electric motor being turned manually to produce a current.

AIM

To investigate the output of a DC motor driven mechanically.

Use gears and a handle to make it easy to turn the shaft of the electric motor.

Safety
Complete a risk assessment before starting the activity.

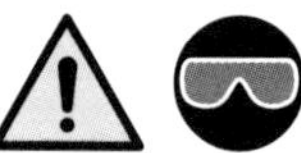

MATERIALS

- centre-zero ammeter or galvanometer (or current and voltage sensors and data-collection system)
- CRO (cathode ray oscilloscope, if not using an electronic measure)
- electric motor
- electrical leads with alligator clips or banana plugs
- gear system

METHOD

1. Connect a small electric motor to a gear system so that the centre shaft of the motor can be turned manually. Connect the leads of the motor to a centre-zero ammeter, or a current sensor. Set up the current sensor following the manufacturer's instructions.
2. Start turning the motor (and start recording data if using an electronic sensor) as slowly and as smoothly as possible. Observe the output as shown on the galvanometer or the graph of the voltage sensor. Increase the speed of rotation gradually and record your observations of the effect on the output.
3. If you are using an ammeter, stop turning the motor after a little while and replace the ammeter with a CRO. Observe the output from the motor on the oscilloscope screen. Sketch two waveforms corresponding to two different speeds of rotation on the same axes in the Results section. Label the waveform corresponding to the higher speed of rotation.

RESULTS

Graph of voltage vs time for two speeds of rotation

ISBN 978 0 6557 0029 6

DISCUSSION

1 Is the electric motor an AC or DC generator? Explain with reference to your graph.

2 How does the speed of rotation affect the frequency and amplitude of the output voltage? Why is this the case?

CONCLUSION

ISBN 978 0 6557 0029 6

PRACTICAL ACTIVITY 14

Experiment

Transformer operation

SUGGESTED DURATION

- 50 minutes data collection + 20 minutes analysis

INTRODUCTION

Transformers are an intrinsic part of any electricity supply system, whether it is solar, wind or hydro. Although a detailed analysis of transformer operation is complex, the basic idea is simple enough. Two coils are wound on one iron core so that the magnetic flux generated by one passes through the other. The coil connected to the AC supply is referred to as the primary, and the coil connected to the 'load' is the secondary. The transformer operates on the principle that, whenever a changing magnetic flux passes through a coil, there will be an induced EMF. In a transformer, the changing flux originates from an alternating current in the primary coil. Because this flux also goes through the secondary coil, there will be an induced EMF in both coils. In this activity, the principles of operation of transformers will be investigated.

MATERIALS

- U-shaped iron cores
- pre-wound coils of different turns
- electrical leads
- low-voltage AC/DC power supply*
- two voltmeters or voltage sensors and data-collection system
- signal generator with sine and square waveform outputs

AIM

To investigate the operation and the volts-to-turns ratio of a transformer.

*Ensure your DC power supply is either a true DC source such as a battery or is fully rectified and filtered.

A power supply that is only half-wave rectified, without filtering, such as those usually supplied in junior laboratories, will give potentially misleading results.

Safety

Always use power supplies with safety cut-outs.

Do not exceed the recommended voltage levels.

Always turn off the power supply between each test.

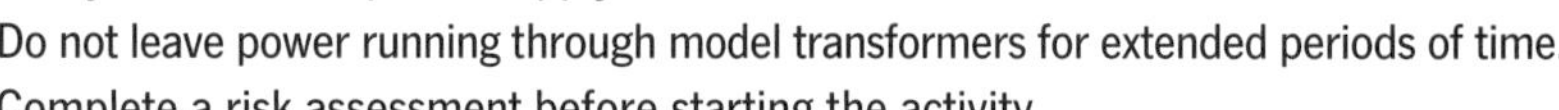

Do not leave power running through model transformers for extended periods of time.

Complete a risk assessment before starting the activity.

METHOD

1 ▪ Set up the coils and core as shown in Figure 3.3.17. In the diagram, the coil to the left will be referred to as the primary coil, and the one to the right will be the secondary coil. An alternating current is being applied to the primary coil and the output is being measured at the secondary.

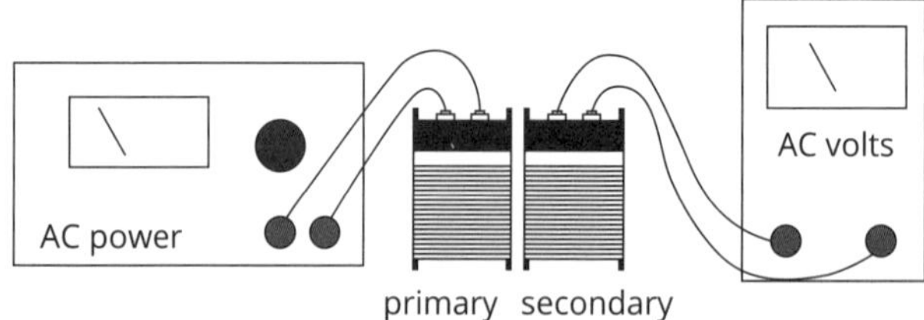

Figure 3.3.17 The coils and iron core set-up

2 ▪ Set up the voltmeters or the data-collection system, following the manufacturer's directions, and connect the two voltage sensors. Set the sample rate to at least 200 Hz and display a voltage versus time graph for each sensor and a digital display of each voltage.

 ISBN 978 0 6557 0029 6

3 ▪ Using two coils of the same number of turns for both primary and secondary, adjust the input voltage to 6 V AC. Connect a voltmeter or voltage sensor across the primary coil and a second one across the secondary coil. Measure the voltages and record the results in Table 1.

4 ▪ Insert a straight iron crosspiece between the two coils, as shown in Figure 3.3.18a. Measure and record the input and output voltage again, keeping the input voltage from the power supply the same. Record the results in Table 1.

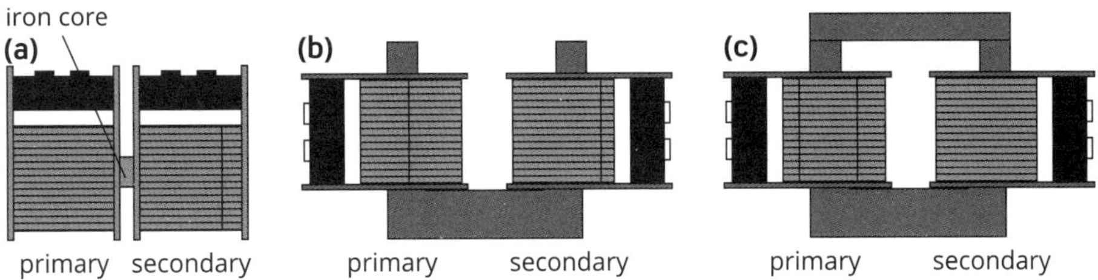

Figure 3.3.18 The coils, with the iron core in different positions: (a) a crosspiece between the coils, (b) a U-shaped core, and (c) both crosspiece and U-shaped core

5 ▪ Place the coils on the sides of an open U-shaped core, as shown in Figure 3.3.18b. Once again, measure and record the input and output voltage, keeping the input voltage from the power supply the same. Record the results in Table 1.

6 ▪ Finally, repeat the measurement after placing the crosspiece over the U-shaped core, as shown in Figure 3.3.18c. Record the results in Table 1.

7 ▪ Using the arrangement that produced the best result for the secondary output, compare each possible combination of primary and secondary coils. Record the arrangement of the coils and the respective primary and secondary outputs for each combination.

8 ▪ Using two coils with equal numbers of turns and the core configuration with the best results, replace the AC power supply with the DC supply. Adjust the output to 6 V DC and measure the input and output voltage. Record the results in Table 2. If using voltage sensors, draw the graph of the output voltage.

You will need voltage sensors for this final section. If using voltmeters, finish the activity here.

9 ▪ Replace the DC power supply with the signal generator. Set the signal generator to a sine-wave output of approximately 6 V amplitude and a frequency of 10 Hz. Record the voltage display for both the input and output voltages on the same graph of voltage versus time. Print out and paste the graph in the Results section or sketch the graphs in the space provided.

10 ▪ Finally, switch the output of the signal generator to a square wave. Keep the amplitude and the frequency the same as that used with the sine wave. Record the voltage display for both the input and output voltages on the same graph of voltage versus time. Print out and paste the graph in the Results section or sketch the graphs in the space provided.

RESULTS

Table 1 Transformer operation

Number of turns						
Primary (N_1)	**Secondary (N_2)**	**Input (V_1) V**	**Output (V_2) V**	**Ratio $\frac{N_1}{N_2}$**	**Ratio $\frac{V_1}{V_2}$**	**Core configuration**
						no core
						straight iron core
						U-shaped core
						U-shaped core with crossbar

PRACTICAL ACTIVITY 14

1 Based on your results, which arrangement induces the maximum EMF in the secondary coil? Why?

Table 2 DC input/output voltages	
DC power-supply input voltage (V)	
Recorded output voltage (V)	

2 Sketch the graph of output voltage for the DC power supply.

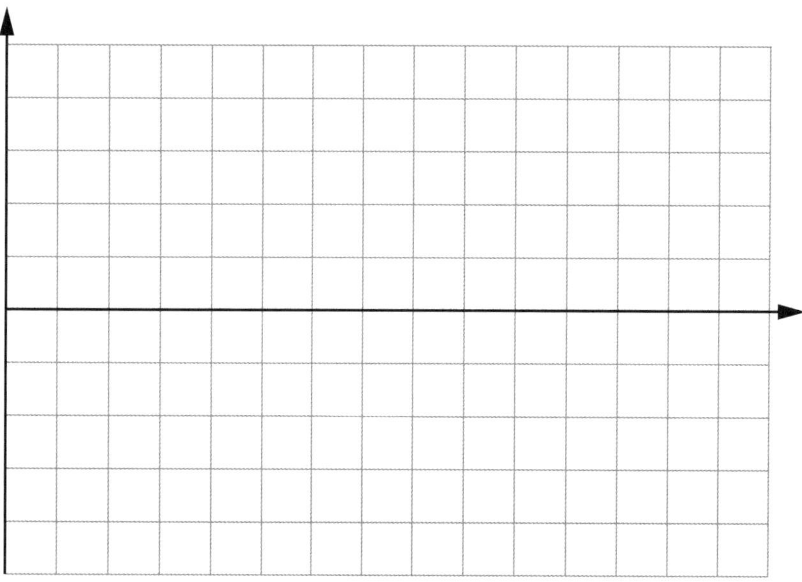

3 Sketch or paste your graph of input and output voltages for the sine-wave supply.

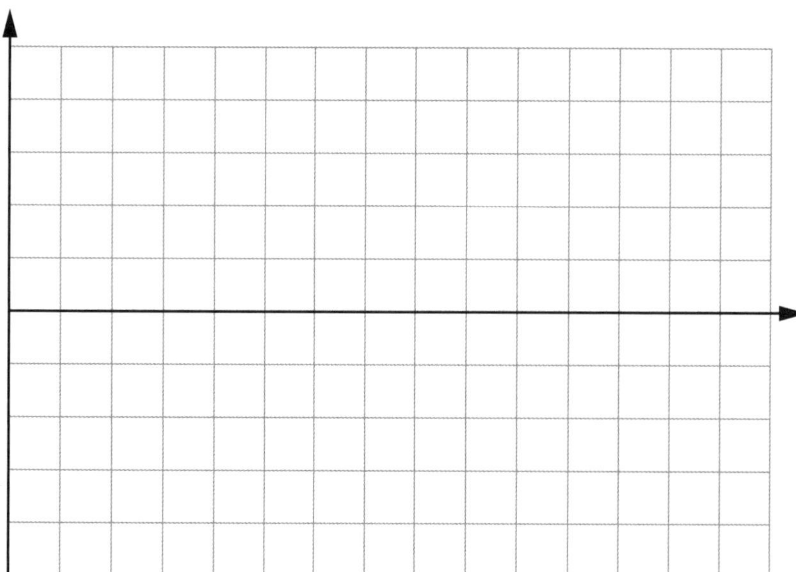

ISBN 978 0 6557 0029 6

4 Sketch or paste your graph of the input and output voltages for the square-wave supply.

DISCUSSION

1 Compare the ratio of the number of turns $N_1 : N_2$ to the ratio of the input and output voltages $V_1 : V_2$. Based on your results, is the transformer an ideal transformer? Explain your conclusion.

2 Why was the voltage of the AC power supply measured at the primary coil? How does this assist the reliability of your conclusions?

3 Under what primary voltage supply conditions will a transformer work? Explain your answer with reference to the results and graphs from each input.

ISBN 978 0 6557 0029 6

4 The induced voltage in the secondary coil varied depending on the configuration of the cores. Explain why this occurred.

5 Eddy currents are set up in the iron core of a transformer and are a major cause of energy loss. Refer to your textbook or other resources, and research the means by which eddy currents can be reduced.

CONCLUSION

 ISBN 978 0 6557 0029 6

PRACTICAL ACTIVITY 15

Case study

Electric power—issues in supply and distribution

SUGGESTED DURATION

- 3.75 hours

INTRODUCTION

Electricity is an indispensable commodity in the modern world. If you don't think so, just recall the last time you had a blackout at home. The reliable and economical provision of electricity is an issue that is rarely out of the public eye and the ongoing efforts to adapt to our changing climate regularly bring new problems.

The story of the provision of electric power started with street lighting around 1880 and quickly spread to power for domestic, industrial and transport applications in the following decades. Today, the provision of electric power continues to be of major importance across the planet, with electricity being generated from a wide variety of resources and transmitted via a range of different systems, including via overhead wires supported by huge pylons, like the one shown in Figure 3.3.19.

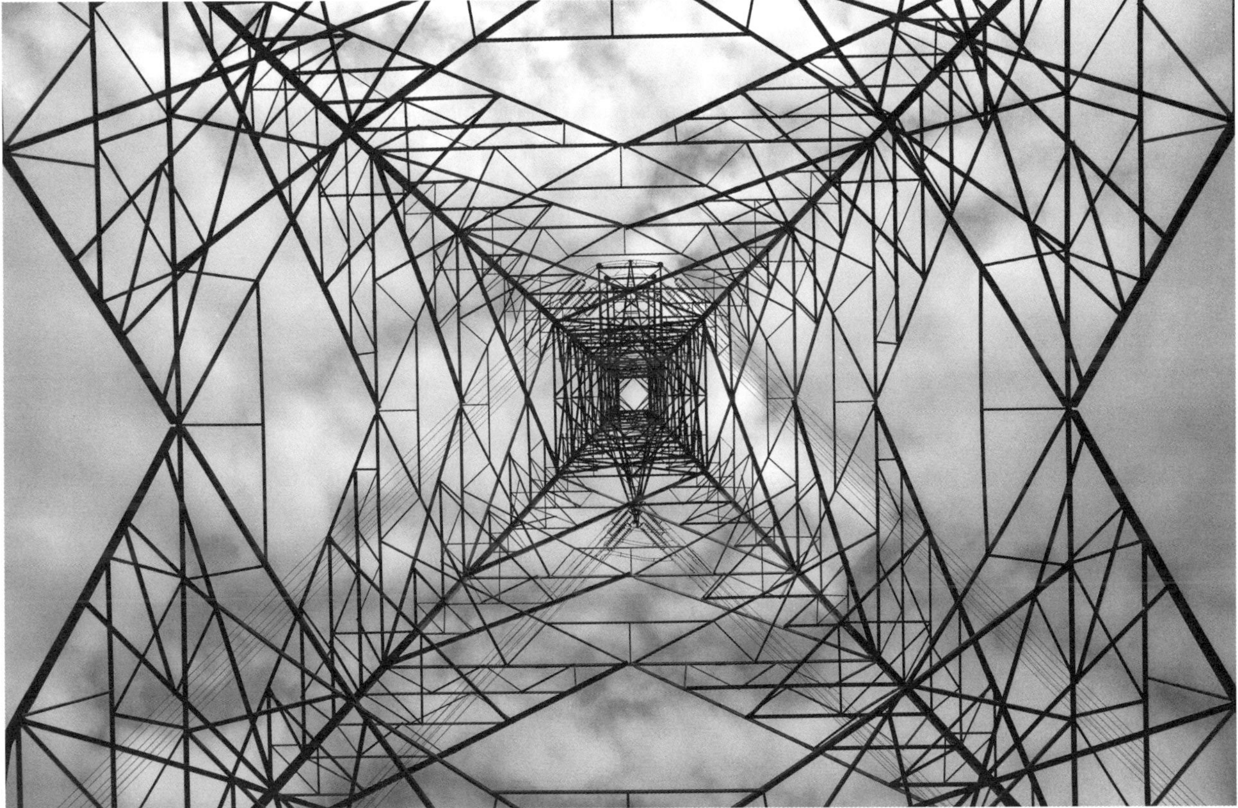

Figure 3.3.19 Looking upwards through an electricity pylon

AIM

Your task is to conduct some detailed research into an aspect of the provision of electric power and its history. You will need to focus on the physics behind the issue, not just the human endeavours. A list of stimulus topics is provided here to help you get started, but don't limit yourself to these.

- The War of Currents: Edison versus Tesla, General Electric versus Westinghouse
- Generation: Spinning generators or solar? Are there other ways in which electricity could be generated on a large scale?
- Transmission over long distances: AC versus DC—a decided issue?
- Transmission overground, underground, undersea, or through space?
- Matching voltages and frequencies between different sources and grids
- High-voltage switching, and three-phase power
- Sunspots and electric transmission grids

PRACTICAL ACTIVITY 15

Your research must be conducted individually. The topic chosen must consist of an issue in the area of AC electricity generation and supply as the primary area of research. The topic must allow for the development of an answer to one clear research question. A topic that has a broad range of resources available is likely to prove better than one for which the resources are limited.

METHOD

1 ▪ Carefully define your topic and define its limits. Perhaps outline what it does not cover.

2 ▪ Phrase your topic as a question or as a number of related questions. For example, 'What's so good about alternating current?', 'How is power shared between different Australian states?', 'How can batteries help balance the demand?' It is important to look at different sources of information before you settle on an area or question.
Many electrical utility companies provide detailed information.

3 ▪ Do some initial research around answering your initial questions. Rephrase your questions to make them as clear and specific as possible. For example, 'How does DC get converted into AC?', 'Why is three-phase power so efficient in generation and transmission?', 'How is the output of a wind turbine synchronised to the grid?', 'Why is switching off 500 kV so tricky?'

4 ▪ Look back at your initial topic question. Construct a hypothesis that can be applied to answer your question. This becomes your working hypothesis and should summarise the answer to your main research question. It will most likely change after some further research.

5 ▪ Look back at your original question. Does it need rephrasing in light of your research? Restate your question as you will present it.

6 ▪ Highlight the physics in your topic. Can you put it into terms your fellow students will understand?

 ISBN 978 0 6557 0029 6

7 ▪ Working in a small group, evaluate other students' research topics. What are the strengths of their research questions? How could you improve your own research question?

8 ▪ Carry out the remainder of your research, summarising the key points as you proceed so that your topic has a clear focus and structure.

DISCUSSION

1 Were you successful in answering your original research question? Did you need to rephrase it?

2 Do your research sources all agree? Are there any dissenting claims or explanations?

Communicate your findings in the form of an individual documentary, media report or other short visual presentation.

3 Did your presentation generate questions from your audience?

CONCLUSION

EXAM QUESTIONS

Multiple-choice questions

Question 1 VCE Physics 2021 (A) 6

A magnet approaches a coil with six turns, as shown in the diagram below. During time interval Δt, the magnetic flux changes by 0.05 Wb and the average induced EMF is 1.2 V.

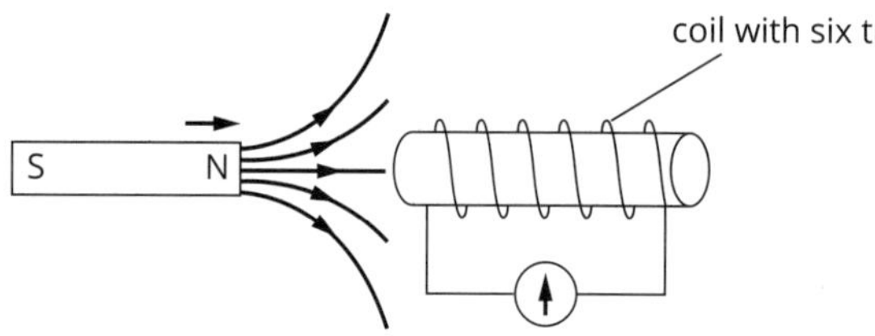

Which one of the following is closest to the time interval Δt?

A. 0.04 s

B. 0.01 s

C. 0.25 s

D. 0.50 s

Question 2 VCE Physics 2020 (A) 6

A single loop of wire moves into a uniform magnetic field B of strength 3.5×10^{-4} T over time $t = 0.20$ s from point X to point Y, as shown in the diagram below. The area A of the loop is 0.05 m^2.

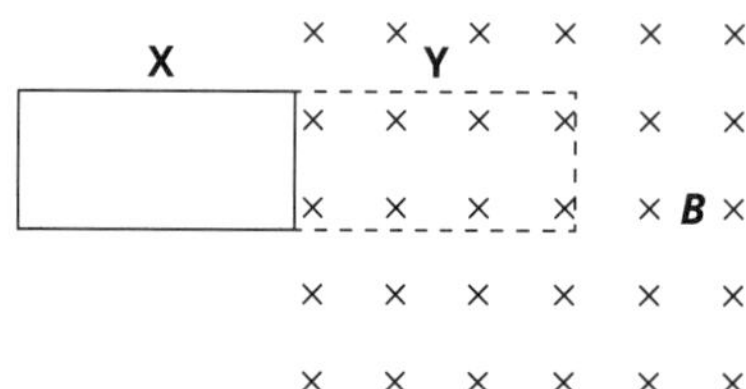

The magnitude of the average induced EMF in the loop is closest to:

A. 0 V

B. 3.5×10^{-6} V

C. 8.8×10^{-5} V

D. 8.8×10^{3} V

Question 3 VCE Physics 2020 (A) 7

An ideal transformer has an input DC voltage of 240 V, 2000 turns in the primary coil and 80 turns in the secondary coil.

The output voltage is closest to:

A. 0 V

B. 9.6 V

C. 6.0×10^{3} V

D. 3.8×10^{7} V

Question 4 VCE Physics 2017 (A) 6

The graph below shows the change in magnetic flux (Φ) through a coil of wire as a function of time (t).

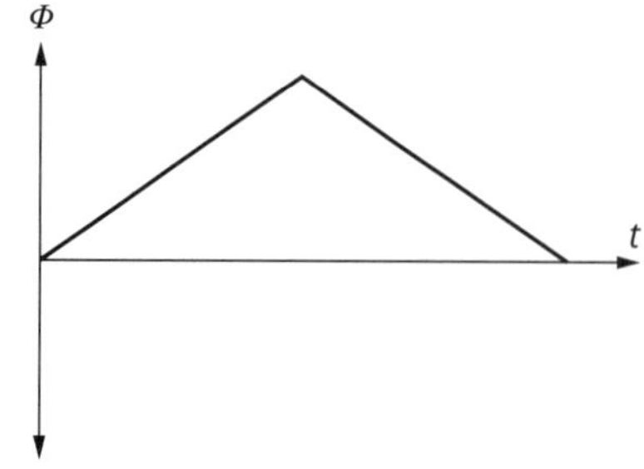

 ISBN 978 0 6557 0029 6

Which one of the following graphs best represents the induced EMF (ε) across the coil of wire as a function of time (t)?

A.

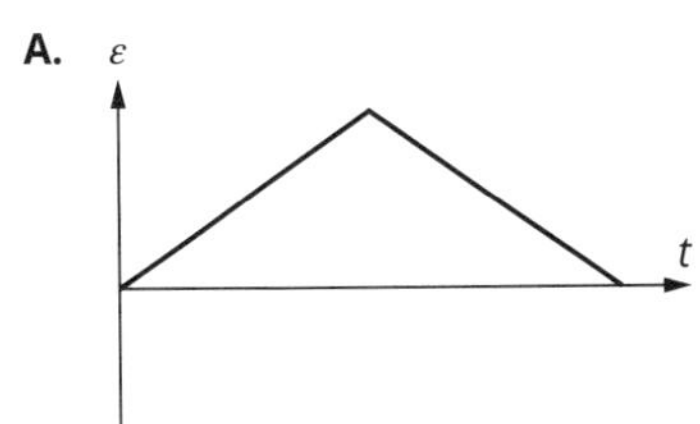

B.

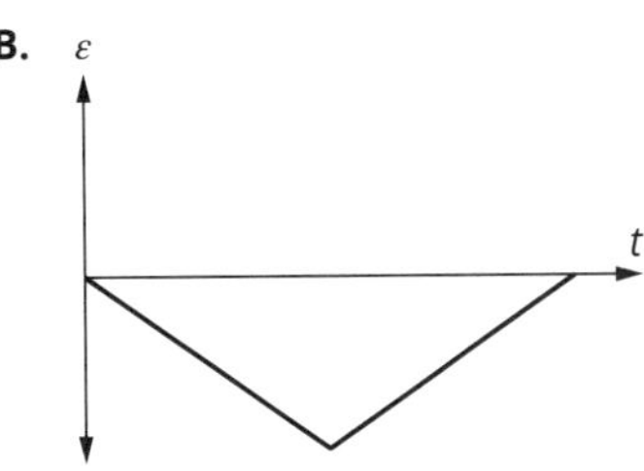

C.

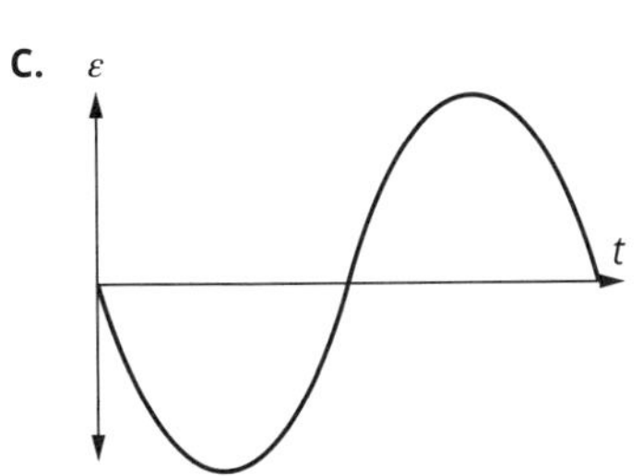

D.

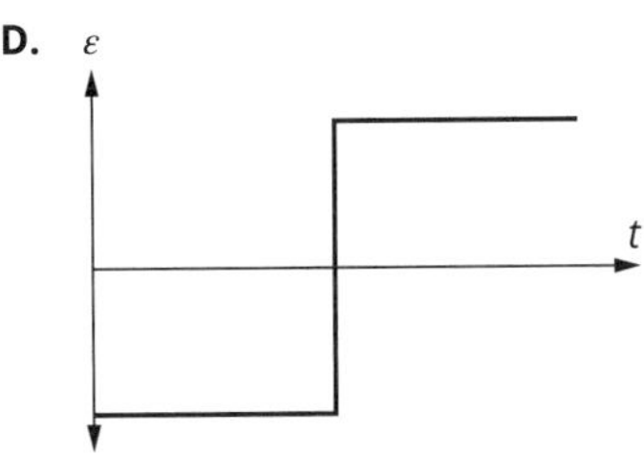

Question 5 VCE Physics 2019 (A) 7

The coil of an AC generator completes 50 revolutions per second.
A graph of output voltage versus time for this generator is shown below.

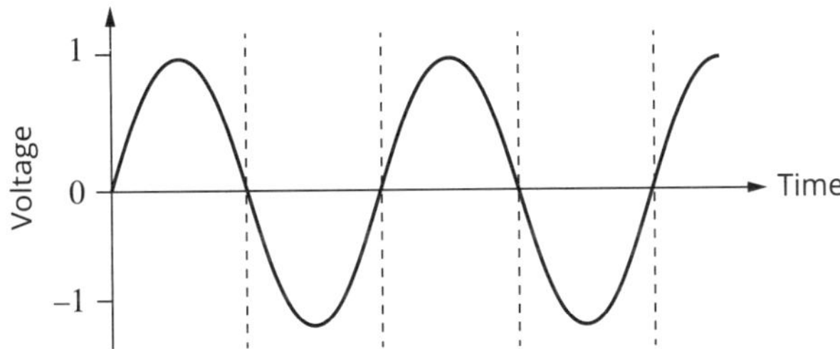

Which one of the following graphs best represents the output voltage if the rate of rotation is changed to 25 revolutions per second?

A.

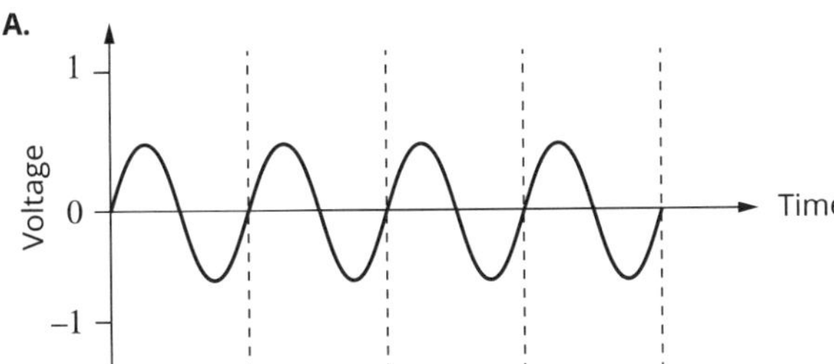

B.

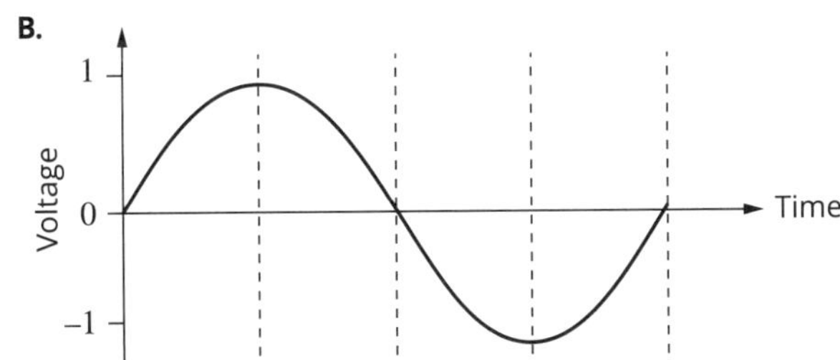

C.

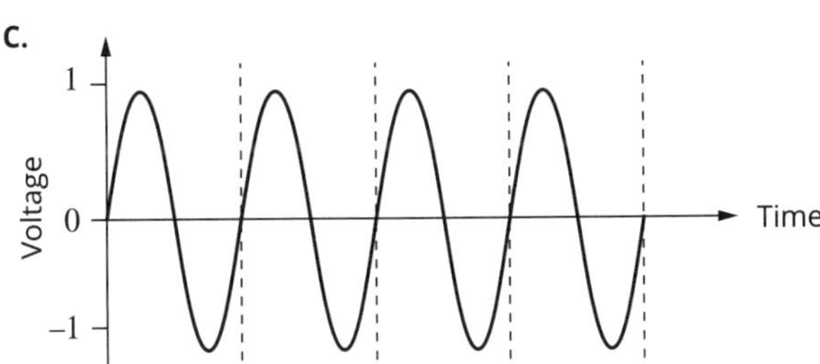

D.

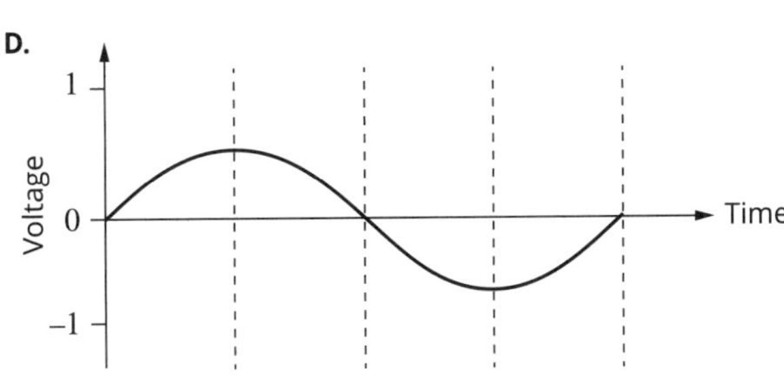

ISBN 978 0 6557 0029 6

EXAM QUESTIONS

Question 6 VCE Physics 2019 (A) 8

An electrical generator is shown in the diagram below. The generator is turning clockwise.

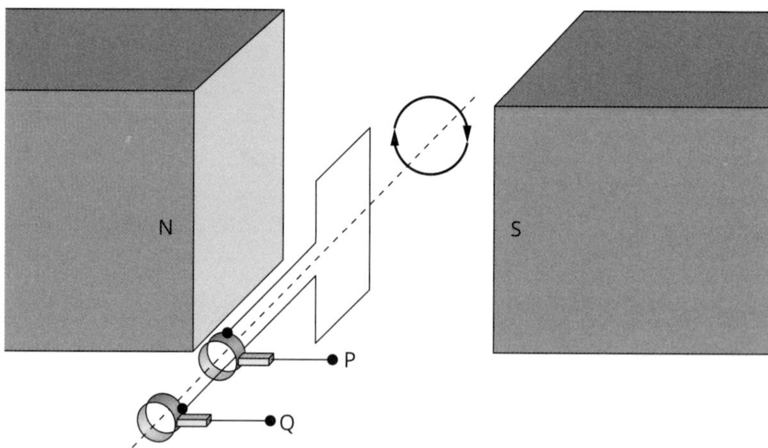

The voltage between P and Q and the magnetic flux through the loop are both graphed as a function of time, with voltage versus time shown as a solid line and magnetic flux versus time shown as a dashed line.

Which one of the following graphs best shows the relationships for this electrical generator?

A.

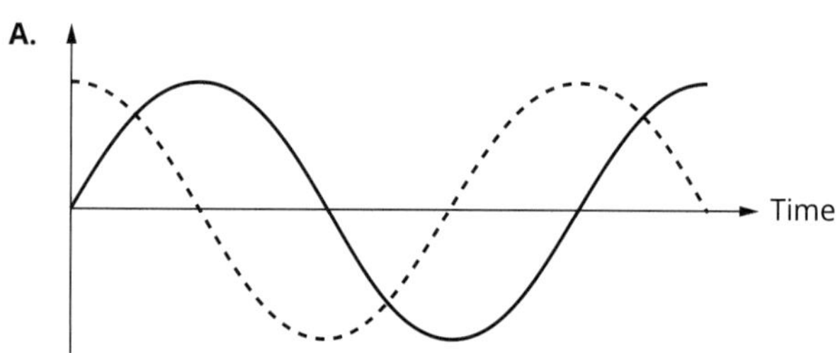

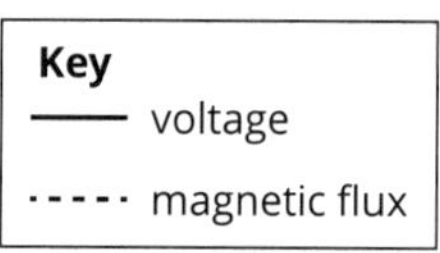

B.

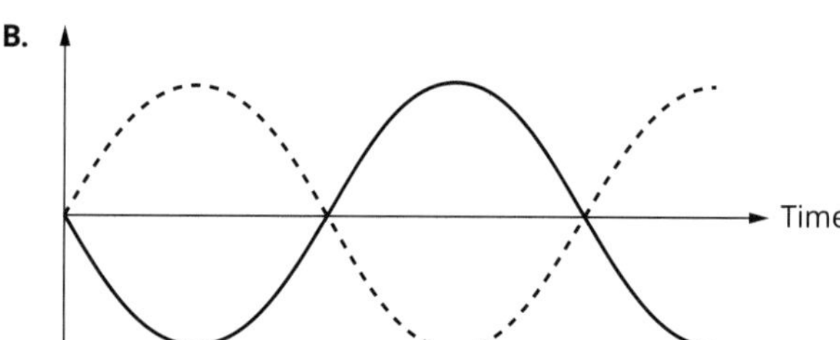

C.

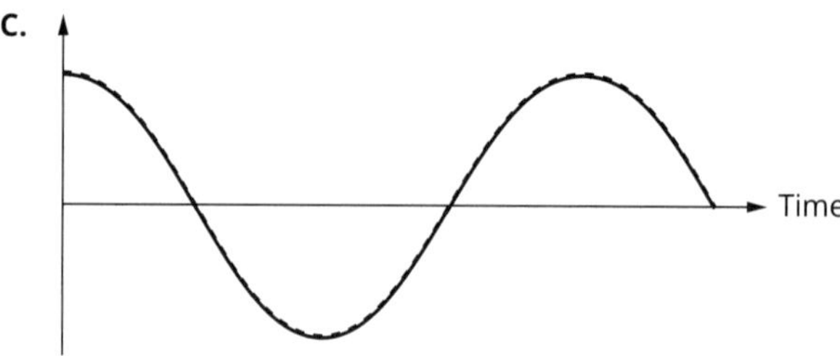

D.

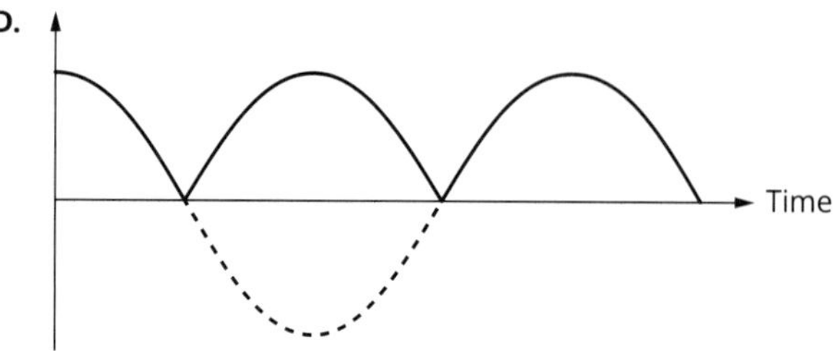

ISBN 978 0 6557 0029 6

EXAM QUESTIONS

Question 7 VCE Physics 2021 (A) 7

A mobile phone charger uses a step-down transformer to transform 240 V AC mains voltage to 5.0 V. The mobile phone draws a current of 3.0 A while charging. Assume that the transformer is ideal and that all readings are rms. Which one of the following is closest to the current drawn from the mains during charging?

A. 48 A

B. 16 A

C. 1.2 A

D. 0.06 A

Question 8 VCE Physics 2021 (A) 8

The diagram below shows a simple electrical generator consisting of a rotating wire loop in a magnetic field, connected to an external circuit with a light globe, a split ring commutator and brushes. The direction of rotation is shown by the arrow.

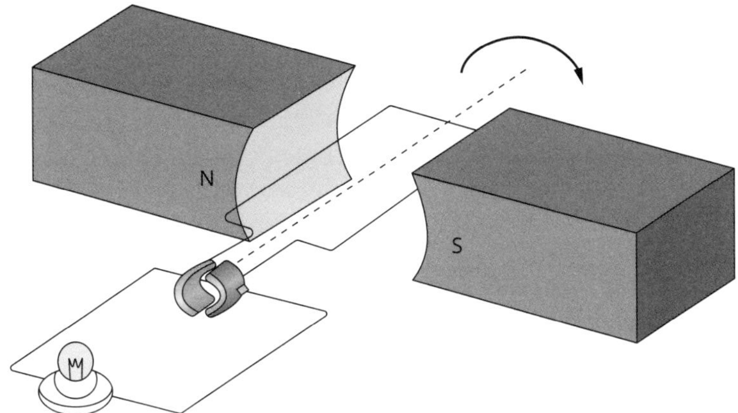

Which one of the following best describes the function of the split ring commutator in the external circuit?

A. It delivers a DC current to the light globe.

B. It delivers an AC current to the light globe.

C. It ensures the force on the side of the loop nearest the north pole is always up.

D. It ensures the force on the side of the loop nearest the north pole is always down.

Use the following information to answer Questions 9 and 10.

Students doing a VCE Physics practical investigation use a step-down transformer with 240 V_{rms} AC to 12 V_{rms} AC.

Question 9 VCE Physics 2017 (A) 4

Which one of the following best gives the ratio of the number of turns, $N_{primary} : N_{secondary}$?

A. 1:4

B. 1:20

C. 4:1

D. 20:1

Question 10 VCE Physics 2017 (A) 5

The transformer delivers 48 W_{rms} to a resistor. Assume that the transformer is ideal. Which one of the following best gives the peak current in the secondary coil?

A. 0.2 A

B. 4.0 A

C. 5.7 A

D. 11.3 A

EXAM QUESTIONS

Short-answer questions

Question 1 (6 marks) VCE Physics 2018 (B) 2

A square loop of wire of 10 turns with a cross-sectional area of 1.6×10^{-3} m^2 passes at a constant speed into, through and out of a magnetic field of magnitude 2.0×10^{-2} T, as shown in the figure below. The loop takes 0.50 s to go from position X to position Y.

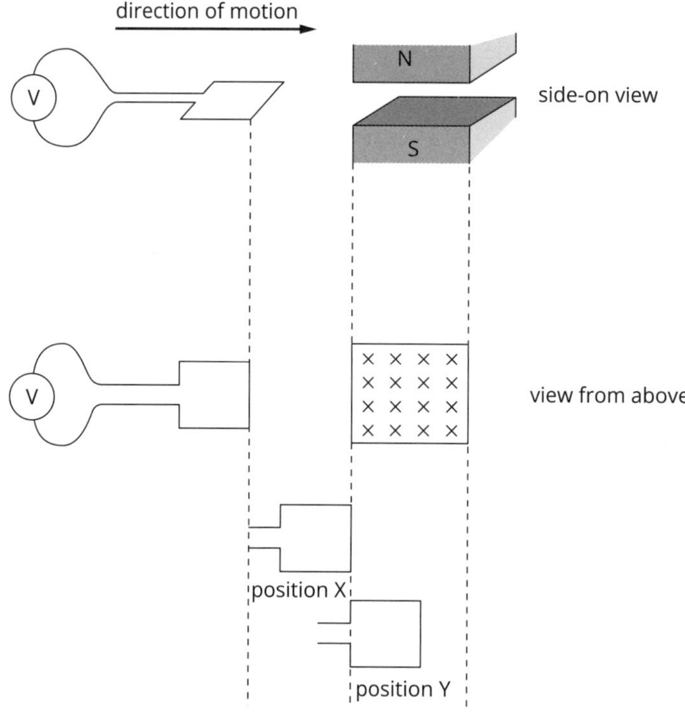

a. Calculate the average EMF induced in the loop as it passes from just outside the magnetic field at position X to just inside the magnetic field at position Y. Show your working. 3 marks

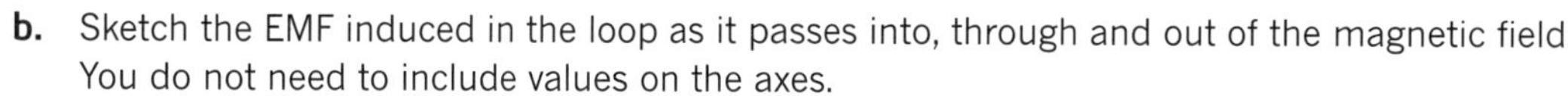

b. Sketch the EMF induced in the loop as it passes into, through and out of the magnetic field. You do not need to include values on the axes. 3 marks

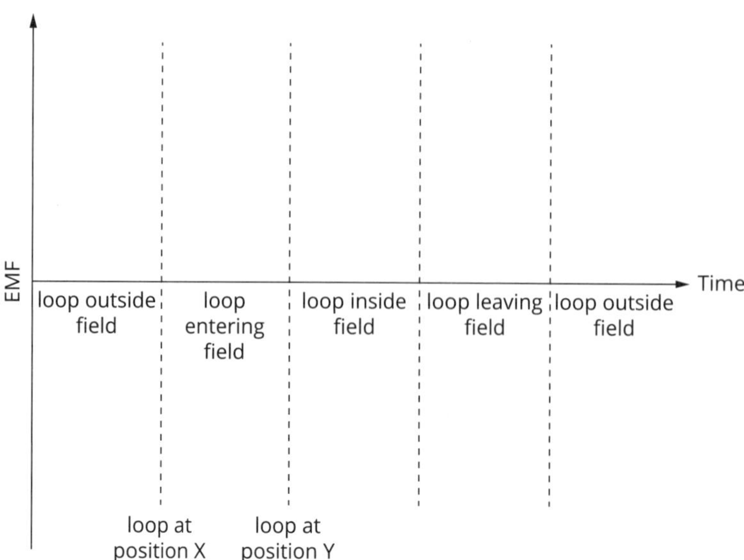

 ISBN 978 0 6557 0029 6

EXAM QUESTIONS

Question 2 (4 marks) VCE Physics 2018 (B) 4

The figure below shows a simple AC alternator with the output connected to an oscilloscope and a light globe. The oscilloscope can be considered as having a very large resistance. The coil is rotated, as shown in the figure below.

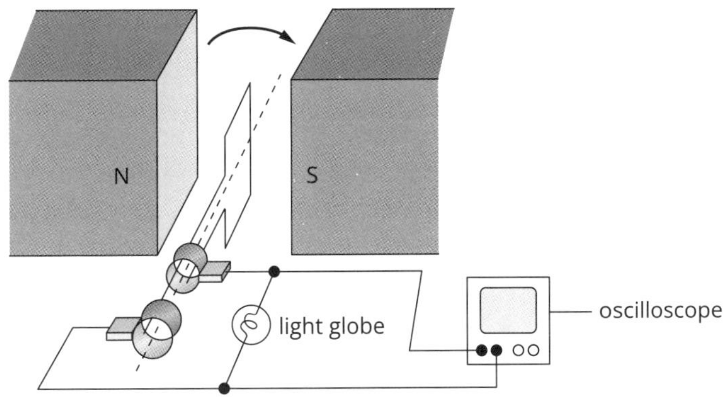

The output on the oscilloscope is shown in the graph below.

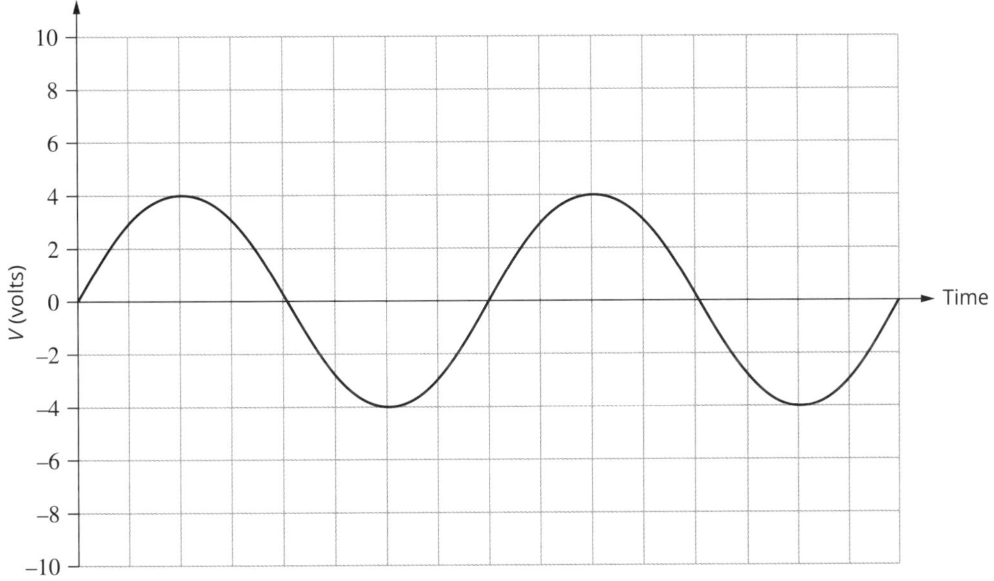

a. The AC alternator is to be replaced with a battery.
What voltage should the battery have for the light globe to light up with the same average brightness as it did with the alternator? Show your working. 2 marks

b. The rate of rotation of the loop is doubled.
On the graph below, sketch the output that will now be seen on the oscilloscope. The original waveform is shown as a dashed line. 2 marks

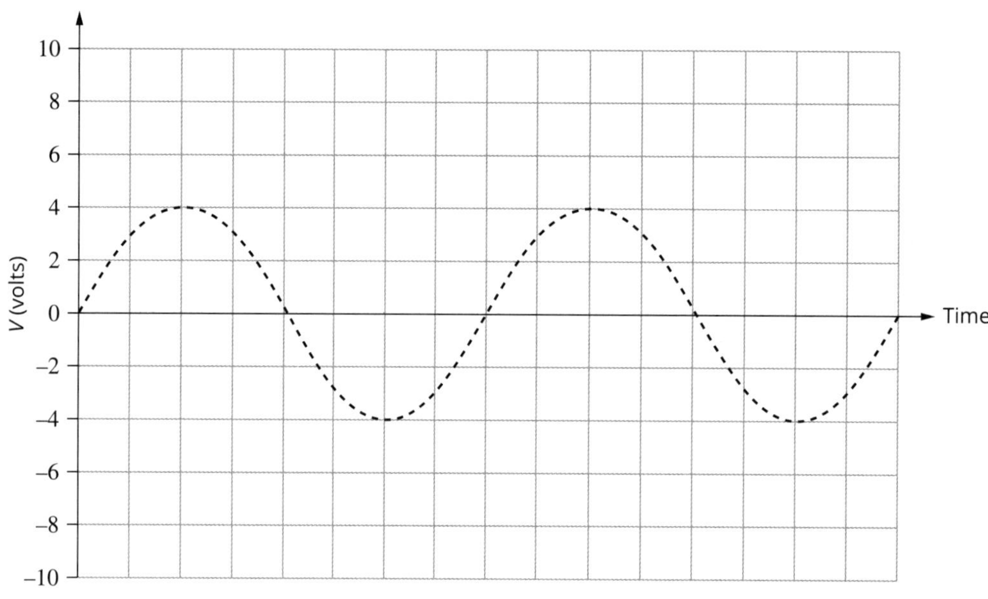

Question 3 (7 marks) VCE Physics 2013 (A) 15

Students are experimenting with an ideal transformer. The circuit is shown below.

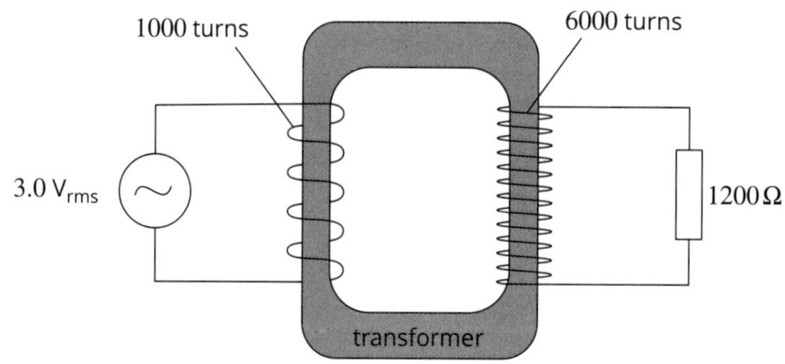

The primary coil has 1000 turns; the secondary coil has 6000 turns. There is a 1200 Ω resistor in the secondary circuit. A 3.0 V_{rms} AC power supply is connected across the primary coil.

a. Calculate the rms voltage across the resistor. 1 mark

b. Calculate the peak voltage across the resistor. 1 mark

c. Calculate the power dissipated in the resistor. 2 marks

 ISBN 978 0 6557 0029 6

EXAM QUESTIONS

The students now modify the circuit, and connect a 3.0 V DC battery and a switch in the primary circuit, as shown in the figure below.

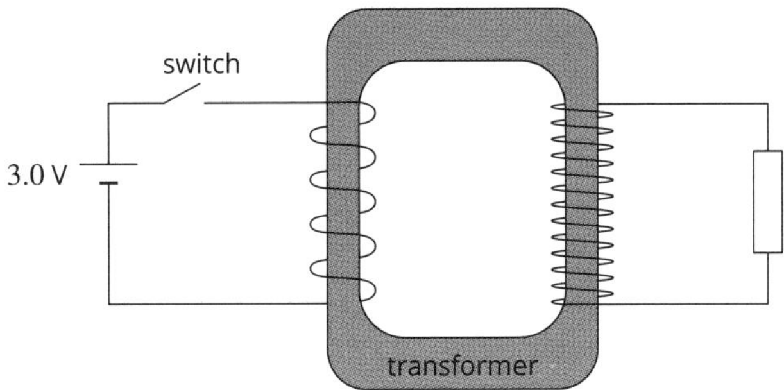

d. The students have been asked to observe the current in the resistor as the switch is closed. Before the switch is closed, there is no current in the resistor. This does not surprise them. When the switch is closed, there is a very short pulse of current in the resistor. When the switch remains closed, there is no current in the resistor.

Explain why there is a short pulse of current as the switch is closed and why there is no current in the resistor as the switch remains closed. No numbers are required in your answer, but you should refer to the relevant law of physics. 3 marks

Question 4 (10 marks) VCE Physics 2013 (A) 18

A bank of solar cells generates DC electricity. The current generated is transmitted along two transmission lines to a toolshed. The voltage loss along the transmission lines is 24 V. The current in the transmission lines is 6.0 A. The output power of the bank of solar cells is 1200 W.

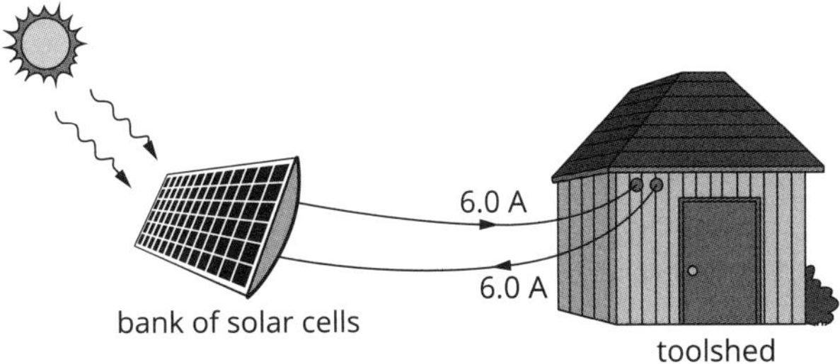

a. Calculate the total resistance of the transmission lines. 2 marks

b. Calculate the output voltage of the bank of solar cells. 2 marks

c. Calculate the value of the ratio (as a percentage). 3 marks

$$\frac{\text{power loss in the transmission lines}}{\text{power input to the transmission lines}}$$

d. The owner of the toolshed wants to reduce the power lost in the transmission lines. She installs a new bank of solar cells that produces the same power (1200 W), but at a different voltage. She also installs new transmission lines with a total resistance of 2.0 Ω. This will change the voltage at the toolshed.

With the new arrangement, the voltage loss in the transmission lines is 10 V.

Calculate the output voltage of the new bank of solar cells. 3 marks

 ISBN 978 0 6557 0029 6

UNIT 4 How have creative ideas and investigation revolutionised thinking in physics?

AREA OF STUDY 1

How has understanding about the physical world changed?

Outcome 1

Analyse and apply models that explain the nature of light and matter, and use special relativity to explain observations made when objects are moving at speeds approaching the speed of light

Key knowledge

Light as a wave

- describe light as a transverse electromagnetic wave which is produced by the acceleration of charges, which in turn produces changing electric fields and associated changing magnetic fields
- identify that all electromagnetic waves travel at the same speed, *c*, in a vacuum
- explain the formation of a standing wave resulting from the superposition of a travelling wave and its reflection
- analyse the formation of standing waves (only those with nodes at both ends is required)
- investigate and explain theoretically and practically diffraction as the directional spread of various frequencies with reference to different gap width or obstacle size, including the qualitative effect of changing the $\frac{\lambda}{w}$ ratio, and apply this to limitations of imaging using electromagnetic waves
- explain the results of Young's double slit experiment with reference to:
  - evidence for the wave-like nature of light
  - constructive and destructive interference of coherent waves in terms of path differences: $n\lambda$ and $\left(n+\frac{1}{2}\right)\lambda$, respectively, where $n = 0, 1, 2, \ldots$
  - effect of wavelength, distance of screen and slit separation on interference patterns: $\Delta x = \frac{\lambda L}{d}$ when $L >> d$

Light as a particle

- apply the quantised energy of photons: $E = hf = \frac{hc}{\lambda}$
- analyse the photoelectric effect with reference to:
  - evidence for the particle-like nature of light
  - experimental data in the form of graphs of photocurrent versus electrode potential, and of kinetic energy of electrons versus frequency
  - kinetic energy of emitted photoelectrons: $E_{k\,max} = hf - \phi$, using energy units of joule and electron-volt
  - effects of intensity of incident irradiation on the emission of photoelectrons
- describe the limitation of the wave model of light in explaining experimental results related to the photoelectric effect

Matter as particles or waves

- interpret electron diffraction patterns as evidence for the wave-like nature of matter
- distinguish between the diffraction patterns produced by photons and electrons
- calculate the de Broglie wavelength of matter: $\lambda = \frac{h}{p}$

Similarities between light and matter

- discuss the importance of the idea of quantisation in the development of knowledge about light and in explaining the nature of atoms

- compare the momentum of photons and of matter of the same wavelength including calculations using: $p = \frac{h}{\lambda}$
- explain the production of atomic absorption and emission line spectra, including those from metal vapour lamps
- interpret spectra and calculate the energy of absorbed or emitted photons: $E = hf$
- analyse the emission or absorption of a photon by an atom in terms of a change in the electron energy state of the atom, with the difference in the states' energies being equal to the photon energy: $E = hf = \frac{hc}{\lambda}$
- interpret the single photon and the electron double slit experiment as evidence for the dual nature of light and matter

Einstein's special theory of relativity

- describe the limitation of classical mechanics when considering motion approaching the speed of light
- describe Einstein's two postulates for his special theory of relativity that:
  - the laws of physics are the same in all inertial (non-accelerated) frames of reference
  - the speed of light has a constant value for all observers regardless of their motion or the motion of the source
- interpret the null result of the Michelson-Morley experiment as evidence in support of Einstein's special theory of relativity
- compare Einstein's special theory of relativity with the principles of classical physics
- describe proper time (t_0) as the time interval between two events in a reference frame where the two events occur at the same point in space
- describe proper length (L_0) as the length that is measured in the frame of reference in which objects are at rest
- model mathematically time dilation and length contraction at speeds approaching c using the equations:

  $t = \gamma t_0$ and $L = \frac{L_0}{\gamma}$

  where $\gamma = \frac{1}{\sqrt{\left(1 - \frac{v^2}{c^2}\right)}}$
- explain and analyse examples of special relativity, including that:
  - muons can reach Earth, even though their half-lives would suggest that they should decay in the upper atmosphere
  - particle accelerator lengths must be designed to take the effects of special relativity into account
  - time signals from GPS satellites must be corrected for the effects of special relativity due to their orbital velocity

Relationship between energy and mass

- interpret Einstein's prediction by showing that the total 'mass–energy' of an object is given by: $E_{tot} = E_k + E_0 = \gamma mc^2$ where $E_0 = mc^2$, and where kinetic energy can be calculated by: $E_k = (\gamma - 1)mc^2$
- apply the energy–mass relationship to mass conversion in the Sun, to positron–electron annihilation and to nuclear transformations in particle accelerators (details of the particular nuclear processes are not required).

- **You will now be able to complete Worksheet 29.**

Light as a wave

To understand the wave-like nature of light, it will help if you have a good understanding of the properties of mechanical waves.

MECHANICAL WAVES

Mechanical waves need a medium to travel through. For example, sound waves need air molecules to travel through.

Sound is a **longitudinal** wave; that is, the wave vibration travels in the same direction as the wave. Sound waves have compressions and rarefactions instead of crests and troughs.

Light is a **transverse** wave. The vibrations of a transverse wave are at right angles to the direction in which the wave travels. The displacement–distance graph in Figure 4.1.1 shows the displacement of particles along the length of a transverse wave at a particular point in time.

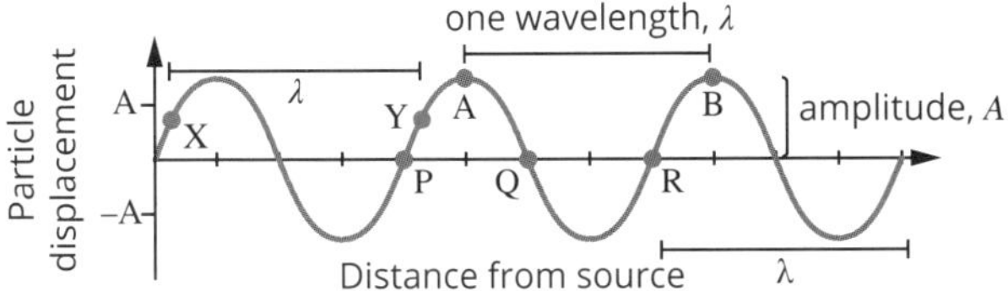

Figure 4.1.1 Particle displacements for a transverse wave

The **amplitude** of a wave is the maximum displacement of the particles from their average or rest position. The peak of the displacement in the positive direction is called a **crest** and the peak in the negative direction is called a **trough**.

The **wavelength**, λ, is the length of a complete cycle or oscillation, measured when the wave is plotted against distance from the source. It is measured between any two successive equivalent points on the wave—for example, between two adjacent crests.

The displacement–time graph in Figure 4.1.2 traces the position of one point over time as the wave moves through that point. The displacement–time graph looks similar to a displacement–distance graph of a transverse wave, so be careful to check the label on the horizontal axis.

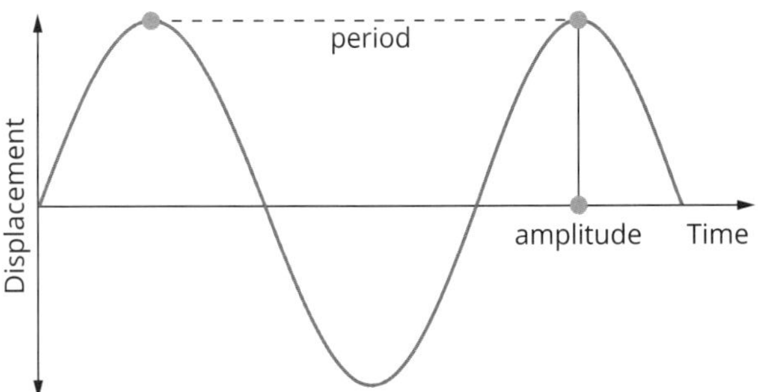

Figure 4.1.2 The movement of a single point on a transverse wave over time as the wave passes through that point

The **period** of a wave, T, measured in seconds, is the time for one complete oscillation (Figure 4.1.2).

The **frequency**, f, measured in hertz, is the number of complete oscillations per second. It is the inverse of the period: $f = \frac{1}{T}$

The velocity of the wave, v, measured in metres per second, is calculated using the wave equation: $v = f\lambda$.

The properties of mechanical waves can be used to illustrate superposition, resonance and standing waves.

SUPERPOSITION

When two waves meet, they can interact by:

- producing a smaller wave (if the crests of one wave meet the troughs of the other wave); this is referred to as **destructive interference**
- producing a larger wave or supercrest (if the crests of each wave meet); this is known as **constructive interference**.

This interference can occur in both mechanical and electromagnetic waves, and is called superposition. The principle of superposition states that when two or more waves interact, the resultant displacement or pressure at each point along the wave is the vector sum of the displacements or pressures of the component waves. The method of superposition is shown in Figure 4.1.3a and b, in which the waves interact to produce a larger wave. The waves then move apart unchanged and continue travelling in their original directions, as shown in Figure 4.1.3c.

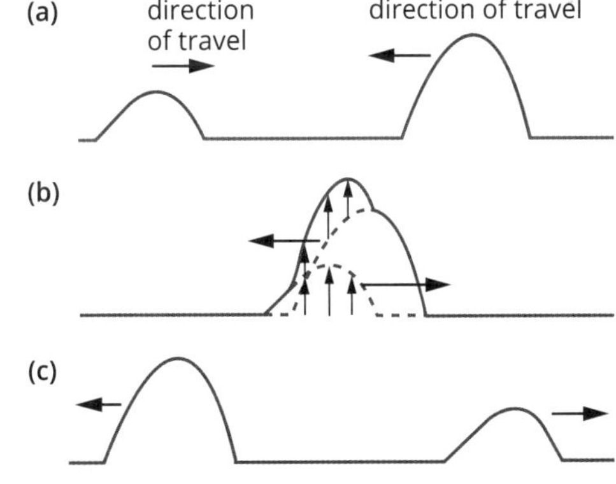

Figure 4.1.3 Superposition of two waves

RESONANCE

An object that can vibrate tends to do so at a specific frequency known as the natural or resonant frequency. Resonance occurs when a source produces a driving frequency (also called a forcing vibration) equal to the natural frequency of the object. Two special effects occur with resonance:

- The amplitude of the vibration increases.
- The maximum possible energy from the source is transferred to the resonating object.

KEY KNOWLEDGE

A child's playground swing is a good example of a resonant system. When the swing is pushed once, the movement of the swing represents an object vibrating at its natural frequency. If the swing continues to be pushed at this natural frequency, the amplitude of the swing increases. However, if the frequency of the pushes does not match the natural frequency of the swing, pushing becomes more difficult and the amplitude will not increase.

STANDING WAVES

Standing or stationary waves occur as a result of resonance at the natural frequency of vibration. They occur when two waves of the same amplitude and frequency are travelling in opposite directions.

Nodes are produced by destructive interference, in which the amplitudes of the two waves completely cancel.

Points on a standing wave where the particles remain stationary are called nodes.

Points of maximum amplitude on a standing wave are called antinodes.

Antinodes represent constructive interference, in which the amplitudes of the two waves combine.

Standing waves can be produced by vibrating a string attached to a fixed point, as shown in Figure 4.1.4. Standing waves with different wavelengths can be produced by vibrating the string at different frequencies.

Standing sound wave frequencies are referred to as harmonics. The simplest mode is called the fundamental frequency or first harmonic. The fundamental frequency has the longest wavelength and the lowest frequency. The fundamental frequency of an instrument depends on the type of instrument and whether the ends are fixed or not. In this area of study we consider only standing waves with both ends fixed.

For a string fixed at both ends, the wavelength of the standing waves corresponding to the various harmonics is given by:

$$\lambda_n = \frac{2l}{n}$$

where λ_n is the wavelength of the nth harmonic (m), l is the length of string (m) and n is the number of the harmonic.

The first four harmonics in a string fixed at both ends are shown in Figure 4.1.5. Note that there is a node at each fixed end.

Using the wave equation, $v = f\lambda$, it is possible to find the relationship between frequency, velocity and string length. The general formula for the frequency of any harmonic is:

$$f = \frac{nv}{2l}$$

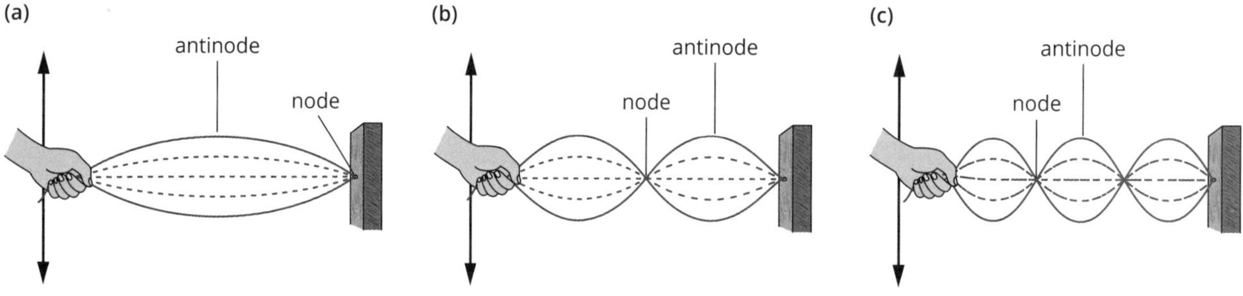

Figure 4.1.4 Standing waves produced by vibrating a string attached to a fixed point. The vibrations are at (a) the fundamental frequency, (b) twice the fundamental frequency, and (c) three times the fundamental frequency.

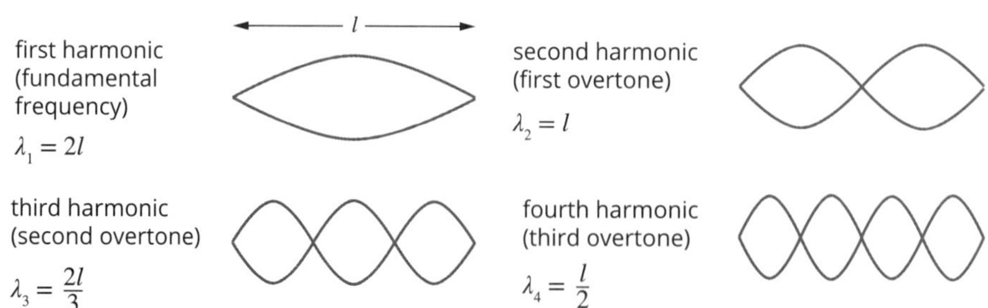

Figure 4.1.5 Harmonics in a string fixed at both ends

ISBN 978 0 6557 0029 6

KEY KNOWLEDGE

ELECTROMAGNETIC WAVES

In many circumstances light behaves like a wave. However, the wave characteristics of light cannot solely be modelled as a mechanical wave because light can travel through a vacuum. Therefore a different model is needed.

The physicist James Maxwell unified the theories of electricity and magnetism to find that light is a form of **electromagnetic radiation** (EMR). Recall that a point charge generates an electric field and moving point charges—a current—generate a magnetic field. Maxwell put these two ideas together, and stated that this would produce two mutually propagating fields, as shown in Figure 4.1.6, known as EMR or electromagnetic (EM) waves.

Electromagnetic waves are transverse waves made up of mutually perpendicular, oscillating electric and magnetic fields. These fields are perpendicular to the direction of propagation of the radiation and the frequency, and therefore the wavelength, λ, of both fields is the same, as can be seen in Figure 4.1.6. Electromagnetic waves cause charges to oscillate at the frequency of the wave. This also works in reverse. Oscillating charges produce EM waves of the same frequency as the oscillation.

The wave equation ($v = f\lambda$) can be used to calculate the frequency and wavelength of EM waves; EM waves travel at the speed of light. Maxwell's theoretical calculations for the speed of EMR closely matched the experimentally determined values for the speed of light—so closely that it provided a clue that light must be a form of EMR. (Light travels through a vacuum at approximately $c = 3.0 \times 10^8$ m s^{-1}, which is so reliable it is a fixed SI unit.) The wave equation can therefore be changed to:

$c = f\lambda$

where c is the speed of light (m s^{-1})
f is the frequency of the wave (Hz)
λ is the wavelength of the wave (m).

EMR can be used for a variety of purposes depending on the properties of the waves, which are determined by their frequency. The **electromagnetic spectrum** is the range of all types of EMR, and is divided into 'bands' according to how the types of EM radiation are used (Figure 4.1.7). The shorter the wavelength of the EM wave, the greater its penetrating power. The most penetrating waves are gamma rays. Long wavelength waves, such as AM radio waves, have such low penetrating power that they cannot even escape Earth's atmosphere.

- **You will now be able to conduct Practical activity 16.**

EVIDENCE FOR THE WAVE MODEL OF LIGHT

Diffraction

When a plane (straight) wave passes through a narrow opening or meets a sharp object, it experiences diffraction. Diffraction is the bending of the wavefronts as they pass through the opening. The diffraction will be large if the wavelength is similar to, or larger than, the width of the opening, as shown in Figure 4.1.8a on page 154. When the wavelength is smaller than the width of the opening, the diffraction will be less (Figure 4.1.8b).

Significant diffraction occurs when the ratio of wavelength to gap or object size is greater than or equal to 1, i.e. $\frac{\lambda}{w} \geq 1$.

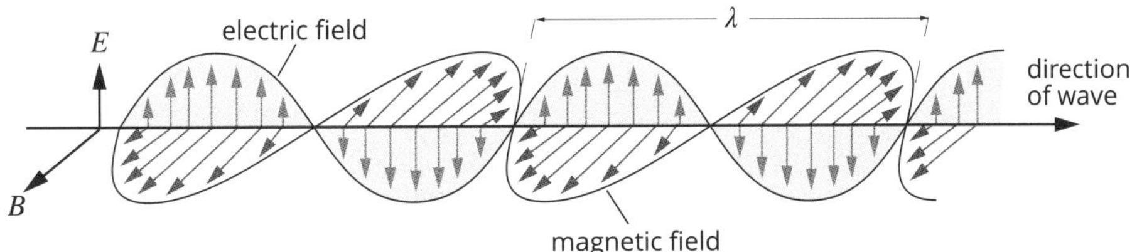

Figure 4.1.6 The electric and magnetic fields in electromagnetic radiation are perpendicular to each other and are both perpendicular to the direction of propagation of the radiation.

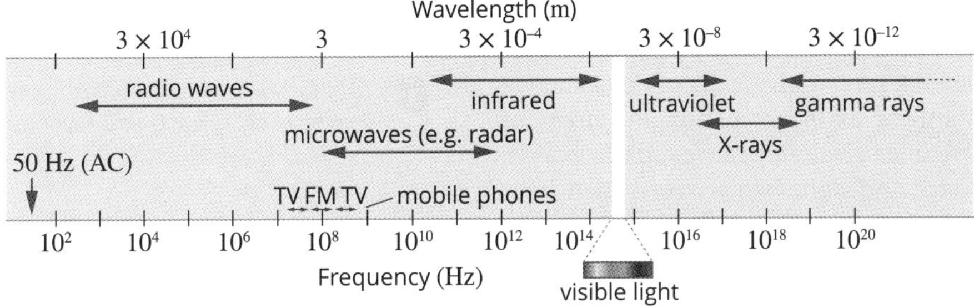

Figure 4.1.7 Electromagnetic spectrum

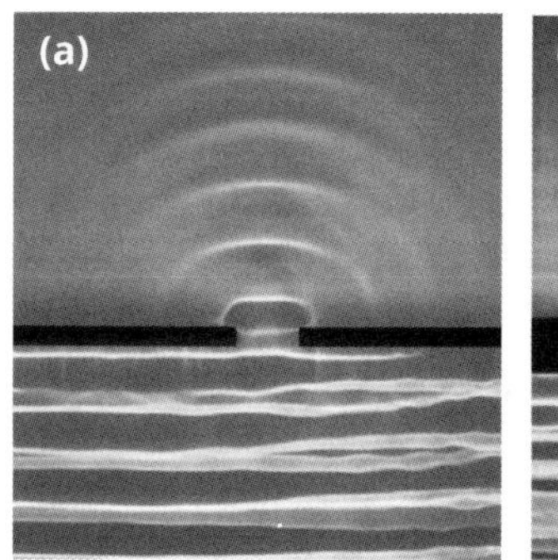

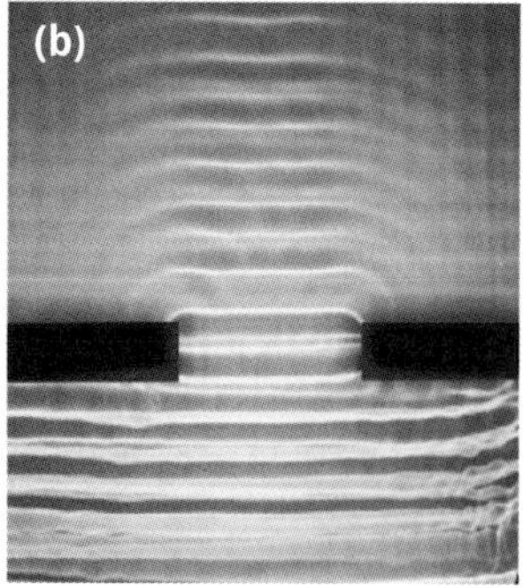

Figure 4.1.8 (a) When the wavelength is similar to or larger than the width of the opening, the diffraction is large. (b) When the wavelength is smaller than the width of the opening, the diffraction is less.

Diffraction and imaging

Diffraction can be a problem for scientists using microscopes and telescopes because it can result in blurred images. For example, a significant problem is that the light from two tiny objects or two distant objects very close together can be diffracted so much that the two objects appear as one blurred object. When this happens, we say that the objects are unresolved. Essentially, the ratio $\frac{\lambda}{w}$, where w is the slit width, indicates the size that can be clearly imaged by a particular instrument. This means that, as a general rule, optical microscopes cannot create images of objects that are smaller than the wavelength of the light they use; otherwise, diffraction effects are too significant.

Diffraction also places a theoretical limit on the resolution of optical telescopes. However, atmospheric distortion usually has a much larger effect on telescope images than diffraction. The Hubble Space Telescope sits above Earth's atmosphere and is not affected by atmospheric distortion. It can resolve images right down to their diffraction limit, i.e. where the separation of the stars is approximately equal to the wavelength of the light.

Diffraction patterns and gratings

Light diffracts as it passes through a very small gap. As the light passes through the gap, some of the wavelets making up the wavefront will diffract at the barriers that form the edges of the gap and some will pass through the centre of the gap. As a result of this, the light waves that emerge from the gap will interact. In some places the interactions will be constructive and in others the interactions will be destructive. When these light waves are made to shine on a screen, the areas of constructive interference will appear as bright bands and areas of destructive interference will appear as dark bands. The pattern of dark and light bands seen when light passes through a single small gap is called a **diffraction pattern**.

The spacing of the dark and light bands in a diffraction pattern, and therefore the width of the overall diffraction pattern, is proportional to the ratio $\frac{\lambda}{w}$. According to this relationship, if the wavelength is held constant and the gap made smaller, greater diffraction is seen. If different wavelengths enter the same gap, those with a smaller wavelength will undergo less diffraction than those with a longer wavelength (Figure 4.1.9).

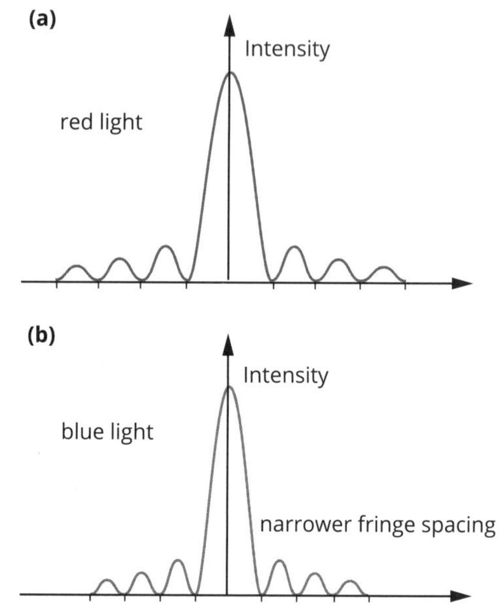

Figure 4.1.9 (a) Red light passing through a single small gap is diffracted to a greater extent than (b) blue light.

Although some diffraction patterns can be observed using natural materials, in practice much clearer diffraction patterns can be generated by passing light through a diffraction grating. Recall that a diffraction grating is a piece of material that contains a large number of very closely spaced parallel gaps or slits.

A **diffraction grating** can be thought of as a series of parallel slits all placed side by side. The diffraction pattern from one slit is superimposed on the pattern from the adjacent slit, producing a strong, clear image on the screen.

Diffraction experiments usually use light that is **monochromatic** (i.e. light of only one colour). When white light, which contains a number of different colours, shines through a diffraction grating, each different colour is diffracted by a different amount and forms its own set of coloured fringes. This results in the light being dispersed into its component colours.

A diffraction grating is used to separate the different colours of light. It acts as a super-prism.

 ISBN 978 0 6557 0029 6

KEY KNOWLEDGE

Young's double-slit experiment

In 1803, English scientist Thomas Young performed an experiment in which he shone monochromatic light onto a screen containing two very tiny slits.

According to the particle theory, light should pass directly through the slits to produce two bright lines or bands on the screen (Figure 4.1.10a). Instead, Young observed a series of bright and dark bands or 'fringes' (Figure 4.1.10b), which you would expect from diffracted waves. Young's double-slit interference experiment provided evidence to support the wave model of light.

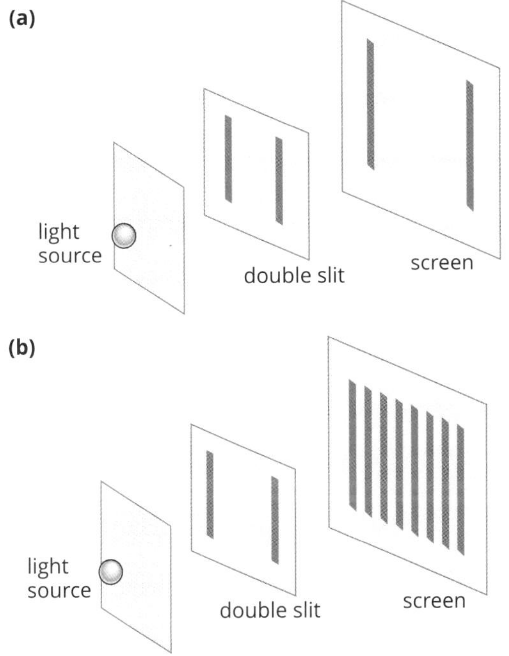

Figure 4.1.10 Young's double-slit experiment. (a) According to the particle theory of light, two bright lines should be seen on the screen. (b) In the actual experiment a series of bright and dark lines were seen, which supported a wave model of light.

Consider a double-slit experiment with coherent light shining through two slits, S_1 and S_2, as shown in Figure 4.1.11. At a particular point on the screen, P, each wave train will have travelled a different distance, i.e. S_1P and S_2P. The **path difference**, pd, is the difference in the distance travelled by each wave train from a pair of slits to the same point on the screen.

In Young's experiment, it is possible to predict where the bright fringes will occur by considering the geometry of the situation. Consider two slits, S_1 and S_2, that are separated by a distance, d. If a line is drawn at right angles halfway between the two slits directly across to the screen, then any point, P, on the screen can be identified by its angle, θ, from this line (shown in Figure 4.1.11). The fringe spacing (Δx) is the distance between adjacent fringes, and the distance to the screen is shown using the variable L.

Constructive interference of coherent waves occurs when the path difference, pd, is equal to a whole number of wavelengths:

> $\text{pd} = n\lambda$
>
> where $n = 0, 1, 2, 3 \ldots$

Destructive interference of coherent waves occurs when the path difference equals an odd number of half wavelengths:

> $\text{pd} = \left(n + \frac{1}{2}\right)\lambda$
>
> where $n = 1, 2, 3 \ldots$

If the viewing screen is moved further from the two slits, the fringes will appear further apart from each other, i.e. $\Delta x \propto L$. Conversely, reducing the separation of the slits increases the spacing of the fringes, i.e. $\Delta x \propto \frac{1}{d}$. Using light of a longer wavelength will result in increased fringe spacing, i.e. $\Delta x \propto \lambda$.

The following equation can be used to calculate the fringe separation.

> $\Delta x = \frac{\lambda L}{d}$
>
> where Δx is the fringe separation
> λ is the wavelength of the light waves
> L is the distance from the slits to the screen
> d is the slit separation.

- **You will now be able to conduct Practical activity 17 and complete Worksheet 30.**

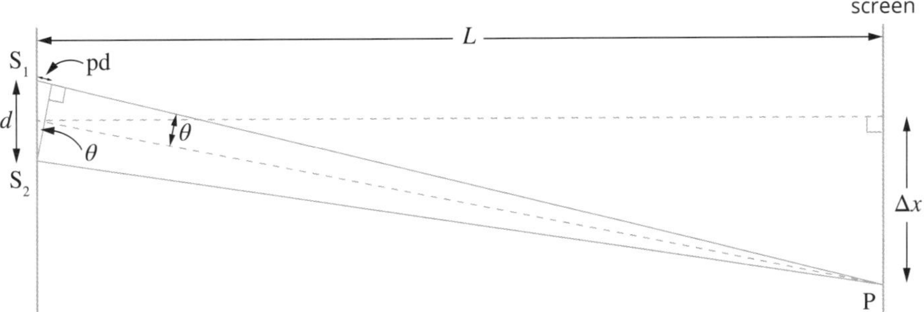

Figure 4.1.11 The geometry of two-point source interference

Light as a particle

THE PHOTOELECTRIC EFFECT

At the start of the twentieth century, a phenomenon that could not be explained using the wave model for light was being observed. Scientists noticed that when some types of electromagnetic radiation (EMR) are incident on a piece of metal, the metal becomes positively charged. This positive charge is due to electrons being ejected from the surface of the metal. The electrons became known as **photoelectrons** because they were released due to incident light or other forms of EMR. The phenomenon is known as the **photoelectric effect**.

The experiment used to investigate the photoelectric effect involves illuminating a metal plate (the cathode) mounted inside a tube that has an oppositely charged plate (the anode) at the end. The resulting electric field helps the photoelectrons cross the gap to the anode (positive potential). A galvanometer is used to measure the current. This is shown in Figure 4.1.12.

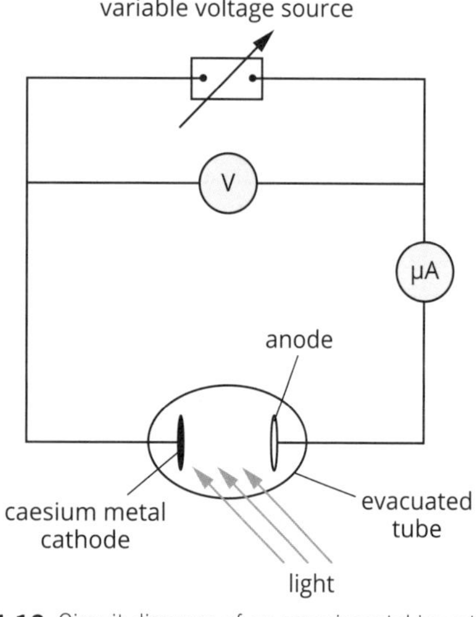

Figure 4.1.12 Circuit diagram of an experimental investigation of the photoelectric effect

The German physicist Philipp Lenard discovered that, for a particular cathode metal, there is a certain frequency of light below which no photoelectrons are observed. This is called the **threshold frequency**, f_0. The photoelectric effect will only emit photoelectrons from a clean metal surface if the frequency of the incident light is greater than a threshold frequency, f_0.

- If $f < f_0$, no electrons are released.
- If $f > f_0$, the rate of electron release (the photocurrent) is proportional to the intensity of the light and occurs without any time delay.

Figure 4.1.13 is a graph of photocurrent, I, plotted as a function of the voltage, V, applied between the cathode and the anode for different light intensities, I_2 and I_1.

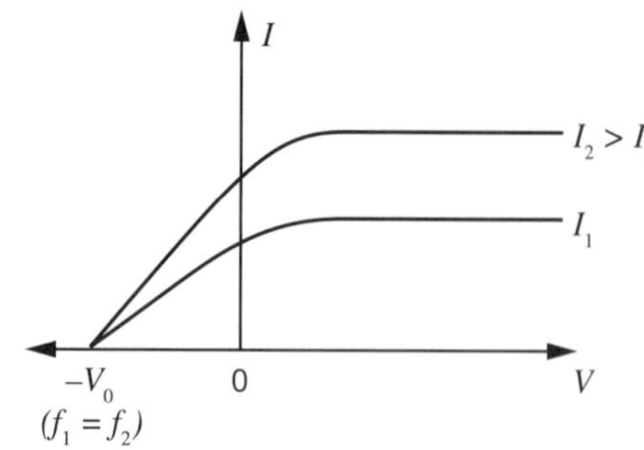

Figure 4.1.13 Photocurrent (I) plotted as a function of the voltage (V)

If the applied voltage is positive, photoelectrons are attracted to the anode until the photocurrent reaches a maximum value. Increasing the voltage beyond this does not affect the rate of electron release.

If the applied voltage is negative, photoelectrons are attracted back towards the illuminated cathode and repelled by the collector electrode (anode), and the photocurrent is reduced until no photoelectrons reach the collector. This voltage is called the **stopping voltage**, V_0.

For brighter light ($I_2 > I_1$) of the same frequency ($f_1 = f_2$), there is a higher photocurrent, but the same stopping voltage. For a particular frequency of light incident on a particular metal, this stopping voltage is a constant. (If two different frequencies of light are compared, the higher frequency light has a higher stopping voltage.)

Several energy transformations are involved when the light source illuminates the metal plate:

1. the energy of the incoming photon ($E = hf$); this is the total energy available in the collision
2. the energy required to overcome the attractive forces acting on the electron in the 'sea'; this is called the work function, ϕ
3. the maximum kinetic energy of electrons after they have been ejected from the surface of the metal.

By experiment, the maximum kinetic energy of the electrons, E_{kmax} (i.e. that of the fastest electron), can be found by using a reverse voltage, the stopping voltage, V_0. The formula is:

$$E_{kmax} = q_e V_0$$

where q_e is the charge on an electron (-1.6×10^{-19} C).

For a given metal, a certain amount of energy is needed to eject the electron. This is called the work function. The **work function**, ϕ, for a metal is given by $\phi = hf_0$, and is different for each metal. If the frequency of the incident light is greater than the threshold frequency, then a photoelectron will be ejected with some kinetic energy up to a maximum value.

The maximum kinetic energy of the photoelectrons emitted from a metal is the energy of the photons minus the work function, ϕ, of the metal:

$E_{kmax} = hf - \phi$.

 ISBN 978 0 6557 0029 6

A graph of $E_{k\max}$ versus frequency will have a gradient equal to Planck's constant, h, and a y-intercept equal to the work function, ϕ. Figure 4.1.14 shows that magnesium has a high threshold frequency that is in the ultraviolet region. The threshold frequency for potassium is in the visible region. The work function for both metals can be taken from the y-intercepts.

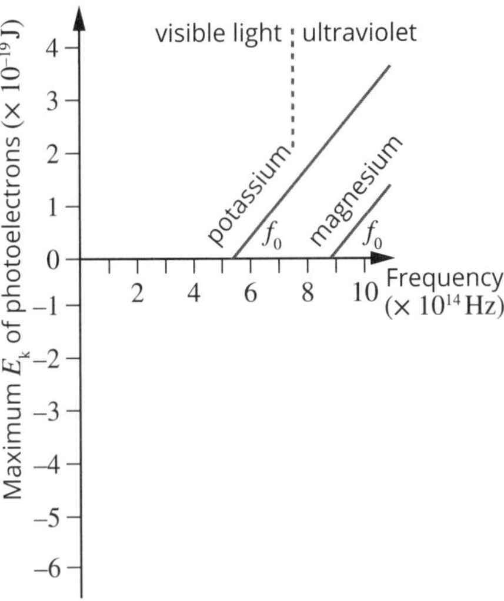

Figure 4.1.14 Maximum kinetic energy of emitted photoelectrons versus frequency of incident light for potassium and magnesium

- **You will now be able to conduct Practical activity 18 and complete Worksheet 31.**

The dual nature of light and matter

A number of phenomena related to the behaviour of light, such as the photoelectric effect, can only be explained using the concept of photons or light quanta. The wave approach to light could not explain various features of the photoelectric effect, such as the existence of a threshold frequency, the absence of a time delay when using very weak light sources, and that the increased intensity of light results in a greater rate of electron release rather than increased electron energy. According to the wave model, the frequency of light should be irrelevant to whether or not photoelectrons are ejected. Since a wave is a form of continuous energy transfer, it would be expected that energy from the wave would build up in the metal over time.

Einstein used Planck's concept of a photon to explain the photoelectric effect, stating that each electron release was due to an interaction with only one photon. The photon model of light explained the existence of a threshold frequency for each metal; the absence of a time delay for the photocurrent, even for weak light sources; and why brighter light resulted in a higher photocurrent.

Light exhibits wave properties in some situations and particle properties in others. The concept of wave–particle duality is used to describe the dual nature of light.

Table 4.1.1 outlines some of the key predictions or observations of the photoelectric effect that differentiate between the wave and particle models of light.

Table 4.1.1 The predictions of the wave model that are not supported by observing the photoelectric effect

Wave model (predictions)	Particle model (observations)
predicts that any frequency should work	there is a minimum frequency (threshold frequency) and energy before electrons are emitted
predicts that increasing the intensity of light would increase the energy of the emitted electrons	the energy of the emitted electrons depends only on the frequency of the incident light
suggests there is a time delay before electrons are emitted when weak light sources are used	explains an absence of any time delay before electrons are emitted when weak light sources are used

- **You will now be able to complete Worksheet 32.**

THE QUANTUM NATURE OF LIGHT AND MATTER

The wave and particle models for light seem to be fundamentally incompatible. Waves are continuous and are described in terms of wavelength and frequency. Particles are discrete and are described by physical dimensions such as their mass and radius. In 1924, French physicist Louis de Broglie proposed a groundbreaking theory and suggested that, as light demonstrates both wave and particle-like properties, perhaps matter might sometimes demonstrate wave-like properties. He quantified this theory by predicting that the wavelength of a particle would be given by what is now known as the de Broglie equation:

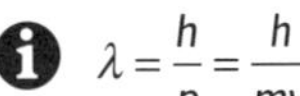

$$\lambda = \frac{h}{p} = \frac{h}{mv}$$

where λ is the wavelength of the particle (m)
h is Planck's constant (6.63×10^{-34} J s)
p is the momentum of the particle (kg m s^{-1})
m is the mass of the particle (kg)
v is the velocity of the particle (m s^{-1}).

It should be noted that when this equation is used for everyday objects such as a cricket ball (with a mass of about 60 g), the wavelength is extremely small (about 9.9×10^{-35} m) and is not noticeable. However, at the atomic level, energy and matter exhibit the characteristics of both waves and particles.

KEY KNOWLEDGE

Like light, all matter has a dual nature. Throughout everyday experience, matter is particle-like, but under some situations it has a wave-like nature. This symmetry in nature—the dual nature of light and matter—is referred to as **wave–particle duality**. For example, Young's double-slit experiment is explained by a wave model, but produces the same interference and diffraction patterns when one photon at a time or one electron at a time is passed through the slits. Figure 4.1.15 illustrates that an interference pattern can be built up over time by a series of single photons passing through an apparatus like that used in Young's experiment, demonstrating the wave–particle duality of light.

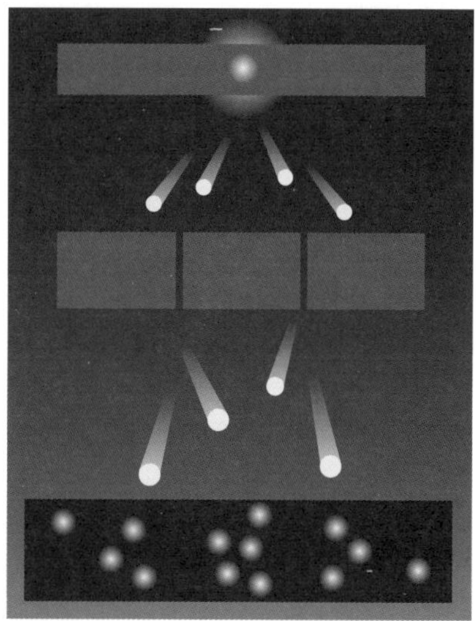

Figure 4.1.15 Young's double-slit experiment using a series of single photons

In 1925, American physicists Clinton J. Davisson and Lester H. Germer were investigating the reflection of electrons by a metal lattice. They found that the scattered electrons produced a diffraction pattern. This was confirmation of De Broglie's hypothesis that particles display wave-like behaviour and have a wavelength.

Further evidence of this was found by the physicist G.P. Thomson in the same year. Thomson produced diffraction patterns for both electrons and X-rays of the same wavelength. Figure 4.1.16 shows the similarity of a diffraction pattern produced by X-rays compared to one in which electrons were used.

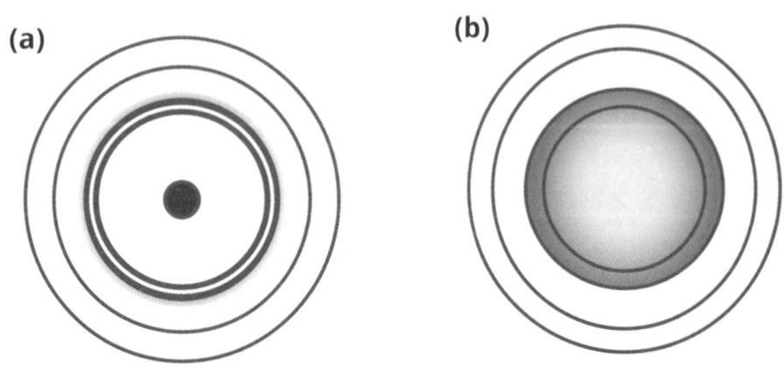

Figure 4.1.16 Diffraction patterns using (a) X-rays and (b) a beam of electrons with the same target crystal

In 1925, the Austrian physicist Erwin Schrödinger built on the work of Niels Bohr by developing a mathematical equation that could describe the wave behaviour of electrons in situations other than the simple hydrogen atom. In Schrödinger's model, the wave properties of electrons are interpreted as representing the probability of finding an electron in a certain location. Quantum mechanics is the name given to the study of the wave properties of electrons.

LIGHT AND MATTER

Spectroscopy is the branch of science that investigates the spectra produced when matter interacts with or emits electromagnetic radiation. A spectroscope is the device used to determine the spectra, and works by combining a diffraction grating with a viewing telescope or a digital converter.

When a graduated scale is added to the spectroscope to make a **spectrometer**, the specific wavelengths in the spectrum can be determined. The spectroscope determines the chemical make-up of a visible source of light because each element has its own distinctive **emission line spectrum** (Figure 4.1.17b). An emission line spectrum shows only certain colours or specific wavelengths of light. When elements are heated to high temperatures or have an electrical current passed through them, they produce light. Atoms within the material absorb energy and become 'excited', and this makes the atom unstable. Eventually the atom will return to the 'unexcited' or **ground state**, and when this happens, the energy that had been absorbed is released. The wavelength of that energy (known as a photon) will depend on the amount of energy released.

In 1819, German physicist Joseph von Fraunhofer reported many dark lines appearing in the spectrum of sunlight. Fifty years later, Gustav Kirchhoff and Robert Bunsen deduced that the dark lines were due to these colours (wavelengths or frequencies) being absorbed by gases as light made its way through the outer atmosphere of the Sun. This is called an **absorption line spectrum** and is shown in Figure 4.1.17a.

By comparing the emission line spectrum to the absorption line spectrum viewed using a spectroscope, we can learn about the chemical make-up of an object. An emission line spectrum is produced by energised atoms, while an absorption line spectrum is created when white light passes through a cold gas. The absorption and emission line spectra for hydrogen are shown in Figure 4.1.17.

Figure 4.1.17 The (a) absorption and (b) emission line spectra of hydrogen

 ISBN 978 0 6557 0029 6

KEY KNOWLEDGE

The emission and absorption line spectra of hydrogen were of interest to scientists, as it had been recognised that lines in the absorption spectrum of hydrogen matched lines in the solar spectrum. This allowed astronomers to determine that the Sun is largely composed of hydrogen and smaller amounts of other elements. Interpreting the line spectra of stars further revealed their temperature, composition, age and rotation.

BOHR MODEL OF THE ATOM

The work of Thomson and Rutherford established the nuclear model of the atom—a positive nucleus surrounded by electrons, but these models had their limitations. For example, Rutherford's model proposed that electrons revolve around the nucleus in circular orbits. According to the law of conservation of energy, the orbiting electrons should emit energy due to their motion. That energy loss would, in turn, cause their circular orbits to shrink.

Danish physicist Niels Bohr published a solution to this instability problem.

1 An electron can exist only in certain energy states, and while in this state the electron does not radiate energy.
2 When an electron undergoes a transition from an upper energy state to a lower energy state, a photon of energy is emitted.

Bohr proposed that the quantum mechanical nature of matter was a better way to understand the structure of the atom.

Bohr applied Planck's quantum theory to Rutherford's model, and suggested that electrons in atoms orbit the nucleus in specially defined energy levels, and no radiation is emitted or absorbed unless the electron can jump from its energy level to another. Energy levels can be shown as a number of horizontal lines on a graph. The graph in Figure 4.1.18 shows the energy levels for sodium gas, where $n = 1$ is the ground state (the lowest energy state of an atom) and the highest level is where ionisation occurs and the electron escapes the atom.

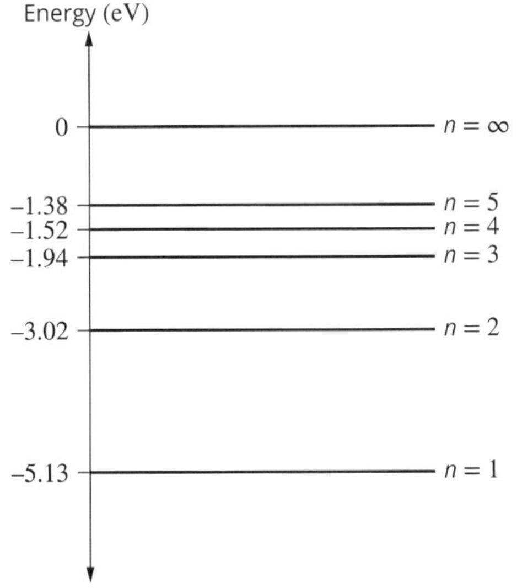

Figure 4.1.18 Energy levels for sodium gas

Bohr's main ideas were as follows.

- The electron moves in a circular orbit around the nucleus of an atom.
- The force keeping the electron moving in a circle is the electrostatic force of attraction (the positive nucleus attracts the negative electron).
- A number of allowable orbits of different radii exist for each atom and are labelled $n = 1, 2, 3$, etc. The electron may occupy only these orbits.
- An electron ordinarily occupies the lowest energy orbit available.
- An electron can jump to a higher energy level by absorbing some energy. The absorbed energy must be exactly equal to the difference between the electron's initial and final energy levels.
- Electromagnetic radiation is emitted by an excited atom when an electron falls from a higher energy level to a lower energy level. The energy of the emitted light will be exactly equal to the energy difference between the electron's initial and final levels.

The last two points of Bohr's idea suggest that electron energies are quantised, since only certain values are allowed, further supporting Planck's model. As discussed earlier, an emission line spectrum shows only certain colours or specific wavelengths of light for a certain element. Bohr proposed that an emission line spectrum is produced by energised atoms as electrons undergo transitions between energy levels. An electron that drops between energy levels emits a photon (light) of energy equal to the difference between the energy levels. The energy of the photon then determines the colour of the light.

Bohr labelled the possible electron orbits for the hydrogen atom with a quantum number, n, and he was able to calculate the energy associated with each quantum number. Using these energy levels, he could theoretically predict the wavelengths of all of the lines of the hydrogen emission line spectrum using Planck's equation:

$$E = \frac{hc}{\lambda}$$

The frequency of a photon emitted or absorbed by a hydrogen atom can be calculated from the difference between the energy levels involved:

$$E_2 - E_1 = hf = \frac{hc}{\lambda}$$

In 1885, the Swiss mathematician Johann Balmer found an empirical equation that predicted the wavelength of the visible lines of the hydrogen emission line spectrum.

The ultraviolet series was later observed by Theodore Lyman, and two different infrared series were observed by Friedrich Paschen and Frederick Brackett. The energy transitions for the Balmer, Lyman and Paschen series are shown in Figure 4.1.19.

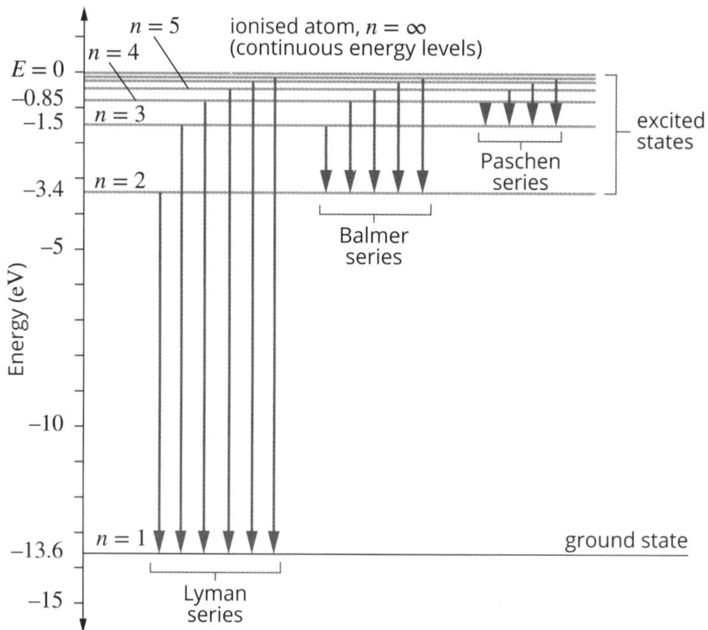

Figure 4.1.19 The energy transitions for the Balmer, Lyman and Paschen series

- **You will now be able to conduct Practical activity 19 and complete Worksheets 33, 34, 35 and 36.**

Einstein's theory of special relativity

Galileo and Newton developed theories of motion. These theories allowed the relative motion of low-speed objects to be modelled mathematically. Galileo's principle of relativity states that you cannot tell if you are moving or not if you are travelling at constant velocity, without looking outside of your own **frame of reference**.

 A frame of reference describes where an observation is being made from.

Based on the work of Galileo, Isaac Newton developed mathematical models to describe motion, and using these equations the velocity of objects can be calculated relative to any frame of reference if the velocity of the frame of reference is known. Newton had referred to these as inertial frames of reference, as the law of inertia applied within them.

Einstein decided that Galileo's principle of relativity was so elegant it simply had to be true, and he was also convinced that Maxwell's electromagnetic equations, and their predictions, were sound. Most physicists believed that the constant speed of light predicted by Maxwell's equations referred to the speed of light relative to a **medium** (a substance it travelled through). However, as light can travel through a vacuum, this medium was no ordinary material and physicists gave it the name **aether**. This was a real problem for Einstein because if the speed of light was fixed in the aether, it must depend on the velocity of an inertial frame in the aether, which would be in direct conflict with the principle of Galilean relativity, which Einstein was reluctant to abandon.

Although Einstein accepted both Galileo's and Maxwell's theories despite the apparent contradiction, this still left the question: how could two observers travelling at different speeds see the same light beam travelling at the same speed? Einstein put forward two simple **postulates**. The two postulates of special relativity can be abbreviated to:

 The laws of physics are the same in all inertial frames of reference.
The speed of light is the same to all observers.

Einstein realised that accepting both of these postulates implied that space and time were not absolute and independent, but were related in some way. For example, consider a train that has a flashing light bulb set right in the centre of the carriage. If Clare, who is outside the train, measures the light travelling at the same speed in the forwards and backwards directions, she will find that the light will reach the back wall first.

 ISBN 978 0 6557 0029 6

This is because that wall is moving towards the light, whereas the front wall is moving away from the light, and so the light will take longer to catch up to it. This is shown in Figure 4.1.20.

Figure 4.1.20 Clare measures the light reaching the back wall of the train carriage before it reaches the front wall, as the train is travelling forwards. An observer on the train would see the light reach the front and back walls at the same time.

Two events that are simultaneous in one frame of reference are not necessarily simultaneous in another. This implies that time measured in different frames of reference might not be the same. This lead to the conclusion that both time and space are related in a four-dimensional universe called **spacetime**.

TIME DILATION

From Einstein's second postulate, for the speed of light to remain the same for all observers, either time or space will need to change to compensate for this. For example, consider the situation in Figure 4.1.21, where Amaya and Binh are riding in a spaceship that can travel at speeds close to the speed of light. Clare is watching from a space station, which according to Clare is a stationary frame of reference. Amaya and Binh have taken along a light clock, which (it is assumed) Clare can read, even from a large distance away. A light clock 'ticks' each time the light pulse reflects off the bottom mirror. Clare also has an identical light clock in her own space station, which she can compare to Amaya's light clock. Like any light clock, this clock is governed by a regular oscillation that defines a period of time. Clare measures that the light pulses travel a zigzag path between the mirrors.

Figure 4.1.21 Time dilation illustrated by a light clock

In their own frame of reference, Amaya and Binh measure a unit of time equal to t_a. Clare, from her frame of reference, measures a different time, t_c. The **proper time**, t_0, is the time measured by an observer at the same point in an inertial frame of reference; in this example it would be Amaya's and Binh's time, t_a. Clare's measured time, t_c, is greater than the time that Amaya and Binh measure, t_a, for the same event. This means the pulses in a light clock in a moving frame of reference have to travel further when observed from a stationary frame ($t = \frac{d}{c}$). Because of the constancy of the speed of light, this effectively means that time appears to have slowed in a moving frame.

This is known as **time dilation**, according to the equation:

$$t = \gamma t_0$$

where t is the time observed from the stationary frame
t_0 is the proper time in the moving frame
γ is the **Lorentz factor**:

$$\gamma = \frac{1}{\sqrt{\left(1 - \frac{v^2}{c^2}\right)}}$$

where v is the speed of the moving frame of reference ($m\,s^{-1}$)
c is the speed of light ($3.0 \times 10^8\,m\,s^{-1}$).

The situation above was from Clare's point of view, not Amaya's and Binh's. According to Amaya and Binh, as they look out their window at Clare in her space station receding from them, they can consider that it is they who are at rest and it is Clare and her space station that are moving away at a velocity near the speed of light. This is what Galileo's principle of relativity and Einstein's first postulate are all about. Observers in relative motion both measure time slowing in the other frame of reference.

In Earth's atmosphere, high-energy cosmic rays interact with the nuclei of oxygen atoms 15 km above the surface of Earth to create a cascade of high velocity subatomic particles. One of these particles is a muon, which is unstable. Time dilation explains how muons can reach Earth's surface after originating 15 km up in the upper atmosphere, when they should all decay within 0.7 km of their journey according to classical physics. Within the stationary observer's frame of reference, the muons' lifetimes are dilated so that they reach the detectors on Earth's surface before we would expect them to have decayed. This distance travelled is actually shorter. This is known as **length contraction**.

LENGTH CONTRACTION

The theory of special relativity states that time and space are related. Motion affects space in the direction of travel. A moving object will appear shorter, or will appear to travel less distance, by the inverse of the Lorentz factor, γ. The **proper length**, L_0, is the length measured by an observer at rest with respect to the object being measured.

Einstein's length contraction equation is given by:

$L = \frac{L_0}{\gamma}$

where L is the contracted length as seen in the moving frame,
L_0 is the proper length in the stationary frame,
γ is the Lorentz factor.

This apparent contraction of an object's length when moving is relative to an observer.

EINSTEIN'S MASS-ENERGY RELATIONSHIP

The problem with the length contraction equation can be seen if you consider a spaceship that gets to the speed of light: the length of the spaceship will shrink to zero, and time inside it appears to stop altogether. Einstein took this to mean that it is not possible to reach the speed of light in any real spaceship. However, the difficulties with time and length for the spaceship were not the only reasons Einstein came to this conclusion. Einstein showed that as the speed of a spaceship approaches *c*, its momentum increases, but this is not reflected in a corresponding increase in speed.

Relativistic momentum (momentum described only by the theory of relativity) includes the Lorentz factor, γ, and hence, as more impulse is added, the mass seems to increase towards infinity as the speed gets closer, but never equal, to *c*. The relativistic momentum equation is:

$p = \gamma mv = \gamma p_0$

where p_0 is the momentum, mv, as you would define it in classical mechanics,
p is the relativistic momentum ($kg\,m\,s^{-1}$).

A term called relativistic mass, γm, may be used to indicate the mass of an object that is moving. As the Lorentz factor increases with the increase in the velocity, the relativistic mass also increases.

Consider the example with the rocket ship that is attempting to increase its velocity to the speed of light. With the increase in the relativistic mass of the rocket ship, it becomes harder for the force of the engines to cause a change in velocity (and therefore a change in momentum, or impulse). The closer the rocket ship approaches to *c*, the greater the amount of impulse that is required to accelerate the ship to the speed of light. This was the reason, Einstein concluded, why an object can never reach the speed of light.

As the momentum of an object increases, so does its kinetic energy. Einstein showed, however, that the classical expression for kinetic energy was not correct at high speeds. The kinetic energy is given by:

$$E_k = (\gamma - 1)mc^2$$

From this equation, and by considering conservation of energy, Einstein found that the total energy of an object is given by:

$E_{tot} = E_k + E_0 = \gamma mc^2$

where the rest energy, E_0, which is the energy associated with the rest mass of an object, is given by:

$E_0 = mc^2$

Mass and energy are seen as different forms of the same thing. This means that mass, *m*, can be converted into energy, and energy can be converted into mass.

Nuclear fission and fusion reactions result in a mass defect (change). It is this difference in mass that is converted to the energy released in nuclear reactions. This mass is related to the energy produced according to:

$$\Delta E = \Delta mc^2$$

Nuclear fusion is the combining of light nuclei to form heavier nuclei. Extremely high temperatures are required for fusion to occur. This is the process occurring in stars. Hydrogen nuclei fuse to form deuterium. Further fusions result in the formation of isotopes of helium.

- **You will now be able to complete Worksheets 37, 38 and 39.**

 ISBN 978 0 6557 0029 6

WORKSHEET 29

Knowledge review—waves and light

1 Rearrange these colours in order of increasing wavelength:

green, indigo, red, orange, violet, yellow, blue

2 Rearrange these radiation types in order of increasing frequency:

X-rays, microwaves, blue light, radio, infrared, ultraviolet

3 Calculate the frequency of electromagnetic radiation whose wavelength is 1.25×10^{-3} m. State the type of radiation it most likely is based on the frequency.

4 A raindrop hits a calm water surface and creates a series of ripples. Identify which of the following quantities changes as the ripples move out from the starting point.

A wavelength

B amplitude

C frequency

D velocity

5 In a ripple tank, a set of parallel waves 1.5 cm apart is travelling towards a shallower region at $7.5\,\text{cm}\,\text{s}^{-1}$. Each wavefront makes an angle of 20° with the straight edge of the deeper section. The wave separation becomes 1.3 cm once it passes into shallower water.

a Calculate the frequency of the waves in the initial deeper section.

b Calculate the new frequency in the shallower section of the ripple tank.

c Determine the angle the wavefronts make with the boundary of the shallower section. (Hint: Use a variation of Snell's law: $n_1 \sin\theta_1 = n_2 \sin\theta_2$)

6 Categorise the following types of waves by whether they are transverse or longitudinal.

sound, radio, guitar-string vibrations, water, sonar, Mexican wave

Transverse waves: ____________________

Longitudinal waves: ____________________

ISBN 978 0 6557 0029 6

WORKSHEET 30

Modelling

Diffraction and interference

DIFFRACTION GRATINGS

Diffraction gratings work on the same principle as the double-slit experiment, except that they have many lines or slits. A diffraction grating is defined by its number of lines per cm.

Consider a grating with 4000 lines per cm. Then the slit spacing is given as:

$$d = \frac{1}{4000} = 2.5 \times 10^{-4}\ \text{cm} = 2.5 \times 10^{-6}\ \text{m}$$

The more slits a diffraction grating has, the narrower the interference fringe and the more precise the diffraction patterns that can be generated. A simple arrangement in which the detector angle can be changed to pick up specific wavelengths is shown in Figure 4.1.22.

The collimator is a lens arrangement that collects the light using one lens and focuses the light onto the diffraction grating using a second lens.

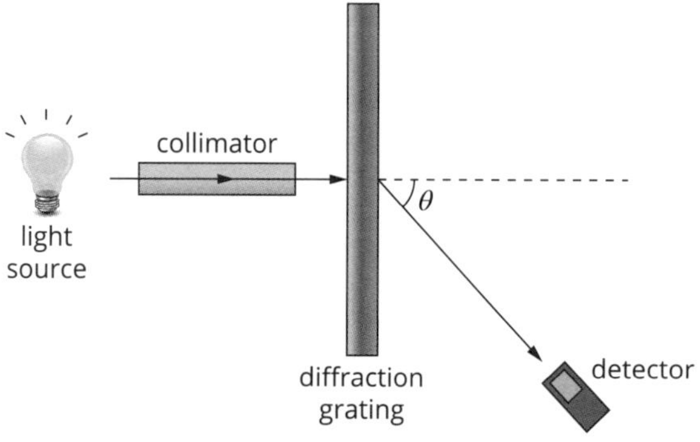

Figure 4.1.22 Experimental set-up for the collimator and diffraction grating

As for a double slit, the condition for constructive interference in a diffraction grating is given by $n\lambda = d\sin\theta$.

1 A HeNe laser of wavelength 633.2 nm is incident on a diffraction grating with 5000 lines cm^{-1}. At what angle does the detector need to be to observe the first-order line ($n = 1$) of this wavelength?

2 A white light source is shone through the diffraction grating. What colour will be seen at the angle calculated in Question **1**?

3 **a** The angle of the detector is changed to 40.0°. What first-order wavelength will be observed?

b What second-order wavelength could be detected?

ISBN 978 0 6557 0029 6

4 In X-ray diffraction, the spacing between atoms becomes the diffraction grating. A crystal is rotated through an angle θ, and the angles at which constructive interference occur give information about the atomic spacing and the crystal structure.

a Figure 4.1.23, look at the path difference between the two rays and write the condition for constructive interference in this case.

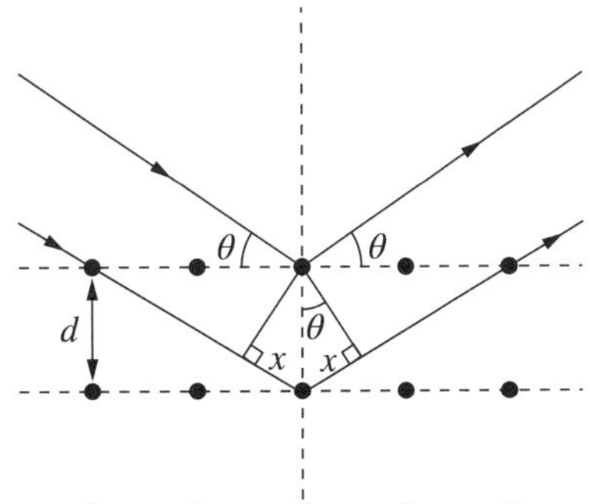

Figure 4.1.23 Diagram of X-ray diffraction

b An NaCl crystal has a spacing between adjacent atoms of 0.2814 nm. What wavelength will the X-ray need to be to observe constructive interference at an angle of 40.0°? Assume first-order effects only.

INTERFERENCE OF LIGHT

5 What property of electromagnetic radiation does Young's double-slit experiment show?

6 For the double slit and screen shown, draw the wavefronts and indicate the regions of constructive and destructive interference.

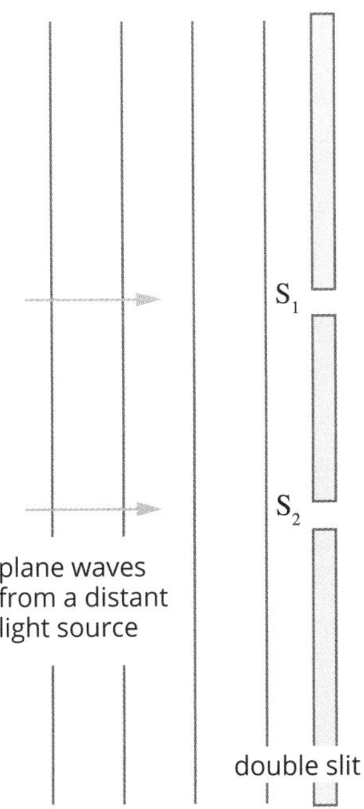

7 The direction of the wave can be indicated by a ray. Consider waves passing through slits S_1 and S_2 to produce an interference pattern on the screen a distance L away, as shown in Figure 4.1.24.

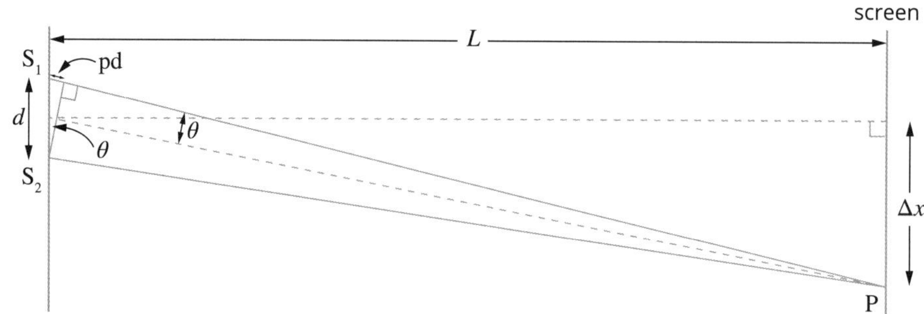

Figure 4.1.24 Waves from double slits incident on a screen

a What does the path difference have to be for constructive interference? Explain your answer.

b What does the path difference have to be for destructive interference? Explain your answer.

8 An interference pattern from a red laser is given in Figure 4.1.25.

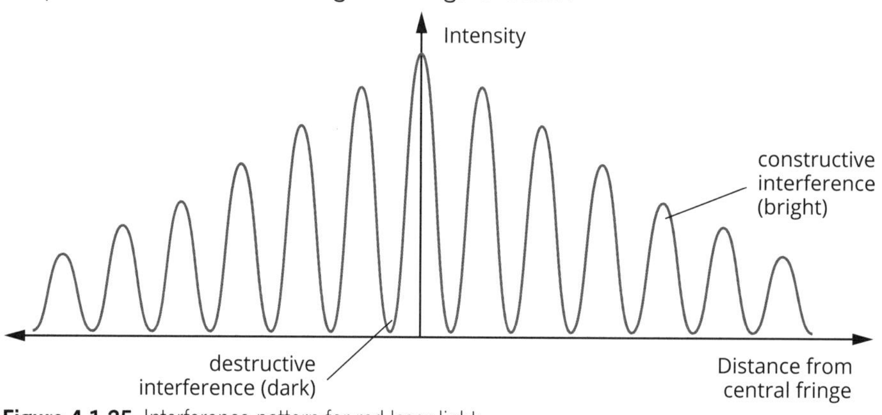

Figure 4.1.25 Interference pattern for red laser light

How would you expect the pattern to change if:

a a green laser is used instead of a red laser?

b the red laser is used but the slit spacing is decreased?

c the red laser is used and the slits are moved closer to the screen?

9 A blue semiconductor laser of 450 nm is directed through a thin pair of slits, 70 μm apart, onto a screen that is 2.5 m away. Calculate the fringe spacing.

 ISBN 978 0 6557 0029 6

10 Light of an unknown wavelength is emitted through a pair of thin slits 30 μm apart. The screen is 1.5 m away and the fringe separation is 2.0 cm. Determine the wavelength and colour of the laser.

11 A Young's double-slit experiment was performed with a semiconductor laser diode of unknown wavelength. To reduce experimental error, the student decided to take a series of measurements. The student changed the distance of the screen from the slits and measured the fringe separation. The double slits were 50 μm apart. Plot the data on a suitable graph and determine the wavelength using a line of best fit and its gradient.

L (m)	Δx (cm)
1.0	1.3
1.5	2.0
2.0	2.6
2.5	3.3
3.0	3.9

WORKSHEET 31

Modelling

The photoelectric effect

A circuit for measuring the photoelectric effect is shown in Figure 4.1.26.

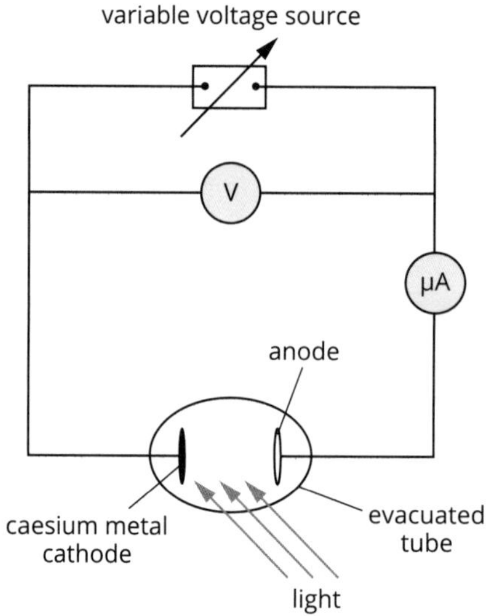

Figure 4.1.26 Circuit for measuring the photoelectric effect

1 The following are some observations of the photoelectric effect. What conclusions could be drawn from each observation?

a There is a threshold frequency below which no photoelectrons are emitted, even if the intensity is increased.

b Above the threshold frequency, increasing the intensity increases the number of photoelectrons produced.

c When a reverse bias is applied, the cathode has a positive potential. There is there still a photocurrent at a small reverse bias.

2 If the stopping voltage is 1.8 V, calculate the maximum kinetic energy of the photoelectrons in eV and joules.

3 Two photoelectric effect experiments are conducted in which the number of photons incident on the metal is the same. In the first, a light of frequency f_1 is used, and a photocurrent I_1 and stopping potential V_1 are measured. In the second, a lower frequency, f_2, is used, and a photocurrent I_2 and stopping potential V_2 are measured. Which is the most accurate statement? Explain your answer.

A Photocurrent $I_2 < I_1$ and stopping potential $V_2 < V_1$

B Photocurrent $I_2 < I_1$ and stopping potential $V_2 = V_1$

C Photocurrent $I_2 = I_1$ and stopping potential $V_2 < V_1$

D Photocurrent $I_2 = I_1$ and stopping potential $V_2 > V_1$

ISBN 978 0 6557 0029 6

4 Explain why the wave model cannot be used to explain the photoelectric effect.

5 The work function for some metals is given below:

calcium	2.9 eV	niobium	4.3 eV
copper	4.7 eV	gold	5.1 eV

a Which metal will emit photoelectrons if light of $1.0^9 \times 10^{15}$ Hz is incident on it?

b For the metals that will eject photoelectrons, what will be the maximum kinetic energy in eV?

6 Beryllium has a threshold frequency of 1.20×10^{15} Hz. Calculate the maximum kinetic energy (eV) of the ejected photoelectrons when UV light of wavelength 200 nm is incident on the beryllium cathode.

7 Determine the work functions of potassium and magnesium from the graph in Figure 4.1.27, using two methods.

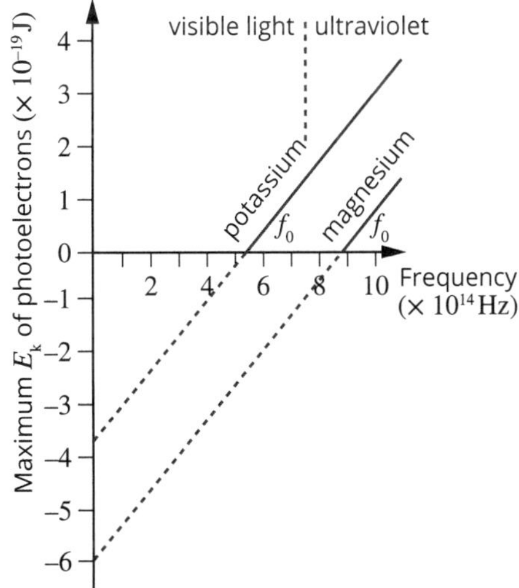

Figure 4.1.27 Graph of kinetic energy of emitted photoelectrons versus frequency of incident light

WORKSHEET 32

Case study

Evidence for the wave model of light

The following is a list of some of the behaviours or properties of light you may have examined.

straight-line propagation	diffraction	photoelectric effect
reflection	colour	Wien's law
Compton effect	dispersion	two-slit interference
absorption	refraction	thin-film interference
double refraction and polarisation	inverse square law	propagation through a vacuum

1 Find out which of these behaviours or properties would have been known to Isaac Newton and/or Christiaan Huygens; which would have been known since ancient times; and which they would not have known. If possible, find a date by which the phenomenon was first noted or discovered.

Known since ancient times	Known to Newton and Huygens	Unknown to Newton and Huygens

2 Briefly outline the model for light formulated by each of these two scientists.

3 Based on your learning from Questions **1** and **2**, sort the behaviours of light listed above into three categories according to which model it supports.

Supports Newton's model	Supports Huygens' model	Could support either model

 ISBN 978 0 6557 0029 6

WORKSHEET 33

Modelling

Matter waves

Ignore relativistic effects in all calculations. Give your answers to two significant figures. Use $m_e = 9.1 \times 10^{-31}$ kg.

1 **a** How was Young's double-slit experiment modified to show matter acting like a wave?

b What other evidence was there for matter waves?

2 The de Broglie wavelength is given by $\lambda = \frac{h}{p}$ or $\lambda = \frac{h}{mv}$.

a An electron is fired with a velocity of $5.0 \times 10^6\,\text{m s}^{-1}$. Calculate its de Broglie wavelength.

b Consider a 900 kg car travelling at $60\,\text{km h}^{-1}$. Calculate its de Broglie wavelength.

c What conclusions can you draw from the wavelengths calculated in **a** and **b**?

3 **a** An electron is accelerated at 2.0 keV in an electron microscope. Calculate the de Broglie wavelength of the electron.

b How does this compare with the wavelength of visible light? Why is this useful in an electron microscope?

4 **a** Photon momentum has been used in solar sails for space flight. Calculate the momentum from one green-light photon with wavelength 510 nm.

b Compare this to the momentum of a 100 g ball travelling at 15 km h^{-1}.

EXTENSION

5 How did de Broglie modify the Bohr model using matter waves? Draw a diagram to assist your explanation.

 ISBN 978 0 6557 0029 6

WORKSHEET 34

Modelling

Quantum mechanical atom

1 For which atom was Bohr's model most successful?

2 The (a) absorption and (b) emission spectra for hydrogen are shown in Figure 4.1.28.

Figure 4.1.28 (a) Absorption and (b) emission spectra for hydrogen. The bright lines in the emission spectrum line up with the 'missing' dark lines in the absorption spectrum.

a Using the energy-level diagram below, explain the conditions under which absorption occurs.

$n = 3$

$n = 2$

$n = 1$

b Using the energy-level diagram below, explain how emission occurs. Draw all of the possible transitions.

$n = 3$

$n = 2$

$n = 1$

3 Refer to Figure 4.1.29 to answer the questions.

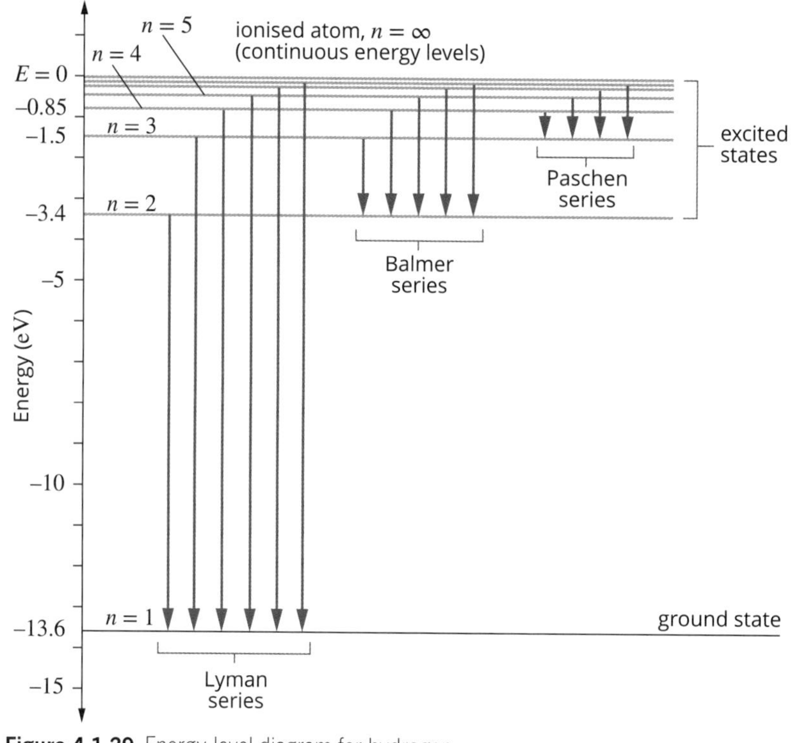

Figure 4.1.29 Energy-level diagram for hydrogen

a Calculate the energy of a photon when an electron drops from the $n = 3$ energy level to the $n = 1$ energy level.

b Calculate the wavelength of a photon emitted when an electron transitions from the $n = 2$ to the $n = 1$ level.

c Light emitted from the centre of the Sun can be treated as a blackbody and therefore emits a full range of colours. As it passes through the Sun's atmosphere some lines are absorbed, giving rise to a series of lines known as Fraunhofer lines. An already-excited hydrogen atom undergoes an absorption transition from $n = 3$ to $n = 4$. Use the Rydberg expression $\frac{1}{\lambda} = R\left(\frac{1}{n_1^2} - \frac{1}{n_2^2}\right)$ to calculate the wavelength of this transition. The Rydberg constant R is equal to $1.097 \times 10^7\,\text{m}^{-1}$. Compare your answer to the wavelength you would obtain using the method from **b**.

ISBN 978 0 6557 0029 6

d For each of the following emission lines, identify the transition and whether it belongs to the Lyman series, the Balmer series or the Paschen series. (Use the expression $E_n = \frac{13.6}{n^2}$ for the last one.)

2.55 eV:

0.65 eV:

13.056 eV:

4 What were the limitations of the Bohr model?

5 Each atom and molecule produces a unique spectrum that can be used to identify the composition of a material, or even the distance to a star. The diagram below shows the energy levels for a mercury atom.

Light with photon energies of 5.5 eV, 8.8 eV and 9.6 eV is incident on mercury. Draw all the possible absorption transitions on the diagram.

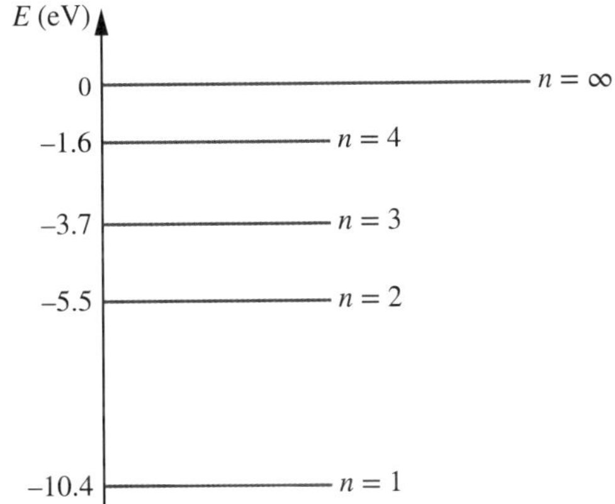

6 An electron with energy of 5.5 eV is incident on mercury. What could happen?

ISBN 978 0 6557 0029 6

WORKSHEET 35

Modelling

Light and matter

1 According to quantum mechanics, all particles can behave like waves. The wavelength of a particle:

A decreases with bigger mass and bigger velocity

B increases with bigger mass and bigger velocity

C decreases with bigger mass and increases with bigger velocity

D increases with bigger mass and decreases with bigger velocity

2 **a** Given Planck's constant, $h = 6.63 \times 10^{-34}\,\text{m}^2\,\text{kg}\,\text{s}^{-1}$, calculate the wavelength of a 700 g grapefruit thrown at $18.0\,\text{m}\,\text{s}^{-1}$.

b Explain how your answer indicates that grapefruits do not seem to behave like waves.

3 The emission spectrum of a strange new isotope has been examined. It contains precisely 10 different wavelengths. How many energy levels are in an atom of this isotope?

A 4 **B** 5 **C** 10 **D** 15

4 The energy level diagram for hydrogen is shown in Figure 4.1.30.

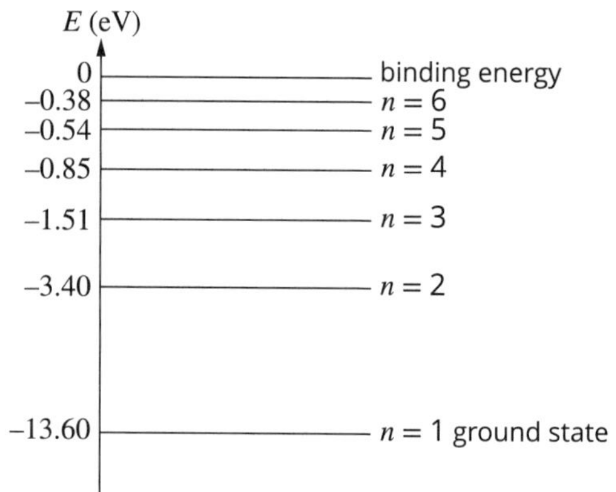

Figure 4.1.30 Energy level diagram for hydrogen

a Calculate the frequency of a photon emitted in a transition from the $n = 5$ level to the $n = 2$ level.

b What wavelength would such a photon have?

c When the absorption spectrum of hydrogen is examined, this particular wavelength is not present. Explain how this occurs.

ISBN 978 0 6557 0029 6

d What happens when a 12.5 eV photon strikes a hydrogen atom in the ground state?

5 The photoelectric effect is usually cited as strong evidence for the dual nature of light. Figure 4.1.31 shows a typical arrangement used to measure the photoelectric effect.

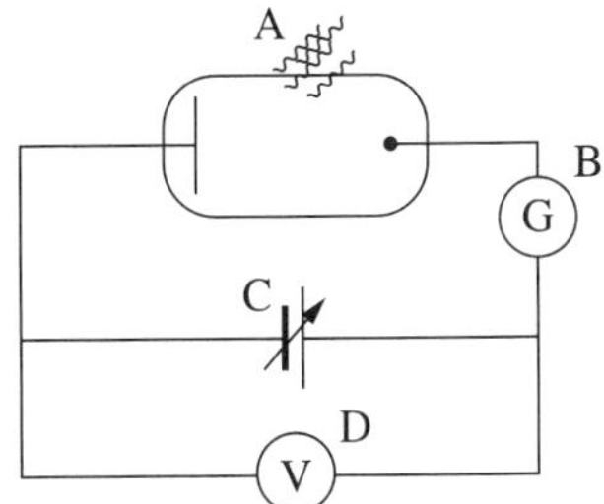

Figure 4.1.31 Circuit diagram for measuring the photoelectric effect

a The letters on the diagram identify the parts of the apparatus. Fill in the blanks in the table below.

Part	Name	What it is for and/or what it does
A	photons/light	
B		
C		
D		

b What factors affect the kinetic energy of the fastest photoelectrons?

c Classical physics predicted that increasing the intensity of the light would increase this energy. Explain how this prediction was made and why it was not observed.

d It is found that the lowest frequency that produces photoelectrons is 5.31×10^{14} Hz. What is the energy of photons produced this way, in joules?

e What is the size of the work function for the metal in this experiment?

f What will be the energy of the fastest photoelectrons produced by light of wavelength 300 nm?

ISBN 978 0 6557 0029 6

WORKSHEET 36

Simulation

Investigating spectra

There are two types of line spectra covered in this physics course—emission and absorption.

An emission line spectrum can be created by passing an electric current through a gas in a discharge tube. A very large potential difference generally needs to be applied across the contacts at either end of the discharge tube to start the current.

1 The discharge inside the tube looks like a steady spark or plasma. Describe what happens to the atoms or molecules in the gas when the discharge takes place.

2 The light coming from the tube is created when excited atoms transition to lower energy states. Each emitted wavelength corresponds to a specific transition. If a wavelength of 451 nm was found in an emission spectrum, what is the size of the energy transition (in joules) that created it?

3 A more common unit of energy employed in this area is the electron-volt (eV). Why is this energy unit given this name? How many joules are equal to one electron-volt?

4 Convert the energy of the transition in Question **2** into electron-volts.

The wavelengths of light emitted from a discharge tube are generally measured with a spectroscope. Newton originally created a spectrum by passing white light through a glass prism. A diffraction grating, either etched on transparent plastic or scratched on glass, will also produce a spectrum.

5 Give two reasons why a diffraction grating produces a much better spectrum than a glass prism.

Your school may also have a HeNe laser that emits light at 633 nm. If not, a red laser pointer in a PowerPoint presentation 'clicker' might be available. These generally emit light at about 650 nm. Shine the laser through a diffraction grating at a white screen about a metre away. Exercise care when using a laser. Do not shine it into anyone's eyes!

You should be able to see a bright spot directly in front of the laser. In addition, you should see a pair of red spots equally spaced to either side of the central spot. (You may need to rotate the diffraction grating to see them.) There may even be another pair of fainter spots further out.

ISBN 978 0 6557 0029 6

6 Measure the distance of a spot from the centre of the screen (Δx) and the distance of the screen from the grating (L), shown in Figure 4.1.32. Use the equation $d \sin \theta = n\lambda$ to find d, the spacing between the lines on the diffraction grating ($n = 1$ for the first spot).

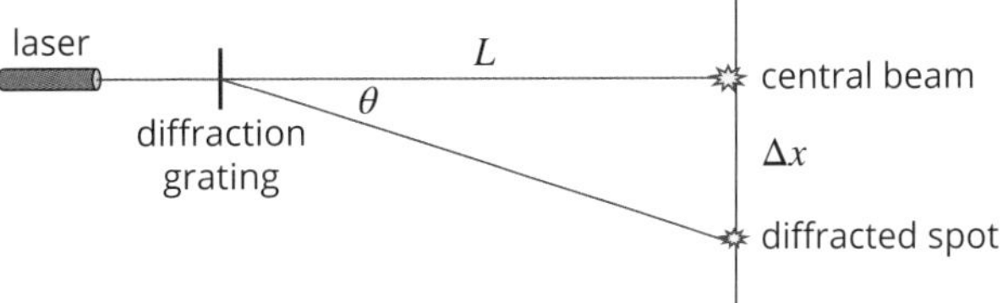

Figure 4.1.32 Experimental set-up for diffraction grating and screen

Now use your spectroscope to examine some different light sources. Discharge tubes would be ideal—as long as you can find a really dark room. Other sources to try would be:

- incandescent light globes
- fluorescent tubes
- low-energy light globes
- LED lights
- LED traffic lights
- street lights—especially the yellow ones
- sunlight reflected from white paper. Do not look at the Sun!

7 Do you see distinct emission lines in all the spectra? Which spectra do not have distinct lines?

An absorption line spectrum is created when light of a range of wavelengths passes through a gas or plasma. The gas may absorb some specific wavelengths, leaving dark lines in the continuous spectrum. Each of these dark lines will correspond to an emission line belonging to the gas. When a specific wavelength is absorbed, the atom is excited into a higher energy state. It immediately returns to a lower energy level by emitting the energy just received—often producing light of the same wavelength.

8 If the same colour that was absorbed is re-radiated, why are dark lines formed at all? Why don't the re-emitted waves fill in the dark gaps?

The absorption line spectra of stars tell us exactly what elements are present in the gases of their outer stellar atmospheres. The width or 'darkness' of the lines indicates how much of each element is present. In addition, the mix of absorption lines can tell us a good deal about the temperature and type of star. For example, a blue star with few lines other than helium will indicate a young star, whereas a yellow star with many lines of metals will be an older star, created from the leftover remnants of a supernova.

9 If the lines in an absorption spectrum are shifted from their usual position, it would indicate that a star is moving towards or away from the observer. What is the name of this effect? What would a shift to the blue end of the spectrum indicate?

WORKSHEET 37

Literature review

Special relativity and muons

Muons with a half-life of 1.56×10^{-6} s are created by cosmic-ray interaction with atoms in the upper atmosphere at a height of 10.0 km. Many of the muons travel down to Earth at 0.98*c* and are detected at Earth's surface.

1 In Earth's frame of reference, how long would it take a muon to reach the surface?

2 How many muon half-lives does this represent?

3 Given that after each half-life, only half of the muons remain, estimate how many muons would be expected to arrive at Earth's surface from an initial population of 10 million?

4 It is found that the number of muons detected is much greater than expected. Show how special relativity explains this by time dilation.

5 Find the travel time in the muon's frame of reference.

6 How many half-lives does this constitute? Out of 10 million muons, how many will reach the surface?

7 Outline how this observation can be explained by length contraction, rather than by time dilation.

8 Calculate the distance travelled by a muon (0.98c) in the muon's frame of reference.

 ISBN 978 0 6557 0029 6

WORKSHEET 38

Modelling

It's all relative—special relativity

If you watch the activity inside a moving train from the platform outside, you would generally think that you would need to add the velocity of the train to any velocity measured inside the train in order to find the final velocity relative to your stationary frame of reference. Einstein realised that this idea of adding velocities was based on a questionable assumption: that time and space are 'absolute' and 'uniform'. Newton also realised that his work was based on this assumption, but he felt, like most of us, that it was a reasonable one. Certainly at the everyday speeds of a train and moving passengers it is.

However, Einstein postulated that light will always travel at the same velocity, no matter what frame of reference we measure it in, and experiments since have established that this is the case. This has strange implications for the nature of space and time. In particular, they become 'relative'.

In this simulation, the speed of light is reduced to 'ordinary' speeds. Your simulation is based on Einstein's own discussions of a light flashing in a train. In Figure 4.1.33, the light from the bulb in the centre of the train carriage, is seen by observers inside the train to reach the ends of the carriage at the same time. But what do observers such as Clare, who is outside this moving train (Figure 4.1.34), measure?

Figure 4.1.33 The observers inside the train see the light reach the ends of the carriage at the same time.

Figure 4.1.34 The observer, Clare, observing when the light reaches the back and front walls of the train.

Observers only 'see' (relativistic effects are not really seen in a real-world sense) the light when it reaches their eyes. However, they can calculate from the known distance and speed of light how long ago the light actually took to reach an object. This is referred to as the look-back time.

In this simulation, you will calculate the time at which the two light flashes reach the front and rear walls of the carriage and compare these values for each observer using $t = \frac{L}{v}$.

To calculate and compare the required times, you can make use of a convenient simplification. Although Amaya and Binh, who are travelling on the train, and Clare all measure the speed of light as c, the time taken for the light to reach the end of the carriage, as Clare measures it, can be found from the apparent speed of light relative to the carriage. Clare measures the light moving backwards at c and the train moving forwards at v, and so the time for the light to reach the rear of the carriage is obtained by dividing the relevant distance by $c + v$ (or by $c - v$ for the light flash that is moving forwards).

No one actually sees the light travelling at $c + v$. Clare sees the train moving forwards and the light moving backwards, so that, to her, the relative speed of light and train appears to be $c + v$. Clare also measures the length of the train contracted by the Lorentz factor, γ, and so the length to be divided by $c + v$ is $\frac{L}{\gamma}$.

1 For this simulation, rather than having impossibly fast trains, light will be slowed down to more 'ordinary' speeds. Is this a reasonable constraint?

____

____

2 Complete the following table by calculating the relevant quantities for train speeds between 0 m s^{-1} and 100 m s^{-1} for a speed of light, *c*, equal to 100 m s^{-1}. The quantities are as follows:

T_A—time for the light to reach the ends of the carriage as measured by Amaya and Binh (equal to the proper time)

T_{CR}—time for the light to reach the rear wall as measured by Clare

T_{CF}—time for the light to reach the front wall as measured by Clare

T—difference in times as measured by Clare

L (m)	c (m s^{-1})	v (m s^{-1})	γ	$T_A = \frac{L}{c}$ (s)	$T_{CR} = \frac{\frac{L}{\gamma}}{(c+v)}$ (s)	$T_{CF} = \frac{\frac{L}{\gamma}}{(c-v)}$ (s)	$T = T_{CF} - T_{CR}$ (s)
10	100	0					
10	100	10					
10	100	20					
10	100	30					
10	100	40					
10	100	50					
10	100	60					
10	100	70					
10	100	80					
10	100	90					
10	100	99					

3 Plot graphs of T_A, T_{CR}, T_{CF} and T against the speed of the train on the graph provided. Label the axes appropriately with both quantities and units.

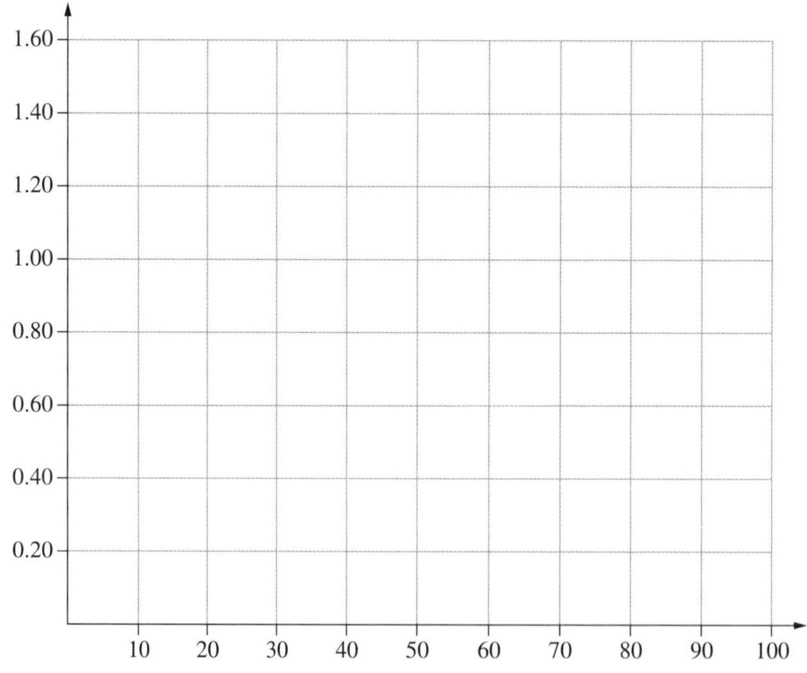

4 Develop a spreadsheet using a suitable program available to you and try other values for *c*. Do all combinations of *c* and *v* work?

 ISBN 978 0 6557 0029 6

5 What happens when the speed of the train is equal to the speed of light? Why is this? What happens, and why, when the train has a speed faster than light?

6 For the situation when the train is at rest, do the observers inside and outside the train agree on their calculations of when the light hits the front and rear walls?

7 Describe the situation as measured by the different observers when the train is travelling slowly. How do Clare's measurements compare with those of Amaya and Binh? What happens as you increase the speed of the train?

8 If you watch a tennis match, you do not always hear the sound of the racquet hitting the ball at the same moment as you see the racquet hit the ball. Why is this? Is this also a case of non-simultaneity?

9 Is the non-simultaneity that Clare observes just a 'trick' of look-back effects? Explain your answer.

10 What happens in your simulation if you put in the accepted value for the speed of light and keep the speed of the train at the same magnitude as used in the table?

11 Investigate and describe one type of experimental evidence for time dilation and/or length contraction.

Examples include the Hafele–Keating experiment or the Frisch–Smith experiment.

WORKSHEET 39

Literacy review—quantum physics and relativity

1 Complete the following table by writing in standard definitions for each of the terms listed.

absorption line spectrum	
atomic energy level	
diffraction	
diffraction pattern	
electromagnetic radiation	
emission line spectrum	
interference	
photoelectric effect	
photon	
Planck's constant	
quantum	
stopping voltage	
threshold frequency	
work function	

2 The following table includes terms that compare and contrast relativistic measurement with Newtonian measurement. Complete the table with a definition for each of the included terms.

frame of reference	
inertial frame of reference	
length contraction	
proper length	
relativistic time	
proper time	
relativistic mass	
rest mass	
spacetime	
time dilation	
simultaneity	

 ISBN 978 0 6557 0029 6

WORKSHEET 40

Reflection—How has understanding about the physical world changed?

The following table lists the key knowledge covered in this area of study.

1 Reflect on how well you understand the concepts listed. Rate your learning by shading the circle that corresponds to your current level of understanding for each one.

Key knowledge	Not confident ◄				► Very confident
The properties of electromagnetic waves	○	○	○	○	○
The formation of standing waves	○	○	○	○	○
Diffraction, including the effect of gap width or obstacle size	○	○	○	○	○
Interference of light, including Young's double-slit experiment	○	○	○	○	○
Quantised energy of photons: $E = hf = \frac{hc}{\lambda}$	○	○	○	○	○
The photoelectric effect, including comparison of the wave and particle models of light in explaining the photoelectric effect	○	○	○	○	○
Electron diffraction and de Broglie wavelength	○	○	○	○	○
Calculations of momentum from wavelength: $p = \frac{h}{\lambda}$	○	○	○	○	○
Emission and absorption spectra, including $E = hf = \frac{hc}{\lambda}$	○	○	○	○	○
Quantised states of electrons in an atom	○	○	○	○	○
Frames of reference and special relativity	○	○	○	○	○
Calculations of time dilation and length contraction for velocities near speed of light	○	○	○	○	○
The relationship between energy and mass: $E_{tot} = E_k + E_0 = \gamma mc^2$, where $E_0 = mc^2$	○	○	○	○	○

2 Consider the points you have shaded from Not confident to Very confident. List specific ideas you can identify that were challenging.

3 Write down two different strategies that you will apply to help further your understanding of these ideas.

PRACTICAL ACTIVITY 16

Experiment • Modelling

Measuring the speed of light

SUGGESTED DURATION

- 25 minutes data collection + 10 minutes analysis

MATERIALS

- microwave oven—must be of the type that requires a turntable
- packet or two of marshmallows—you can also use a large chocolate block or choc chips
- microwave-safe plate or dish
- ruler
- heatproof or ovenproof gloves

INTRODUCTION

Today, manufacturers of high-quality science equipment produce apparatus for the laboratory measurement of the speed of light. These rely on the high-speed measurement of the reflection of monochromatic light over a measured distance or Foucault's method of using rotating and fixed mirrors.

There is a simpler method that, although making some assumptions, can determine the speed of light with reasonable precision based on the wave-like behaviour of light.

AIM

To determine the speed of light based on the wave-like behaviour of light.

Safety

Take care to ensure the microwave is closed prior to turning on. Do not leave metal objects inside. Carefully follow all other manufacturer's safety guidelines.

Materials will be very hot when being removed. Use appropriate safety apparatus, including heatproof gloves.

Complete a risk assessment before starting the activity.

METHOD

1. Remove the turntable from the microwave oven.
2. Open the bag of marshmallows and arrange them in the base of the dish, completely covering it with one layer of marshmallows. If you're using chocolate blocks, break the block up and arrange the individual squares up in a similar way.
3. Place the dish in the microwave and cook on a low power level. Microwaves don't heat evenly and normally require a turntable to ensure that the heat is distributed evenly. As the dish isn't being rotated, the marshmallows will begin to melt unevenly, melting more quickly in the 'hottest' parts of the oven. Continue to heat the marshmallows until around four or five distinct melted spots are observed.
4. Carefully remove the dish from the microwave using the ovenproof gloves to avoid being burned. Allow the dish to cool.
5. Using the ruler, measure the distance between any two of the melted spots and record them in the table in the Results section. Repeat this for the distance between two different melted spots, until you have filled the table.
6. Record an estimate of the error in each of your distance measurements and calculate the percentage uncertainty in each measurement. Record your results in the table.
7. Recall that the velocity of a wave is given by $v = f\lambda$, and that the speed of light $c = f\lambda$. The frequency of the microwaves in the oven will be recorded on the specifications panel fixed to the back or side of the microwave oven. Record this in the table in the Results section.

RESULTS

Results and calculations

Distance between melted spots (cm)	Measurement uncertainty (cm)	% uncertainty	Distance between melted spots × 2 (m)	Microwave frequency (Hz)	Speed of light, c ($m\,s^{-1}$)

ISBN 978 0 6557 0029 6

PRACTICAL ACTIVITY 16

1 The distance between melted spots corresponds to half the wavelength of the microwaves. Why is this the case? Use a diagram to support your explanation.

2 Using twice the distance between melted spots as the wavelength of the microwaves, in metres, calculate the speed of light for each pair of melted spots. Record the average value.

DISCUSSION

1 How does your calculation of the speed of light compare with the currently accepted value for the speed of light in air?

2 Comment on the reliability of the conclusions you can draw from this investigation.

CONCLUSION

PRACTICAL ACTIVITY 17

Experiment

Interference of light—Young's double-slit experiment

SUGGESTED DURATION

- For one set of slits: 100 minutes data collection + 30 minutes analysis

MATERIALS

- double slits—preformed of varying sizes
- retort stands
- three-finger clamps
- laser pointer/s with known wavelength (a spectrometer can be used to confirm the wavelength)
- white paper
- pencil
- ruler
- tape
- measuring tape

INTRODUCTION

In this activity a key wave behaviour of light will be investigated. In 1801, Thomas Young obtained convincing evidence of the wave nature of light. Light from a single source falls on a slide containing two closely spaced slits. If light consists of tiny particles (or 'corpuscles' as described by Isaac Newton), we might expect to see two bright lines on a screen placed behind the slits. Young observed a series of bright lines. Young was able to explain this result as a wave interference phenomenon. Because of diffraction, the waves leaving the two small slits spread out from the edges of the slits. This is equivalent to the interference pattern of ripples produced when two rocks are thrown into a pond.

The equation that describes the spatial conditions for constructive interference (interference maxima) in a double-slit interference pattern is:

$d \sin\theta = n\lambda$

where d is the spacing between the slits

θ is the angle at the centre line and the nth-order maxima in the interference pattern

λ is the wavelength of the coherent light source

n is an integer (n = 0, 1, 2, ...).

In practice, the angular position θ of each interference maxima can be expressed in terms of linear position, x, where x_n is the linear distance between the 0th-order maxima and the nth-order maxima observed in the interference pattern on a screen some distance L from the double-slit aperture, as shown in Figure 4.1.35, and:

$$x_n = n\frac{\lambda L}{d}$$

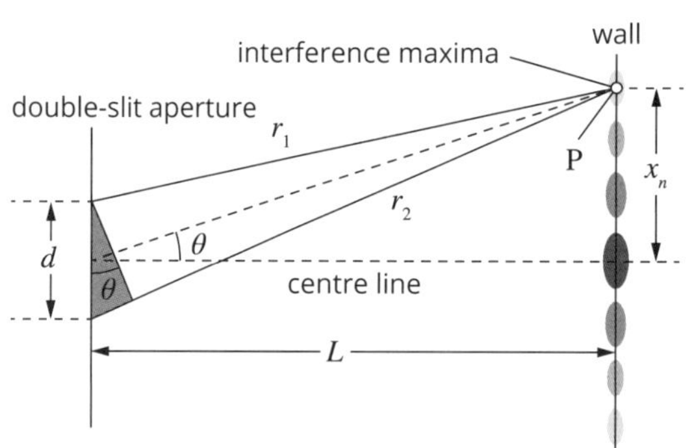

Figure 4.1.35 Interference of light from double slits

AIM

To investigate quantitatively the interference of light through two parallel slits as a wave-like behaviour of light.

Best results are obtained in a darkened room.

Safety

If using a laser as the light source, take particular care not to look into its beam or shine it directly into other people's eyes. Permanent damage to the eye could result.

Complete a risk assessment before starting the activity.

 ISBN 978 0 6557 0029 6

PRACTICAL ACTIVITY 17

METHOD

1 ▪ Assemble your equipment and align the laser as shown in Figure 4.1.36.

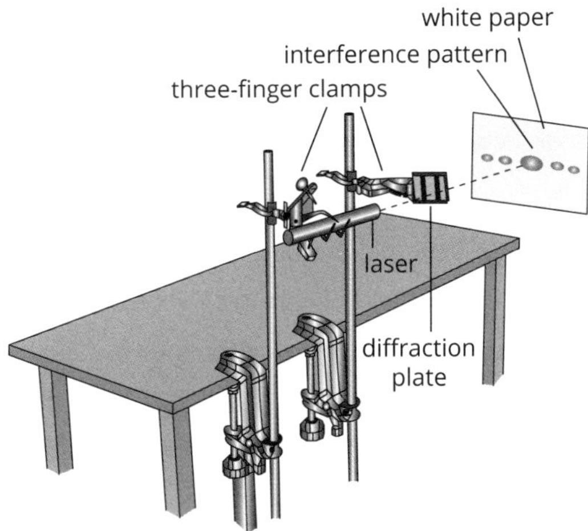

Figure 4.1.36 Experimental set-up

2 ▪ Find an area on your lab table with enough space to align the components, with the laser aimed away from other lab groups, and towards a wall or other flat rigid surface on which you can attach the white paper.

3 ▪ Use tape to hold the white paper in place against the wall or other surface.

4 ▪ Lightly clamp the edge of the diffraction plate (the edge parallel to the slits on the plate) in the three-finger clamp. Be certain the double slits on the plate are vertical and the fingers of the clamp touch only the edge of the plate. Over tightening may damage or distort the plate so be careful.

5 ▪ Adjust the set-up so that the laser beam is perpendicular to the diffraction plate, and the white paper and diffraction plate are parallel to each other.

6 ▪ Allow at least 1 metre of space between the diffraction plate and the paper. Use as large a distance as possible while ensuring visibility of the light on the paper. A darkened room can help.

7 ▪ Adjust the laser so the beam shines on the diffraction plate. A clear image of the interference pattern should appear on the white paper. Record the distance between slits on the diffraction plate in the Results section, including an estimate of the uncertainty in the measurement.

> **Aim the laser slightly downwards at the diffraction plate to prevent stray reflection of the laser beam travelling upwards into a classmate's eyes. You might also want to place an object behind your set-up (behind the laser) to catch any reflection of the laser beam from the diffraction plate.**

8 ▪ Once aligned, tighten the set-up components so the laser and diffraction plate do not move during data collection.

9 ▪ Use the ruler and pencil to draw a horizontal line through the center of the interference pattern on the paper.

10 ▪ Make a small mark on the line you just drew at the centre of the 0th-order (central brightest) maxima, as shown in Figure 4.1.37.

11 ▪ Continue to make small marks at the centres of the neighbouring five maxima to the right or left of the 0th maxima.

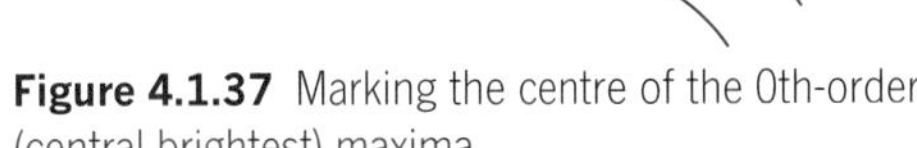

Figure 4.1.37 Marking the centre of the 0th-order (central brightest) maxima

12 ▪ Turn off the laser, and then record its wavelength, λ, in the Results section.

> **The wavelength is usually printed on a sticker on the outside of the laser. If it is not printed on the laser, ask your teacher for this value or use a spectrometer to measure it directly.**

13 ▪ Use the measuring tape to measure the distance L between the diffraction plate and the white paper. Record this value in the Results section, together with an estimate of the uncertainty in the measurement.

14 ▪ Remove the white paper and place it on your lab table.

15 ▪ Use the ruler to accurately measure the distance from the 0th maxima mark ($n = 0$) to each higher order maxima ($n = 1, 2, 3, 4, 5$). Record each distance (x_n) in the table in the Results section.

RESULTS

List the variables in this experiment:

Independent: ______________

Dependent: ______________

Controlled: ______________

Stated width between slits, d = ______________ m ± __________

λ = ______________ nm ± __________

L = ______________ m ± __________

Distance to each maxima	
Integer order maxima n	**Distance from 0th maxima x_n (cm) ± ________**
1	
2	
3	
4	
5	

1 Plot a graph of distance of interference maxima from 0th maxima (x_n) versus integer order (n) in the blank graph axes. Label both axes with the correct scale and units, and add uncertainty bars where appropriate. Describe the shape of the graph produced and what that implies regarding the relationship between maxima and integer order.

2 Draw a line of best fit through the data in the graph and determine the equation of the line here.

ISBN 978 0 6557 0029 6

3 Use the gradient from the line of best fit to determine the spacing, d, between the parallel slits on the diffraction plate.

i.e. gradient $= \frac{\lambda L}{d}$

DISCUSSION

1 State the experimental value for the spacing between the double slits. Compare this with the stated value.

2 Based on the difference between actual and experimental values, comment on the reliability of conclusions you can draw from this investigation.

3 Discuss factors that may have caused an error in your experimental value for the slit spacing. Explain how each factor you list could have been avoided or minimised.

4 Explain how your data would differ if you had used slits spaced twice as far apart and half as far apart.

5 Would the data in your experiment differ if the distance between your laser and the diffraction plate had been much greater? Justify your answer.

CONCLUSION

PRACTICAL ACTIVITY 18

Experiment

Photoelectric effect

SUGGESTED DURATION

- 50 minutes data collection + 30 minutes analysis

MATERIALS

- photoelectric effect kit, which may include all of the following:
  - current detector and amplifier or current sensor and data acquisition system
  - voltage meter or sensor
  - lamp to suit kit (generally mercury vapour, but may also be incandescent)
  - set of coloured filters (may be part of kit or not required)
  - voltmeter or voltage sensor
  - variable resistor or rheostat
  - switch
  - DC power supply
  - electrical leads

INTRODUCTION

The photoelectric effect refers to the emission of electrons from the surface of a metal when light of low wavelength is incident on the surface. This phenomenon cannot be sufficiently explained using the wave theory of light, and its explanation led to the development of the photon or particle-like dual-nature model of light we have today. In the photon model, a beam of light consists of a stream of photons, each carrying energy $E_{photon} = hf$, where h is Planck's constant (6.63×10^{-34} J s) and f is the frequency of the incident light (Hz).

The work function for the metal is given by $\phi = hf_0$, where f_0 is the minimum threshold frequency and is different for each metal. If the frequency of the incident light is greater than the threshold frequency, a photoelectron will be ejected with some kinetic energy up to a maximum value $E_{k\,max} = hf - \phi$.

By experiment, the maximum kinetic energy for the electrons (i.e. the fastest electron) can be found using a reverse voltage called the stopping voltage, V_s, so that $E_{k\,max} = eV_s$.

AIM

To investigate the photoelectric effect quantitatively.

Safety

If you are using a mercury lamp, avoid looking directly at it. It is advisable to wear protective glasses.

Complete a risk assessment before starting the activity.

METHOD

Figure 4.1.38 shows a typical circuit for a photoelectric effect kit. Check your kit's instructions for the particular circuit that applies.

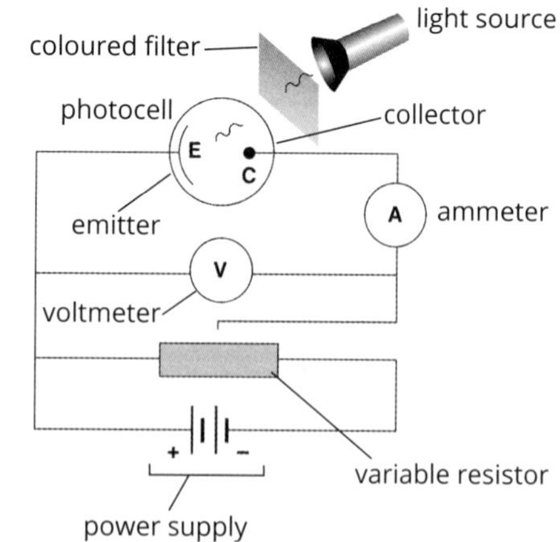

Figure 4.1.38 Circuit for a photoelectric effect kit

1 • Set up the kit for the photoelectric effect using the method recommended by the manufacturer. The general form of the circuit is shown in the diagram. Follow any directions that are specific to your kit. (You may find most or all of the circuit is built into the kit.) The relative positions of the light source and the photocell should stay fixed. Start with the filter or LED that transmits the longest wavelength (usually red).

2 • Turn on the light source and allow at least 5 minutes until the lamp has warmed up and stabilised.

3 • Using the first filter (red) and a fixed intensity for the light, direct the light through the filter onto the anode of the photoelectric cell. Adjust the variable resistor until the current sensor reads exactly zero ampere. Wait a few seconds to be sure that the current is exactly zero. Record the reading on the voltmeter—this will be the stopping voltage. Record these values, including the wavelength of the filter and estimates of the uncertainties in each measurement, in the table in the Results section. Have different people repeat the measurement up to three times.

4 • Repeat step 3 for each of the other colours available, working progressively through to violet. Record the results in the table in the Results section.

ISBN 978 0 6557 0029 6

PRACTICAL ACTIVITY 18

RESULTS

List the variables associated with this experimental method.

Independent: ______

Dependent: ______

Controlled: ______

1 Explain why it is essential to allow at least 5 minutes until the lamp has warmed up and stabilised when beginning this experiment.

______

______

2 Complete the following table.

Stopping voltage and frequency results for an unknown photocell

Filter wavelength (nm)	Frequency ($\times 10^{14}$ Hz) ±	Current (A) ±	Stopping voltage (V) ±			Average voltage (V)
			Trial 1	Trial 2	Trial 3	

3 Plot a graph of stopping voltage versus frequency on the grid provided. Add uncertainty bars for each point and draw a line of best fit.

4 Determine the gradient of the line.

______

5 From the graph, determine the *x*-intercept and *y*-intercept. Record both values.

______

______

DISCUSSION

1 Summarise your results for the quantities found.

2 State the significance of each of the values you have determined and the relevant units. Discuss the reliability of your results and the comparison with accepted values.

3 Discuss the likely causes of errors in this experiment and the means by which you attempted to reduce them.

4 In the first part of the experiment, a lower current was obtained with a less intense light. Explain this in terms of a particle-like model of light.

5 Explain why the stopping voltage depends only on the frequency of the incident light and not on the intensity.

CONCLUSION

 ISBN 978 0 6557 0029 6

PRACTICAL ACTIVITY 19

Experiment

Light and spectra

SUGGESTED DURATION

- 50 minutes data collection + 20 minutes analysis

INTRODUCTION

In Part **A** of this activity, you will create and examine a continuous spectrum of light. In Part **B**, you will observe the spectral lines from gas emission tubes using a spectrometer.

AIM

To investigate how emitted light can be used to identify an element and provide evidence for atomic energy levels.

Safety

Handle hot spectral tubes with care. Do not touch any tube with bare hands—use a soft cloth to handle the tubes or they may be permanently damaged. Read all accompanying safety notes before starting the experiment.

Complete a risk assessment before starting the activity.

MATERIALS

- clear filament globe and power supply (a standard light box will also work)
- screen with single slit
- solid screen
- convex lens
- prism
- spectral tubes
- spectral tube power supply and mount
- spectroscope, diffraction grating glasses; or spectrometer and computing device
- multiclamp
- retort stand

METHOD

Part A • Creating a continuous spectrum

1 • Set up the equipment as shown in Figure 4.1.39. The filament globe acts as a white light source. After first passing through the slit, the light is dispersed into a continuous spectrum by the prism.
Do not exceed the rated power of the globe supplied.

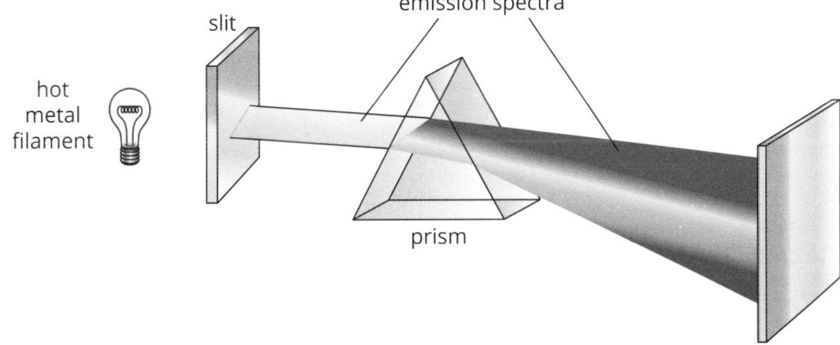

Figure 4.1.39 Experimental set-up for a continuous spectrum

2 • Place the convex lens between the slit and the prism. Move the lens backwards and forwards until a clear spectrum is produced on the solid screen. You may need to darken the room to see the spectrum clearly. Record the order of the colours in the spectrum in the Results section.

Part B • Observing spectral lines from gas emission tubes

Set up the spectral tube power supply and mount with a spectral tube—your teacher may have already done this. Do not turn on the tube at this stage. Spectral tubes should only be illuminated for short times when they are about to be observed.

If you have a hand-held spectroscope or diffraction glasses, no further preparation is needed.

PRACTICAL ACTIVITY 19

Using a spectrometer

1 • Turn on the spectrometer and connect it to your computing device.

2 • Connect the fibre-optic cable to the spectrometer, following the manufacturer's instructions.

3 • Use a multiclamp to secure the probe or rounded end of the fibre-optic cable on a retort stand, as shown in Figure 4.1.40.

4 • Place the end of the probe a distance of 2 cm or less from the gas tube. Adjust the probe to point towards the tube. Do not allow the probe to directly touch the tube.

5 • Open the spectrometry application and choose 'analyse light', following the manufacturer's specific instructions.

6 • Turn on the power to the spectral tube mount (your teacher may wish to do this—always check!). Start recording with the spectrometer software or start carefully observing the spectrum produced by the light.

7 • Adjust the fibre-optic cable or angle of observation until a clear spectrum is seen.

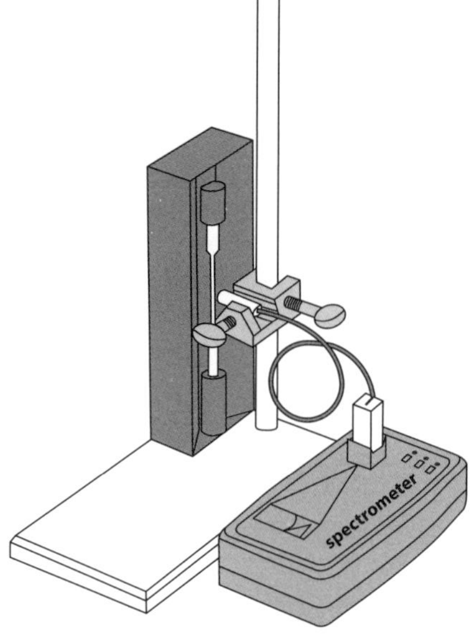

Figure 4.1.40 Experimental set-up for a spectrometer

RESULTS

Part A • Creating a continuous spectrum

1 What is the order of the colours produced?

2 What does the order of the colours imply in terms of the respective wavelengths of the light?

3 What effect would placing a cloud of gas between the source and the slits have on the spectrum?

4 If possible, direct a beam of sunlight through the slits so a spectrum is formed on the viewing screen. Is this spectrum the same as the one from the filament globe? Comment on any differences. Be very careful not to look directly at the sunlight.

Part B • Observing spectral lines from gas emission tubes

1 Record up to five significant peaks or lines in the following table. Using the tools available to you, measure and record the corresponding wavelength for each line.

Emission spectra		
Colour of peak or line	**Wavelength (nm)**	**Energy (J)**

ISBN 978 0 6557 0029 6

2 Based on your observations, what gas is contained in the spectral tube? You may need to check a suitable reference to find the expected spectrum for particular gases. (Some spectrometer software will include profiles for standard gases.)

3 Astronomers use high-powered spectrometers to analyse light throughout space. Explain how it is possible for an element to have the same line emission pattern every time it is energised, whether the element is in outer space or in a gas spectrum tube in a classroom.

4 For each spectral line identified in the table above, calculate the equivalent energy of the emitted photons. Record your answer in the table.

DISCUSSION

1 Using your particular results and observations, explain how spectroscopy can be used to identify particular elements.

2 What type of spectra are produced by the spectral tubes and by sunlight—continuous, emission or absorption? Explain your answer.

CONCLUSION

ISBN 978 0 6557 0029 6

EXAM QUESTIONS

Multiple-choice questions

Question 1 VCE Physics 2018 (A) 12

A teacher sets up an apparatus to demonstrate Young's double-slit experiment. A pattern of bright and dark bands is observed on the screen, as shown below.

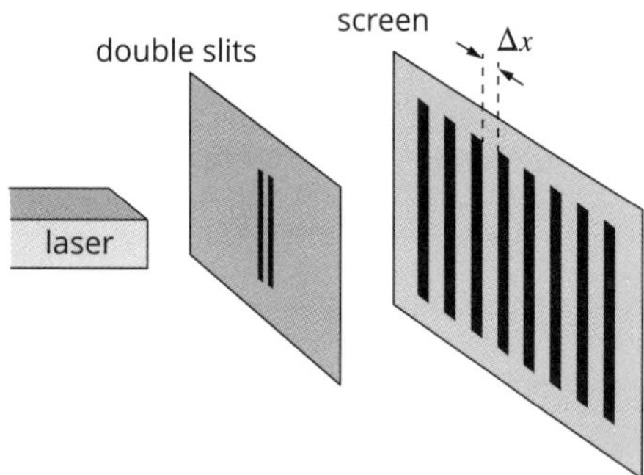

Which one of the following actions will increase the distance, Δx, between the adjacent dark bands in this interference pattern?

A. Decrease the distance between the slits and the screen.

B. Decrease the wavelength of the light.

C. Decrease the slit separation.

D. Decrease the slit width.

Question 2 VCE Physics 2018 (A) 13

Which one of the following diagrams best represents the graph of γ (the Lorentz factor) versus speed for an electron that is accelerated from rest to near the speed of light, c?

A.

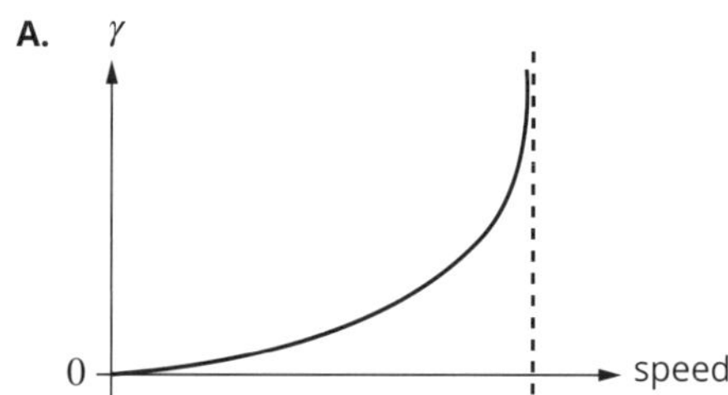

B.

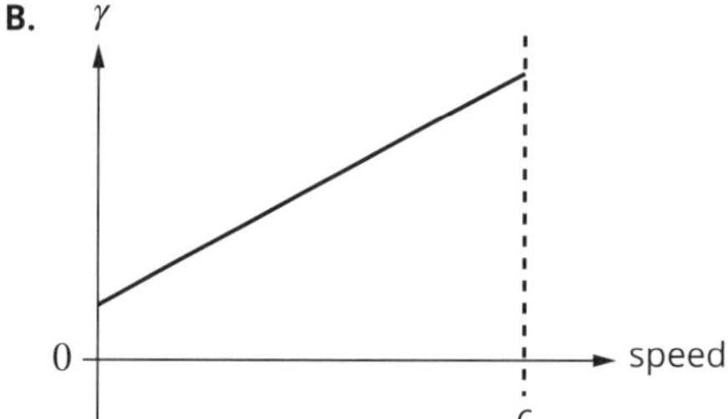

C.

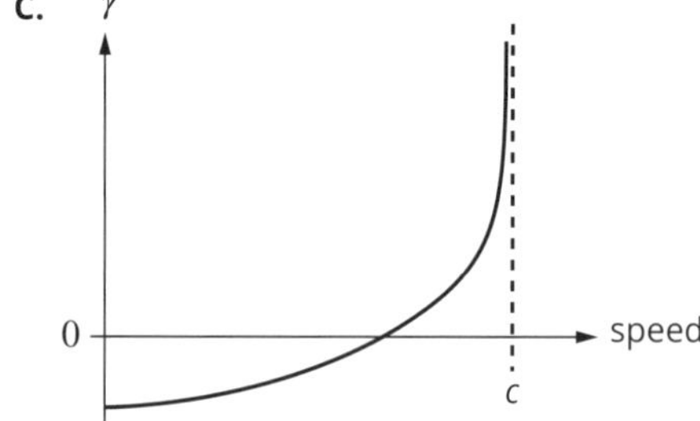

D.

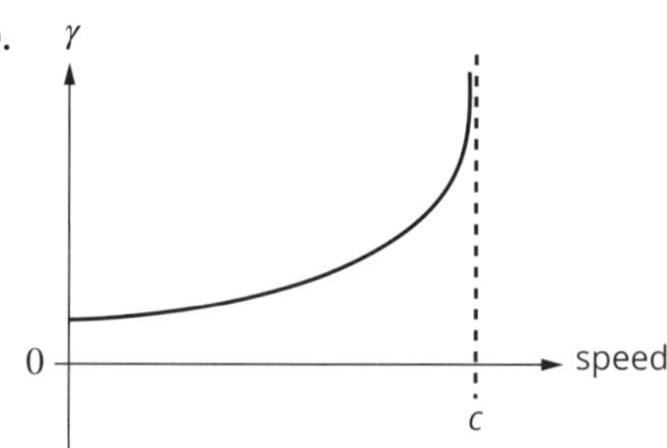

Question 3 VCE Physics 2018 (A) 14

Which one of the following statements about the kinetic energy, E_k, of a proton travelling at relativistic speed is the most accurate?

A. The difference between the proton's relativistic E_k and its classical E_k cannot be determined.

B. The proton's relativistic E_k is greater than its classical E_k.

C. The proton's relativistic E_k is the same as its classical E_k.

D. The proton's relativistic E_k is less than its classical E_k.

ISBN 978 0 6557 0029 6

EXAM QUESTIONS

Question 4 VCE Physics 2018 (A) 17

The results of a photoelectric experiment are displayed in the graph below. The graph shows the maximum kinetic energy ($E_{k\,max}$) of photoelectrons versus the frequency (f) of light falling on the metal surface.

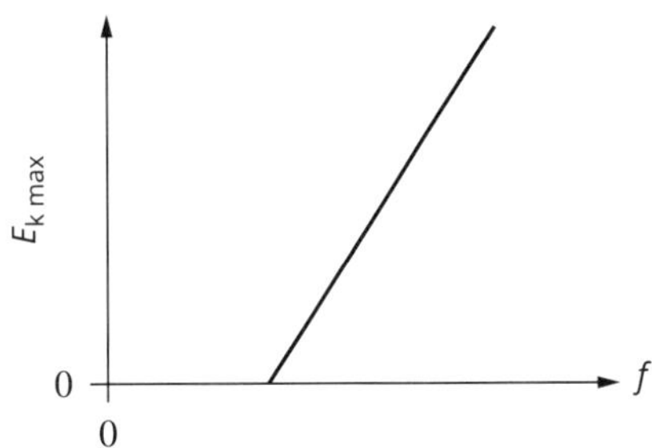

A second experiment is conducted with the original metal surface being replaced by one with a larger work function. The original data is shown with a solid line and the results of the second experiment are shown with a dashed line. Which one of the following graphs shows the results from the second experiment?

A.

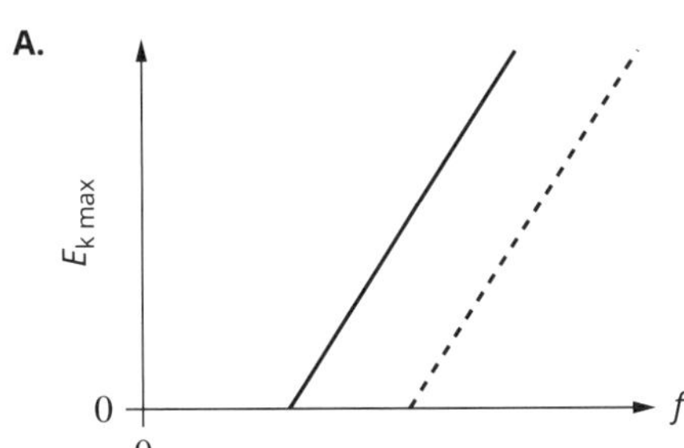

B.

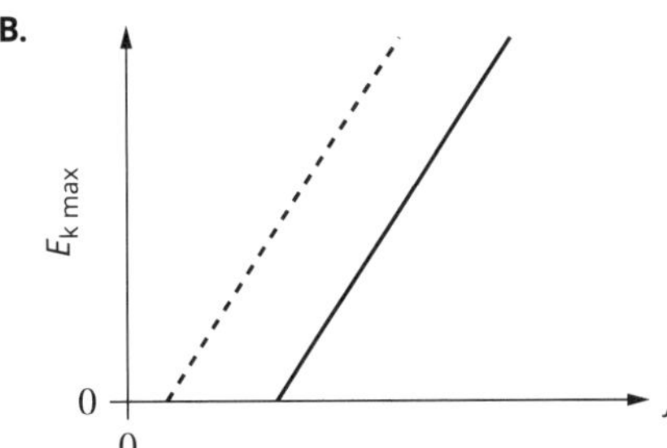

C.

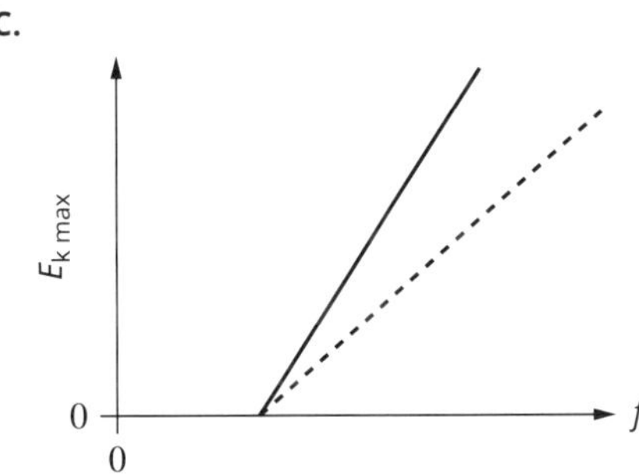

D.

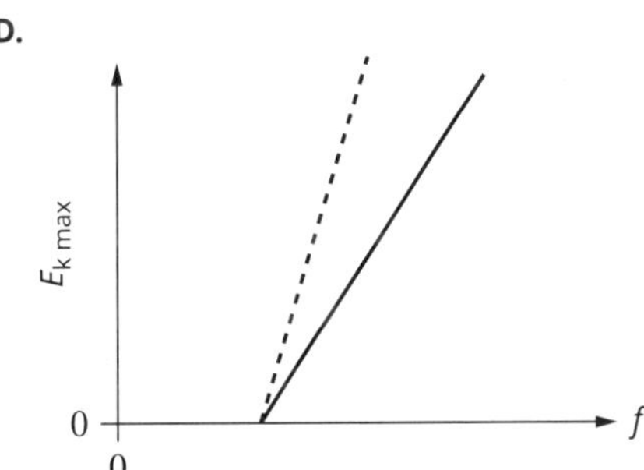

Question 5 VCE Physics 2020 (A) 17

The diagram below shows some of the energy levels for the electrons within an atom. The arrows labelled A, B, C and D indicate transitions between the energy levels and their lengths indicate the relative size of the energy change.

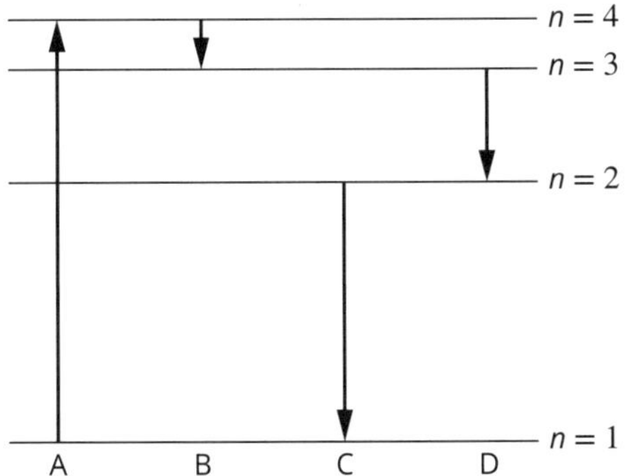

EXAM QUESTIONS

Which transition results in the emission of a photon with the most energy?

A. A

B. B

C. C

D. D

Question 6 VCE Physics 2020 (A) 18

Quantised energy levels within atoms can best be explained by:

A. electrons behaving as individual particles with different energies.

B. electrons behaving as waves, with each energy level representing a diffraction pattern.

C. protons behaving as waves, with only standing waves at particular wavelengths allowed.

D. electrons behaving as waves, with only standing waves at particular wavelengths allowed.

Question 7 VCE Physics 2013 (B) (1) 1

James is stationary ($v = 0$) on a footpath while Amanda drives past at a constant speed of 60 km h^{-1}. Which one of the following statements is correct?

A. Amanda is in a non-inertial reference frame because she is moving relative to James.

B. James must be in a non-inertial reference frame because he is stationary at the moment.

C. James is not stationary in his reference frame because he is moving in Amanda's reference frame.

D. Amanda is stationary in her reference frame even though she is moving in James's reference frame.

Question 8 VCE Physics 2013 (B) (1) 4

The spaceship *Andromeda* (A) is travelling at 0.7*c* towards the asteroid Ceres (C). It sends a light pulse to the nearby ship *Bradbury* (B), which is approaching the asteroid from the far side at 0.8*c*, as shown in the figure below.

0.7*c*

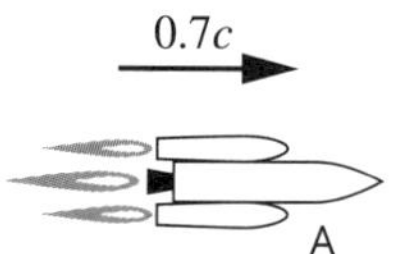

0.8*c*

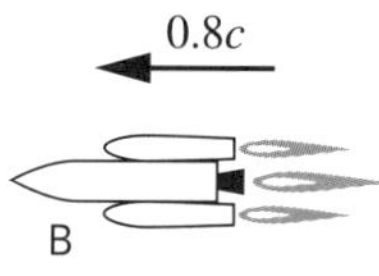

The speed of the light pulse as measured from each body is:

A. greatest for A and least for B.

B. greatest for B and least for A.

C. greatest for C and least for B.

D. the same for each body.

Question 9 VCE Physics 2013 (B) (1) 5

A physicist purchased a limousine, but found that it was twice as long as her garage. She reasoned that in the garage's reference frame, it should be possible for a moving limousine to fit exactly inside the garage for an instant.

What is the minimum speed at which the limousine would have to travel in order for this to work?

A. $\frac{c}{\sqrt{2}}$

B. $\frac{3}{4}c$

C. $\frac{\sqrt{3}}{2}c$

D. $\sqrt{3}c$

ISBN 978 0 6557 0029 6

EXAM QUESTIONS

Question 10 VCE Physics 2013 (B) (1) 8

Which one of the following statements is correct?

A. Proper time cannot be measured on a moving clock.

B. Proper time is the time interval between two events that is measured by a stationary clock.

C. Proper time is the shortest possible time interval between two events that any observer can measure.

D. An observer who measures a proper time is the only observer performing a correct measurement of the time between two events.

Short-answer questions

Question 1 (9 marks) VCE Physics 2013 (A) 22

The apparatus for a Young's double-slit experiment is shown in the figure below.

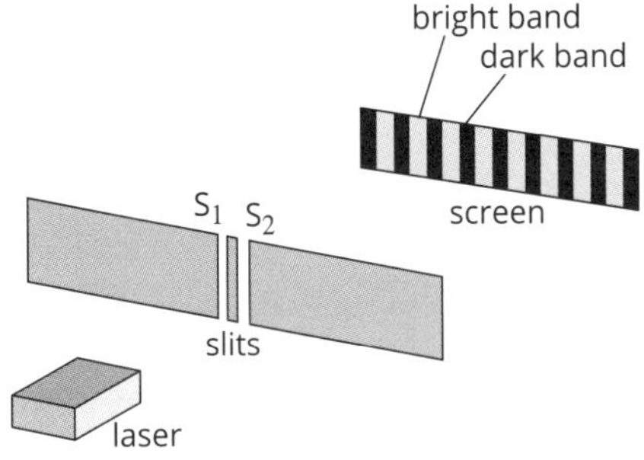

not to scale

a. A beam of green light ($\lambda = 550$ nm) is incident on the slits.
Describe the intensity at the exact centre of the interference pattern on the screen and give a reason for your answer. 2 marks

b. The beam is now replaced with light of a lower frequency.
The second dark band from the centre of the interference pattern would 1 mark

A. become narrower.

B. remain in the same position.

C. move closer to the centre of the pattern.

D. move further away from the centre of the pattern.

c. The path difference from the slits to the second bright band from the centre of the interference pattern is 1.4×10^3 nm. Calculate the path difference (in metres) from the slits to the first dark band from the centre of the pattern. 3 marks

d. A student reads on a website that 'Young's experiment supports the particle model of light'. Explain, with reasons, whether the statement is correct or incorrect. 3 marks

Question 2 (2 marks) VCE Physics 2013 (A) 19

A photon of blue light has a frequency of 6.7×10^{14} Hz.

a. Calculate the energy (in joules) of the photon of blue light. 1 mark

b. Calculate the wavelength (in metres) of the photon of blue light. 1 mark

Question 3 (2 marks) VCE Physics 2018 (B) 14

Jani is stationary in a spaceship travelling at constant speed.

Does this mean that the spaceship must be in an inertial frame of reference? Justify your answer.

Question 4 (7 marks) VCE Physics 2018 (B) 17

To investigate the photoelectric effect, Sai and Kym set up an experiment. The apparatus is shown in the figure below.

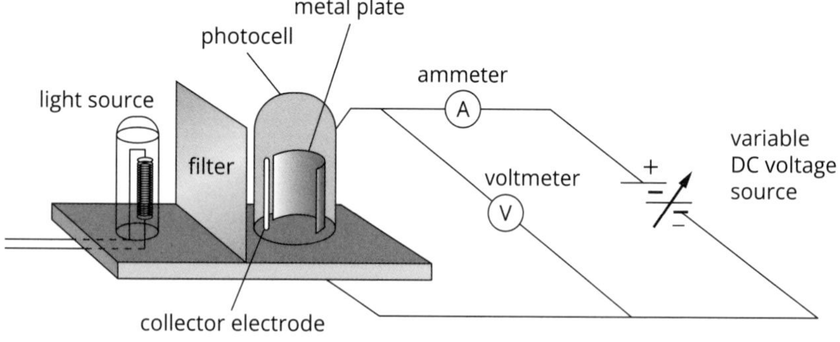

With the light source on and a filter in place, Sai and Kym measure the maximum kinetic energy of emitted photoelectrons by gradually changing the collector voltage until the current measured by the ammeter just falls to zero.

They record this voltage (the stopping voltage) for each frequency of the incident light and plot their results in a graph of stopping voltage, V_S, versus frequency, f ($\times 10^{14}$ Hz), of the incident light, as shown below.

 ISBN 978 0 6557 0029 6

EXAM QUESTIONS

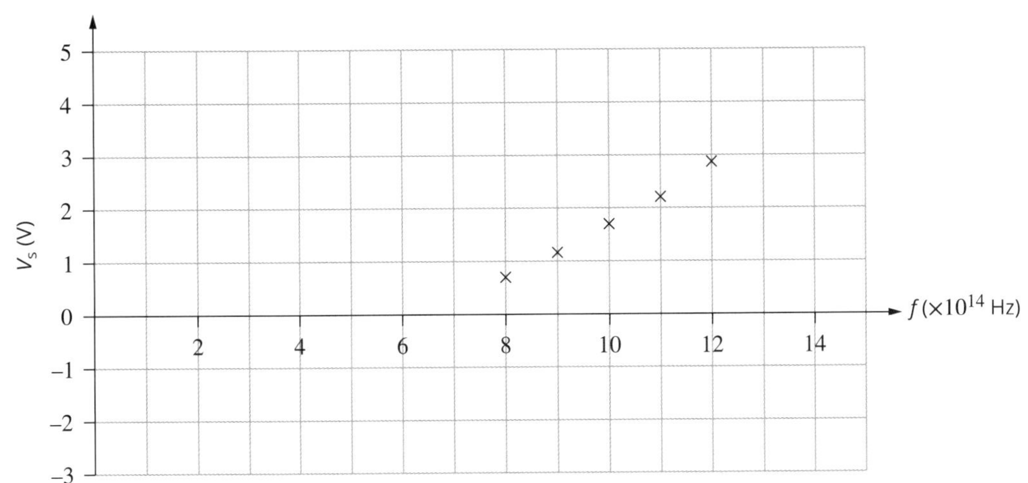

With 6.0×10^{14} Hz light, the ammeter always shows zero. Sai wants to repeat the experiment for this frequency with a much brighter light source and wants to expose the metal to the light for much longer. Kym says photoelectrons will never be ejected with this frequency of light.

a. **i.** Who is correct—Sai or Kym? Write the name in the space below. 1 mark

ii. What explanation might Sai give to support her opinion that by waiting longer and using a brighter light source, photoelectrons could be ejected from the metal with light of a frequency of 6.0×10^{14} Hz? 2 marks

b. Use the graph to calculate Planck's constant. Show your working. 2 marks

c. Determine the work function of the metal from the graph. Give your reasoning. 2 marks

ISBN 978 0 6557 0029 6

EXAM QUESTIONS

Question 5 (4 marks) VCE Physics 2021 (B) 19

A simplified diagram of some of the energy levels of an atom is shown in the figure below.

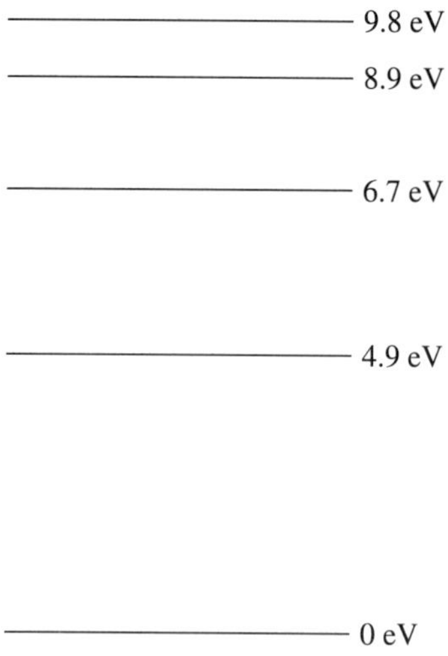
9.8 eV
8.9 eV
6.7 eV
4.9 eV
0 eV

a. Identify the transition on the energy level diagram in the figure above that would result in the emission of a 565 nm photon. Show your working. 2 marks

b. A sample of the atoms is excited into the 9.8 eV state and a line spectrum is observed as the states decay. Assume that all possible transitions occur.

What is the total number of lines in the spectrum? Explain your answer. You may use the diagram below to support your answer. 2 marks

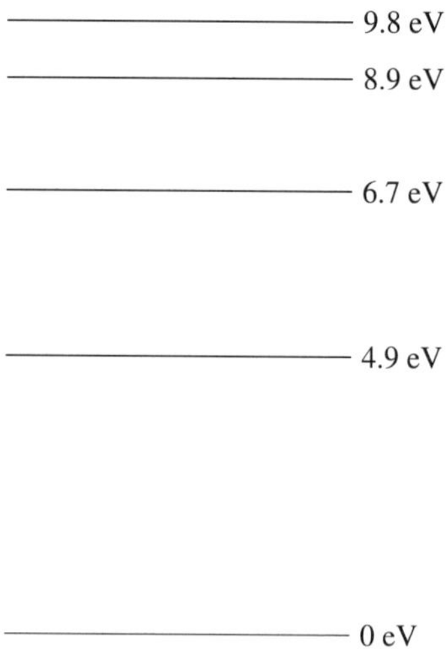
9.8 eV
8.9 eV
6.7 eV
4.9 eV
0 eV

ISBN 978 0 6557 0029 6

UNIT 4

How have creative ideas and investigation revolutionised thinking in physics?

AREA OF STUDY 2

How is scientific inquiry used to investigate fields, motion or light?

Outcome

Design and conduct a scientific investigation related to fields, motion or light, and present an aim, methodology and method, results, discussion and a conclusion in a scientific poster.

Key knowledge

Investigation design

- identify the physics concepts specific to the investigation and explain their significance, including definitions of key terms and physics representations
- explain the characteristics of the selected scientific methodology and method, including: techniques of primary qualitative and quantitative data generation relevant to the selected investigation; and appropriateness of the use of independent, dependent and controlled variables in the selected scientific investigation
- identify and apply concepts of accuracy, precision, repeatability, reproducibility, resolution and validity of data; and the identification of, and distinction between, error and uncertainty
- identify and apply health, safety and ethical guidelines relevant to the selected investigation

Scientific evidence

- discuss the nature of evidence that supports or refutes a hypothesis, model or theory
- apply methods of organising, analysing and evaluating primary data to identify patterns and relationships including: the physical significance of the gradient of linearised data; causes of uncertainty; use of uncertainty bars; and assumptions and limitations of data, methodologies and methods
- model the scientific practice of using a logbook to authenticate generated primary data

Science communication

- apply the conventions of science communication: scientific terminology and representations; symbols, equations and formulas; standard abbreviations; significant figures; and units of measurement
- apply the conventions of scientific poster presentation, including succinct communication of the selected scientific investigation, and acknowledgment of references
- explain the key findings and implications of the selected investigation.

How can the width of a hair be measured?

SCIENTIFIC INVESTIGATION

Students undertake a student-designed scientific investigation in either Unit 3 or Unit 4, or across both Units 3 and 4. The investigation involves the generation of primary data relating to fields, motion or light and involves one continuous variable. The investigation draws on knowledge and related key science skills developed across Units 3 and 4 and is undertaken by students in the laboratory and/or in the field.

ASSESSMENT FOR OUTCOME 2

Communication of the design, analysis and findings of a student-designed and student-conducted scientific investigation through a structured scientific poster and logbook entries. The poster should not exceed 600 words.

SUGGESTED DURATION

A minimum of 10 hours of class time should be devoted to undertaking and communicating findings related to Area of Study 2. As per Area of Study 1, your teacher will be your primary guide. To assist you, the key steps to follow, relevant poster section and suggested time allocation are set out below.

The sample investigation on the following page steps you through a controlled experiment, conducted following the designing and planning phase of the investigation.

The suggested duration for this part of the investigation includes 15–20 minutes for set-up, and 90 minutes for observation and recording. The sample investigation also provides a guide for writing your scientific report in the format of a scientific poster.

USING THIS GUIDE

There is scope for developing an investigation on a range of topics relevant to Units 3 and 4. This sample investigation is drawn from Unit 4 Area of Study 1 with a focus on the key knowledge and skills related to light as a wave, and in particular diffraction and interference. In particular, it further explores how properties of light can be used for practical purposes, including to measure the width of a human hair.

In this student-designed investigation, it is important to carefully consider how to monitor the variable under investigation to achieve valid and reliable results. Safety considerations must also be addressed in the planning process. This guide is intended to take you through approaches to planning, conducting and reporting on scientific investigations.

A risk assessment must be completed prior to beginning the investigation. Relevant social and ethical issues should also be addressed.

Refer to the Toolkit at the beginning of this book for more detailed information on designing and conducting scientific investigations, and presenting a scientific report.

Scientific investigation section	Key step	Relevant poster section/s	Suggested time allocation
Designing and planning your investigation	Step 1: Developing aims, hypotheses and predictions	Title Introduction	60–120 minutes
	Step 2: Determining appropriate methodology and methods	Methodology and methods	60–120 minutes
Conducting your investigation and recording and presenting data	Step 3: Conducting your investigation to generate primary data		120–240 minutes
	Step 4: Recording, organising and presenting your data	Results	120–180 minutes
Discussing your investigation and drawing evidence-based conclusions	Step 5: Analysing and evaluating your data	Discussion Conclusion	60–120 minutes
	Step 6: Referencing	References and acknowledgements	30 minutes
Reporting on your investigation	Step 7: Preparing your scientific poster	All sections	60–180 minutes

ISBN 978 0 6557 0029 6

INTRODUCTION

BACKGROUND

Historical experiments over many years have refined our understanding of light. Those same historical experiments were often developed as a solution to a practical problem. This is particularly true where reliable measurements of very small objects are required.

This investigation requires you to research the application of an experiment on the behaviour of light. The question under investigation is: Can light be used to measure the width of a human hair?

AIM

To use diffraction, a wave property of light, to measure the thickness of a very thin object, in particular the width of a human hair.

HYPOTHESIS

The separation of the nodes and anti-nodes (dark and light lines) due to the diffraction of a monochromatic light source around a very thin object will be related to the width of the object. This can be used to determine the width of a human hair.

METHODOLOGY AND METHODS

Remember, your methodology is broader than the methods you have selected for this investigation. It includes a rationale for the approach taken and why this is important to the investigation. The methods are the specific steps taken to generate data during your investigation.

METHODOLOGY

Several factors need to be considered in planning this investigation. These may include:

- identification of variables
- how the experiment will be controlled to ensure accuracy, precision, reproducibility, repeatability and validity of measurements
- the length of time for which the experiment should be conducted to achieve meaningful results.

METHODS

After you have considered your methodology, prepare your methods, outlining each step. Always consider any potential hazards and make sure your procedure allows for a valid and reliable investigation. Remember that these instructions should be clear and easy for someone else to follow. You may want to talk to your teacher before proceeding.

MATERIALS

Record a list of all of the materials you will need for your investigation. The following list is provided as a guide.

- cardboard
- small laser pointer
- sticky tape
- viewing screen
- ruler, scale or other measuring device

RESULTS

The results will be qualitative and quantitative. Everything should be included in your logbook, which is your essential authentication document. Include any difficulties that occurred, as well as all the positive outcomes. Consider presenting the results in tables and graphs, to illustrate trends and summarise relationships. Include any uncertainty within your final results; for example, an estimate of the uncertainty involved in measuring the separation of the diffraction pattern nodes and antinodes.

DISCUSSION

The discussion is a critical section where you will analyse, interpret and evaluate the primary data collected. You will also need to evaluate the methodology, methods and the impact of any limitations, and suggest improvements for later, similar, investigations. Your results should be linked to specific physics concepts, the aim and the hypotheses.

Here are some questions to guide your discussion:

1 What is the underlying behaviour of light that is applicable to your topic?

2 Look at other students' investigations. Comment on the critical thinking skills, problem-solving and scientific processes they employed, which made some more or less effective in determining a reliable result.

3 What would you change in your final methodology to make it more reliable? Outline suggestions for further research.

CONCLUSION

This is a summary of research findings linking your question (title), aim and hypothesis to the results of your investigation.

REFERENCES AND ACKNOWLEDGEMENTS

Remember to reference and acknowledge all secondary sources used in the course of planning and conducting your investigation. These may include:

- your logbook—primary data, conversations, research etc.
- material supplied by your teacher and the school
- internet research and sources.

When referencing published sources, follow accepted protocols for presenting bibliographical data, such as APA citation style. For example:

Black, L., Dommel, A., Dommel, N., Fisher, T., Jobson, K., Lewis, G., Moran, G, Nardelli, D., & White, G. (2023). *Heinemann Physics* 12 (5th ed.). Pearson Australia.